$8⁷⁵
6/16
MB

TENNYSON

PETER LEVI

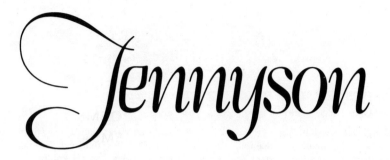

Charles Scribner's Sons
New York

Maxwell Macmillan International
New York   Oxford   Singapore   Sydney

Charles Scribner's Sons
Macmillan Publishing Company
866 Third Avenue
New York, NY 10022

Macmillan Publishing Company is part of the Maxwell Communication Group of Companies.

Thanks are due to Oxford University Press and Harvard University Press for permission to quote excerpts from *The Letters of Alfred Lord Tennyson* edited by Cecil Y. Lang and Edgar F. Shannon Junior, copyright © 1982, 1987, 1990

Library of Congress Cataloging-in-Publication Data
Levi, Peter.
    Tennyson / Peter Levi.
      p. cm.
    Includes bibliographical references and index.
    ISBN 0-684-19662-X
    1. Tennyson, Alfred Tennyson, Baron, 1809–1892. 2. Poets, English—19th century—Biography. I. Title.
    PR5581.L48 1994
    821'.8—dc20
    [B]   93-11805   CIP

10 9 8 7 6 5 4 3 2 1

Printed in the United States of America

FOR DEIRDRE AND
MATTHEW
WITH THANKS FOR
LINCOLNSHIRE
CORNWALL
THE LAKES
AND
WEST WIGHT

CONTENTS

LIST OF ILLUSTRATIONS

FOLLOWING PAGE 178

The author and publishers are grateful to the following for permission to use pictures:

Ashmolean Museum, Oxford: number 23
The *English Illustrated Magazine* (Christmas 1892): number 30.
Henry Jennings's *Lord Tennyson*, Chatto & Windus, 1884 (frontispiece): number 24.
The National Portrait Gallery, London: numbers 7, 9, 12, 16, 25 and 31.
John Spedding, Mirehouse, Keswick, Cumbria: number 13.
All other pictures are from the Tennyson Research Centre, Lincoln, by permission of Lincolnshire County Council.

ACKNOWLEDGEMENTS

I AM very grateful to the Master, the Fellows and the librarians of St Catherine's College, Oxford, where I was once a Fellow, and did much of the research for this book, over many years, and to the librarians of the Bodleian Library, Mr Tomlinson in particular, the London Library, Mr Matthews in particular, and Trinity College, Cambridge, Diana Chardin in particular. I am most grateful for help with books to my long-suffering wife Deirdre, to Cressida Connolly, and to Fram Dinshaw who first lent me Volume One of the *Letters*. I am very grateful to Lord and Lady Briggs for Tennyson's only limerick, to Anthony Hobson for reading me Winny Seebohm's visit to Tennyson, and to Katie Owen for many acute suggestions. I had unforgettable kindness and helpfulness from the Rector of Louth Canon D. W. Owen, who sent me Mr Sturman's useful Fytche article, from Dr G. A. Knight of the Lincolnshire Archives in St Rumbold Street, Lincoln, and above all from the hardworked Librarian of the Tennyson Research Centre, Free School Lane, Lincoln, Miss Gates. Finally, at a time when I was many miles from Oxford, and helpless without a text of Quintus of Smyrna's *Post Homerica*, Professor Parsons of Christ Church came as swiftly and efficiently to my aid as Jebb or Jowett ever came to Tennyson's.

FAMILY TREE OF THE TENNYSONS

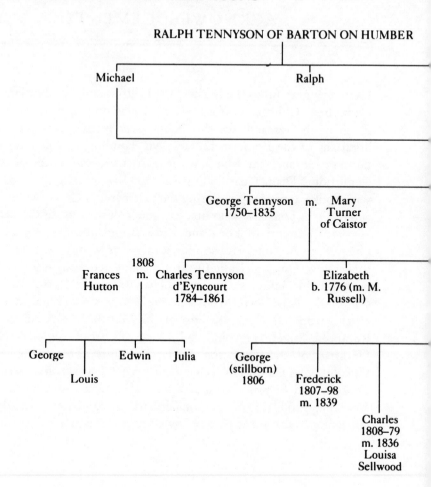

RALPH TENNYSON OF BARTON ON HUMBER

Michael

Ralph

George Tennyson m. Mary
1750–1835   Turner
                      of Caistor

1808
Frances m. Charles Tennyson   Elizabeth
Hutton   d'Eyncourt   b. 1776 (m. M.
              1784–1861   Russell)

George   Edwin   Julia   George
                                  (stillborn)   Frederick
      Louis   1806   1807–98
                                                 m. 1839

                                                        Charles
                                                        1808–79
                                                        m. 1836
                                                        Louisa
                                                        Sellwood

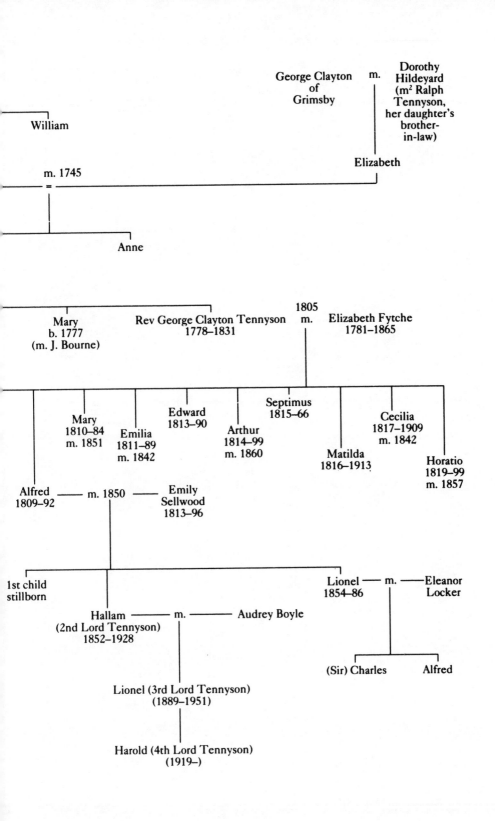

George Clayton
of
Grimsby
m.
Dorothy
Hildeyard
(m² Ralph
Tennyson,
her daughter's
brother-
in-law)

William

Elizabeth

m. 1745
=

Anne

Mary
b. 1777
(m. J. Bourne)

Rev George Clayton Tennyson
1778–1831

1805
m.

Elizabeth Fytche
1781–1865

Mary
1810–84
m. 1851

Emilia
1811–89
m. 1842

Edward
1813–90

Arthur
1814–99
m. 1860

Septimus
1815–66

Matilda
1816–1913

Cecilia
1817–1909
m. 1842

Horatio
1819–99
m. 1857

Alfred
1809–92 — m. 1850 — Emily
Sellwood
1813–96

1st child
stillborn

Lionel — m. —Eleanor
1854–86   Locker

Hallam ——— m. ——— Audrey Boyle
(2nd Lord Tennyson)
1852–1928

(Sir) Charles   Alfred

Lionel (3rd Lord Tennyson)
(1889–1951)

Harold (4th Lord Tennyson)
(1919–)

INTRODUCTION

I HAVE always found Tennyson a deeply attractive and somewhat mysterious poet, and for many years have read what I could about him and his friends. To write a book that will take time to write is like undertaking a long journey with a friend: the friend and your friendship must have staying power, and Lord Tennyson has that abundantly. To put it another way, the writing of a new biography is like the expert cleaning of an old picture: it will pose a whole series of detailed problems, which call for solutions, and only slowly does one's sense of the complete picture come to light. I think having written this book that I do now understand this great poet; the long series of problems solved has left him much clearer, and yet because of his genuine greatness just as mysterious as before.

I have followed him step by step, and seldom or never enjoyed anything more; it is a bonus that he casts a light on the whole nineteenth century, but he casts it also on the art of poetry. Poetry itself is what makes him mysterious. Some things about his poetry have been obscured by the passage of time: he died a hundred years ago, though when I was born it was less than forty years, and for that reason I have hoped to bring him more clearly before a generation which does not know Latin or Greek and has little sympathy with the theological entanglements or the social struggles of the last century. It requires an effort of the imagination from all of us, after all, to think what England was like when Tennyson was born, between Trafalgar and Waterloo.

So much is recorded about the life of Lord Tennyson that the difficulty today is as much in the selection of detail as the establishment of the truth. Many small questions remain, but so much has been published that it is possible to discover solid ground almost everywhere. We have all his letters in print at last, in an exemplary edition, and his poems in an edition that is fully annotated and contains the numerous manuscript variations, some of them of great interest, that Trinity College has now allowed to be made public; the editor, Christopher Ricks, is the most learned, the most careful and tactful of scholars.

There have been biographies of Tennyson before; small but not negligible ones by Evelyn Waugh's father and by Henry Jennings written in his lifetime, then the monumental and magnificent *Memoir* by his son, written with the widow's help, revised later but never superseded. Numerous articles followed; there was a small, incisive book by A. C. Benson, and much later a clever but somewhat lamentable book by Lord Dufferin's nephew, Harold Nicolson (who repented later), followed by a stern but quirky essay by Auden. I am leaving out the pure critics, and have mostly ignored them in writing this biography. The twenty years between the world wars were the trough of Tennyson's reputation, which was already beginning to plunge at the time of his death. That it has now recovered is largely due to the activities of Sir Charles Tennyson, Lionel's son and the poet's grandson, who was thirteen when his grandfather died and who, late in life, after a successful career (hence his knighthood), devoted himself to the lives of his grandfather and the large Tennyson family. The best of the shorter lives of Tennyson by a long chalk apart from his, is Joanna Richardson's *The Pre-Eminent Victorian* (1962) which marks the change of tone.

Lord Tennyson has been lucky enough to attract some of the finest of American scholars, firstly to deal with his papers, which were severely weeded by Hallam with the best advice and the best of intentions, yet even in their censored state still threaten to overwhelm one, and secondly to probe into his life. Where Sir Charles had built a scaffolding, they have constructed a solid edifice. In one or two matters I have differed from the generally received opinion of scholars: about Rose (or Rosa) Baring, for instance, with whom the poet had only an insignificant flirtation or hardly even that, and about the curious suggestion that Tennyson had epilepsy, inherited from his father, which is extremely unlikely or impossible for medical reasons. There are other explanations that cover the phenomena; the suggestion of epilepsy dates from the days of William James, who deals with it.

Other differences are a matter of emphasis; I suppose that in general I find Tennyson more sympathetic as a man than some of his biographers have thought him. That may be because I have never got over the *Memoir*, which I first read forty years ago; it is also true that I read Philip Larkin's review of R. B. Martin's large biography, which was a severe rebuke, before I had read the book. Having now worked my way through Martin's *Tennyson, The Unquiet Heart* (1980), I think it a brilliant and amazing reconstruction of a life. The same scholar's life of FitzGerald (*With Friends Possessed*, 1985) is almost equally important for students of Tennyson's life, and his

Hopkins is a great step forward; but of the three books, his Tennyson is the most massively documented: it is surely a lifework.

Can one really ever know the subject of a biography? I have heard Lord Bullock say that in the end they always elude you. Yet I feel as if I do know Tennyson, and as if he were a familiar friend. It is possible to snuffle out most of his secrets. He himself hated biographies; when Charles Milnes Gaskell first privately printed his Eton memoirs, and Gladstone then sent him some letters from Arthur Hallam, Tennyson uttered a cry of rage, almost as if he were Hallam's widow. He did not like intimacies dragged into the daylight, because he distrusted journalists and hated tourists, in both cases with good reason. He complained once to the Queen at Osborne of barbarous invasions of his privacy, and when she said she had no such trouble in the Isle of Wight, he replied that no doubt if he could post a sentry with a gun at his gate, he would have no trouble either. And he was also extremely shy and self-conscious. He told a conventional little girl he was walking with in London, the future Mrs Kenneth Grahame, that her mother ought not to dress her so queerly, because people were staring, though at the time he was wearing his vast cloak and his magician's hat.

But he chose to be written about by his son Hallam, who did a better job than was done for any of his contemporaries. Luckily Hallam was not perfectly organized, so scholars can have the pleasure of correcting him; further, he left masses, not to say haystacks, of material (now at the Lincoln Tennyson Research Centre), which represent early stages of the making of his father's glorious memorial. We are free therefore to observe what was smoothed over and left out, such as Tennyson's brother Charles's drug habit. The danger for a biographer now is to be too knowing, to question too much: there is after all a certain important truth in the family love which has sought to cover the poet's sores and to reduce him (as in life he could never be reduced) to late Victorian propriety. Hallam's other book, *Tennyson and His Friends* (1911), helps one a lot to get behind the marble façade and, taken together with his papers and Emily's journal[1] (censored by herself in old age but revealing enough), which has now been printed, opens new possibilities, though it is a hundred years since the laureate's death, of really knowing Alfred Tennyson. Even Arthur Hallam, with his letters and papers in print,[2] is more knowable than he was.

Hallam Tennyson imitated his father in preparing a trial version of his book before the one that he published. It was Tennyson's habit to produce one or more trial editions of a few copies before he would issue any of his books to the public, so that quite apart from the intricate problems of manuscripts, which are best appreciated by a study of the full Shatto and Shaw edition of *In Memoriam* (1982),[3] the problems of Tennyson's proofs and trial editions add some obscurity to the history of his publications. The subject of his bibliography, which fell into the hands of the forgers Wise and Buxton Forman, has never since then been thoroughly elucidated by anyone, although its remaining mysteries appeared to me of minor importance.[4]

One of the most useful instruments for a biographer is the Lincoln list of the books that Alfred, the Rector his father, Emily, his brother Charles, and his son Hallam once owned, many of which are now in the Research Centre (*Tennyson in Lincoln*, 1971). It is not compiled to the highest standards of modern librarianship, and it is possible to make discoveries among the books not revealed by the published list, but still it is very useful indeed. An even humbler instrument, which is not in every detail reliable but which I at least found most useful, is F. B. Pinion's *Tennyson Chronology* (1990), a simple catalogue of whatever the poet is known to have been doing on every day of his life. He knew few people who kept records before he went to Cambridge, and even his entry to the University was mysteriously casual, but once there he fell in with a set of friends who, together with the friends of friends, made up a most unusual group. They included Thackeray, FitzGerald, Gladstone, Monckton Milnes (later Lord Houghton), Spedding who edited Bacon, Arthur Hallam, numerous future deans of cathedrals, and some heads of colleges. Behind them looms the fascinating and influential figure of F. D. Maurice, and they cluster around his club, the Apostles. They had almost all been written about before 1910, and all throw light on the poet. As he grew older Tennyson met other writers like Leigh Hunt, Wordsworth and the Brownings, and he naturally went more and more into the world, so that in the end there is almost no one he appears not to know; yet still they all have things to say about him. His relations with Carlyle, Browning, Swinburne, Charles Kingsley (who quarrelled with him), Tom Hughes (who illustrated him), Henry James, and a swarm of minor writers like Patmore and the Palgraves, add both glamour and substance to his life.

There are even forgotten nuggets to be found about him in

pamphlets intended for the tourist, in Sir Charles Tennyson on his houses, and R. J. Hutchings on 'Literary Haunts' in the Isle of Wight, which tells us that Tennyson began work on a botanical dictionary, and that the Briary, a cottage where G. F. Watts lived, was burnt down in 1934; it also identifies one of Tennyson's terriers, Winks, and the deerhound (Russian wolfhound?) Lufra, and reproduces Richard Doyle's enchanting painting of the view from the drawing room. There are vital photographs in J. S. English's pamphlet *The Postcard World of Tennyson* (1984), and even in the flimsy *Tennyson's Lincolnshire* (1985). In themselves these are small matters, but they are just an example of the bewildering profusion of what is known. In 1939 after all he was still clearly remembered in Haslemere. Fifty years after the death of Lord Tennyson, I was a child of nine: his death seemed long ago to me, but people of sixty or seventy had known him. Now the living tradition has almost died out, though not quite, since I got an unpublished limerick from Lord Briggs only the other day. But the contents of the Trinity manuscripts of the poems have been a secret so well guarded that they are like a new discovery: the three-volume Ricks edition appeared only in 1987, and without it I could not have written this book.

Or it would have taken very much longer, and the same may be said even more vehemently of the *Letters*, the third and final volume of which appeared only in 1990. The first had appeared in 1981, but with so thorough and so vast an edition that was not slow progress. The notes to the three volumes, and the passages quoted from diarists and memoirists, would be enough on their own to make them invaluable, though readers should be warned that the notes, which settle many uncertainties about Tennyson's life, are not indexed: one must simply work through every single one. I had delayed starting to write this book until the third volume of the *Letters* was available, and had already reached that bad stage of research when one can no longer remember what one's notes are about, and no longer find one bit of paper among the many, so that in this biography of Tennyson there are bound to be more errors of detail even than has been usual with me. The reader may be assured that they do not arise from undue hurry or from any lack of affection for this great and extraordinary poet.

There are two manuscript sources I have failed to exhaust. Lord Houghton's papers are now at Trinity, and they include in the course of his journal some records of Tennyson's conversation, which to judge by the bits quoted in James Pope-Hennessey's life of Richard Monckton Milnes (1949 and 1951) would be worth sifting through. But my eyesight is no longer good, and nor is Lord Houghton's handwriting. The journals are already being studied: let us hope the relevant parts will be published. The other source is also hard to read, though not impossible: it is Hallam's record of his father's anecdotes and jokes, of which he tells a number in the *Memoir* (some were told more than once, it is clear). The manuscript is at Lincoln; it was plundered by Sir Charles Tennyson, but there is plenty more unpublished. I have been able to date this manuscript, which is a Marlborough school exercise book, a little later than it is usually dated, at the beginning of Hallam's work as his father's secretary. I have read it with much pleasure, but there is no sense in printing it as an appendix, so that also must be someone else's task.

One cannot really know a poet without knowing his world, and his relations with the changes in it. Tennyson's social world is hard to place, because the whole of England altered so much in his lifetime. But the nineteenth century was probably the best time financially there has ever been for a writer to live, and Tennyson in particular did extremely well. It was the age of the cheap book and mass circulation even of poetry. But this means that the torrents and cataracts of what was published and lies in libraries are so vast that no single scholar, even of those who devote their lives to the enterprise, could really read it all. Tennyson at some times of his life read a novel every day at bedtime; much that he read was by women who are now more or less forgotten, yet they influenced him greatly.

Even if one restricts oneself to poetry, it is a subtle balance that must be found between what he admired, what he remembered, and what he had discovered in unlikely places. How should one justly weigh Smith and Dobell, memorably called the Spasmodics,[5] and the Lushington brothers, or Lord Houghton as a poet, or the Arthurian stories in Percy's *Reliques*? I have not attempted to trace all the musical settings of his verse: I know the few that are famous, and have heard some of Lear's, though they do not encourage one to probe any further. Hallam Tennyson's friend Stanford is an improvement, but I have never heard for example the lute music Elgar wrote for Tennyson's play *Queen Mary*. The laureate hated most of his illustrators, though he was polite to Doré and did no worse than grunt about Tom Hughes; he seems to have liked only his daughter-in-law Audrey Boyle's aunt, or was that a mere flirtation? Yet a pretty page of 'The Progress of Spring' decorated by Thackeray, more delicate than one would expect, hung on the wall of his study nearly all his life long.

It is not a simple task to reduce all these ways of considering Lord Tennyson to a single volume of narrative text. And there are some tracks that lead nowhere, some conundrums that make one pause and nothing more. For instance the saying went round the clubs, so that several people heard it, at the time of Tennyson's peerage, that it was a disgrace to make a man a peer just for writing a few verses. Lear heard it abroad, for example, and Grant Duff heard it in London. But Grant Duff also heard someone claim that the printers of Tennyson always ran out of certain letters because the word 'love' occurred so often in his poems. I had not of course attempted to check this assertion, but when I came to examine the index to *In Memoriam* published privately and anonymously by Lewis Carroll in 1862, which is some forty pages listing the principal noun in each clause, and giving the references, I was amazed to see that there are twenty-two entries under soul, thirty-six under spirit, and sixty-six under love. So did a printer really make the remark? I have filed this under dead ends, like the Kelmscott *Maud* (1893), which sounds like a moving tribute from William Morris but turns out to be only a sign that Macmillan had just bought the Kelmscott Press. On the other hand the closeness of Tennyson's house to the Royal School of Military Music at Twickenham may not be a dead end, yet it is a road that dies out.

Until yesterday Farringford on the Isle of Wight vividly recalled Tennyson. The Rectory where the poet was born has been rebuilt, but it survives, and so does the large stone monument Knowles built for him in Surrey; both are still in use as houses, and neither is generally (or I think ever) accessible to the public. Innumerable lodgings can be traced in London where he stayed, and at least the sites of houses in Epping Forest and in Cheltenham. But the house that most strongly conveys his atmosphere and recalls his days is undoubtedly Mirehouse, near Keswick on Bassenthwaite, which has been sold only once in its history, in 1688, and is still the home of the Spedding family, who were Tennyson's friends. Even the walled garden still called the Bee Garden, in the potting shed of which James Spedding drew him while it rained, is to be seen. The gardens and the trees are richer now than when Archdeacon Froude drew them, but I am inclined to think Tennyson's Gothic windows and embellishments to Farringford were modelled on Mirehouse rather than his father's house. Mirehouse was built by Lord Derby in 1666 with seven bays, and sold to his agent in 1688. The Gothic towers were added in 1790, and the last kinsman of Lord Derby's agent, who had no heir, left the house in 1802 to Mr Spedding of Armathwaite, the father of Tennyson's friend. I believe that it haunted Tennyson's imagination.

Finally, I am not able to epitomize what I think or feel about Lord Tennyson. But the most vigorous and intimate summary I have ever found of him is by Benjamin Jowett. It is printed in *Tennyson and His Friends* and represents the smoother pages Jowett contributed to the *Memoir* in a succinct and slightly earlier form. I give it here because *Tennyson and His Friends* is a book as rarely to be found nowadays as the *Memoir* is common.

Absolute truthfulness, absolutely himself, never played tricks.

Never got himself puffed in the newspapers.

A friend of liberty and truth.

Extraordinary vitality.

Great common-sense and a strong will.

The instinct of common-sense at the bottom of all he did.

Not a man of the world (in the ordinary sense) but a man who had the greatest insight into the world, and often in a word or a sentence would flash a light.

Intensely needed sympathy.

A great and deep strength.

He mastered circumstances, but he was also partly mastered by them, e.g. the old calamity of the disinheritance of his father and his treatment by rogues in the days of his youth.

Very fair towards other poets, including those who were not popular, such as Crabbe.

He had the high-bred manners not only of a gentleman but of a great man.

He would have wished that, like Shakespeare, his life might be unknown to posterity.

PETER LEVI
Prospect Cottage
Frampton on Severn
19 February 1992

CHAPTER ONE

The Birth of the Poet

ALFRED TENNYSON was born at Somersby Rectory in remotest Lincolnshire on 5 August, 1809 (or so the baptismal register records: his mother used to celebrate his birthday on the 6th, her wedding anniversary, and his son Hallam followed this tradition). The doctor thought he had a fine pair of legs. George III was on the throne, Trafalgar had been fought but Waterloo was still in the future. The King did not die until 1820, when Tennyson was eleven years old, and George IV did not die until he was twenty-one. He was brought up under the Regency, which lasted from February 1811 until the old King's death, and he should not be considered simply as a Victorian poet, since Queen Victoria was ten years his junior and came to the throne when he was nearly thirty. Indeed, if one thinks of Victorian poets as those brought up under Victoria, the list runs more or less from Swinburne to Robert Graves. She can no more lay claim to Tennyson than she can to the Duke of Wellington: they were both tall, elderly men who were very kind to her, but their backbones and their manners were forged in a severe and more formal age.

The reason for dwelling on the date of Tennyson's birth is that confusion about him sometimes arises from an apparent discontinuity in English poetry during his boyhood, as if, when he became famous as a poet, he stepped forward into a vacuum. Burns (1759–96) was dead, though it is true that Blake (1757–1827) was still alive,[1] as were Wordsworth (1770–1850) and Coleridge (1772–1834). Wordsworth's reputation continually increased after his two volumes of new and collected poems of 1809, his first successful publication (*Lyrical Ballads*, published in 1798, had sold only a few hundred copies). Coleridge was fashionable before Wordsworth, but survived only as an eccentric sage. It was these two more than anyone else who represented for Tennyson's generation the living tradition of English poetry. Scott (1771–1832) might be added to swell the list, but as a poet he was painfully short of talent. It might seem that English poetry was headed for a grim season.

The obvious trouble was the death of three great and striking poets, all of whom were born at the end of the eighteenth century, and all of whom died young: Byron (1788–1824), Shelley (1792–1822), and Keats (1795–1821). Of these three, it was the death of Byron, who of course was a national hero,[2] that most upset Tennyson; he was thirteen when he heard the news, and went off alone into the woods, where he carved Byron's name on a rock. But Shelley was very much the discovery of Tennyson's circle of friends at Cambridge: *Adonais* was promoted and republished by them because Arthur Hallam, on holiday in Italy, came across a copy of the original Pisa edition and brought it home. (The last remaining copy in London had been bought for Browning in 1828 for his sixteenth birthday, from Ollier of Vere Street.) Keats was the youngest of the three, and the nearest to being Tennyson's contemporary. He was far closer to him in manner than the others, and in the same way enchanted by Greek mythology, though less educated, and by English scenery, though a touch lusher and less subtle than Tennyson. Keats was the son of an ostler and horse dealer, Tennyson was a clever clergyman's son; that difference in social background and in education is almost all that divides them.

There are other poets whose lives are relevant to the apparent dislocation, the exaggerated divide which is thought to separate Tennyson from his predecessors. It is of course true that death makes older poets look immeasurably grand, but what about John Clare (1793–1864)? When Tennyson was born he was eighteen, and living in obscurity just a county away (but a county of impassable roads) in the poorest circumstances. Doubtless that accounts for the truthfulness and sheer force of his tone and for the intellectual brilliance of his satires, but probably it is also what drove him mad. Yet in one way he is what Tennyson could and should have been. I do not think Tennyson was conscious of Clare, whose brief vogue was in his boyhood. Clare's first book appeared in 1820; in 1837 he went to a private asylum in Epping Forest that Tennyson by coincidence visited as a friend of the manager, and in 1841 to the Northampton asylum where he died.

Other poets, who are forgotten today, were important to him. Melodious Thomas Moore (1779–1852) and the melancholy Cowper

(1731–1800) scarcely affected him; from Thomas Hood (1799–1845) he took only a certain sprightliness, and a wrong-headed idea of what a ballad was, either of which he might have picked up anywhere, even from his father. It is strange how utterly he was cut off, like the rest of middle-class England, from whatever was left of genuine popular or folk poetry, but his education slammed the gate on it.[3] He did admire Crabbe (1754–1832)[4] but Crabbe was a very old-fashioned writer. What was fashionable was in the *Annuals* – Hood's 'I remember, I remember' in 1823 and Macaulay's 'Armada' in 1833.

It may well be from Crabbe and not from other models that he took the idea of the modern short story in verse which is the ruling form of so many of his longer poems. And as a boy he loved and adored James Thomson (1700–48), as Clare did too. Modern readers find Thomson unreadable, and his long moralizing descriptions and sub-Miltonic blank verse do fall heavily on the ear, but in short doses he can captivate, and Tennyson learnt a great deal from him. In particular he learnt a certain delicate and intimate verbal music which became almost as instinctive in his poems as birdsong. That is a great gift to pick up from a minor poet, and no doubt its sources are complex, as we shall see, but the rudiments of Tennyson's skill clearly derive from James Thomson.[5] Who would be certain at first glance that this couplet

> Infinite wings! till all the plume-dark air
> And rude resounding shore are one wild cry

and these lines

> The blackbird whistles from the thorny brake,
> The mellow bullfinch answers from the grove

were not by Tennyson? But they are by Thomson, and the mellow bullfinch recalls what Tennyson several times said was his favourite line in his own poetry: 'The mellow ouzel fluted in the elm.'[6] I take it that this is a case of subconscious memory, not of clever adaptation, but he was particularly proud of the observation that the blackbird 'fluted'. He did perhaps consciously learn Thomson's habit of Miltonic or freshly coined compound epithets, such as hollow-whispering and dewy-bright, which Tennyson alters in 'Œnone' to dewy-dark.

Since Tennyson broke out virtually from his cradle as a poet, mastering stanza form at the age of eight, it is particularly interesting to record whatever we know of the roots of his poetry. We are told for example that his mother Elizabeth, who was dragged around the lanes in a wheeled chair drawn at first by a large dog, later by a small pony, and attended by her children, used to read to them from Mrs Hemans, and from Beattie's *Calendar*. (When the poet had come to his height and his strength he would lift up the pony and carry it round the garden or, according to his friend FitzGerald, the dinner table.) The habit of reading in the lanes, once acquired, was never lost. On occasion Tennyson as a boy was walking and reading in snow, so that the coach crept silently up on him. When shouted at, he was startled to find a horse breathing heavily over his shoulder. Mrs Hemans got more attention than she usually gets.

She was born in 1793, and her early poems were printed privately and disastrously in Liverpool in 1808. She swiftly recovered from this reverse, and published enough verse to fill seven volumes of collected poems in 1839, though she was dead by 1835. She attracted Shelley's attention and he attempted to correspond with her, but was rebuffed by her parents. Her chosen friend was Bishop Heber, and she was one of the revivers of romantic Wales. It is hard to know which of her books Mrs Tennyson got hold of; it could have been *Domestic Affections* of 1812, the year of her marriage, or *Dartmoor*, a Royal Society of Literature prize poem of 1821. She wrote a long poem about the freedom of Spain, where her brothers fought against Napoleon, and one about the state of Greece. She was extremely popular. Her poetry hardly alters with changes of subject; it just flows on and on, sugary, tedious and fluent. If she was ever an influence on Tennyson, she was soon forgotten by him. Only the subjects of Spain, of exotic Greece, and wild Dartmoor wake echoes in his later life. She embodies the conventional taste of the reign of George IV, and was respectable reading for a clergyman's wife. Wordsworth, whom she met in 1829, wrote her epitaph soon afterwards.

James Beattie is a much more surprising and interesting choice for Tennyson's mother. The first intriguing thing about Beattie is that he never wrote a poem or book called *The Calendar*.[7] Whoever began this confusion, which more than one Tennyson makes, he was probably half thinking of Thomson's *The Seasons*. If Alfred himself was confused, which I am unable to credit, then Beattie was to him the vaguest of far-off voices. None the less, Beattie did influence him. He was a Scottish poet who lived from 1735 to 1803; his works were still being reprinted as late as 1831 (with an introduction by Dyce). Alfred's brother Charles owned a selected Beattie (ed. Alfred Howard, 1834) which he apparently bought for himself. Beattie wrote 'A Triumph of Melancholy', and translated Virgil's *Eclogues*, mostly into couplets of a devastating propriety. But the poem Mrs Tennyson liked was surely his *The Minstrel, or The Progress of Genius* (1771/74), about the education of a poet in a wild place. The poet 'drank the living water from the rock', he was 'strange and way-ward', and 'oft the craggy cliff he loved to climb'. The hero is slightly reminiscent of Clare's peasant boy poet, Lubin. This is strong meat for a little boy already writing verses. In book two, the poet grows up and meets a hoary sage, but the poem unfortunately breaks off, because Beattie says his friend died. He does at least provide Tennyson with the 'lin-lan-lone' noise that he thought bells made,[8] in a line about 'many a long-lingering year in lonely isle'. The line 'down the rough slope the ponderous waggon rings' has similar echoes. But it will be better to quote a longer passage that makes an unmistakably Tennysonian sound:

> But who the melodies of morn can tell?
> The wild brook babbling down the mountain-side;
> The lowing herd; the sheepfold's simple bell;
> The pipe of early shepherd dim descried
> In the lone valley; echoing far and wide
> The clamorous horn along the cliffs above;
> The hollow murmur of the ocean tide;
> The hum of bees, the linnet's lay of love,
> And the full choir that wakes the universal grove.

I do not of course suppose that Tennyson was Beattie's apprentice, only that this was one of the things poetry meant to him. Poetry is multiple even to a child, and we know that the poet's father read it and wrote it down in notebooks. His eldest brother Fred wrote it too and when they were young men, Coleridge thought Alfred's elder brother Charles was a better poet than he was.[9] Alfred's earliest recorded lines written in childhood point in more than one direction, none of them that of Beattie. But one is pleased that a poet now so totally neglected[10] went on working at some level of his mind, and that his mother, who was a good and simple lady, contributed something to his genius.

In the crowded literary households of the early nineteenth century, poetry and fiction arose from a shared feeling and a shared children's world. The Tennyson family was extremely odd, and unlike other families, except perhaps for the Brontës in some aspects. On his mother's side Alfred was a Fytche.[11] They were a dull, solid family some of whom went to universities: his cousin Lewis went to Lincoln College, Oxford. The family descended from a Louth grocer (d. 1751) whose shop goods were valued at his death at £1000, though his son Stephen, Alfred's grandfather, was Rector of Louth (1774–80), a dull, solid appointment. His wife was a niece of John Green, Bishop of Lincoln.[12] Stephen Fytche was a ten-year man at St John's, Cambridge who got his degree by leaving his name ten years on the college books. He then took the Louth living at once, and resigned it within a year of his marriage. Tennyson's mother appears to have been born after her father's retirement from Louth, when he was Vicar of Withcall, a wold village eight miles away to the west, but his grandmother lived on at Louth in Harvey's Alley, now Westgate Place, with the poet's aunt, the unmarried daughter Mary Anne Fytche (b. 1782). This aunt was important to the young Tennysons. Alfred's first recorded letter was to her about poetry, and the Rev Mr Waite wrote in 1866 that the 'poetic genius' of the boys was 'inherited and fostered by their parents, and excited by a good and kind aunt'. Who knows? Alfred's mother was beautiful and had some money: in the marriage market of those years, which are also Jane Austen's, she was a catch. She had a number of connections and friendships in the county, with the Massingberds for example, and her family was a power in Louth. When she was old, one of her sons, thinking her asleep, said she had had twenty-four proposals of marriage in her day. She opened her eyes, smiled, and said 'twenty-five', and went back to sleep. Later in life, Mary Anne moved in with her widowed sister Elizabeth Tennyson. They died within weeks of each other, and they are both in Highgate Cemetery. They were given each other's gravestones, a mistake put right only in the 1940s.

For Alfred Tennyson's early years, his brother Charles is by far the best witness, even when he tells the stories with a personal nuance: he is bound to be right about their mother, but it is possible that the Rector may have favoured Alfred. Charles spoke with an innocence of his own to Canon Rawnsley, a family friend who wrote a memoir of the Tennysons published in 1900:

> We should none of us probably have written poetry if it had not been for her. When our father almost mocked at our attempts, she gave us her warm encouragement. She would let us go with her, she in her donkey chair, or dog-chair – for a Newfoundland Mastiff was her steed – as she went through the Somersby Lanes, she would listen to our bits of verse and read to us from Beattie's *Calendar* or Thomson's *Seasons* the passages she loved the best.

Whenever the dog was tired it would lie down and take a rest. 'I think you would like her,' writes Mary Tennyson of Elizabeth in 1805, 'she is particularly fond of and tender to animals, and quadrupeds conversation she enters with more interest into than any other.'

The Tennyson family were farmers in Holderness, on the long belt of land narrowing to a spit which lies north of the Humber, between Hull and the sea. It is a strange and peaceful area, much loved by Philip Larkin and before him by Andrew Marvell. The Tennysons may originally have been Vikings. For several generations before Alfred was born they were moving upwards in society, and southwards in their houses. One was a surgeon, but mostly they were lawyers and agents, advocates in small cases in provincial towns and agents in small matters within the county. But they had been marrying money and acquiring claims to grander lineage. This mixture proved indigestible to them, and the resulting explosions happened in Alfred's father's time. In the seventeenth century a collateral branch had the sleepy distinction of producing two or three bishops, and in the eighteenth the southward drift of the Tennysons began slowly and tranquilly. Ralph settled south of the river at Barton on Humber. Michael married a Clayton and founded the family fortunes. The Claytons were landowners and Michael's wife, Elizabeth, was a Hildeyard on her mother's side. Her son George, Alfred's paternal grandfather, later made a claim to noble ancestry through this connection. George was apprenticed to a lawyer in Hull, and then set up at Market Rasen. At twenty-five, in 1775, he married Mary Turner of Caistor House. Her brother Sam was a parson, a gambler, a furious drinker and a banger of rum glasses on the table (he smashed a glass of rum and water, inveighing against Lord Byron; his sister Mary on the other hand read young Alfred 'The Prisoner of Chillon' 'very tenderly'). Sam died in 1835, leaving estates to Alfred's elder brother Charles, who consequently changed his name to Charles Tennyson Turner. George was sharp, ambitious, mean, suspicious and fierce: he had many of the characteristics of a peasant, and his grandchildren called him the Old Man of the Wolds. He was all but crooked; that is, he was a schemer and a groveller until the victim fell into his clutches, but then he was ruthlessly avaricious. His wife did not count for much in his household; she died in 1825. She always maintained, no one knows why, that Alfred's literary genius came from her side of the family.

The future Rector of Somersby, Alfred's father George, was born in 1778 and his brother Charles in 1784; two girls, Elizabeth and Mary, were born in 1776 and 1777. Mary and George were boarded with their grandmothers in Holderness and Caistor until George was ten, on the grounds that it would 'save trouble and expense'. When he visited Market Rasen, his mother wrote, 'I think I never saw a child so rude and ungovernable'.Old Michael Tennyson, George's grandfather, would take the child into his bed in the early morning and tell him about the stars, a tradition that took root for several generations. The story of each of these children is hair-raising in its own way, except for George's eldest sister Elizabeth, who married a coal millionaire from Durham, Matthew Russell, owner of Brancepeth Castle and a couple of rotten boroughs. They married in 1798 when she was twenty-two; she had twenty-five happy years with him and lived to be eighty. But Mary was morose, a hypochondriac, a wanderer between health resorts and an addict of dramatic quarrels with landladies and intimates. She was a crazy Calvinist, married to a dissenting squire called John Bourne of Dalby. When she met Alfred in the street she remarked how sad it was that he, unlike herself, was going to hell. She often wept at this thought. Their house was a few miles from Somersby, though it burnt down in 1842. While it stood, the young Tennysons frequented it. George's brother Charles was late-born, unwanted by his mother and adored by his father. Charles became a practical and successful minor politician, but was not by nature a gentleman and made himself ridiculous by his pretensions to be one. To judge from his letters he was a crashing bore and a fusspot, as well as an irritating snob; his family was affected by him, as if boredom could be transmitted by blood.

At some time early in George's boyhood his father decided, if not to disinherit him, then at least to change his place in the pecking order with his younger brother. A country neighbour called Heneage who owned 10,000 acres in Lincolnshire warned him he would be damned to hell if he did such a wicked thing. (I am not clear when he said this, but maybe after the marriage of George Clayton Tennyson.) The Heneage family were Fytche sympathizers; Mrs Heneage came to tea at Mrs Fytche's house on the wedding day in 1805; she 'had four horses to her coach'. Why did he do it? No one knows, except that it was the old man's whim.[13]

Young George went to school at St Peter's, York, at the age of nine, then for a year to a private coach, and finally in 1796 to St John's, Cambridge. He was a dextrous versifier in Latin and Greek and coped well with examinations (there are prize bindings with the college arms among his books), though he opted for a pass degree: honours 'would neither suit my health, time or inclination,' he wrote to his father. He always wished he had gone to Eton for the sake of the verses, which seems a sensible velleity. Eton Latin verses of the period are of an extraordinary brilliance, which was produced by sound tuition and by rivalry. The syllabus had scarcely altered since Shakespeare's day. It was the most intense moment of the neo-classic age, Horace was intellectually the ruler of the squirearchy with Virgil as runner-up. If you died lucky, you got a monument of an urn with some crisp decoration and some loose drapery, carved in relief in white marble on black. In spite of anxious probing about idleness and dissipation, George's father received only courteous reassurances from St John's. Young George's only recorded exploit was making a hole in a Trinity chapel window with a pistol shot, but he was not discovered. Yet he must have founded his remarkable taste for antiquarian learned books in his college library,[14] a remarkable collection which includes a gift of several hundred from Shakespeare's friend the Earl of Southampton.

George Clayton grew up fond of poetry and a player on the harp. His friends valued him and his parishioners accepted him; his mother can be presumed to have fostered his genuine taste in verse and his remarkable learning. He was or became a liar on a mythological scale, he drank too much and sometimes broke down altogether. No doubt bringing up a huge family in a tiny house might have had these dire consequences, but he had shown signs of them earlier in life, and the root cause seems to have been resentment against his unquestionably disgusting old father. He did his children no service by bringing them up to feel bitterly about their ill-treatment as a family by their grandfather and their cousins. He resented among other things being forced into the Church: a good living in his time and a constant resort of county families such as the Tennysons had become, but a limited and humiliating career, particularly if one scarcely believed the Creed. George Clayton Tennyson apparently did his duty without belief, as so many did.

In 1790, the Old Man of the Wolds was already thinking about livings for George; he took his degree in spring 1801 and became an ordained deacon in May. It happened that the Tsar of Russia was assassinated that March, and the new deacon set off to attend the coronation at Moscow. The British delegation to which he attached himself was led by Lord St Helens, an old member of St John's, who carried a lavish present of diamonds. This adventure went badly wrong, and George seems to have spun a romantic lie about it which he repeated or elaborated all his life. Even Alfred repeated it. According to the fiction George arrived late, but went to a state dinner at St Petersburg. There he naively mentioned the assassination at table, and was at once told by Lord St Helens to leave and ride for his life, because both the noble assassins had been present and heard him. There follows a long tarradiddle about his homeward journey through southern Russia, an illness in a cottage, listening out for the trumpet of a King's Messenger, and hearing it and being rescued. Alfred in later life did not express incredulity, though he did wonder whether it was true.

In fact it is improbable from beginning to end. The likeliest truth, since he certainly went to Russia, is that Lord St Helens sent him home in disgrace for some reason he found too humiliating to tell his family. Still, the illness in the Crimea, with no medicine but the country people dancing round his bed and chanting incantations, is a good touch. During Napoleon's retreat from Moscow, French prisoners were tied to logs and beaten to death with flails to the chanting of folk songs. The deacon arrived home in February 1802, having probably travelled by Moscow and Hamburg; he had never expected to arrive before January.[15]

However this may be, in December 1802 he was ordained priest and became Rector of Benniworth, near Louth. The Heneage family gave him the living, and that of Great Grimsby in 1815; he held both livings until his death. In August 1805 he married Elizabeth Fytche. His sister wrote:

> Last Tuesday morning, Charles and I turned our half rested limbs out of bed at five o'clock to go to Louth and attend the nuptials of our brother George . . . She had on a white beaver hat and lily muslin gown. The happy pair proceeded to church at 8 o'clock, teeming with chastened delight . . . After breakfast we danced 'Come Haste to the Wedding'. Cotillions and waltzes followed, fandangos and minuettos closed the revels of the morning . . . We had three outriders, all of which together with postillions and every horse had good white satin favors at a shilling a yard, tyed up by the bridesmaids, but trouble was nothing, expense was all!!! . . . Eliza is really a sweet tempered creature and the very woman for George.

At the end of 1806 George became Rector of Somersby with Bag Enderby, another tiny settlement a mile or two away. The Rector paid £35 a year to a curate at Benniworth but the income of that parish was £500. Somersby brought in £180 a year; it had seventy people. The Rector had to do a good deal to improve the Rectory, so it was 1808 before they moved in. The patron of this living was an old friend of his father's who owned the beautiful castellated brick house next door, something like a piece of Hampton Court. It was apparently designed by Vanbrugh, who did other work in this county; all the same it was let to a tenant farmer.

Meanwhile in 1784 the new Rector's father, old George, had bought some land at Tealby with an unpretentious house called Bayons on it. His other son Charles later knocked that down to build between 1836 and 1840 a giant Dracula's Castle, once more called Bayons, of the most expensive and in other ways undesirable kind. The old man launched Charles into politics, and finally agreed in the early 1830s that they should alter their name to Tennyson d'Eyncourt, in pursuit of a Norman connection with many dog-legs through the female line and some degree of improbability. One must remember that the Eglinton Tournament, the final crazy attempt to restore ancient chivalry in the form of jousting, took place in 1839. The Somersby Tennysons deeply resented the splendours and pretensions of their cousins; county society appears from letters to have despised them and thought them ridiculous. All the same, Alfred was a little impressed even in spite of himself; when his peerage came to him many years later he thought of calling himself Lord d'Eyncourt.

The Rector raised his large family in pleasant, slightly hilly country, which is unusual for the county and much more typical of southern English landscape than anything else in Lincolnshire. The countryside is gently rolling, though the infinite flat fens begin only two or three miles away. The two houses stood side by side, divided from the church only by a lane. The Rectory was a small white Georgian house with additions that made it look long and low. The drawing room was yellow-curtained and book-lined, and woodbine crept in at the bow window of the nursery. Alfred Tennyson's room as a boy was a small attic looking west towards the woods. The most surprising addition was a dining hall in Gothic taste with buttresses and stained glass, designed by the Rector and built by himself and his servant and coachman, Hollins, in 1819. The Rector is said to have carved the Gothic chimneypiece himself.[16]

The Rectory has been several times altered since the Rector's day, and the old dining hall was pulled down and rebuilt in the 1970s. The house is not open to visitors, and is not worth investigation in any detail, having been transformed for modern use. But it does give a strong impression of the shell that once sheltered the family. Behind it, the garden slopes down into a little valley; once the garden had its own stream, a tributary of the local brook, but that dried up almost beyond living memory. The two churches of Somersby and Bag Enderby must have been tumbledown places; they have both been repaired with brick. Somersby has a late medieval stone cross, and Bag Enderby the boss of a Danish shield, and an oak tree where Wesley, who was a local man, is supposed to have preached. The Rector was often to be seen running along the lanes between the two churches, with his gown tucked up.

Inside Bag Enderby church stands a pleasing map of the area which claims to show the exact whereabouts of every detail of Tennyson's poem 'The Brook' marked with a pin; from each pin a string leads to a photograph and a quotation. Alas, when Tennyson as an old man was asked about these and many more locally accepted identifications, he grumbled that they were all untrue. All the same, his poetry is quite specific at times about Somersby, and it is often deeply interfused with memories of his childhood. The woods where there was a holy well are still full of snowdrops in season, another wood a mile or so away has a wonderful crop of orchids, the landscape is still agricultural, and Somersby is still deeply lost on the edge of nowhere. Harrington Hall near by, and Langton church which is not three miles away and looks as if it were specially built for Dr Johnson's first visit, belong to another and a grander world.

And yet the processes of agriculture have altered and were altering even in the poet's lifetime. It is not just that there were once no railway trains, no hydraulic rams or mechanical threshers, but that other noises of the countryside have changed and increased. Alfred's older brother Charles Tennyson Turner wrote of the lowing of the working oxen, the hum of spinning wheels, the bat as silent as a snowflake, pigeons in flocks where 'a hundred wings are dropt as soft as one', and the dull sound of the flail. Charles is almost fuller of feeling and memory than Alfred. Alfred remembers poplars and an elm, but Charles remembers growing marigolds, and the sight of green wheat 'surging through shadows of the hedgerow elms'. Alfred broods on the music that 'sleeps in the plain eggs of the nightingale', but Charles sets 'the mute eggs of the nightingale' under a breeding thrush. The 'plain' colour of the eggs really depends on what the bird has been eating. They may be vermilion, or have golden whirls. Alfred Tennyson is a particularly innocent poet.

The little Tennysons passed their boyhood in the world of Peter De Wint. English watercolour painting was at its height when they were young men, but Cotman, perhaps the most brilliant of them all, already had to seek out wild places as he sought out the picturesque (his famous and very beautiful picture of the bridge at Rokeby greatly exaggerates the wildness of the place), and with Ruskin and Hopkins a few years later conservation was a serious issue. (Charles Tennyson protested at the felling of trees by an absentee landlord.)

We know that the Rector played the harp (and Alfred the flute and Charles several instruments). Both of them wrote poems about harps, though Charles's was about an Aeolian harp, but there is no necessary connection of the poems with the Rector. Later in life, one of their sisters played. Charles wrote more than once about pictures: once, in Sonnet 163, about a picture remembered from childhood. It was of Armida and Rinaldo, and a likely romantic subject for one of

those Italian paintings of his father's which in later representations
appear quite black. No doubt the candle smoke of a century had
done its work thoroughly. It is pleasing to know the subject:

> The man asleep, so near to love or harm;
> The wingèd boy, that stays Armida's arm,
> The siren girl, all hushed lest he awake;
> While, in the background of that pictured tale,
> Sown with enchanted herbs, and clad with gloom,
> A sombre eminence o'erlooks the vale

It is not one of his better poems, but he does remember the picture
extremely clearly. Sir Charles Tennyson, Alfred's grandson, recalled
the pictures as quite a good collection of minor old masters. The
romantic influence of paintings and illustrations must be taken into
account when one is thinking about children crazy about poetry.

Not all influences are literary; Alfred's memories are intermingled
with his dreams. He used to dream poems; one was a very long one
about fairies with the lines getting shorter and shorter, ending in fifty
or sixty of two syllables each. He forgot them of course when he
woke, but he did tell Lewis Carroll about them in 1859. When he
was about ten, he dreamed:

> May a cock-sparrow
> Write to a barrow?
> I hope you'll excuse
> My infantine muse.[17]

His poem 'Memory' muses about some water buffaloes from a
book of his father's about Egypt, but what he secretly has at the back
of his mind or at the bottom of his dream is some naked girls in the
shallow water. The poem censors them. His 'Ode to Memory' is just
as unpromising at first, but suddenly at line 56 he breaks into reality,
with

> The seven elms, the poplars four
> That stand beside my father's door
> (56–7)

Then he is off again, with the brook about which he wrote often and in which as he claimed he summarized many brooks. But I believe in the reality of the

> . . . bleat
> Of the thick-fleecèd sheep from wattled folds,
>   Upon the ridgèd wolds,
> When the first matin-song hath wakened loud
> Over the dark dewy earth forlorn,
>   What time the amber morn
> Forth gushes from beneath a low-hung cloud.
>
> (65–71)

Of course this is early Tennyson: written in boyhood. His father 'considered this one of the best of his early and peculiarly concentrated Nature-poems', so the poet said to Hallam. One can sense influences, but concentrated is the right word, and the point to notice is that Alfred Tennyson really has experienced all these things. Matthew Arnold's shepherd is out of Theocritus, in spite of his 'wattled cotes', but these sheep and the dawn chorus and the sunrise ring true.

Alfred was brought up in a close huddle of children, many of whom wrote poetry; the three eldest boys were serious in their attempts. Alfred began at about eight. The others went to church but he was kept in by a cold, so Charles told him to write a poem. He filled the slate with a recognizable imitation of Thomson's *The Seasons*. The earliest lines of his of which we have any record survive only as fragments. Around this time he was said to have written a neat four-line stanza that might as easily be by Campbell.[18] 'Before I could read, I was in the habit on a stormy day of spreading my arms to the wind, and crying out "I hear a voice that's speaking in the wind," and the words "far, far away" had always a strange charm for me.'[19] Walking in the fields with Charles, writing verses in their heads, and walking on different sides of the same hedge so as not to distract each other, Alfred yelled out '*A thousand brazen chariots rolled over a bridge of brass*', so Charles told his curate in later life.[20] One of his most treasured compositions was the line '*With slaughterous sons of thunder rolled the flood*'.[21]

At about ten or eleven he took to Pope's *Iliad* and wrote hundreds of lines in Pope's style. He could improvise Pope's couplets, and so could both his brothers, 'for my father was a poet and could write regular metre very skilfully'.[22] The boys competed in storytelling. This must haved been the time of Alfred's long episodic story 'The Old Horse', which kept the children enthralled for months. 'At about twelve and onward I wrote an epic of six thousand lines à la Walter Scott' (that is, in octosyllabic stanzas). It is fair to discern a falling off, if not in his achievement at least in his taste. He was going downhill towards adolescence. By about 1822 he used to go for long rambles in the fields with his brother Arthur (b. 1814), and said to him, knowing he was going to be a poet, 'Well, Arthur, I mean to be famous.' It is a little like Auden, who as a youth was asked by Neville Coghill what he wanted to be. 'A poet.' 'Well then, reading English should be very useful to you.' 'No, sir, you don't understand. I mean a great poet.'

There is no doubt that Alfred grew up sweetly into a brilliance that surprised everyone and which his father noticed with pride. The stories of his ability are easy to believe; only his abundance is unusual. It should be stressed that it was very common in his day to write poetry; it was hardly more than a gentlemanly accomplishment in his circles, and many friends of his wholly without talent published books of verse. Families even in our lifetimes produce children's newspapers in manuscript. I myself, for example, at ten or eleven wrote an act or two of a play in 'Shakespearean' blank verse, and started an epic about the 1914 war, for no particular reason; nor was that at all abnormal behaviour as late as the 1940s. The difference is not just Tennyson's wonderful ear and intellectual superiority, but the fact that in his generation people read poems like Beattie's *The Minstrel or The Progress of Genius*, and took them seriously. It is fascinating that Beattie himself learnt to versify by studying Ogilby's translation of Virgil,[23] a neglected book since Dryden, which was written and published under the Commonwealth, but does have a special hold on Virgilian music; children were thrilled by its illustrations. The only other English poets to be such elegant and accomplished beginners as Tennyson are Milton and Blake.

The line I have mentioned about a voice in the wind is interesting in other ways. It may be adapted from some poem he had read. Auden thought it implied a deep anxiety about his identity. The poet tells us later in life that he used to go into a kind of trance, and recent scholars have sought to diagnose epilepsy, or the fear of epilepsy, which he is supposed to have caught from his father. But his father was not epileptic, nor is epilepsy inherited, and there is not the slightest evidence that Alfred had epilepsy. His brothers and sisters were all eccentric, one mad, but none of them was epileptic. Scholars have been seduced by connecting 'epilepsy' with sexual guilt, and insinuating its presence because it used to be imagined that masturbation was a cause of epilepsy. But this does not hold water. The only epilepsy which just possibly could have affected the Rector is temporal lobe epilepsy, which is extremely rare. A doctor told the Rector's mother his fits were 'catalepsy, not epilepsy', and drink is a much likelier cause of his ailments. As for Alfred, William James dealt with the case in his *The Varieties of Religious Experience*, basing his view on the poem 'The Two Voices', and in a letter Tennyson wrote to B. P. Blood, of Amsterdam, NY, in May 1874 describing 'a kind of waking trance I have frequently had, quite up from boyhood, when I have been all alone'. He induced it by repeating his own name until his individuality 'seemed to dissolve and fade away into boundless being'. His friend the scientist Tyndall remembers him saying, 'By God Almighty! There is no delusion in the matter! It is no nebulous ecstasy, but a state of transcendent wonder, associated with absolute clearness of mind.' James calls Tennyson's experience an extremely frequent phenomenon, and so it is;[24] he goes on to attack the view of Sir James Crichton-Browne that 'they connect themselves with the perplexed and scared disturbances of self-consciousness which occasionally precede epileptic attacks'. James calls that 'a rather absurdly alarmist view'. His whole chapter is a remarkable example of tact and common sense.[25]

There is nothing queerer about Alfred's trances than there is about Charles becoming addicted to drugs on medical advice as an adult and finding them hard to shake off, or about Fred's addiction to Mozart or poor Edward's adult madness. Alfred grew up rather normally. When his father was drunk or in a bad temper, he ran outside and hid and wept among the tombstones. But that did not occupy his entire youth. When Cecilia was about four, Alfred was twelve and living at home. An anecdote of hers can scarcely be any earlier, in which she remembers sitting on his knee on winter evenings by the firelight with Arthur (who was then seven) and Matilda (five) leaning on him on either side, and the baby Horatio (two) between his legs, while he enchanted them with stories about knights and forests and dragons and mountains, and Indians and demons and witches. The period of the story fits his turning to Scott, and suggests also *The Devil and the Lady*, which he wrote at fourteen, as his father certifies.[26]

By then his childhood was over. The fortified camps with a willow wand for king and a guard of strong sticks which the brothers stoned to death were abandoned. When all the elder brothers together put on Elizabethan plays in the drawing room, it was Alfred with his mastery of verse and his fine voice that his parents picked out as the future actor; when he was ill and almost died, his father said England had nearly lost one of its great poets. There is no doubt that by that time the family knew what they were dealing with. But what about his schooling? The curious episode of Louth grammar school, which he and Charles both bitterly detested, calls out for an explanation.

By 1816, when he already had two younger sisters and three younger brothers,[27] Alfred was sent away to school at Louth with the two eldest boys, Fred and Charles. They were day boys with lodgings in their mother's family's house,[28] which Fred remembered later had an enormous garden. Alfred was seven, but he took a dim view of the school, and it entered only slightly into his poetry. At eleven he left Louth. Fred went on to Eton, where he passed into the hands of Keate, a famous flogger; Alfred and later Charles were taught at home by their father.[29] At some stage there was a little tuition in elementary mathematics from a village schoolmaster.

Alfred told his children[30] in later life that he was given the choice of school or the navy. That is an odd choice for so tiny a boy, but it does confirm that the three older boys were sent away in turn as soon as possible, because the Rectory was too small for so many children. By going more or less together they at least had some solidarity. Fred remembered their games together in the big old garden at Louth, where they would each have their own kingdom in a different corner, which they named after the resonant provinces of China. But Alfred's only good memories of the place were a wall with some moss on it, and the Latin phrase *desilientis aquae*, which enchanted him. He would never willingly walk down the street where the school was, once he had left it, and nor would Charles. It is somehow symbolic that an older boy saw Alfred Tennyson weeping on the stairs and kicked him in the stomach for good measure. (He always hid the name of the boy who kicked him, who grew up 'the kindest of men' and a local doctor, but his name is to be found in the Lincoln manuscript of this conversation. He had never forgotten it.)

The place was a two-storey brick building of 1766, where the upper room had long desks along the side walls, a fireplace and an usher's seat. At one end sat the head, the Rev John Waite, at the other the second master and the writing master. The centre of the room was an open plain. A tiny side room called the library was reserved for beating. The steps were outside the building but roofed. On the ground floor lived 'certain almswomen'.[31] A gravel playground ran round two sides of the school; a garden with fruit trees in it was walled off. The Rev Mr Waite was bald, ruddy and bespectacled; he wore knee-breeches, white stockings and low shoes. He was a smallish, fattish man, who appeared in 1866 to be still quite unconscious of his wickedness which after all was nothing out of the ordinary in his times.

The schooling was pitiable. Reading was taught from the Bible, with a Collect or the reader to be learnt once a week. A very few boys learnt French once a week. The writing master taught spelling and mathematics.[32] The rest of the time was spent on Latin and Greek, but only the very cleverest boys, destined for universities, 'had often read a little Euripides'. The usual fare was Caesar, 'eclogues' (that is, selections) from Ovid, and a book called *Collectanea Graeca Minora*. The boys seem to have read a Latin text about English history in 1520: *Audito regem Doroberniam proficisci*.

'Teaching and flogging were convertible terms . . . The very air seemed resonant with the shrieks of all the generations.' The headmaster brandished a birch. He would begin by merely boxing boys' ears with his hand or a convenient book, then he would find a stick and beat any target he could reach, but 'these were but gentle hints he was among us'. He would at last unlock his desk and produce his special cane, 'a knotted thing' thought to have been cut from the Tree of Knowledge.

All this is described in an article by John W. Hales MA which was luckily reprinted at the time of the poet's death in the *Gentleman's Magazine*.[33] There were also better times of course. Hales was a happy, rather mutton-headed fellow, who loved the occasional holidays. 'What an overvaulting of desks, what glad clamours, what wanderings on hills, what bathings in clear brooks, what noises of battling with "louts".' He remembers 'tender interchanges of vows and oranges'. The countryside was thrilling, and the headmaster was building up the school, which had all but died out. He solicited pupils far and wide, and the young Tennysons fell into his net. Their

father may not have seen his mistake, because in 1825 he sent Arthur
for two years, and in 1827 Edward, Septimus and Horatio. Horatio
suffered four years, Septimus three and Edward only one. In the first
half of the century it was not extraordinary for boys to be taught at
home; schools were wild places. Yet one should remember by
contrast the exceptional grammar school Samuel Parr ran at Norwich, and the one at Bury St Edmunds where a lot of Tennyson's
Cambridge friends had gone, and where Bishop Pretyman of Lincoln
went, who became Pitt's tutor and lifelong friend.

The enchanting phrase that Tennyson remembered all his life,
'*sonus desilientis aquae*' comes from *Fasti* (IV, 428), a book of Ovid he
cannot possibly have read complete. The *fasti* are the festivals of the
Roman year, with the antiquarian stories and queer customs attached
to them. Modern sixth formers find them fiendishly difficult.
Tennyson must have read them as an 'eclogue', and what more suitable selection from Ovid could there be than the story of Proserpine?
The couplet Tennyson liked occurred at the very beginning, but the
word *sonus* is invented by him. Ovid's couplet goes like this:

> *Valle sub umbrosa locus est aspergine multa*
> *uvidus ex alto desilientis aquae*

(In the shadows of a valley wet with clouds of spray from water
leaping downwards from a height)

It is something to acquire a feel for the rhythms of elegiac
couplets, which did enter deeply into Tennyson's idea of poetry. It is
important, as he always saw, for an English poet to be conscious of
'quantitative' values, and the system of scansion by the length of
syllables, in English as in Latin. Indeed it is this finesse of the ear that
makes him so different from other poets. The particular phrase about
falling water has echoes in his own poems, but more interestingly it
has the melting 'l' sound and the haunting vowel pattern that he
cultivated. The whole passage of Ovid is about girls gathering
flowers. The list is pretty: *calthae, papavereae comae*, hyacinth, *amarantus*, thyme, rosemary, *melilotos*, roses, lilies,flowers without names.
Amarantus and *melilot* stuck in his head, and the sense of variety of
the flowering earth impressed him. He is at root an Ovidian poet,
and in searching for the source of *desilientis aquae*, one is delighted to
come on a bit of Ovid which is so Tennysonian.

The other textbook he said he came across at school leads to a passage equally apt. James Murray of the *Oxford English Dictionary* wrote to him in old age to know where he got the peculiar word 'balm-cricket', there being surely no such creature recorded. The problem is not so simple, because James Murray had collected 1783 Bailey, *Cicada*, the Baum-cricket, and 1783 Ainsworth Lat. dict. *Cicada*, a sauterelle, or according to others, a balm-cricket, then the passage Tennyson referred him to, which he dates 1787, and finally Tennyson's 'A Dirge' (1830)[34]:

> The balm-cricket carols clear
> In the green that folds thy grave
>
> (47–8)

Tennyson told Murray[35] the mistake of translating *Baum-grille* as Balm-cricket occurred in a poem by Theocritus in Dalzel's *Analecta* which he read as a boy. Theocritus appears on the first page, but that is numbered p. 215, so one need not think that Tennyson was flung into quite such deep water immediately.[36] The difficult dialect in which Theocritus wrote ensures that his poetry is not usually encountered nowadays before the sixth form, but undoubtedly Tennyson came to love him. The note that invents 'balm-cricket' is on p. 265 and it is more or less as Murray reports it: *cicada orni* Linn. Angl. the Balm Cricket (*orni* means the mountain ash).

To take the simpler problem first. Linn. must mean Linnaeus, who identifies the *Baum-grille* from nature. There is indeed a tree-cricket in southern Germany, though it is unknown to Greek lands. One might ask how this curious creature got coupled with the Greek word *tettix*. Apparently because some classical scholar in Scotland, perhaps Rutherford who is quoted by Dalzel, had coupled the cicada of Theocritus, a puzzling insect he had never heard performing, with a moment in the *Iliad* (III, 152) where Helen appears on the towers of Troy and the people buzz like cicadas in a tree. Aha, thought the scholar, who knew his Linnaeus as educated people did; he means a tree-cricket. Some lesser scholar who knew no German turned *baum* (tree) into Balm, and young Tennyson was duped into his enchanting neologism.

It would not be worth explaining this at such length if it were not that the queer bundle of texts brought together by Dunbar and Dalzel really did influence Tennyson. It is fascinating that he came across Theocritus early in life, because of all classical poets this is the one closest to Tennyson in style. He was at that time seldom translated and hardly exploited in English, but Tennyson went for him as a bee goes for honey. The poems selected are the first idyll, the second, the third and eighth, but this note is at line 148 of the first idyll. All the Tennysons had editions of Theocritus, which are now at Lincoln. Dalzel was used at Louth, but the Rector bought his Dalzel when Alfred left Louth and came home to be taught.

> Goatherd, that Pine-trees boughs by yonder spring
> In pleasing murmurs mix, and sweetly sing:
> And Thou doest sweetly pipe

That is Thomas Creech's version (1684) of the famous opening verses. I admit that Tennyson would not have known it, because Creech's reputation was sunk by his later version of Lucretius, but it conveys some idea of the original. When Creech came to the cricket he just called it an insect:

> Dear Thyrsis! O! may Hony drops distil,
> And Honey Combs, thy mouth, dear Shepherd, fill!
> It fills thy sweetness, youth, for Thyrsis sings
> More sweet than Insects bred in flowry springs.

Alfred Tennyson took other judgements from Dalzel, or from his father (his manuscript notes have never been thoroughly examined). Sappho's ode to Aphrodite, which Charles translated, and Simonides, whose *Larnaki en daidelea* Charles also attempted, remained for Alfred among the high points of all poetry. In Catullus he pursued into Latin the same taste that he had for Sappho. It was intensely romantic: of all lines he loved Sappho's about the topmost apple on the topmost branch. He was thrilled by the few handfuls we have of ancient Greek lyrics, though he found tragedy more difficult. Given the pedantic and unclear editions of those days, that is small wonder, and given his young age, it was inevitable.[37]

Meanwhile he went on growing up. He jumped the brook and defended the garden bridge with his 'sword'. Fred introduced an element of reality by bringing home a genuine fencing foil. Alfred smoked his first cigar, which the saddler's boy in Louth gave him, with entire satisfaction, and realized then he was doomed to be a smoker. His future wife first noticed him about that time, waiting in a carriage outside her father's house. He was then fourteen. His mother was worn out, though she would have a new lease of life when the Rector died. The Rector was breaking up. As a young man he had been popular in the houses he visited, and for years he kept up appearances, acquiring a coach when Alfred was about six, and sending his children to the country assemblies. In 1813 he had organized a doctorate from the University of Cambridge and was appointed Chaplain to the High Sheriff. At Spilsby Sessions the barristers rejoiced in him as a conversationalist. But the end of his life (he died at fifty-three) was terribly sad. His relations with his father had soured by 1820 when he was forty-two, if not much earlier.[38] 'You have long injured me by your suspicions. I cannot avoid them, for the fault is not mine. God judge between you and me.'

We know that when the poet was six in 1815, and the Old Man got the living of Grimsby for his son, the Rector wanted to move there, but the old fellow prevented him. There must have been a row then about the size of the Rector's family. But it was from 1820 onwards that he went downhill. His brother Charles had used his brother-in-law Matthew Russell's pots of money to become MP for Grimsby in 1818.[39] This he had accomplished by giving a cellar of coal, a stone and a half of flour and the same of beef to each of the voters, and standing godfather to ninety-two of their offspring at a bottle of wine per child. It may well be that foreseeing Grimsby as the theatre of his son Charles's parliamentary splendours had decided the old man not to let the Rector live there.[40] By 1820 Charles and his brother the Rector were on very bad terms. Still, the old man's response to the furious letter I have quoted was first a longish silence and then the settlement of £20,000 on the Rector's children. The Fytches seem not to have helped, though John Fytche (1783–1855), the head of the family, was Warden of Louth five times, the first in 1820, and a Deputy Lieutenant of the county.[41]

The Rector drank a lot. In April 1822 he went to Cheltenham for a cure and reported to his mother the doctor said 'a cirrhus' had 'not yet formed' on his liver. In November his father offered through John Fytche of Louth to pay £60 a year a head for any or all of the boys he sent to Louth or anywhere similar. Charles's wife Fanny was then at Cheltenham, and wrote to the Rector's wife, 'You will be surprised to hear he has a new suit of clothes, Hat and Boots which I vowed to buy him myself rather than he should appear in his nasty old schoolmaster's shoes.' So that is where the tradition of ragged and eccentric dress among male Tennysons began. The wealthy husband of his sister Elizabeth Russell died in 1822; at Cheltenham the Rector had been very kind to her, but now he became bitter. 'You would scarcely believe that she told me, a little time before her husband died, that my family could live well and be educated genteelly for £800 a year!!!'

Next year he had fits, and the family imagined he had epilepsy. He had 'violent Paroxysms' and was unfit for duties. His wife feared he was going mad, but of course he continued to drink. In August 1825, when Alfred was sixteen, he wrote to his Uncle Charles, the MP, 'my poor father is not any better than before. He had another violent attack of the same nature yesterday.' The attacks left him very weak, so that the slightest shock would bring them on again, and sometimes he had three in a night. The doctor treated him with large quantities of laudanum and calomel. It would be another seventy years before a doctor was likelier to cure you than kill you.

Fred went to Cambridge in autumn 1826 and his grandfather offered to pay. His grandmother had died, and Alfred wrote a poem about her: his grandfather tipped him half a guinea saying that was the first and the last money he would ever make out of poetry. The family feud smouldered on, bursting into flame whenever the Rector wrote another letter. Still, on the good side, he did not believe in eternal hell, would not say the Athanasian creed, and took plenty of snuff in the pulpit.[42] But the people said he was 'amazing sharp' with his children.

Even in that doom-laden and bottle-strewn atmosphere, the only injuries he did to Alfred were apparently temporary and did not affect his poetry. That was a strong growth that found its own nourishment, both in the Rector's library,[43] in books like the four-volume Burns (1809) and the six-volume works of the orientalist Sir William Jones (1799), and above all in the language and the strong, pure Lincolnshire dialect that surrounded him. The lyrics of Burns, which he adored all his life, were the first dialect poetry to be thought respectable in England; Alfred had an accent to his dying day, which sounds in modern terms like a strong touch of Yorkshire, and he was fond of reciting his Lincolnshire dialect poems, which he wrote late in life; they were his memorial to the lost world of his childhood.[44] They are salty and fascinating observations of provincial and peasant life, and no account of his boyhood could be true that failed to refer to them. To those innocently outspoken servants and peasants, the best witness is Canon H. D. Rawnsley. His family were Lincolnshire vicars before him and old friends of the Tennyson family.

> I remember as if it was nobbut yisterday, my man, as was a fiddler bit of a fellow, was off to Hildred's theer at Skegness, to play for quality at a dance, and he was cooming hoam in the morning early, and bedashed, who should he light on but Mr Alfred, a roävin and raävin upon the sandhills in his shirtsleeves an' all; and Mr Alfred said, saäys he, 'Good morning,' saäys he; and my man saäys, 'Thou poor fool, thou doesn't know morning from night,' for you know, Sir, in them days we all thowt he was craäzed.
>
> As for Mr Halfred, he was a 'dacious one. He used to be walking up and down the carriage drive hundreds of times a day, shouting and holloaing and preaching, with a book always in his hand and such a lad for making sad work of his clothes . . . down on his heels and his coat unlaced and his hair anyhow. He was a rough 'un was Mr Halfred and no mistake.

The Canon as a young man found a farmer at Gibraltar Point who complained about the earwig destroying his pear crop. Nobody ever liked pears, he said, as much as young Mr Alfred as a boy. What Mr Alfred?

> Why Mr Alfred; you know Mr Alfred. Ivvery one in them daäys, knew Mr Alfred here'bout howivver. You've heard tell of Mr Alfred Tennyson, the owd Doctor's son, strange friend of owd Mr Rownsley, as built the house at Skegnest?[45] He was straängen fond o' the jam as well as the pears, was Mr Alfred. My missus 'ud saäy, 'Now here's Mr Alfred a-cooming; we must git the jam ready'; and she would open the door and let the cat out, for he was a regular boy for the cats was Mr Alfred. I remember our cat, poor thing, went up smoke-hole one time when he comed in the door, and Mr Alfred said 'Your cat's is so shan Mrs G—', and like enough poor things. Not that he meant owt, but cats is sensible things, and they know who's who mind ye.

The Tennyson servants naturally spoke the same dialect. 'If you raäked out Hell with a smaäll-tooth coämb you weän't find their likes,' said the cook about the Rector and his wife. 'I remember the oud doctor,' said the rat-catcher. 'What a clip he used to goä betweeän them chooörches.'

Yet Alfred's poetry after his childhood became at its best neo-classical. He already knew Horace, and claimed later he could hardly bear to look at him again until he was forty.[46] By this of course he meant the lyric poetry of Horace. (One can see all the same that Horace did enter into him from his later poem to F. D. Maurice.) As a boy he was not ready for the lessons of Horace, yet his marvellously polished version of Claudian, a less demanding author, really is extraordinary, in the same way as the youthful Pope's version of Statius. The story is the rape of Proserpine again, the style Popean couplets. Claudian was popular because Addison, who quoted him at length, was popular. Tennyson probably wrote this at twelve or thirteen:

> A vine-clad thyrsus with celestial grace
> Sustains his reeling feet and props his falling pace.
> Ye mighty Demons, whose tremendous sway
> The shadowy tribes of airy ghosts obey,
> To whose insatiate portion ever fall
> All things that perish on this earthly ball
>
> (25–30)

The poem that follows this in the same notebook was certainly written at fourteen, because the Rector annotated the fact. We have three manuscripts of it though, the earliest being now at Harvard. The title is *The Devil and the Lady*, and it is nothing less than a blank verse play, complete down to line 63 of act III, scene iii. It is very jolly and spirited, and excessively macabre; as a boyish performance it is stunning and unparalleled, but all the same I do not know that it should have gone beyond home. Jowett told Hallam Tennyson to print it, and he did print two or three pages. 'Most original,' said Jowett, and so it is; with this ambitious work we come within the circle of poems considered for publication in 1827. Alfred and Charles held this play back, either because it was never finished, or because it would not appeal to public taste. At least that is true of taste as they understood it. Its vein is satiric and Shakespearean, its plot a morbid

folk tale set in Germany. Its true place is set against the early plays of
Browning and the preposterous plays of Byron and Shelley. Other
boys (and girls) of that generation had published as early in life, and
Alfred said later he had written far better things but decided against
printing them. It is a constant problem with him that poems do
suddenly appear at any time in his life which may have been written
long ago, though he does revise and recast; indeed he often shows
his genius in revision and not composition.

The 1827 book is *Poems by Two Brothers*, which turned out years
afterwards to have been by three brothers. What happened to Fred?
He went up to his father's old college of St John's in 1826 but
migrated later to Trinity. At Eton he had been Captain of the School,
and there he learnt to stand up to Keate with a degree of stylish
insolence. He was cool and ironic and while at Cambridge treated
the dons, his father and even his grandfathers as he did Keate. The
Rector wished he had never sent him to Eton.[47] Fred was clearly not
willing to be embarrassed by association with juveniles. In fact as a
poet in English he was dead silent for many years. We know that as
a boy he told Alfred he had a poet equal to Byron, and that he
brought home in triumph the line 'Waterfalls leap among wild islands
green' from Shelley, of whom Alfred never read a page before
Cambridge. He won a Greek verse prize there, and quite creditably,
to judge from a fragment. A few of the poems in this first collection
are certainly by him, and it must be allowed, since no one was quite
certain fifty years later which they were, or precisely who each of the
others was by, that all three of their styles were indistinguishable. I
am inclined to believe I can usually detect Alfred because he is a
shade better, but only just and not always. Fred must have been their
leader at least until he went to Eton; at Cambridge he was perhaps
less identified with them. This secret and rather negligent sharing in
their publication marks his withdrawal. Alfred's second publication
in 1830, which was planned to be with Arthur Hallam, though in
fact Alfred printed alone, marks the withdrawal of Charles.

Alfred Tennyson's juvenilia, like most works reflecting adolescence, advance in several directions at once. His 1820 notebook was
sixty-four pages labelled 'Vol. 1, The Poetry of Tennyson, Vol. 2,
The Lyrical Poetry of Tennyson, Vol. 3, The Prose Writings of
Tennyson', but its contents were all Latin elegiacs. In 1820 he was
eleven. At one moment we catch him with Fred bathing in the brook
(it was scarcely deep enough to swim) and running around with a

tiny brother admiring his tiny beauty, at another telling himself 'It won't happen', in the hope that wishes may go by contraries, at another hiding among the tombstones at night praying to die; we have glimpses of him dropping in to tea at cottages, reading to the old, and letting wild animals out of traps to the fury of the local gamekeepers, who intended to duck him in a pond if they ever caught him: we have a nice vignette of him flinging a heavy iron bar over a haystack, which a couple of village boys who were there thought no other young man in Lincolnshire could have done. His poetry in its neo-classic direction was becoming perfect, like a perfectly polished, perfectly useless rococo mirror. But *The Devil and the Lady* and the Claudian translation and 'The Coach of Death' and 'Armageddon' have something in common: they are all about devils and death. The whole Tennyson family, from his aunts to his brothers and sisters, carried the mark of their gloomy variety of the disturbed religion of the day like the plague. At their best they were intensely preoccupied with doing good. At their worst they were all subject to shivering breakdown and fear of damnation. Their father read plenty of Voltaire and refused to believe in hell, and Alfred followed in his footsteps. This battle went on all through his lifetime, but in his adolescence the devils had the upper hand.

It is not clear where the boys got their idea of what was 'acceptable to public taste', as Alfred put it, but the likeliest source is their father, whose poems would fit easily enough among theirs apart from an occasional older-fashioned phrase. It was from the Rector in more satiric mood that Alfred acquired his habit of mocking George IV:[48]

> O, I have passed a Southern summer's day,
> The dazzling landscape dim'd th' astonish'd sight,
> And in that overpowering blaze of light
> Entranc'd and lost I lay.
>
> The sun is set, and indistinctly seen,
> The fading visions wear a graver hue,
> And softer prospects open to the view
> Less vivid, more serene.[49]

That is the Rector. Alfred is more ambitious, particularly in unpublished poems like the Miltonic and Virgilian 'Armageddon'. His education shows through only in a mild mathematical obsession with cones. He enjoys long sentences, and is obviously spreading his wings for an ambitious flight: over-ambitious maybe, in the melodramatic style of Byron. At some stage his uncle Charles offered to show his verse to the fashionable Thomas Moore, Byron's friend, but we do not know the result.

The poems Tennyson published in 1827 were more restrained and ran in stanzas. Some lines are absurd, but no more so than the average of Hood and Campbell and their like. I remember how we found as schoolboys that the poems of this period were particularly easy to parody. Canning had noticed this quality in Southey in the 1790s,[50] and Alfred Tennyson used to like a joke about Campbell's 'Iser rolling rapidly' in which the poet falls downstairs and says 'We Sir, rolling rapidly.' (I was told that joke at school.) I recollect smoking-room humour about Tennyson's own 'Oriana', and about the end of a poem on Iphigenia where the sword 'touched her fair throat, no more'. 'What more did the good lady want?' a critic is supposed to have written. And consider this, from 'Memory':

> Round every palm-tree, springing
>   With bright fruit in the waste,
> A mournful asp is clinging,
>   Which sours it to our taste.
>
> O'er every fountain, pouring
>   Its waters through the wild,
> Which man imbibes, adoring,
>   And deems it undefiled,
>
> The poison-shrubs are dropping
>   Their dark dews day by day;
> And care is hourly lopping
>   Our greenest boughs away!
>
> (29–40)

This awful poem appears to be a blend of Sir William Jones and Lord Byron. It was not reprinted after 1827, and the other unreprinted early verse is not much better: take two lines from 'I wander in darkness and sorrow':

As dismally gurgles beside me
The bleak river's desolate moan

(3–4)

Charles was between fifteen and eighteen, Alfred between fifteen and seventeen, when the collection was put together, which suggests that Charles began writing well a year before Alfred.[51] It was Charles who opened the batting with some heroic couplets, the first sentence twenty-three lines long. Readers were asked not to examine with a microscope, because 'Distance on all a mellow haze bestows', and in that haze it is best to leave a large part of the tiny book. But there are good and characteristic Tennysonian lines, like 'winding through the whispering ranks/Of sedges on the willow banks' in 'The Vale of Bones', and it is never precisely his ear which is at fault. Alfred's longing for the sensuous exotic has already taken root: in 'Did not thy roseate lips outvie' he takes from Ulloa's *Voyage to South America* in his father's library the blossom of the West Indian Anana, 'of so elegant a crimson as even to dazzle the eye', as 'the gay Anana's spicy bloom'. In 'Persia', what he notices first is

blooming bower
Of Schiraz or of Ispahan,
In bower untrod by foot of man,
Clasps round the green and fragrant stem
Of lotos, fair and fresh and blue,
And crowns it with a diadem

(6–11)

which he imagines as a kind of sunflower. His syntax is vague here but he is excited by geography; his father's teaching will certainly have included 'work with the globes', and the store of general knowledge that imparted: at one moment ('On Sublimity') he speaks of Stromboli, Antiparos and the Geyser, at another ('Persia') of Cydnus, Trebizonde and the Euxine. He had already written an ode to Time and one on the Sublime (both on the heavy side), a lament of the Peruvians and a fall of Jerusalem, and followed Byron and Mrs Hemans in exhorting the Greeks to recover their ancient virtues in 'Exhortation to the Greeks': more importantly for the future, he wrote a poem 'Written During the Convulsions in Spain', praising a revolution against the reactionary monarch Ferdinand VII. That was

left out of the 1827 book 'for some forgotten reason'. The revolution
was put down in 1820 by the intervention of the Duc d'Angoulême,
to furious English protests, but I scarcely suppose the lines were
written at that time; they are simply Byronic:

> Fresh be their tombs who fall,
> Green be they one and all,
>   There may the red rose and wild laurel wave!
>
> (7–9)

Yet among all these youthful attempts one suddenly encounters
a stanza, almost a whole poem, of wonderful clarity and force. There
is one first printed in 1969 from the notebook kept precisely between
the ages of fifteen and eighteen, 'The musky air was mute':[52]

> The musky air was mute
>   Through the green alley's latticed length of shade;
> Her small and naked foot
>   Shook the pale dewdrop from the drooping blade.
>
> She came: her sad eyes glistened,
>   Her hot tears fell on my embracing arm;
> She spoke no word but listened
>   And in her eye stood fixed unquiet calm
>
> (1–8)

One feels this verse is too perfect to last, and indeed it does fall away
in the third and fourth stanzas, and could be criticized earlier for
artificiality of phrase. All the same it is a striking performance, and it
is the beginning of a vein in Tennyson which will lead to some of
the finest of his earlier poems, those about mysterious women often
encountered at night, often associated with the Lincolnshire countryside. They are fantasies, and they culminate in *Maud*. There is one
other surprising foretaste lurking among his early papers, 'In deep
and solemn dreams', once again unprinted (this time until his
grandson Sir Charles noticed it in 1931). It occurs in two of the
poet's Cambridge notebooks, watermarked 1825 and 1826, both of
which include poems of 1830. But it appears to draw on Savary's
Letters on Egypt, which was in the Rector's library, and it seems to
have gone through a number of versions. It contains one stanza

which immediately brings to mind one of the unforgettable images of *In Memoriam*. In the early poem it is the moment of daybreak:

> Brothers, come! the twilight's tears,
> Are heavy on the barley spears,
> And the sweet winds tremble o'er
> The large leaves of the sycamore.
>
> (46–8)

In *In Memoriam* these pleasant lines are transformed into:

> And sucked from out the distant gloom
> A breeze began to tremble o'er
> The large leaves of the sycamore,
> And fluctuate all the still perfume
>
> (XCV, 53–6)

Alfred at seventeen was poised on the edge of Cambridge, just at the opening of his tightly furled petals, but he was still a boy and his huge family filled one part of his mind. All his friends were local, family friends. His studies entered more deeply into him than a schoolboy's,[53] but it is clear that he still saw his future as a poet's without much thought of the university and less of how he was to earn his living. He felt he was a gentleman, however poor; the existence of his grandparents must have tempted him, and his father's hopeless expectations confirmed him, in an optimistic view of life. When one considers his brothers and sisters, it is odd how little any of them did except in the ministries of religion: Fred lived in Italy, then in Jersey, but to his dying day aged 92 did nothing at all.[54]

Poems by Two Brothers were published by Jackson of Louth, whose building survives, not much having happened in Louth since the Panorama was drawn from the church steeple. They were to be paid £20, £5 of it in books from Jackson's bookshop.[55] They got a polite notice in the *Literary Chronicle* for May 1827, which suggests that they scored a hit on the duller kind of public taste, and another in the *Gentleman's Magazine* in June acknowledging 'amiable feelings . . . elegance and correctness'. Charles maintained later that the two of them hired a carriage to celebrate, and trundled off to Mablethorpe, which was fourteen miles, to 'share their triumph with the winds and the waves'. Alfred could not remember. It is certain that they both adored Mablethorpe, Alfred in particular. Nothing could be heard there behind the barrier of sand dunes, Rawnsley says, but the hum of bees and the swish of the scythe. An early life of Tennyson by H. J. Jennings (1884) records the rumour that he once ran all the way there, which was not an impossible feat for a country boy. Mablethorpe was then the loneliest of hamlets, connected by a long barrier of miles of sand dunes southwards to what was still the small village of Skegness. The Rector's snooty brother Charles preferred Cleethorpes, now a suburb of Grimsby. This whole coast has now of course altered utterly. Alfred became a connoisseur of sea waves and of foreshores at Mablethorpe; indeed, he never saw such huge seas except in western Ireland and western Cornwall. At Skegness the families would stay at Miss Walls's New Hotel,[56] at Mablethorpe they took cottages, but we hear a great deal about Alfred on his own, northward from Skegness to Mablethorpe or southward to Gibraltar Point. Family seaside holidays were an important occasion of getting away on one's own to many generations of adolescents. Alfred as a young man sometimes expressed a preference for the religion of the Methodists with their sincerity and honesty: it was at Mablethorpe apparently that he knew some.[57] It was also at Mablethorpe that the sound of the *Iliad* became inextricably mingled for him with the noises of the sea.

Many questions we would wish to ask about *Poems by Two Brothers* cannot now be answered. We know that Alfred as a schoolboy at Louth once wrote an English poem 'for one of the Jacksons'. Sir Charles Tennyson thought the publication might have been first attempted in Lincoln, but that is conjectural. Jackson had a London distributor in Simpkin Marshall (the head of that firm had recently died in Louth, in 1814, and they had some Lincolnshire connections). There was a rumour that the idea of making money by a book of their poems came from the coachman, but that has been discredited.[58] We know that the two brothers wrote to Louth to have their names removed, though not kept a secret: this seems to have been out of cautiousness and genuine modesty. It is not clear how many copies were printed; we know only that it was too many, because a large number, bound and unbound, came to light in 1870. If Jackson printed 1000 at 5s. 0d. each, with 200 'large paper' at 7s. 0d., which was the price, then a royalty of 10 per cent on the first thousand would more than cover the £20 advance, so probably Jackson printed fewer. But in 1892 the original manuscript sold for

CHAPTER TWO

Cambridge

WE CAN easily enough imagine Tennyson's boyhood through experiences of our own. Even the remoteness and obscurity of the Lincolnshire countryside seem distant from us in time only as they are in space, and it is not too difficult to think of a world before motor cars and railways, a world in which the fields and farms are densely populated with labourers and a few men own everything; our own world can touch hands with it. But Cambridge in the 1820s is another matter: it is precisely to be dated because, sleepy as it was, it belonged to the broad streams and long processes of national life. The strange Tennyson quirk of building Bayons as a palace of fantasies in the late 1830s might have taken confidence from the amazing Gothic stonework of the Rector's old college of St John's, where the Gothic revival had already started in 1624 (if Gothic was ever abandoned in Cambridge); certainly by the 1820s it must have seemed venerable, and the New Court by Rickman and Hutchinson was going up, in all its monumental elaboration, between 1825 and 1831. Trinity's New Court (1823–5) by Wilkins was also Gothic, but much less grand (Wilkins had also submitted a classical scheme).

It is the architecture of Cambridge, more than anything else, which amazes the modern visitor and overwhelmed Tennyson. The university is like a town full of monasteries, in which one quadrangular court leads on to another and college confronts college until the mind begins to reel. Oxford has mysteries, it is full of nooks and crannies, but Cambridge lies more open, revealing its full brilliance in one short walk. Capability Brown had offered to lay out the Backs as a single great park or garden, and Hawksmoor to rearrange the whole city like the Vatican; both schemes were rejected, alas. In Tennyson's day, life was medievally confined to one's own college, or more so than it is nowadays, and although King's is the most obviously beautiful college and until 1960 used to be the most noble (it was founded, like Eton by Henry VI, and used to be full of

Etonians), Trinity, the foundation of Henry VIII, was in Tennyson's time – and I think is still – the biggest, architecturally the grandest, and intellectually the most distinguished of all Cambridge colleges. One does not forget the first impression of the vastness of its peacefully mouldering Great Court, or the baroque dignity of the Wren Library, or its avenue of limes marvellously insinuating age.

But this was Cambridge before university reform: its finances were mean and chaotic, its fellowships filled by nepotism, its studies undirected and ill-organized. In the generation before Tennyson, Richard Porson of Trinity was Professor of Greek, and the best scholar of his subject in the world since Bentley nearly a hundred years before. He was paid only £40 a year, because that was what Henry VIII provided; he found no suitable room in Trinity for teaching, so he lived in London in the Temple and visited Cambridge only to examine. He is said to have mocked the poet's father's Greek verse. Porson was the son of a parish clerk and a cobbler's daughter; he failed to get a Trinity teaching fellowship because the Master was reserving that for his nephew.[1] The Master in Tennyson's day was Christopher Wordsworth, youngest brother of the poet, a clergyman without charm or talent or learning, who was appointed because as an undergraduate he tutored a boy whose father became Archbishop of Canterbury and recommended him to Lord Liverpool. He had held various clerical appointments for sixteen years; he was now a severe widower and a staunch conservative; he fought a running fight with the young about their irregular attendance at chapel services.[2] Still, he built Trinity New Court, and in 1821 proposed a system of public examination for degrees, in classics and theology combined; this was presumably intended for future clergymen. The classical tripos was not his idea, but it swiftly followed in 1822. In Tennyson's day it was still a comparatively new institution; its three legs were mathematics, philosophy and classical literature. The first cemented, crenellated block of lecture rooms at Trinity was built only in 1833. The most striking and successful new building in Cambridge when Alfred Tennyson arrived there was the eccentric and beautiful Wilkins Screen which barred strangers from King's; that was finished in 1828. Thorwaldson's Byron (1829) proposed for the Abbey came to rest at Trinity a little later.

The number of new students in Cambridge in 1660 was 280, and in Oxford 305, yet by 1800 the numbers had sunk to 150 and 255: now with the new buildings it was increasing again. Education was beginning to come to life. So in the same generation was science, and even theology was emitting quarrelsome grumbles (in theology the result was the Tractarian movement). The Natural Science tripos at Cambridge dates from 1851; other subjects followed swiftly after that date. In 1810, Trinity alone admitted 75 new students; in 1820 there were 97 and in 1830 the number was 124. At St John's the new admissions rose from 57 to 84 in the same period. The young Tennysons therefore arrived at Trinity when the place was beginning to stir like a beehive. It was at Trinity that the movement began which was to carry Cambridge studies so high. Both Herschel the astronomer and Faraday were already Fellows. There were a lot of new prizes: in 1813 the Duke of Gloucester founded the Chancellor's Medal for poetry, and the Rector insisted Alfred should compete. Teaching was beginning to be taken more seriously, which is not of course always pleasant for those who are taught. Still, to any member of a later generation the undergraduate lives of the Tennysons would appear unbelievably amateur. Alfred, for example, does not seem to have bothered his head much about a degree, because he could not willingly undertake the necessary mathematics. The college did not mind, since he added to its prestige in other, more traditional ways. He was not what was called a reading man. 'I have met some once,' said Thackeray, '. . . nice fellows, but they smelt of the shop.' Those were dull, innocent, laborious scholars destined to work in the public schools and grammar schools, or more probably the Church. He was not much of a sporting man either, though he swam and rowed and fenced. He was perfectly fitted only for friendship, for poetry, and for the Cambridge Conversazione Society, known as the Apostles, who were founded in 1820 but first flourished in 1824 under F. D. Maurice, just in time to entertain him. There were about a dozen of them, and old members swelled the ranks.

Cambridge is not only buildings, which in the excitement of youth one may scarcely notice more than once: it is essentially people. In Tennyson's day there were not as many as there are today, but still Trinity was a respectable size with three or four hundred undergraduates. Edward FitzGerald the poet and W. M. Thackeray the novelist were both there, while the lugubrious W. M. Praed, sharpest of Eton versifiers, and the little rouged and dandified poet and novelist Edward Bulwer, preposterous in both pretensions but a worldly success, had recently gone down.[3] Macaulay was a very slightly earlier old member, and no doubt the servants remembered

Byron. But on one's first entry to a university one is conscious only of a sea of new faces, one's own contemporaries. It will be worth digging a little deeper into some of their lives as Tennyson meets them, because they were friends for life and they most deeply influenced him.

Alfred Tennyson got down from the top of the Lincolnshire coach to Cambridge in the early dusk of a cold, misty November afternoon in 1827. It was the 10th and he was late for term. Dinner in hall at Trinity was at four in those days, so he missed it, but anyway he had not yet been admitted to the College. Charles and Fred were already in residence at 12 Rose Crescent, and it was there that Alfred set up shop. He paid about a guinea a week all found, which was a little cheaper than living in college. His only resources were £100 a year from Mrs Russell, so he needed to economize. In order to be admitted to Trinity he had to be examined by his prospective tutor and by the Dean, but this was not too demanding.[4] His approach to Cambridge was in fact vague; he seems to have followed Charles there as the tail follows the dog, and surely the Rector was as relieved to be rid of them both as they must have been to get away from him.

Charles matriculated in Lent 1828, and picked up a scholarship. Fred had a scholarship at St John's but lost it when he migrated to Trinity in May 1827; his medal for a Greek Ode (1828) and Alfred's Chancellor's Medal for English verse (1829) were signs of competitive prestige, but less valuable than a scholarship. Still, the English verse medal gave one a first dose of fame, at least within the college. Macaulay and Praed had won it in their day; so had Bulwer. (Praed won it two years running, and the Greek Ode prize two years running as well.) Charles and Alfred both seem to have had their eye on the prize in 1828, when the subject was 'The Invasion of Russia by Napoleon Buonaparte'. Of Charles we know that he did tackle the subject, though his poem is lost. Alfred's attempt has some good ominous weather, a heroic or Byronic Napoleon, and a Moscow sunset which is recognizable today:[5]

> Her proud Pavilions and her mingled trees
> And Pomp of Oriental palaces,
> The pillared front of many an airy Hall,
> Crescent and gorgeous cross and golden Ball
> Glistening and flashing with the restless play

Of rainbow hues beneath the waning day

(37–42)

How did he know about the reflection of the rainbow hues in the golden domes? In moonlight they look like green silk. Alas, his poem was unfinished and never submitted, and the prize was won by the younger Christopher Wordsworth, third son of the master.

His lasting friends at Cambridge were not made at once. It is fair to call them a clique within Trinity. They were upper-middle-class young men mostly from the same few schools, of which Eton, Charterhouse and Bury St Edmunds spring to mind. In later life a few were politicians or writers, many were scholars, a great number became deans of cathedrals. He seems to have strayed into their number in 1829 when he won the medal. Until then there is a faint suggestion that the brothers felt out of things. They had altered their lodgings to 57 Corpus Buildings at the end of Alfred's first term; they had better rooms there, but they were now some way along Trumpington Street, beyond King's Parade, and Alfred found the distance inconvenient. When his mother met her brother-in-law Charles at a county ball in Lincoln[6] and was told his son was living in lodgings, she said it was a pity, because her sons were in need of a friendly room in college (this information was relayed with scornful underlinings to their cousin). When Charles and Alfred were summoned to be inspected by their young cousin George, the two friends they produced to impress him were John Frere, son of the Master of Downing, and de Vere, the heir to an Irish baronet. John Frere was an Eton friend of Fred's who became a curate in Essex and finally Rector of Cottenham near Cambridge. Neither of them figures again in Alfred's life, although they were friends of his older brother, and de Vere's younger brother became Alfred's friend later.[7]

He had his first encounter with Cambridge authority before he got to his lodgings on that first evening. He was stopped by a Proctor, a university official whose grisly duty was to patrol the streets, and asked, 'Pray, sir, why are you not wearing your gown?' 'Pray, sir,' he replied, 'what possible business can that be of yours?' It was the law to wear a gown after dark, so as to be more easily spotted in evil-doing; so Alfred was summoned the next day and had to explain himself. Inside Trinity he got on better. His tutor William Whewell was a formidable Lancashireman known as Billy Whistle, later the Master, and hyperactive in Cambridge academic reforms.

He had won the poetry prize in 1814 with his 'Boadicea', had become a Fellow, a Tutor, then with one colleague Tutor of a Side (that is, head tutor in one of the three subjects). He examined, lectured on mathematics, dived deep into Kant, scorned later German philosophy[8] and produced a bulky *History of Inductive Science*. He even coined the word Scientist. His writings include a theory of the origins of Gothic architecture, a treatise on astronomy and natural theology, and a theory of the tides, computing their behaviour worldwide; its pages were dense with mathematics and greatly admired by Darwin. When Alfred as an old man was told the Balliol rhyme about his great friend Benjamin Jowett, 'I am the Master of this college. And what I don't know ain't knowledge,' he thought it unjust to Jowett, but perhaps fair comment on Whewell. Yet they got on fairly well: Alfred used to read Virgil during his mathematics classes, but Whewell winked benignly at him. When Whewell emerged one day from the Senate House to be greeted by a crowd of undergraduates shouting ribald and hostile comments, he noticed Tennyson among them shouting, so he summoned him at once to his rooms. 'But I was shouting for you,' complained the indignant poet. Whewell was pleased and invited him to breakfast.

Whewell was still in his thirties at this time; he was excited about the new British Association for the Advancement of Science (which people called the British Ass), founded in 1831; one would have predicted a practical future for him rather than the years of theorizing which he lived. At one time he appears to have held a chair in mineralogy: perhaps only in the same amateur spirit as he chased an expelled undergraduate right round Trinity New Court, and man-handled him out of the college doors. When Richard Monckton Milnes asked permission to go up in a balloon from the college premises, he wrote on half a sheet of paper, 'Ascendat R. Milnes'. He is probably more interesting to read about than he was to talk to, but one cannot say that his pupils had any right to be bored.

Trouble did overtake Fred, as one might expect. He was 'always distrait' as a friend kindly put it, and none of the brothers went to chapel much, although the Master insisted on five mornings a week. The undergraduates resisted this new measure, and kept a list for a time of Fellows who failed to observe it. Fred went least of all, and when he was set an imposition neglected to do it; when asked why, he replied with sarcasm about the young Christopher Wordsworth, who had got a lesser punishment for the same crime. The Dean referred him to the Master, who rusticated him for a year. He was reinstated only with laborious heavings and family machinations.

Alfred was still preoccupied with home. He hated the 'disgusting flat country' of Cambridge, and his most moving poems were still about Lincolnshire. Meanwhile his father was accelerating on a downhill road: it was his father's death, when that came a little later, that suddenly severed his connection with Cambridge before its time. We know that the Rector urged him to enter his 1829 prize poem on Timbuctoo, which gives every appearance of having been cobbled together from the older 'Armageddon'. The winning verses were accomplished without any serious expenditure of constructive energy, but the days of flinging himself down among the graves and praying for death were over, and there is no evidence that he worried continually about his family. He was sorry not to have written home. He cared, but only in passionate fits. On the night his father finally died he slept in the old man's bed in the hope of seeing his ghost. It may of course have been Alfred's only chance of a bed to himself: the corpse lay in a barn that night because typhoid was suspected. In 1824 there had been 23 people sleeping in the one small house. When Alfred came home it was known in the district that he used to put up barricades of mats and rugs to keep the noise out of his room, and in 1832 when he wrote a poem about this beloved room it still had two beds in it.

There are small traces of continuity with home in his life at Cambridge. Alfred had a pet snake there, and 'brooded over its sinuosities' as it went weaving across the carpet. At home he had a pet owl which first arrived by perching on his shoulder when he hooted to it out of his attic window. There was already a pet monkey then, which was jealous of the owl and used to creep up on it to push it over. Many years later, his mother owned a black monkey in Cheltenham, which must have been a successor. The owl died in a rain butt in the end: from Narcissism, Tennyson said. A little later he seems to have had a dog, but that was really his little sister Cecilia's. It was a King Charles spaniel, which attacked a vicar in 1832 when Alfred had issued out at midnight with his sister and the cook, to ring the bells to celebrate the Reform Act becoming law.[9] He was always fond of dogs: at the end of his life he had a Russian wolfhound called Karenina (the only evidence that he ever read Tolstoy).

It is hard to know in what detail to trace his father's downward course, which was fuelled with laudanum and drink. The early letters

are tense with domestic hysteria between the grandfather's head-
quarters at Bayons and the Rectory at Somersby. As late as 1824,
Alfred just sounds spirited and happy, but then he was not a
protagonist. He had written in 1825 to warn his Uncle Charles, then
in the summer of 1826 Fred and Alfred were both ill, but hoped the
sea would cure them. The elders sounded worried. Alfred and
Charles got taken to London for the first time in June 1827, while
their mother visited a sweet-natured cousin near St Albans, so an
aunt reported on Alfred to their grandfather: 'I wish he had something in life to interest him as well as his beautiful poetry –
Westminster Abbey was the only thing.'[10] Suddenly the Rector's
wife was unable to visit her father-in-law because the Rector would
not let a child go with her, and she dared not leave the children alone
with him. He would not let her have the carriage unless she would
agree to stay away six months. In October 1827, his violence was
getting worse, which may lie behind Alfred's sudden descent on
Cambridge: he was already staying with his grandfather at that time.
In November the Rector had a breakdown and went off alone to
France. Two of Alfred's sisters and a governess were already taking
refuge with their grandfather, who picked up Septimus as well;
Edward was ill. The two elder sisters were Mary and Emilia,
seventeen and sixteen; Edward, who would later go mad, was
fourteen, and Septimus was twelve; the three youngest were between
eight and eleven.

　　Alfred's brother Charles proved himself one of nature's great
letter-writers in this crisis. He wrote to his grandfather: 'Travelling
chafes the desponding mind and gives it resuscitating friction . . .
these drowsy, hazy, obnubilated, gloomy, wet, blue-devil-begetting,
sunless, hopeless, joyless days of November.' Unfortunately he could
not resist a note of impertinence: 'I can fancy you taking your
afternoon's nap, inhaling comfort and complacency from an odorous
Havannah.' Grandfather spotted that Charles was in love with the
governess Miss Watson, who was in debt (there is a lot about debts).
He plotted to send the younger boys into the navy or the army or at
the least to Louth grammar school, except for Edward who could
become a solicitor's clerk. Before the end of November, grandfather
had written the strongest of letters to young Charles, who was
caught secretly writing to the governess: he threatened him with
financial and social extinction. 'Take no clandestine steps.'[11] The

poor girl soon disappeared northwards, pursued by creditors, and we hear no more of her.

In April 1828, the Somersby cook set fire to her dress. The Rector naturally tried to rescue her but he got badly burnt, and the cook died in a few days. This incident appears to have marked a steeper stage in his decline. The servants and the peasants whispered that he installed a new water butt so that if it happened again his cook could jump straight in and not bother him. Why should that rumour have so upset him? Did the pain drive him to more laudanum, more alcohol? The dialect poems that Alfred wrote in later life are thickly salted with black humour; he even quotes a Somersby cook in the subject of his parents, in 'The Village Wife, or The Entail' (1880):

Ya wouldn't find Charlie's likes – 'e were that outdacious at 'oām,
Not thaw ya went fur to raäke out Hell wi' a small — tooth coämb[12]

(75–6)

Whatever the mechanics of his mood were, the Rector was undoubtedly upset. He must have buried the cook and he may have loved her. His attacks were 'severe and harassing', and he was 'excessively ill from spasms of the chest', so that by the end of the year 'I am sick in mind and body, and have indeed great reason to be so.'[13] Then grandfather uttered again, displeased with Alfred and Charles and inquisitorial about debt. 'They did not act disrespectfully to me, but they are so untoward and disorderly and so unlike other people, I don't know what will become of them . . . Those three boys . . . are worse since they went to Cambridge.' The Rector was rather pleased with this severe view, and begged his father to confirm it in writing to Alfred and Charles; but Fred was too far out of hand to be sent for an inquisition. 'I regret the day I ever sent Frederick to Eton.' The Rector sent next door for Mr Baumber the local constable to expel Fred from the house, but the constable only took him in for the night. This time the row was about horses, and their use for running up debts in the small towns: the Rector sent away all his horses on loan to his father, and threw in the girls' ponies as a present. 'I can have no private communication either to or from my wife.' So Mrs Tennyson wrote demanding to have her personal pony back. 'I am extremely ill now and I don't intend to bear it much longer,' she told him. Still the old monster refused to return the animal. Meanwhile, Fred was sent off to Louth with £25 a year, ten less than the curate got.[14]

The drama over the pony continued like a soap opera. By the end of February 1829 the Rector had got hold of a large knife and a loaded gun, and accused Fred (untruthfully) of threatening to murder him. He cursed and swore at his wife until the air was blue. They separated in the end; when he was abandoned in his Rectory he took refuge with the Rawnsleys of Halton Holegate, his old friends, and for the past few years his neighbours.[15] But no arrangement of his lasted, he was desperate, and the noise of bitter quarrelling echoes from letter to letter like dry thunder in the mountains.

It will be best to finish this subject at once, even though it ends later than Alfred's season of Cambridge glory in summer 1829. In late July of that year the Rector was writing to his father and his brother from Geneva. They wondered, as his wife had earlier, whether he was going mad. Young Charles wrote a very funny letter about his father's reports of amazing adventures and miraculous escapes in Europe, from a coach that crashed into a ravine for example, and it is reasonable to suppose Alfred took the same gleeful view. They were neither of them morbidly oppressed by the thought of their father, though if they had all been at home together it would have been another matter. It appears that one of the girls, probably poor limping Mary who was most like Alfred and whom the others admired, tried in haste and distress to run away from home in January 1828, but unsuccessfully. Perhaps anyway she would not have fled far.

By 1828 Alfred had a number of new friends, and by 1829 he really need never be alone again. His life gives every evidence of continuing on its happy and spirited course, and the brilliance of his poems was becoming delightful. He entertained his friends by reciting old ballads, and he published another book. Meanwhile his mother was in despair. In July 1830 she wrote that 'when under the influence of liquor George is dreadfully violent.'[16] His convulsive difficulty in breathing suggests the long-term effects of opium. His final illness was from mid-February to 16 March 1831; his sons were there at the end. He died in his study chair, but all the windows of the house were flung open in a panic, and his corpse was carried out to a barn. Probably that is why there was a rumour of typhoid. That night Alfred slept in his father's bed, but next morning the Rev Mr

Rawnsley arrived and had the Rector's corpse carried indoors again. His pitiable deathbed in the country was such another world from Cambridge that we should surely regard it from Alfred's point of view as just a distraction, admittedly a grievous one, from a life which had been full for nearly a year. The Rector's symptoms were numerous, and very likely it was the doctors who killed him. In considering the hypochondria of all male Tennysons from the grandfather downwards, the inadequacy of medicine must be remembered. The Rector's lungs were bad, his stomach very bad, he talked wildly and had 'Depression of the brain'. His own obstreperous father lived on to be eighty-five (in 1835), still bickering grimly over financial arrangements.

The dark side of Alfred's feelings about childhood at Somersby came to light later, in 1834, when he had occasion to write to his Uncle Charles about the nineteen-year-old Septimus. Edward had gone mad by then, and Charles was heading for ordination, but the case of Septimus was urgent.

> My grandfather talks of letting him stop at home two or three months longer – if this is acted upon I have very little doubt but that his mind will prove as deranged as Edward's . . . I have studied the minds of my own family. I know how delicately they are organized, and how much might be done in this instance by suddenly removing Septimus from all those objects and subjects with which he has been familiar, and upon which he has been accustomed to brood, into some situation where he might be able to form his own friendships with those of his own age, and to feel there is something to live and care for.[17]

Septimus was afflicted with deep depressions and fits of ungovernable tears, which was how Edward's madness had begun. Alfred's letter is both passionate and sober. Septimus was in fact sent away to study medicine, but that did not last, and he is famous only for once uncoiling himself from the rug when D. G. Rossetti entered a room, and introducing himself with 'I am Septimus, the most morbid of the Tennysons.'

Alfred had his own fits of gloom at Cambridge, as many young men do. 'I know not how it is, but I feel isolated here in the midst of society. The country is so disgustingly level, the revelry of the place is so monotonous, the studies of the University so uninteresting, so much matter of fact. None but dry-headed, calculating, angular little gentlemen can take much delight in them.' Yet it was noticed in his circle that he had a Johnsonian common sense and a singular power of expression. All his life he gave tongue to whatever came into his head. When his Trinity friend D. D. Heath remarked on the dirtiness of his shirt, he simply said 'Yours wouldn't be half so clean if you'd been wearing it for a fortnight.'[18] He became at Cambridge liberal, for a time in politics and more permanently in theology, and all speculation. He welcomed science, or at least had the intelligence to notice it, and to respect and consider it. Alfred understood evolution in a Lamarckian sense before Darwin took ship in the *Beagle*: the foundation of his views probably lay in his being brought up by his father (no ordinary clergyman) on Buffon, that wonderfully calming and philosophic naturalist. Buffon had been translated and sections of his work circulated in handy little volumes in French, apparently for children.

I am not sure whether his generation or the Apostles within it were as amazing or important as has sometimes been said: I believe that they were. Their habits were severe: wine was forbidden at formal meetings for fear of quarrels; they stuck to coffee and anchovy sandwiches, which they called whales. Still, they were bursting with free speech, anti-slavery, equality of religions, and all the liberal causes they could put a name to, but social relations with their seniors were still formal and stiff; Tennyson remembered that a few years before his time you had to wear a white waistcoat in hall at Trinity. Ease of the young with their elders was the greatest change that he noticed in Cambridge when he returned there later in life. The most exciting thing in his own life at Cambridge was his friendship with Arthur Hallam, and their most important cause and adventure was their journey to Spain together. Even in their politics they behaved like poets, they did what Shelley or Byron might have done.

It is useful to distinguish Alfred's new friends by the year of their arrival in Cambridge, since very few of them were senior to the Tennysons. Within the Apostles, F. D. Maurice had been a strong influence both on the group as a group and on liberal speculation about theology, but he had left Cambridge by the time Alfred arrived. Connop Thirlwall was equally brilliant, but he had become a don and at the moment influenced only his pupils. In 1834 he wrote a good, vigorous pamphlet about admitting dissenters to Cambridge, with a sideswipe at compulsory chapel, so the unutterable Master of Trinity demanded his resignation. He did resign, proceeded to write a solid learned work about ancient history, then was luckily made Bishop of St David's by Lord Melbourne. He built and restored a phenomenal number of churches, and began to preach in Welsh within a year of his appointment (but the Welsh did not like him as much as I do).

In 1825 Trench and Charles Buller had arrived at Trinity. Buller was a Harrow boy who was rescued from that (at the time) failing institution and tutored by Thomas Carlyle. He went first to Edinburgh. He liked the Cambridge Union, and debated there successfully with Praed and with Macaulay. Richard Trench had also been at Harrow; his later life was highly energetic and successful, since he became Dean of Westminster, where he instituted the public evening services in the nave, and set the ball rolling that led to Murray's *Oxford English Dictionary*; he was then made Archbishop of Dublin, where he felt it his duty to undertake an honourable rearguard battle against Gladstone. But at Cambridge he was still literary, and crazy about Spanish: indeed he wrote a Spanish tragedy which was nearly performed, and his *Poems* (1865) are a respectable monument, still readable without disgust. However, no serious purpose will be served by quoting the poems. They are the products of a Scottish holiday, entitled 'The Isle of Mull' and 'The Herring-fishers of Loch Fynne', or at times comments about foreign tyrants like the Tsar, or bits and pieces of old mythology, or 'Poems from Eastern Sources'. They are charming and often tackle Tennyson's hollower kind of subject, such as the battle of Inkerman, and the wedding of the Prince of Wales. Trench is a man of abundant energies, who among other things sits down quite seriously to write poems.

Many of these young men wrote and published poems: theirs was the last age of the amateur, and they set poetry in a high place among their ambitions. The rules of the English poem were well known and appeared solid in their day like those of Latin Verse, so why should they not? We shall not see such a generation again. Yet to do them justice they knew at once that Tennyson was the real thing, and suspected they themselves were not: that is why they took him up so warmly.

In 1826 two wonderful eccentrics arrived, J. M. Kemble the Anglo-Saxonist, and Edward FitzGerald the poet. Kemble was the actress Fanny's brother, and drew many friends into a passion for the theatre unusual for intellectuals at that time. Charles Kemble was his father and Sarah Siddons his aunt, but it is Fanny's memoirs that are worth reading. She was known by all Jack Kemble's friends, and in November 1829 she suddenly went on the stage, saved the family fortunes which were tottering on the edge of bankruptcy, and became famous overnight. She thought later that Tennyson had been the hero of his generation and that this was the general view.

J. M. Kemble had uncharted adventures. We hear of him throwing his wife out of doors and flinging his slippers after her. The policeman who attempted to retrieve these missiles got a furious sermon on the Englishman's home being his castle. His degree was deferred until he could prove he had read Locke and Paley, since his answers on their works had taken the form of pure demolition. Paley's *Evidences for Christianity* was indeed the public enemy or Aunt Sally of the Apostles. Kemble was a fan of German philosophers, and at one time bore down headlong on ordination in the Church. The only good result of the Spanish affair, which I will discuss later, was that after long discussions with Trench over pots of beer at Gibraltar, he gave up the idea of life as a clergyman, and turned to Anglo-Saxon, in which subject he did valuable work. Later he took to prehistoric archaeology in continental Europe with the same enthusiasm. Thackeray, a good witness in these matters, calls him Black Jack and suggetss that he dipped into low life.

FitzGerald did not know Tennyson until his own Cambridge career was over, but he became a close and treasured friend of all three brothers, particularly Fred. The link there was music, Mozart in particular since Mozart was the advanced enthusiasm, the commoner level being Handel. His life was a sad one, but his character is subtle and captivating. Fitz thought Alfred looked like a god out of Keats, only with a pipe between his teeth. It was Fitz who spoke in later life of the champagne quality of Alfred's youthful poetry, because to him it was also a lost mood, a drowned time, a dead Cambridge. His parents were the richest commoners in England, and he kept on his Cambridge rooms for years.

Charles Merivale came up in the same year, to St John's rather than Trinity, but he had been at Harrow with Trench and was drawn into the same Cambridge circle. We have a letter from Alfred written to him in late June 1829, begging him to recite the prize poem 'Timbuctoo', perhaps because Alfred was too shy, or could it not be was worried about his accent? They knew each other already by

April 1828, when Merivale wrote to his father: 'I have got the third of the Tennysons in my room – who is an immense poet, as indeed are all the tribe – was the father so?' He writes to his mother: 'For conversation I fly to Birkbeck or Tennyson at Trinity, with the latter of whom especially I exercise dialectics by constant argument.'[19] There is a touch of stiffness about Merivale. He became Dean of Ely and was quite liberal, but his rhyming version of the whole *Iliad* is unacceptable and his Latin version of the entire *Hyperion* of Keats crushes a butterfly with a dictionary.

In 1827 James Spedding, whose family were from the Lake District, and Richard Monckton Milnes arrived at Trinity with the Tennysons, and J. W. Blakesley from St Paul's arrived at Corpus Christi, but as all his friends were at Trinity he migrated there in 1830. Spedding, whom Tennyson called 'our Pope' and the wisest of the Apostles, his best friend and adviser after Hallam died, devoted his life to Bacon, a Trinity man immortalized in the college by Roubiliac. He had intended to rescue Bacon's reputation as a moralist, but his friends thought he left it worse than he found it. Still, he was a talented historian, and Froude was his cousin. James Spedding was the second son of a squire who had been to school with Wordsworth. James could draw with an astonishing skill: his Hallam, his self-portrait and his Tennyson all convey much that we would not otherwise understand. No one else shows Hallam with a lute, or fencing foil or a cigar, as James Spedding does. He was also a distinguished collector of books and manuscripts. But he never married, and roosted in the end with some sisters at Westbourne Terrace, where he was not allowed to smoke. Tennyson claimed not to know where it was. Even at Mirehouse, the family home, the smoking room contained arrangement for washing after one had smoked. The whole south side of that house was rebuilt in 1830 with higher rooms; James was happy there. He won the college declamation prize in 1830, and in later life refused the Under-secretaryship of the Colonies (£2000 a year) in 1845, the Cambridge chair of History in 1869, and an honorary degree in 1874, but he died an honorary Fellow of Trinity.

When Tennyson first spotted Richard Monckton Milnes he thought him 'the best tempered looking man I ever saw' and longed to have him as a friend. He was an amusing, lively figure who became a successful newspaper poet, a book collector, and a politician, though he lost his youthful verve as a debater. However, he remained a man of various liberal causes, a rich and worldly third-generation MP. He was generous in praise and always a somebody, not a nobody; that is the best one can say. He fell in love with Hallam but was severely rebuffed. He had been privately educated, had to live abroad as a boy because of some financial troubles of his father, but had solid English county roots, and added to those an enormously wide European acquaintance. Palmerston made him Lord Houghton. He was not light enough, or rather not pretentious enough, to be called a charlatan, though Tennyson compared him when he produced a book on his journey through Greece to an iridescent soap bubble. His principal Apostolic quality was vigorous energy and liberalism.[20]

But it was in the year junior to him that Tennyson was to make his most important friendships, with Edmund Lushington, a Greek scholar of the greatest brilliance who went on to marry Alfred's sister Cecilia, and with Arthur Hallam. They were both poets, and if Arthur had lived to marry Emily Tennyson, which was how his affection for Alfred resolved itself, they would both have been his kinsmen. Four members of the Apostles at least planned at one time or another to marry Tennyson sisters. But it is also true that Charles and Alfred married sisters, and so did Arthur and Horatio Tennyson. The reason is partly a tendency to cuddle up, and to want what one's brother or close friend has got. The tendency is rarer today, when families are not so big or so close, and social opportunity has enormously increased. Even in my lifetime it was considered a boy's duty to produce possible suitors for his sisters: or rather it was a past duty still spoken of, the shadow of a disappearing reality. In my father's day when a soldier died his brother felt obliged to marry his widow. What appears to us mildly incestuous was to Alfred Tennyson and his friends perfectly normal. Something similar should be said of his relations with Arthur Hallam. That was a normal, boyish friendship; long after Hallam's death it became a deeper heart-wound through years of brooding, and through the success of the long poem inspired by his death, *In Memoriam*.

Arthur Hallam was a bright boy who grew up to join the Eton Society, which in those days was an intellectual club that had a tiny room of its own and took in newspapers, but chiefly a debating club. It was called The Literati and is now called Pop. Keate threatened to suppress it, like the Vice-Chancellor at Cambridge who dispersed the Union under Connop Thirlwall and his friends in the same period

(1817 at Cambridge, the 1820s at Eton). The Eton Society was supposed to be confined to history and not allowed to debate subjects more modern than 1688, but it was clearly aimed at British politics as a career: Canning was an influence on young Etonians. Liberals did not always have the upper hand in its debates. The Apostles were high-minded, and the influence they exercised in later life was largely on the Church, education and literature. Political and dogmatic debates were excluded from their formal discussions. The old Apostles in London bought the periodical *Athenaeum* and ran it very well for several years.

Arthur was not just a wonderful debater, but a poet who had published verses in a school magazine and was described by his friends as the unofficial laureate of Eton. His father was Henry Hallam the historian, son of a Dean of Windsor and the Provost's daughter; Arthur was therefore not a first generation Etonian. His mother was an Elton of Clevedon near Bristol, the sister of Sir Charles[21] (a poet of real distinction fit to be named with Charles Tennyson) and the daughter of the Rev Sir Abraham.[22] This fierce old patriarch lived to be eighty-seven and was strong against Dissenters; his son Charles eloped with a Dissenter and was pursued by the galloping old man into Bristol, where he declared himself a Unitarian and had no more communication with his father until they were reconciled in 1827. The old man lived mostly in a seaside hotel in which he had shares. He married for a second time at the age of sixty-eight, in 1823. The Hallams saw rather little of the Eltons: Arthur went to Clevedon once, and writes with a certain tartness about it. He appears unconscious of his Uncle Charles as a poet, and the beautiful old house might as well have been the hideous Bayons.

An able boy with an allowance of £300 a year, Arthur Hallam was the son of a well-known man,[23] and the world was his oyster. His great debating friend at Eton had been the future prime minister W. E. Gladstone, in some ways a tormentedly self-conscious figure as well as an ambitious one. When Hallam was a cheerful small boy jumping off Windsor Bridge for a dare, Gladstone was in love with him. He wrote in his journal, which as an Etonian he already kept, an analysis of their relationship. In 1829 he wrote:

It began late in 1824 more at his seeking than mine.
It slackened soon: more on my account than his.
It recommenced in 1825 late, more at my seeking than his.

It ripened much from the early part of 1826 to the middle.
In the middle—[24] rather took my place.
In the latter end it became closer and stronger.
Through '27 it flourished most happily, to my very great
    enjoyment.

In early 1828, when Hallam was leaving Eton, 'it varied but slightly',
but when in mid-1828 Hallam returned to England, 'he thought me
cold'. Early in 1829 expostulation followed. 'I didn't increase my *rate*
of writing as I perhaps ought.' In 1826 Hallam had written to his
sister: 'Walking out a good deal and running the changes on
Gladstone, Farr and Hammer.' At the end of Arthur Hallam's life,
he had begun corresponding with Gladstone again.

Gladstone went to Christ Church, Oxford, but he remained so
subject to Hallam's magnetism that he founded an Oxford Club in
imitation of the Apostles.[25] The Cambridge club might as easily have
perished in a year or two as the imitation did. The tinge of
homosexuality that has clung to the Apostles in modern times
scarcely then existed, and of course Gladstone's and Arthur Hallam's
boyish affair was as pure as snow: Gladstone simply imagined it in
terms of a real love affair. The same is true of Alfred Tennyson's
deep literary and intellectual involvement with this young man. The
only thing abnormal about Arthur Hallam, apart maybe from his
father heavily breathing on the sidelines of his life, was that after
concentrated work he went very pink, suffering a rush of blood to
the head.[26] The Tennysons do not seem to have noticed that, but it
was a symptom of what killed him.

When he left Eton, Arthur spent some time in Italy where he fell
in love, not perhaps very deeply but more deeply than a ballroom
flirtation, with a pretty English girl called Anne Wintour. Another
Eton boy who was his contemporary, called Milnes Gaskell, succeeded at the time in claiming her affection.[27] One result of his Italian
journey which one might not have foreseen is the English fame of
Shelley's *Adonais*. That had reached England by August of 1821
when Keats was not a year dead, but it was treated with extreme
savagery in the periodicals and sold almost no copies.[28] The objection
was to Keats, and to Leigh Hunt's 'Cockney School': that is, it was a
piece of political and class warfare. The same periodicals had been
polite to Shelley in 1819 and 1820. By 1828 that water was far gone
under the bridge, and yet *Adonais* remained virtually an unknown

poem. Arthur Hallam came across a copy in Pisa where it was first printed, and bore it home in triumph. Monckton Milnes and Hallam republished it in 500 copies in Cambridge and it did become better known, though the Cambridge edition is said to be rarer today than the Pisa edition. It was an Apostolic enterprise, perhaps the first to have any serious importance. Shelley was not even Hallam's favourite poet, though they all admired him. All the same, Mrs Shelley would surely have included it in her coming edition anyway.

W. H. Thompson, the future Master of Trinity, who was apparently not much liked (except by Tennyson later in life, when they sat together in a garden in the Surrey hills talking poetry as old men), arrived in the same magical 1828. In 1855, when he was already no chicken, he married his old tutor's widow. That year was a famous vintage for Greek scholars (Shilleto was one), but E. Lushington, who left almost no writings except for Tennyson's 'Œnone' in Greek, was its champion. D. D. Heath, in whose house, Coldharbour near Leith Hill, Thompson and Tennyson would meet late in life, was another 1828 man. Three others in the list of friends arrived only in 1829: Henry Alford, who edited Donne's sermons as a young man (in an edition still useful) and went on to edit the New Testament, and indeed to produce 48 volumes of highly various literary works, starting with his own poems when he was twenty-one; William Brookfield, who worked his way through Cambridge as what was called a 'servitor', offering labour in lieu of fees, and W. M. Thackeray. Thackeray's deepest friendship was with Fitz-Gerald; they suffered together from a therapeutic class in mathematics for which they were farmed out to another college. Drawings commemorate it. Thackeray was on the fast side as an undergraduate; later in life when Brookfield had married an Elton (they met when he was twenty-seven and she was fifteen), and when Isabella Thackeray had gone mad, Thackeray had a long affair with Mrs Brookfield.

Thackeray and Brookfield had been allies in low life excursions. Old Brooks, as Tennyson called him, was the funniest of men, much loved by all the Apostles. He could make a whole roomful of them roll around on the floor with laughter. But his life was a sad one. His opium addiction may have been one of the reasons why he missed high promotion in the Church; but the Bishops were conservative, well bred and well connected, and no Apostle attained a mitre unless Dublin is held to count. Even the Canons of Westminster shared a grandeur of social origin in those days that would have excluded poor Brooks. Tennyson loved him deeply. He loved Thackeray too and rather secretly preferred him to Dickens. He said of the Waterloo scene in *Vanity Fair*, for example, that Dickens could never have written that; in fact he admired a kind of prose like the purpler passages of Evelyn Waugh.[29] But he saw little of Thackeray, and Dickens was his friend, so matters were awkward; there are very few references to the poet in Thackeray's letters. It is not recorded what Tennyson thought of Thackeray's verse, although we know that the poet used to entertain his friends with a mime of George IV, with his collar up, his cheeks puffed and his hair frizzed.

In the 1840s, Thackeray was to write of Tennyson: He 'seems to me to have the cachet of a great man . . . reads all sorts of things, swallows them and digests them like a great poetical boa-constrictor as he is.' Thackeray was first read 'some beautiful verses by Alfred Tennyson' by Kemble in May 1832. 'Perhaps it is his big yellow face and growling voice that has made an impression on me. Manliness and simplicity of manners . . .'[30]

Not all these men were elected Apostles; some of them were Apostolic fellow-travellers so to speak. But years afterwards Alfred Tennyson gave his son a list of his friends, and it was a rule that anyone up for election must know all the existing members, even though the society was a secret one. There are three others he mentions: Lord Dynevor's son Stephen Spring-Rice, and the two Scottish squires, Monteith and Tennant.

We have a list of the formal debates that took place in Alfred's day, starting in November 1829.[31] Should the clergy sit in the Commons? Hallam voted against, Alfred paid five shillings for missing the debate. Did the law of libel work well? Hallam voted against. Have Shelley's poems an immoral tendency? Tennyson and Hallam say no. Is there any rule of morals except general expediency? Tennyson and Hallam say yes. Hallam reads an essay on whether an intelligent God can be deduced from the phenomena of the universe, and both Hallam and Tennyson say no. Did the monasteries or the Islamic invasions have a better effect on literature? Hallam stays neutral. On 13 February 1830 Tennyson has to read an essay, but he resigns instead. This essay was about ghosts but he said he felt shy about delivering it. The temper of the society was sceptical, his subject was deeply romantic, and he felt passionately about it. (We know he thought ghosts do appear, but never to imaginative people.) He had really put himself in an awkward position by offering this, rather than for example something about standing armies or the game laws. Only a fragment has survived, which contains some introductory remarks, but it claims our attention because it is the only formal piece of English prose beyond letters and notes that we have from his hand, and it offers some hope of assessing the quality of his mind as an undergraduate.

He who has the power of speaking of the spiritual world, speaks in a simple manner of a high matter. He speaks of life and death, and the things after death. He lifts the veil, but the form behind it is shrouded in deeper obscurity. He raises the cloud, but he darkens the prospect. He unlocks with a golden key the iron-grated gates of the charnel house, he throws them wide open. And forth issue from the inmost gloom the colossal Presences of the Past, *maiores humano*; some as they lived, seemingly pale, and faintly smiling; some as they died, still suddenly frozen by the chill of death; and some as they were buried, with dropped eyelids, in their cerements and their winding sheets.

The listeners creep closer to one another, they are afraid of the drawing of their own breaths, the beating of their own hearts. The voice of him who speaks alone, like a mountain stream on a still night, fills up and occupies the silence. He stands as it were on a vantage ground. He becomes the minister and expounder of human sympathies. His words find the heart like the arrows of truth. Those who laughed long before, have long ago become solemn, and those who were solemn before, feel the awful sense of unutterable mystery. The speaker pauses; Wherefore, says one, granting the intensity of the feeling, wherefore this fever and fret about a baseless vision? Do not assume, says another, that any vision is baseless.[32]

This is a good bit of English though a little mannered. It is not as linen-crisp as Jane Austen; it might be Peacock or Mary Shelley. It indicates a feast not of philosophy but of rhetoric; the style might be that of some admirable preacher. The whole piece indicates a mind with powers and reserves, but not a wrangler, not a lawyer or a bishop or even a dean. He has difficulty with the final transition to a philosophic dialogue, but the transition is achieved and the questions are well articulated and neatly pinned in place. I estimate it to be better than the prose of Landor or FitzGerald's *Euphranor*, which

Alfred so admired. It is a pity he had to resign, but he only formally ceased to be a member, and his circle of friends remained the same.

In June 1829 Alfred became very well known in Cambridge, because the prize he won with 'Timbuctoo' was not a college but a university prize. For Arthur Hallam, another candidate, the contest was scarcely more than good fun, since boys like him were brought up to be competitive. Gladstone at school had prayed for the visit of an old Etonian (he knew Canning) 'to settle Hallam a little, and teach him he is not to triumph every Saturday'. When the Etonian Farr abandoned the quest for honours at Cambridge, Gladstone and Hallam had both reproved him, citing Fred Tennyson for his emulation.[33] The most memorable comment on the poetry prize was a parody said to be by Thackeray:

> Would I were a Cassowary
> On the coast of Timbuctoo,
> I would eat a missionary,
> Coat and hat and hymn-book too.

Thackeray published a different parody in a magazine called *Snob* which is quoted by Trollope in his life of Thackeray. 'Timbuctoo' is not in the same metre as these four lines, which none the less do sound like Thackeray. Monckton Milnes felt his own entry was 'the most powerful thing I ever wrote', and Hallam's 'the finest thing since the days of Shelley'. W. B. Donne felt he 'should have given the prize to Hallam'.[34] But when Alfred's poem was printed with the Cambridge prize compositions of the year, Monckton Milnes recognized at once and wrote to Gladstone, that it showed 'splendid imaginative power. I consider Tennyson as promising fair to be the greatest poet of our generation, perhaps of our century.' Hallam was delighted as well. They must have known each other already, since he thought that 'although Tennyson deserved it, he borrowed the pervading idea from me.'

The young men did slop their superlatives about, but they had probably seen something of the poems that were going to appear in 1830, where one can indeed for the first time discern a great poet in Tennyson. In March 1830, Charles published *Sonnets and other Fugitive Pieces*. Arthur Hallam, forbidden by his father to publish as Alfred's partner as he had wished, issued his own poems privately in late May, and Alfred published *Poems, Chiefly Lyrical* in June.

Meanwhile in Oxford in November 1829, a Cambridge–Oxford debate took place on the merits of Shelley and Byron, Shelley being supported by Cambridge against Byron supported by Oxford. Byron won, fifty against twenty-three, though the future Cardinal Manning who was at Oxford was greatly impressed by the Cambridge side. It was the new poetry that made an impression. All the same, Monckton Milnes claimed to have made up some of his Shelley quotations, and maintained later that no one at Oxford had ever heard of Shelley. The debate was arranged between Etonians, which is why Hallam took part, but not Alfred Tennyson. In the coach on the way one of them told Hallam that 'the trouble with you Apostles is you are too gregarious.' Gladstone, who took part on the Byron side, was already crazy about poetry, and Coleridge was a mighty personal influence on him. 'I have always loved poetry – though it is only during the last year that I have had an insight into its real nature, and have learned to establish the faith of the heart on the conclusions of reason . . . Oh Robertson, it is a hot atmosphere I am breathing . . . but since I have read Coleridge . . .' Coleridge's special contribution to this generation, and to people as different as Cardinal Newman and Matthew Arnold, was that accepting a religious belief was like accepting a poem. Vague as it seems today, that view was an inspiration then. It had repercussions for Arthur Hallam, and a resonance for Alfred Tennyson. In November 1828 Hallam wrote to Gladstone showing some reluctance: '*Shelley* is the idol before which we are to be short by the knees . . . I am sorry my taste is so stubborn,' but six months later he was 'a furious Shelleyist'. As for Byron versus Shelley, ten years earlier bets were being placed in Oxford on Byron versus Scott, to be decided by sales of their new books.[35]

It is tempting to write at some length about these extremely articulate and often amusing Cambridge boys, if only because so many of them have left letters and memoirs. Not all the memoirs were false, and they often kept journals as well. It is only their jokes that come faintly to us, like voices from far away: Lincolnshire did not exist, Alfred's address was the Grand Caucasus, Spedding's dome was bald because no hair could live at that altitude, it was mistaken for the white cliffs of Dover, ships fired salutes to it. Richard Monckton Milnes, whom his friends called the Bird of Paradox, is to be found in sly correspondence with Swinburne about the Marquis de Sade, and in trouble with the Customs over pornographic books which he bought on the death of his friend the Duc d'Aumale, fifth son of Louis-Philippe. He knew a man in Paris who bound books in human skin. He also appears to be the channel for a story that reached Tennyson about a King of Dahomey who liked to warm his feet in the slit bellies of freshly slaughtered girls: Alfred told his son Hallam that as a schoolboy.[36]

Most of what we know about them all is more sedate; its only fascination is the chance to see them through one another's eyes. But the light they cast on Alfred Tennyson is rather single: they hero-worshipped him. He was a striking figure, queerly dressed, tall and broad as a guardsman, dark as a Spaniard. When he first entered the dining hall and stood for a moment awe-struck and short-sighted, one undergraduate, W. H. Thompson, remarked to another, 'That man must be a poet.' From about 1829 or 1830 his poetry circulated in manuscript quite widely in Cambridge; indeed manuscripts of it still come to light in other people's handwriting.

He and Hallam hero-worshipped one another. In spite of Hallam senior's grim and canny suppression of letters and poems that might reveal or suggest too much, the papers have survived and been published, so that one can now face the question squarely: how promising was he? As soon as he died, at a pitifully young age, he was haloed in the memories of his friends; and *In Memoriam*, by being so obviously great a poem, canonized him. Alfred admitted as an old man that Hallam's future would probably not have been as a poet; and although his poetry is not negligible, being about as good as Moore's, intellectually stronger than much of Campbell's, and technically at least as able as Bishop Heber's, abler for example than Archbishop Trench's, that is probably true. All the same, he either subtly and lightly influenced his friend Tennyson, or their streams ran close together for a while. The lady of the lake entered into Tennyson, but then they both knew Scott: Arthur Hallam actually met him. It may be more important that Hallam would turn at once to any work of metaphysics, German or English, and drink it up like beer, on any occasion and under any circumstances when he had the chance. Gladstone thought he could have been a great statesman.

Among his published papers there is a long one about Cicero's moral philosophy which leaves me cold, because no one today thinks Cicero's philosophy at all interesting: it is derivative and in every sense minor. But another paper, about which his father had grave doubts, concerns the central issues of natural theology. It is certainly original, daring and most carefully considered, and I would be inclined to see in it a high degree of intellectual talent. It was read as a paper to the Apostles, but its most obvious and possibly its only lasting influence was on Alfred. There is no doubt that *In Memoriam* is among other things a dialogue with the dead. Fifty years ago it used to be thought a woolly poem, probably because of T. S. Eliot's serpentine judgement in the 1930s that Tennyson was 'the most instinctive rebel against the society in which he was the most perfect conformist', who faced neither the darkness nor the light in his later years.[37] Yet there are flashes of something sharper in that mass of poems, and Tennyson was not a conformist: he was an enraged old man from the Regency and the years of Waterloo who outlived his generation. If there is any note of strained piety, that is because as he finished *In Memoriam* he was trying to persuade his fiancée he was an orthodox Christian. However that may be, Hallam's essay, '*Theodicaea Novissima*', is courageously clear, though he ties himself in a strange knot in the end, arguing that 'the existence of moral evil is absolutely necessary to the fulfilment of God's essential love for Christ,' beginning from the principle, 'Can man by searching find out God? I believe not.'[38]

It is strange and sad to look through poems that seem so close to Tennyson's as a young man, or haunted by the same shades of Shelley and the other favourites of that bright, distant group of undergraduates:

> There is another world: and some have deemed
> It is a world of music, and of light,
> And human voices, and delightful forms . . .

> With all green leaves nothing but green around me,
> And through their delicate comminglings flashed
> The broken light of a sunned waterfall

Hallam's poem to Ben Lomond contains some unexpected prefigurings of evolutionary theory from one who died in 1833:

> Before the mystic garden and the fruit
> Sung by that Shepherd-Ruler vision-blest,
> Thou wert . . .
>   mammoth huge

And formings rare of the material prime,
And terrible craters, cold a cycle since! . . .
With moss-dark waters of a placid lake.

His Timbuctoo poem really was in some ways more interesting than Tennyson's. It was a Coleridgean vision with a bow towards Shelley's *Alastor*.[39] His epigraph came from Wordsworth, Tennyson's 'came from Chapman', though it appears that he made it up himself; certainly no one has ever discovered its precise source. Arthur Hallam's confidence stretched to sonnets in Italian. The Italian influence on our literature was the subject of his brilliant prize declamation in Trinity Chapel, which was when Lushington first set eyes on Tennyson, sitting with head bowed, intently attentive, just below the pulpit.

Alfred's own poems were becoming more and more beautiful. He chose stern iambic blank verse for his prize poem, which is said to have been a new idea at Cambridge; he now delighted in metrical experiments, not all of which he published, and many of which, having thrown them off as lightly as air, he probably forgot. In his 1830 volume he published a number of metrically inventive poems to girls – Claribel, Lilian, Isabel, Madeline, Juliet, and so on: they are not unlike album verses, but more clearly individualized, rhythmically as well as personally. The girls are fantasies surely; he is flirting, but only with his shadow. Even 'To a clear-headed friend', a poem he intended for Blakesley, wandered off into something quite imaginary.[40] Yet suddenly in the middle of this series comes 'Mariana'. There is something real and numbing about the depression of it, and 'The rusted nails fell from the knots/That held the pear to the gable-wall' is both so precise as to be startling and quite universal as a symbol. The poem is awful in its sadness, and as a poem absolutely perfect. It has a fine fennish gloom full of lowing oxen.[41] The pear was substituted for a peach only in 1862: a correction of genius that wonderfully dims and sobers the picture. The second poem, or rather two poems, in the 1830 collection that indicate a great poet are pastiches of Shakespeare as perhaps 'Mariana' is of Keats; they are songs called 'The Owl'. 'Alone and warming his five wits,/The white owl in the belfry sits.' In the second song he recalls and obviously wants to relive the moment when the owl really came to his window and sat on his shoulder. Of all the magical moments in his life, that one surely must have ranked very high.

The 1830 *Poems, Chiefly Lyrical* is on the whole a happy book, even the 'Ode to Memory' is happy, with the charming three-line compliment to Arthur Hallam, the rest of the poem being classed very early by scholars:

> My friend, with you to live alone,
> Were now much better than to own
> A crown, a sceptre, and a throne!
>
> (119–121)

This is not great poetry, and in 1830 all his great poems are about sadness. Indeed, almost the only other poem undoubtedly great in the collection is another song written at Somersby: 'A spirit haunts the year's last hours', with its oddly unforgettable refrain, 'Heavily hangs the hollyock,/Heavily hangs the tiger-lily.'[42] Others are just touched with genius in a stanza or a few lines, or they give way wonderfully to the sway of a metre: in the case of 'Recollections of the Arabian Nights' fatally, but in 'Leonine Elegiacs' and 'Ilion, Ilion' and 'The Grasshopper' beautifully. One should notice his range too, from playful humour to sharp satire, and his ability to cope with and to better his sources. The poem that began for Blakesley ended like this:

> Like that strange angel which of old,
>   Until the breaking of the light,
> Wrestled with wandering Israel,
>   Past Yabbok brook the livelong night,
> And heaven's mazèd signs stood still
> In the dim tract of Penuel.
>
> (24–9)

It is a fine Miltonic flourish. Or may it be a Methodist flourish, conscious of Charles Wesley's 'Wrestling Jacob'? Someone told H. D. Rawnsley, 'There was a Wesleyan Minister Master Alfred used to have a deal of talk with in them days, and he said he'd go to church on account of his mother, but he could well have liked to get up a meeting hissen, for the church persons were such hypocrites.'

Another poem with passages that touch a nerve is his 'Dying Swan', which appears to be based on Ovid's 'Dido': 'With an inner

voice the river ran'. The swan floated down to a great city like the
Lady of Shalott a little later, yet we are always in the fens:

> And the silvery marish-flowers that throng
> The desolate creeks and pools among,
> Were flooded over with eddying song.
>
> (40–3)

Finally, the 1830 volume contains 'The Kraken', fifteen astonishing lines, almost a sonnet. It may be Britten's music that makes one
love it more than it deserves; but it is certainly a boldly drawn
picture, and a gripping bit of verse. No explanation of influences
impinges on it. The best sonnet otherwise was to J. M. Kemble,
whom Alfred saw as a new Luther, a future priest of extraordinary
energy. That phase in Kemble's life did not last of course, but the
sonnet does come close to a Miltonic tone. Most of his early sonnets
are irregular, and the others are not as good, but Tennyson had
Milton's bare-faced delight in artifice.

Effingham Wilson, a radical and perhaps crooked London bookseller,[43] printed 600 copies of the volume in June 1830, with Hallam
almost certainly as the author's intermediary. In the last stages of
preparation in April 1830 Alfred lost his entire manuscript walking
home from Spilsby; it was never recovered but he was able to supply
it from memory.

Arthur first visited Somersby for a few days before Christmas in
1829, and at least in retrospect he felt he had fallen in love with
Alfred's sister Emily at first sight. She was just seventeen; her local
accent, like Charles's, was stronger than Alfred's. Just before that
momentous event he had taken Alfred and Charles to stay with him
in London, to meet his friends[44] there and to see Fanny Kemble in
her amazing, triumphant first appearance on the stage. They stopped
a day or two in Cambridge to hear a Union debate on Milton, and
proceeded into the depths of midwinter Lincolnshire. If Arthur was
not really smitten in December, he surely was in April 1830, when
he came back to Somersby to help prepare the new book. Charles
had already published *Sonnets and Fugitive Pieces* in Cambridge on 14
March and Alfred and Arthur had intended to publish a volume
together. Only Arthur's father's veto prevented him at the last
moment.

Alfred was delighted to leave practical negotiations to his friend, and promotion and puffs to the Apostles in general. Arthur Hallam was busy on his behalf, wrote a review essay himself, and got Leigh Hunt to write one on Alfred and Charles together. There were other reviews, one of them by W. Fox in January 1831, fourteen pages of praises; in fact Tennyson was beginning to have a little reputation.

Life at Somersby greatly resembled the first act of some lost Shakespearean comedy, at least when the Rector was away, as he was for Arthur's December visit. The first point of resemblance is that Somersby was overcrowded with sweetly innocent and spirited girls and boys. They were all in love with Arthur Hallam, so one of the sisters said years later. The overcrowding in the house drove them out of doors at every opportunity. The 20th of December when he arrived was a mild day, and they played in the garden with Billy, their mother's monkey. On summer evenings, the tea urn, which I take to be a samovar, a boiling water supply, was trundled out, and Alfred would manhandle the harp. One or other of his sisters would play it and everyone would dance by moonlight. Or if friends or brothers or sisters chose, they might walk in the fields at night.

In April of 1830 the Rector was still away, and Arthur Hallam confessed to being in love with Emily Tennyson. There can be little doubt that Arthur was in love with love, and Emily a little in love with her brothers; Alfred was no more than flirting with a masquerade of love, though his affections like Arthur's were passionate. When Emily and Arthur fell deeply in love with one another, Alfred was delighted. One day Arthur was walking in the spring woods with another girl from Horncastle called Emily Sellwood, who had driven over with her sister Louise. Louise married Alfred's brother Charles not many years afterwards and they may easily have been already in love: Charles seems to have got over Miss Watson the governess quite rapidly, and it was apparently only his opium habit, which he is supposed to have contracted under medical advice soon after Cambridge, that delayed his wedding until 1835. The Sellwood family were old friends; Sellwood was a solicitor from the declining gentry, born in Berkshire, who had settled in Horncastle. He was a widower whose wife had been one of the seven sisters of a famous local explorer, Sir John Franklin.[45] As Arthur Hallam and Emily Sellwood wandered along, a tall and handsome Tennyson stepped out from the trees. 'What are you?' he said, 'A Dryad or an Oread?' Alfred Tennyson had met his future wife. She was going to be seventeen that year.

It is worth pausing over what might seem so casual, not only because two boys so passionately friendly each fell within weeks for a girl called Emily introduced by the other, and not only because the atmosphere of Somersby that April really was like that of an enchanted wood, but also because Alfred recorded his feelings in poetry. The poem 'The Talking Oak' is a humorous and technical experiment, which no doubt for that reason has attracted little attention. It was not written until 1837 or early 1838,[46] and not published until 1842, but it surely goes back to the incident in Holywell Wood. The poet has a conversation with an oak tree in which he has carved a girl's name taken from Shakespeare: unusually for Tennyson's shorter poems, quite robust and sexual play is indicated, though only between the oak tree and the girl. She kisses it, it pops an acorn between her breasts. She loves the tree because her human lover cut her name on it, but the tree takes this personally:

> 'I, rooted here among the groves
>   But languidly adjust
> My vapid vegetable loves
>   With anthers and with dust:
>
> 'For ah! my friend, the days were brief
>   Whereof the poets talk,
> When that, which breathes within the leaf,
>   Could slip its bark and walk.'
>
>   (181–8)

When they marry, 'she, Dryad-like, shall wear' a wreath of acorns. The tree longs to 'have paid her kiss for kiss,/With usury thereto.' Let us assume that when Tennyson wrote his charming verses, after Hallam was dead but before he was seriously linked with Emily, he had forgotten the day they met, though she remembered it. The liberated amour at which the poem hints is free only because it is fantasy: the flirtatious verses to Rose Baring, and to Sophie Rawnsley when she was twelve, are conventional where this one rings oddly real. The bells rings, 'low thunders bring the mellow rain', and he discusses the 'baby-oak'[47] within the acorn. The poem is provided early on with a family of characters, as if it was once meant to have a plot, but no plot develops. The girl is modern – 'she left the novel half-uncut . . . she left the new piano shut' – and the scene is perhaps

Epping Forest, but it is impossible not to connect it with Somersby in 1830. Perhaps in some earlier form it had rolled around the back of his head for several years, until he forgot its origin. We are at least right to feel it as Shakespearean, since it owes something to *As You Like It* (III, ii), though also a little bizarrely to Aeschylus (*Prometheus Vinctus* 832) which he read more in 1830 than later. The poem has seventy-five brief stanzas, but it runs briskly and a number of them are in their Ovidian way extremely beautiful:

> 'Her eyelids dropped their silken eaves
> I breathed upon her eyes
> Through all the summer of my leaves
> A welcome mixed with sighs . . .'

> Nor ever lightning char thy grain,
> But, rolling as in sleep,
> Low thunders bring the mellow rain,
> That makes thee broad and deep!
>
> (209–12: 276–80)

I do not think the seven years that passed between 1830 and 1837 constitute the least bar to this argument. After all, Alfred and Emily did not marry for twenty years. But the day in the woods in April was magical, and Emily never forgot it.

In the summer of 1830 came the Spanish adventure. That July the Rector was due back in England and his family were consequently in a disturbed state. His wife had the greatest dread of what might happen:

> You know as well as myself that when under the influence of liquor George is dreadfully violent. Alfred is very ill and went to London to consult an eminent physician, as he supposed, on a case of life or death. He writes me now that the Physician hopes he is mistaken, but desires him to remain in London for a fortnight, and then come to him again, and has given him some medicine to take.[48]

Maybe he misled his mother, but he does seem to have been very nervous at the time, and his sight was bad. By the age of eighteen or so, he saw spots as in a liver attack, and he was very short-sighted: he had to use spectacles to read and a monocle to see what he was eating. There was a rumour he was trying to make his eyes worse, hoping for an aegrotat, a degree without examinations. His poetry was largely unaffected, since he knew it by heart and preferred to 'roll it round' in his head, sometimes for years, before he committed it to paper. When he recited poems Hallam would secretly write them down. Even in his extreme old age, 'Crossing the Bar' was composed on a walk and only written down when he got home. But it probably is true that his famous eye for detail comes from the intense peering of a short-sighted man. And, by his own accounts, he makes mistakes: the 'ringing grooves of change' in 'Locksley Hall' are railway lines, which he thought worked like tram lines. All his life, he was excited by enormous landscapes that he could see, and never more so than in the Pyrenees.

By the time his father reached England, Alfred Tennyson and Arthur Hallam were on their way to Spain. Fred had gone with them, but stopped at Bagnères, at the foot of the next valley. When they went to find him all they found was a cool letter, 'verging on insolence', Hallam says.

This story has been told many times, probably best in Carlyle's biography of John Sterling, who was a friend of F. D. Maurice and a founding father of the Apostles a few years older than the poet.[49] After the Napoleonic wars were over, the Spanish monarchy had been restored, but the present monarch, who was Ferdinand VII, turned out to be extremely reactionary. The *Edinburgh Review* for February 1815 had already uttered a formidable blast against him:

> The policy of some of the restored Governments in other countries of Europe was extremely injurious to the Bourbon administration. Spain, governed by a Bourbon Prince, threw discredit, or rather disgrace, upon all ancient Governments. The conduct of Ferdinand at Valencay was notorious in France. It was well known that he had importuned Napoleon for a Princess of the Imperial Family, and that he wrote constant letters of congratulation to Joseph on his victories over the Spanish armies, whom Ferdinand called the rebel subjects of Joseph. It was known that, besides all those imbecilities of superstition which disgraced his return – besides the re-estab-lishment of the Inquisition – besides the exile, on various grounds or pretexts, of several thousand families, he had thrown into prison more than five thousand persons, for no other crime

than that of administering or seconding a Government which all Europe had recognized – which had resisted all the offers of Bonaparte, and under whom the resistance was made to which he owed his Crown.

It is a grim thought that this was Goya's Prince of the Asturias, the Spanish 'Prince of Wales'. He abolished the elected Parliament, and re-established the Spanish Inquisition. These drastic actions were badly viewed in liberal England: Hallam was already indignant about Spain as a schoolboy at Eton, and London attracted a crowd of Spanish liberal exiles: first sixty or seventy, then several hundreds. In those days the royal family used to attend charity balls for the support of such people, though of course not all exiles were liberal. In 1830 the Duke of Brunswick came to London to begin his exile, with a grim, romantic face and wild hair looking rather like a Tennyson; he had been thrown out of his duchy for tyrannical incompetence. All over Europe the struggle for constitutional government and equality under the law was raging. Spain was just another case, which drew the attention of the Apostles through John Sterling's father, who knew General Torrijos. The General arrived in London as an exile in 1824, but by 1830 his affairs had reached a crisis point.

Let Carlyle take up the tale, writing in 1851: 'Twenty-six years ago, Spaniards were among the new phenomena of London. Daily in the cold spring air you could see a group of fifty or a hundred stately tragic figures in proud threadbare cloaks perambulating mostly with closed lips the broad pavements of Euston Square.' Torrijos had been in London then for five years; he was 'valiant and gallant . . . a lively intellect . . . he knew romantic Spain, he was . . . a kind of living romance.' One of his key connections was Charles Barton, the son of a lieutenant-general in the Life Guards: through Barton he bought a saddle and a sword. Sterling's cousin Robin Boyd, formerly of the Indian army, was even more important. He had £5,000 which he invested with a friend in an old royal gunbrig lying in an Ulster creek. Boyd's first idea was to wander away with Sterling to the Philippines and live there as pirates, but Sterling won him round to the Spanish cause, and Torrijos offered to pay him off with a colonelcy of Spanish cavalry. The Treasure Island atmosphere intensified, with visits to Cambridge, pleas for absolute secrecy, escapes from the Thames police, and gatherings of the exiles at Deal. Boyd's ship was arrested in the Thames and he had to swim for his life; Sterling jumped into a passing boat. Sterling at some stage made a dash to St Valery, but when the time for serious action came he could no longer take part; his health broke down, in November 1830 he married, and his first son was born on a sugar estate in St Vincent in the autumn of 1831. The end came in November 1831. After delays, abortive attempts and frustrations, Torrijos and his men were expelled from Gibraltar, chased at sea, besieged in a Spanish farmhouse, lined up and all shot on the Promenade at Malaga; poor Robert Boyd's body was delivered to the British Consul.

In the final act no Apostle took part, though Trench and Kemble were at Gibraltar. The crazy, doomed little expedition cannot really be understood except as a gesture of despair, and a small part of the powerful European reform movement which in many places, including England, was successful.[50] Alfred Tennyson and Arthur Hallam had a small, clear, concrete part to play, which was in itself a defensible action and which they carried through successfully. They were couriers with coded instructions to carry money to the revolutionary Ojeda across the Pyrenees; Ojeda was to raise a rebellion in the north. In the event he failed to do so. Alfred disliked him on meeting, thought him jealous of Torrijos, and seems to have been shocked by the fraternal sentiment, *Nous allons couper la gorge à tous les curés, mais vous connaissez mon coeur!* Alfred still felt ill, so when the money was handed over he lingered for a while in the mountains at Cauterets with Hallam. The end of the main expedition, of which at first he got only a garbled version, gave him a severe shock. When he had got home, a rumour reached him at Somersby that the Spaniards had captured Kemble, and he raced to Lincoln in search of someone who might help. Within a year of Tennyson's expedition, the King of Spain was dead, and the Spanish exiles almost all went home, though the constitutional quarrel in Spain was settled only by a long civil war (1834–40). But the new movement was inchoate and amateur almost everywhere in Europe;[51] it set up transmigrations of exiles, and consequent unexpected influences for 1830.

Cauterets today is a tiny spa town high up in the Pyrenees above Lourdes. Beyond it lies the Pont d'Espagne among a mountainous countryside of lakes and waterfalls. It is south-south-west of Tarbes and due east of Pamplona. As a mecca for connoisseurs of hot, sulphurous springs the place is historic and illustrious, but as a way into Spain it is negligible: to this day no direct road leads from Cauterets to the frontier. That is clearly why it was chosen. Alfred was thrilled by his expedition with its intoxicating blend of secrecy, excitement and the high mountains, and haunted by the landscape around Cauterets. He wrote a poem directly about it ('In the Valley of Cauteretz') on a second, much later visit in September 1861. Until 1850, it is likely that he felt mountains, lakes and above all waterfalls belonged to Scott or Wordsworth: 'The cataracts blow their trumpets from the steep' is a bold and incomparable line, and it might be typical of Tennyson, but Wordsworth wrote it in his 'Intimations of Immortality'. Now he had some mountain landscape of his own, to match *desilientis aquae*, the falling water of Ovid's *Fasti*. The first part of 'Œnone', Tennyson's Ovidian retelling of the Judgement of Paris, was actually written with Hallam at Cauterets; the 1842 version is the best, but the 1832 version gives a more immediate sensation of the time and place, so that I prefer to quote it here.[52] The habit of running double words together without a hyphen was a passing mania in 1832 and led Coleridge to believe Tennyson could not scan. He corrected the habit in 1842.

> There is a dale in Ida, lovelier
> Than any in old Ionia, beautiful
> With emerald slopes of sunny sward, that lean
> Above the loud glenriver, which hath worn
> A path through steepdown granite walls below
> Mantled with flowering tendriltwine. In front
> The cedarshadowy valleys open wide.
> Far-seen, high over all the Godbuilt wall
> And many a snowycolumned range divine,
> Mounted with awful sculptures – men and Gods,
> The work of Gods – bright on the darkblue sky
> The windy citadel of Ilion
> Shone, like the crown of Troas
>
> (1–13)

The shadows of the mountains, the caverns in the rocks, the crickets, which he now called 'cicalas', the violets and 'amaracus, immortal asphodel' recall the classics, but also the Pyrenees. Amaracus is a flower from Catullus, which Tennyson's generation thought was marjoram, but no doubt Milton was also swimming in his memory.[53]

The famous line 'Self-reverence, self-knowledge, self-control' has a churchy, even a low-church flavour: all three of those words were at least a hundred years old, though the formulation is apparently Tennyson's, and this brief philosophic passage surely reflects conversation with Hallam, who was a high-minded fellow and a moral philosopher. The whole poem is a dazzling performance for a young man, but it is still a young man's performance.

They went north through the sand dunes of the Landes to Bordeaux, and found the *Leeds*, a ship headed for Ireland. The voyage took them four days to Dublin. They made friends on deck with John Harden, who drew them, and whose daughter Jessie told H. D. Rawnsley all about it as an old lady:

> The weather was fine and we were sitting on deck. Mr Hallam was a very interesting, delicate-looking young man, and we saw nothing of him the first day; he was in the saloon. The second day was warm, and he came on deck, and kindly read to us some of Scott's novels, which had recently been published in one volume. In my father's original pencil sketch Mr Tennyson had a large cape, a tall hat, and a very decided nose.

Better still, Arthur Hallam wrote a brilliant letter to Alfred's brother Charles from Dublin (12 September 1830):[54]

> We remained at Cauterets, and recruited our strength with precipitous defiles, jagged mountain tops, forests of solemn pine, tavelled by dewy clouds, and encircling lawns of the greenest freshness, waters in all shapes and all powers, from the clear runnels babbling down over our mountain paths at intervals, to the blue little lake whose deep, cold waters are fed eternally from neighbouring glaciers, and the impetuous cataract, fraying its way over black, beetling rocks.

It can easily be seen how closely intertwined the two of them were at this time, in language and in the experience of life. As time went on, Arthur showed a tendency to communicate in sonnets, which until Wordsworth and the dull Bowles and now these young men, had been the reserve of personal feelings and the speciality of women poets writing in the magazines. Whenever an Apostle asked

Alfred for a poem or the mood took him, he would now respond with a sonnet like a snapshot.

On 20 September they took the first train that ever ran from Liverpool to Manchester, the one that killed the politician Mr Huskisson. Both Charles and Alfred felt ill and were two weeks late for the Cambridge term in October, but by early November Alfred looked 'better than ever'. One notices that Arthur Hallam was warmly concerned about Alfred's health but became as the years passed distinctly humorous about his ailments. There seems to be little doubt that as a young man Alfred was a hypochondriac. But moments of excitement always found him ready for action.

In December there were riots and rick-fires in Cambridgeshire. A mob is said to have threatened to attack the town and burn down the university library, which occupied the old teaching schools and was soon to have Cockerell's fine 'Old Library' built for it, which is now the Law Library. An undergraduate militia happily defended the colleges, and in this cheerful enterprise the Apostles were prominent, armed with sticks. Alfred always liked the idea of a fight, and late in life he gleefully passed on to his son Hallam the instruction he got from an old Waterloo sergeant in London street-fighting.[55] The idea was to lunge at your adversary's belly with the point of your umbrella. He was, as Garlyle said of him, a spoiled Life-guardsman. He helped at that time in the saving of a farm at Coton, where the undergraduates' misplaced enthusiasm for dismantling thatched roofs had the farmer begging them for mercy. Alfred met a peasant who declared with glee that now we shall have potatoes cheap; the poet warned him of the opposite: liberal and generous as he was, one observes he was essentially conservative, as poets tend to be.

In December he took Arthur Hallam home to Somersby to get him formally engaged to Emily, presumably with the Rector's consent. Both were nineteen and Alfred was twenty-one. By being in Lincolnshire, they missed a visit of William Wordsworth to the Master's Lodge at Trinity. He met some Apostles at coffee in James Spedding's rooms, because John Spedding, James's father, had been at school with him, and they were neighbours. Tennant wrote to Somersby that the poet was 'furiously alarmist – nothing but revolutions and reigns of terror and all that . . . upon the whole he said nothing very profound or original, but I enjoyed his talk till one o'clock in the morning; he was also pleased with his hearers.'[56]

In late February 1831 Cambridge was suddenly over. Alfred was summoned home for his father's death, which took place on 16 March. The night he left, the Apostles held a dinner in the old rooms in Corpus Buildings, in Trumpington Street. They ended with dancing, as they so often did, and the dancing ended with a solemn quadrille. Alfred's last sight of Cambridge was Thompson's handsome face under a streetlamp. Later on Charles took his degree, and became a clergyman, but Alfred withdrew, and refused his grandfather's direction into the Church. He was still writing under the influence of the previous summer. In fact to judge from his poetry his father might not have died and he might not have left the University. 'Mariana in the South' began to circulate in mid-February. Alfred Tennyson was quite obviously going to be a great poet; small wonder that the Apostles were gleeful or that his brothers fell silent. There stretched before him a whole lifetime of poetry, in some ways a thrilling prospect, in some ways a dreary one. He was trained in the classical languages and knew the English poets, but he was essentially an oral poet, who rolled his poetry around his head before he wrote it down; one in whose work memory and imagination were inextricable.

He left Cambrige mutinous against its authorities and negligent of most of its studies. The one thing the Master of Trinity could have given him, acquaintance with William Wordsworth, he missed. He was both fortunate and courageous to avoid priesthood and the status of minor poet that it would probaby have imposed on him. He was fortunate also not to fall into the fashionable trap of social poets like Praed[57] and the awful Bulwer, but his taproot went deeper than theirs. His unpublished poem 'Milton's Mulberry'[58] indicates something of his mood. It is of course unreasonable: Milton's college did not only whip or rusticate him and by the time of Milton's death no public monument to him would have been permitted; the mulberry tree was something after all:

Look what love the puddle-pated squarecaps have for me!
I am Milton's mulberry, Milton's Milton's mulberry –
But they whipt and rusticated him that planted me,
Milton's Milton's mulberry, Milton's Milton's mulberry.
Old and hollow, somewhat crooked in the shoulders as you see,
Full of summer foliage yet but propt and padded curiously,
I would sooner have been planted by the hand that planted me,

Than have grown in Paradise and dropt my fruit on Adam's knee –
Look what love the tiny-witted trenchers have for me.

This is oral poetry, composed to be recited, as it were with hammering on the table, and among friends: it requires declamation.[59]

CHAPTER THREE

The Bud Nipped

WHEN THEIR father died, the eldest Tennyson brothers took it hard and solemnly: they wrote grave letters about it and realized that they must soon leave home. The next Rector was going to be Mr Burton's son, who was with them at Trinity; once that was made plain they gained a postponement, since Mr Burton lived at Spilsby, and had no use for the Rectory house until his son should marry and be ready to take over the living. Mrs Tennyson could go on living at Somersby a few more years, provided she employed curates to do the work. Naturally she did so, but the monstrous old man at Tealby now bore down on her and all the children as head of the family. His favoured son Charles was busy in London, where he held the minor office of Clerk of the Ordnance, and his daughters were coming out, a delicate operation at any time, but particularly for him since it involved jockeying for advantageous marriages. His ultimate and hopeless hope was to be Speaker of the House of Commons and to retire with a peerage. He had not attended his brother's funeral; only the crazy Calvinist sister Mrs Bourne arrived.

Meanwhile, Henry Hallam had decided his son was falling into a trap. Father and son were already on uneasy terms in 1830, when Arthur found himself bored by Cambridge after the excitement of Spain:

> I cannot find that my adventures have produced quite the favourable impression on my father's mind that his letter gave me to expect. I don't mean that he blames me at all; but his old notions about the University begin to revive, and he does not seem to comprehend, that after helping to revolutionize kingdoms, one is still less inclined than before to trouble one's head about scholarships, degrees and such gear.

At that point, Arthur was refusing to read for honours, Brookfield took to opium, so probably did Charles Tennyson,[1] and Fred was in London 'under Stanley's care for a stricture'. All the same in early 1831 Arthur was extremely cheerful. 'He has recovered his amiability of late,' wrote Monteith. 'He is not so dissatisfied with *himself*, not so morbid as he used to be.' But Henry Hallam had written to the Rector and got his agreement that Arthur should be 'released' and should not visit Somersby until he was twenty-one, in 1832. Henry assumed (though it was not stated, so the Rector had not formally agreed) that there was to be no exchange of letters. When the Rector died, Arthur was in London trying to shift his father: the underlying reason for that not unworldly man's attitude, as for the Rector's agreement, was certainly financial anxiety, and he was not shifted. When Arthur suddenly died he was generous to the Tennysons, but that was another matter.

The cold season in the Hallam household in Wimpole Street was nothing to the blizzard at Tealby. When their father died, the three boys were found to be in debt at Cambridge (Alfred for very little); we have a list of the tradesmen to whom they owed money, which does not represent a high-flying style of life, but the whole sum, including presumably their college fees and dues, was over £600. Old George was furious: to start with he offended Mrs Tennyson by refusing the trouble and expense of having the Rector buried with his mother; 'he could not undergo the bustle which would be occasioned by having the funeral here.' Mr Rawnsley had drummed up six clerical pall-bearers and reported that the ceremony passed off with calmness and propriety at Somersby.

Fred at first promised to go to the Bar, and as for the other boys, 'I set before them their *entire dependence* on the good opinion they induce their *grandfather* to entertain towards them.' Alfred wanted to go back to Cambridge to take a degree, but was told that was useless unless he would enter the Church. He said in May that he would. Fred then said the same, but wanted a pupil so that he could go back to Eton as a tutor. Alfred gave warning that Edward might easily go mad. Arthur Tennyson had no talent but drawing, so the idea was discussed of putting him into an agent's and surveyor's office. Septimus was clever, so Uncle Charles decided he could be articled to a solicitor; Horatio at eleven was still young enough to go into the navy.

Grandfather replied crushingly to these suggestions. 'I don't know what Arthur is fit for. He still does not know the multiplication tables, or anything useful.' Then in October, 'I have many things troubling and vexing me, but none so much as the Somersby family. I think there are *extra* bills to pay for the three eldest boys amounting to more than £1000.'[2] He borrowed this money, making the boys enter into a contract to repay the whole amount to the younger children instead of money he would have left them by will. The Old Man paid Mrs Tennyson £1000 a year (£200 due to her by contract as his son's widow, and the rest for looking after his grandchildren) and she also had £300 a year of her own from some land; her case at least was not hopeless.

It was settled that Charles was to read for a degree the next year, with James Spedding as a fellow-sufferer and ally. Fred had been restored to the college books at Trinity by the intercession of the weighty Dr Maltby whose wife was somehow a cousin of his mother's, and took his degree only a year late, at the same time as Charles took his. Charles then took to laudanum, and Fred continued to infuriate his grandfather, developing a career as an adventurer until his grandfather's death left him independent in 1835.

In September Emily was ill with a bad pain in the side, so Alfred took her to Cheltenham.[3] Arthur Hallam travelled there and met them, but now it was Alfred's physical condition as much as Emily's that alarmed him. He was still as deeply in love with her as ever.

Throughout the year of his father's death Alfred saw the public results of his *Poems, Chiefly Lyrical*, published in 1830. Arthur Hallam knew a young London poet turning publisher, Alfred Moxon, and interested him in a long, full trumpet-blast of an essay about Alfred written by himself, for the August 1831 issue of Moxon's new *Englishman's Magazine*. The *Westminster* magazine had already been ample and favourable. Hallam's article has been said to embody a new aesthetic and to prefigure the theories of the symbolists: I can only say that it is readable and sensible and certainly fresh compared to prevalent criticism, but it reads like a more coherent Leigh Hunt, who by the way soon turned out to be another fan. Unfortunately, as so often happens with the attempts of an author's friends to promote his work, the effect was partly counter-productive, because it appears to have been Hallam's essay 'On some of the characteristics of modern poetry, and the lyrical poems of Alfred Tennyson' that drew the heavy fire of the critic Christopher North, as we shall see. The *Englishman's Magazine* printed a Tennyson sonnet, and a Hallam poem, 'I see her now an elfin shape', at the same time. Meanwhile Alfred gave a push to Brookfield, with whom he had a boisterously cheerful correspondence, to print a sad sonnet by his young brother Edward in the *Yorkshire Literary Annual*.[4] Edward was eighteen then, and published no more poems. By October 1833 it was obvious to the doctors that he should be in an asylum. His mother did what she could to find a milder cure, but he was not cured: he lived on in his asylum at Lincoln until 1890. Edward and Alfred were very close; they understood one another, and the poem that Edward had published has a mysterious likeness of feeling to the sonnet by Alfred in Moxon's magazine, 'Check every outflash'. which deals with Melancholy:[5]

> Through yonder poplar alley
> Below, the blue-green river windeth slowly,
>   But in the middle of the sombre valley,
>   The crispèd waters whisper musically
>
>   (4-7)

It will be better to give the whole of Edward's poem, not that it is better than this, but because it is harder to find:

> Why do I weep when gazing on that field
> Where happy lambs their airy rounds repeat,
> Or stretch'd beneath yon bloom'd enclosure shield
> Their tender age from the fierce mid-day heat –
> A fence of roses wild yet full as sweet
> As those which in the cultured garden bloom?
> Is it a bootless spell, a vain conceit
> Of thoughts that cannot to perfection come
> Fading like gleams of distant Paradise
> Which makes me mourn and weep when evening dyes
> The West in crimson, faint and fainter glowing
> Or when the glory of the first sunrise
> Along the beauteous East is deeply growing,
> And from the reedy eve the wakeful swallow cries.

What was a slight, at best a delicate piece of writing becomes by force of circumstance heartrending. In its *naïveté*, it enters rather deeply into Alfred Tennyson's sadness also. Alfred's poem is the closer to great art, though it is only a touching of the strings in a minor key, and as a statement it appears to be fantastical: 'When in this valley first I told my love.' That may easily be the reason why he never reprinted it. Edward's poem on the other hand is an attempt at a major statement which he cannot quite encompass: it is about his condition, and his 'thoughts that cannot to perfection come'.

Alfred's poetry was now within a few years of its full power, yet it continued to develop slowly, through the same glassy neo-classic calmnesses and airy verses to girls that had plagued him for some time. He does not appear to have noticed their radical weakness except that they more often remained unprinted as time went on. The most morbid sonnets got rejected as well as one or two that were really beautiful: in particular the magnificent attack on Cambrige, 'Lines on Cambridge of 1830', which he became ashamed of having written. It is the only English poem that does justice to such a theme, and the only one by Tennyson that apparently echoes the polemics of William Blake. The old version ('your bridges and your busted libraries') is preferable to the version he finally consented to print ('your gardens, myriad-volumed libraries'), but the startling trumpet-blast comes at the end of the sentence:

> Shall not avail you, when the Day-beam sports
> New-risen o'er awakened Albion.
> Nor yet your solemn organ-pipes that blow
> Melodious thunders through your vacant courts
>
> (6–9)

There is something wilfully unconfident about his self-criticism, and the politeness or loyalty that made him suppress this poem is disgraceful.

As an undergraduate he seems from his friends' reaction to have toyed with despair and considered atheism, from which dark-looking water Hallam drew him back. Not everyone was so encouraging; Trench wrote sternly to W. B. Donne that Tennyson's friends 'will materially injure him if he does not beware – no young man under any circumstances should believe that he has done anything, but still be forward looking.' Applied to poetry this advice is surely nonsense. A year later Trench thought Tennyson 'certainly the best of the young Poets and the perversest, but this must chiefly be laid to the charge of his Cambridge advisers (Hallam, Blakesley, Kemble and company) who in a short time did much to spoil and pervert him, flattering in every way his Antinomian Spirit.' The word antinomian is nicely chosen, but Tennyson had to find his own way as a poet; his originality even in the construction and texture of verse, and in that verbal precision of music which was Tennyson's strength, is essentially antinomian. If one suspects that Trench as a young man implied something further about politics or religious dogma, then one must choose one's side.

Alfred was deeply preoccupied by the problems of poetry. He wrote a poem hundreds of lines long about Poland, fiery stuff no doubt, but a maid used it to light a fire. He wrote and rightly abandoned another poem of prodigious length, called 'The Lover's Tale'.[6] He worked at it on and off from 1827 until 1832, but the thing had set hard and could not develop at the pace his own growth between eighteen and twenty-three demanded. It was a Keatsian, enamelled exercise with an intricate surface more like a Fabergé egg than a real wild bird's egg. It is unreadable, plotless and far too long: 1064 lines of blank verse when he abandoned it. He intended it for his *Poems* of 1832, but at the last moment he withdrew it, in spite of Hallam's agonized wails. Here he showed an independence and a soundness of judgement that his friends could not match. In the late 1860s he considered it again more than once, but always withdrew it. Finally it was pirated, so he published it with a fourth part which in spite of its melodrama is much more ably written.

It was thought important in that generation to have composed a work of serious length. Nothing was known about the ways in which genuine epic, which is essentially oral and traditional even when it is written, differs from poetry composed at a desk in a library. Nearly all these long poems were failures, but always in different ways. Long narrative poems were at best entertainments of a kind: the last of them in the old manner was probably Yeats on 'The Wanderings of Oisin', which is nearly unreadable, like Tennyson's 'Lover's Tale'. As soon as he dropped that, he began to consider writing a vast epic cycle about King Arthur. His first approach towards this new subject was 'The Lady of Shalott', a substantial ballad in the ballad stanza revived by Drayton, who had of course heard Welsh harpers. It is a pretty, even a delightful poem, but in his graver mood he could do better. He had in fact begun to touch the strings in his classic manner in verses he rejected from 'The Lover's Tale', where their tone was unfitting, and cannibalized for use elsewhere. Four lines, including 'Through all the silent spaces of the worlds', occur word for word in *The Princess* (1848), and a passage about the stars a little later in the same rejected fragment is often quarried but never bettered, and bequeaths to 'Tithonus' several of its most beautiful lines:

> Low in the East
> The bickering Dog-star danced in sparkles – higher
> Mars, glaring by the lonely sisters seven
> Followed white Venus, whiter than all stars,
> Down to the quiet limit of the world.
>
>   (12–16)

'The Lady of Shalott' as we now have it has been perfected in melody and in tonal continuity by prolonged revision. The 1832 *Poems* is a fine and promising collection, but when Tennyson revised and severely selected, one might say weeded the 1830 and 1832 volumes, and republished them with his new poems in 1842, the result was beyond comparison strong. It was one of the great moments in the history of English poetry. That lay ahead, and yet Tennyson's restless and continual revisions make it unfair to consider his early poems without taking a glance at their final and perfect form. The story of 'The Lady of Shalott' was Italian, just like 'The Lover's Tale'; the poet cut out King Arthur and his Queen, and as he revised put in more of his own inventions and forgot his original. Indeed he said he had never heard of the Arthurian 'Maid of Astolat' at that time, though scholars have determinedly pointed out ways in which Malory could have been an influence on his poem. The only actual loss in the revised version of it is an amazing image of what appears to be a drowned water-meadow in spring, scarcely consonant alas with the reapers:

> The yellowleavèd waterlily,
> The greensheathèd daffodilly,
> Tremble in the water chilly
> Round about Shalott.
>
>   (6–9)

George Eliot was surely right to demur about a change that gave us 'Till her blood was frozen slowly,/ And her eyes were darkened wholly' instead of 'Till her eyes were darkened wholly,/

And her smooth face sharpened slowly'. Tennyson made a note of that later, so it sounds as if he felt she might be right to prefer the old version.

When he revised 'Mariana in the South', he cut what had been his very sharp consciousness of southern France, to leave something metrically smoother and more English, so that one regrets the loss. It is interesting that Hallam had it by February 1832, and that its idea came from the Spanish expedition, though its metre was transformed as it was written. In the original,

> At noon she slumbered. All along
> The silvery field, the large leaves talked
> With one another, as among
> The spikèd maize in dreams she walked.
> The lizard leapt: the sunlight played
>
> (37–41)

In the revised version he had changed it to:

> Nor bird would sing, nor lamb would bleat,
> Nor any cloud would cross the vault,
> But day increased from heat to heat,
> On stony drought and steaming salt;
> Till now at noon she slept again

Tennyson left a sonnet unfinished, which he gave to Hallam to write the end. In the first eight lines, which are unmistakable Alfred, the trees talk. For example, 'the grim fir, rejoicing in the night/ Hoarse mutters to the murmuring sycamore.' The final six lines are by a stiffer hand and a lesser poet, therefore by Hallam. The date of the poem is probably about 1831.[7]

His attempts to impress reality on his poems were not confined to what is moving in nature, or even to the idyllic, a type of writing which even when the Greeks invented it could never confine itself to the rules and limits of a genre. He felt Sappho had an influence on his lyrics about love, though that is hard to discern today, perhaps because papyri have given us a clearer idea of Sappho. But his 'The Miller's Daughter' is strongly (if one can use that word about so mild an author) influenced by Mary Russell Mitford. Her fresh charm is more durable than it looks and she is still in print and enjoyable; she derives probably from Goldsmith. Tennyson must have read her in the 1820s or in old magazines. He did consume a huge quantity of fiction and unclassifiable 'light reading', much of it by women, but he had an eye for this kind of anecdote wherever he came across it.[8] Were he alive today, he would have surely written novels as well as poems, though the novel as we know it did not exist in his youth. Even Thackeray wrote anecdotal essays before he came to the novel.

'The Miller's Daughter' reuses the props of old poems with splendid verve and freshness (nature interrupting sleep as in 'Mariana', and flooded meadows as at Shalott), as well as a certain sense of reality from Miss Mitford, whose stories are usually true. She wrote them as stories or essays for magazines but the form in which she cast them, with a lot of nature and a certain eye for social structure, underlies the form of what Alfred Tennyson came to call his 'English Idyls', mis-spelling the word deliberately to distinguish them from Greek Idylls. 'The Miller's Daughter' is splendid, quite original as a poem, and deals with a world he intimately knew. The fact that nothing happens but the gentlest of love affairs is due to the gentleness of Mary Russell Mitford. When he ventured on similar ground a little earlier without the influence in 'The May Queen', his poem was limp and absurd.

'Œnone' by contrast is neo-classical, and at the best does not surpass Ovid on whom it is based. In spite of 'all the charm of all the muses, often flowering in a lonely word', and in spite of the fine Virgilian cadence of its corrected version, which was not so evident in 1832, 'Œnone' is condemned by its nature not to rise above the neo-classic, even though in Tennyson's poetry that Latin sweetness flourishes as it had virtually never done in English until now. And it has memorable lines, like 'The swimming vapour slopes athwart the glen' (1842). He elaborates too much, he will not leave well alone, but this is still an improvement on 'The Lover's Tale':

> For now the noonday quiet holds the hill:
> The grasshopper is silent in the grass:
> The lizard, with his shadow on the stone,
> Rests like a shadow, and the winds are dead.
> The purple flower droops: the golden bee
> Is lily-cradled
>
> (24–9)

The list is too long, the purple flower and the golden bee are otiose and 'lily-cradled' gilds the poem yet again. Even in the first four lines each one detracts ever so slightly from the one before. What is worse, the refrain 'Dear mother Ida, hearken ere I die') does not quite work: 'Ida' and 'I die' clash strangely, and 'hearken ere' is an archaism that sounds like translatorese. Still, his friends loved this poem, Lushington put it into Greek, and it is one of the prettiest essays in its style that the English language had seen since the sixteenth century. If you still think of Alfred Tennyson as a young man unknown in London, a new poet just bursting out of bud, then this poem is an amazing achievement, and at 264 lines its length is serious.

'The Palace of Art' is longer, though its four-line stanzas are less solemn. Trench had said to him at Trinity, 'Tennyson, we cannot live in art,' and this poem was his riposte or response: a short introductory poem goes with it. He calls the palace 'a sort of allegory . . . of a soul/A sinful soul possessed of many gifts'. The doctrine of course is perfectly orthodox, but the poem is long and its detail rich and sleepy. Europa's mantle blows back:

> From one hand drooped a crocus: one hand grasped
> The mild bull's golden horn.
>
> (119–20)

Ganymede's rosy thigh is halfburied in the eagle's down, and after that it is no use to say he was like a flying star. What he really had it in mind to say, apart from this profusion of ornament, is succinctly put by Hallam in a letter to W. B. Donne, on 13 February 1831. 'An artist, as Alfred is wont to say, ought to be lord of the five senses, but if he lacks the inward sense which reveals to him what is inward in the heart, he has left out the part of Hamlet in the play.' All the same, some of the ornament is beautiful. 'No nightingale delighteth to prolong/Her low preamble all alone', and 'She lit white streams of dazzling gas' (1832). The story does not in itself detain our attention.

His 'A Dream of Fair Women' on the other hand has both Chaucerian and classical bones to it, the wood of vision really is mysterious and his own, the whole poem is less laden with ornament than his earlier writing, yet it was written in 1831 or 1832. It is conceivable that this comparative meagreness of language may be due to Chaucer or to a biblical source: at any rate it is unusual. In the

1832 version he began with four stanzas of ascent in a balloon, which I am sorry to lose;[9] he must surely have been thinking of Monckton Milnes rising up above Trinity. The morning in the elm wood is fresher still:

> At last methought that I had wandered far
>   In an old wood: fresh-washed in coolest dew
> The maiden splendours of the morning star
>   Shook in the stedfast blue.
>
> Enormous elm-tree-boles did stoop and lean
>   Upon the dusky brushwood underneath
> Their broad curved branches, fledged with clearest green,
>   New from its silken sheath.
>
> (53–60)

The sense of early morning in Tennyson, and maybe his equally impressive sense of languorous afternoon, might have come from Keats, a poet just becoming known, but by the 1830s Tennyson was closer to the Keats of the handful of great odes; he was casting off the heaviness and density of his more ambitious early style. When Browning writes that 'the brushwood sheaf/Round the elm-tree bole is in tiny leaf', he is probably imitating Tennyson.

'The Lotos-Eaters' is altogether different and completely original. It is a classical tale of course, and in Tennyson's special Baxter-print-style orientalizing, but it more deeply concerns his friends like W. H. Brookfield, and probably his brother Charles, who did take opium. It enters into melancholy, the family affliction of the Tennysons, and by substituting the gods for God, it is able to deal tartly with Christian dogma. In the last lines of his poem he speaks of 'an ill-used race of men that cleave the soil', and 'they suffer – some, 'tis whispered – down in hell/Suffer endless anguish'. He could claim to be within the classical convention, but the attack on Christianity seems quite clear. Leaving this aside, the poem is 173 lines long and very beautiful. The tone is caught from a few lines of Thomsons's 'Castle of Indolence', but the poem is filled out with experience. The afternoon world has Pyrenean waterfalls:

> And like a downward smoke, the slender stream
> Along the cliff to fall and pause and fall did seem.

A land of streams! some, like a downward smoke,
Slow-dropping veils of of thinnest lawn, did go;
And some through wavering lights and shadows broke,
Rolling a slumbrous sheet of foam below.

(8–13)

When I was a child, the whole poem irritated me like a conundrum: I could not see why everyone was so melancholy. Now I find it exquisite and understand the poet's sadnes for his friends, and their sadness too, as he feels it to be. In fact the poem is an astonishing exercise in real sympathy. As for the waterfalls, when Tennyson discovered that lawn was used on the stage to simulate a distant cascade, he did not know whether to be delighted or annoyed. The downward smoke recalls Ovid's *desilientis aquae* more insistently than ever.

The final poem in the 1832 *Poems* is to James Spedding, whose young brother had suddenly died. From a biographer's point of view this was an important turning point in Tennyson's life. It rehearsed the pain and some of the themes of *In Memoriam*, and moves to an intimacy of friendship with James Spedding, which had many results. Spedding became after Hallam's death Alfred's closest adviser, and probably his best friend: one thing led to another; the poet visited him at home in the Lake District, probably because of Spedding's glowing review, and took his wife there when the time came. Spedding got work for £150 a year in a government office, because Henry Taylor, a civil servant, a bad poet and a vain fellow, had spotted his talent from a speech on liberty made in the Cambridge Union as an undergraduate and printed. Spedding was a detailed and useful but rather pedantic private critic of Tennyson's verse before it was published: his queries can be studied on the Trinity manuscript of *In Memoriam*. His cast of mind was formidably academic; he worked for forty years on the works of Bacon, yet he refused the offer of an honorary degree from Cambridge and also the offer of the chair of History, where he would have followed Charles Kingsley. 'I have already had some religious consolation from Blakesley,' he wrote at the time of his brother's death, 'which would have been amusing enough to anyone not the object of it.' Tennyson in his poem noticeably avoids it, and this 1832 poem set a seal on their familiarity.

Yet there is more to these very personal lines than an act of

friendship. From the second to the sixth stanza Alfred Tennyson
adduces his own experience of grief, which was, he says, at his
father's death two years ago:

> In grief I am not all unlearned;
>   Once through mine own doors Death did pass;
>   One went, who never hath returned.
>
>   (18–20)

Had he really mourned his father so long and so deeply? It is possible.
'Your loss is rarer,' he says, and goes on to discuss the loss of a
younger brother, Edward Spedding. When he wrote these lines he
had suffered a more recent, intimate loss of his own younger brother
Edward, who had just become incurably mad and gone away for
ever; this loss must have been present in his mind. As a figure in the
poem, his father fails to evoke the real pain he feels for James
Spedding, and Spedding of course, as his friend, knew the true state
of his feelings. The pain is obviously real, and must have been about
Edward Tennyson. If the reader should deem this a perverse conjecture, let him consider this stanza:

> Your loss is rarer; for this star
>   Rose with you through a little arc
> Of heaven, nor having wandered far
>   Shot on the sudden into dark
>
>   (25–8)

When the book appeared, its author had clearly been at work on
it until the last moment; in fact he continued to revise it. At one
point there was a plan to reissue the 1830 volume revised and with
new poems added to give two poems on each theme. There is
something endearingly amateur about the first edition. The last bit
of 'The May Queen' had been cut, but it reappeared in tiny type
crammed on to a single page with a footnote to express the hope,
'Perhaps the following lines may be allowed to stand as a separate
poem; originally they made part of the text, where they are mani-
festly superfluous.' At the classical line about the grasshopper in
'Œnone', a disarming note reads, 'In the Pyrenees, where part of this
poem was written, I saw a very beautiful species of Cicala, which
had scarlet wings spotted with black. Probably nothing of the kind

exists in Mount Ida.' The publisher was Moxon of 64 New Bond Street. Charles was still being published in Cambridge, by B. Bridges of Market Hill, and can scarcely have expected a wide distribution, though he was well reviewed, and one should remember that at this stage both Wordsworth and Coleridge thought he might do greater things than Alfred.

Moxon had been a friend since 1824 and kinsman of the Lambs (he married Charles Lamb's adopted daughter); he set up as a publisher of poetry in 1830 with a loan of £500 from Samuel Rogers, whose attractive *Italy* was one of his first books. Monckton Milnes alerted Hallam to his existence, and their first contact was in July 1831; Merivale was despatched in August to negotiate terms for contributions to the *Englishman's Magazine*, in which Alfred's 'Check every outflash' and Arthur's review of *Poems, Chiefly Lyrical* appeared that month. By March 1832 Alfred's 'spirits are better; his habits more regular, his condition altogether healthier. He is fully wound up to publication, and having got £100 from Mrs Russell [his aunt] talks of going abroad.'[10]

The new book was suggested by Moxon to Hallam in June; he pounced on the idea. Alfred had to be tempted to London because it was impossible to keep up a correspondence with him. The inability to write letters and a degree of hypochondria that alarmed his friends were already ingrained in him. Yet face to face he was excellent company, and his Cambridge friends flocked around him. 'The great Alfred is here, in Southampton Row, smoking all the day,' wrote Spedding to W. A. Thompson. 'Kemble is in town;' wrote Blakesley, 'he is reading law five hours a day (or at least was doing so before Alfred Tennyson came up to town, for now those five hours are consumed, together with much shag tobacco, in sweet discourse on Poesy).'

> He is still here, and the greater part of his money is here no longer: further I know not, but he can hardly get to countries 'of colour' as he calls it, on his present resources. Yesterday he dined here, and was dreadfully nervous about it: he was silent a long while, but on mention of some water-insects of his acquaintance he suddenly became eloquent

wrote Hallam to Emily.[11] In the end the two young men went up the Rhine for three weeks: Alfred returned 'bugbitten, flybitten, fleabitten, gnatbitten and hungerbitten', deploring the Rhine and claiming he could have designed a better mountain himself than any he saw in Germany.

In October he was correcting proofs: he wanted to revise them all twice, but he still had no idea how long the book was going to be. 'My manuscripts', he remarked innocently, 'are far from being in proper order.' In December 1832, 450 copies of *Poems* appeared at 6 shillings each. His friends had chivvied him, supported him, promoted him, discussed details of every change with him (and there were many), and loved him deeply. The only one he had reservations about was Trench. 'I have no faith in any one of his opinions,' but even so 'it is impossible to look on Trench and not to love him.' The poems of Alfred Tennyson were all but a group project.

The first angry noise came from an unknown critic in the *Literary Gazette*: it came with a parody of 'The Lady of Shalott'. But it was the reviews of the 1830 *Poems, Chiefly Lyrical* by John Wilson, writing in the *Edinburgh Review* as Christopher North, and Croker's review in the *Quarterly* that came as a bombshell. We know how bitterly Alfred felt about these attacks, both because he never forgot them and because of his response, the verses against Christopher North (which against Hallam's advice he insisted on printing in 1832, though he apologized to North in April 1834 in a private letter[12]). The verses do not appear to warrant the fuss made about them,[13] though 'Tipsy Kit', which originally stood, would have been sharper than 'Crusty Christopher', which came from a rhyming dictionary. Wilson was not a person with whom it was possible to engage in civilized discourse or to preserve propriety. Of the many blackguarding, sneering and malignant critics of the day, he could perform among the worst. He is credited by scholars with having silenced Alfred Tennyson for ten years, but that was the effect not of one critic but if of any, then of all of them taken together, particularly Croker in the *Quarterly*. Moxon the publisher thought the attacks did more good than harm to sales, and Hallam did his best to persuade Tennyson in the same direction: the *Quarterly* after all was a Tory Party review. It may still be that the attacks overbalanced Alfred Tennyson's self-criticism and crushed his confidence; yet in spite of his sense of injury, which formed like a scab over the wound, there are other reasons that account for his silence. He did not stop writing: he simply spent longer revising and reselecting his poems, a process that had already begun while he was an undergraduate.

John Wilson (1785–1851) was in youth a pugnacious physical bully of a nasty kind, a strong, *nouveau riche* boy from Paisley. From Glasgow he arrived at Magdalen College, Oxford, where he did well and took his MA in 1810.[14] He had already engaged Wordsworth in polemic correspondence (he recanted later) and was credited at Oxford with marrying a gipsy during a summer spent wandering. (If he did so, he was later a bigamist.) He lived for five years as a gentleman in the Lake District. Then, having lost £50,000 through an uncle, he turned to journalism in Edinburgh, where his first associate was Jeffrey, and his first target canto IV of Byron's *Childe Harold's Pilgrimage*, which he bespattered with banalities.[15] The state of periodical literature then is to us almost inconceivable. Thomas Moore had attempted a duel with Jeffrey over a malign review of 1805, and then tried to challenge Byron for mocking him in verse (that is how they met). In 1817, Wilson joined *Blackwood's* at its foundation. They viciously attacked Coleridge, Leigh Hunt and Keats, though De Quincey persuaded them to some restraint over Shelley.[16] James Mill said the thought of Wilson made him sick; even the scum Jeffrey would have nothing more to do with him, and John Murray gave up his connection with the magazine. Wilson appeared as Christopher North in his series 'Noctes Ambrosianae' (1825–35), a farrago of Peacockian dialogues, and it was here that he went for Alfred Tennyson.

In February 1832 he was mild, and interlarded blame with praise: this is the point of Tennyson's reply, that to be praised by North was a worse insult. He attacked Tennyson only as an affected young man whom 'the Cockneys' were doing their best to spoil, though he had genius, a fine ear and a rich imagination. It was in May that he took up his heaviest cudgel, and its first object was Arthur Hallam's essay in the *Englishman's Magazine*, already defunct. 'An essay on the genius of Alfred Tennyson sent it to the grave . . . awoke a general guffaw, and it expired in convulsions.' This was knockabout stuff, and Arthur Hallam did not take long to discover he was not hurt by it. The poems themselves, or rather those of them Christopher North selected for punishment, were 'drivel, dismal drivel, feeble, fantastic, silliness, and clumsy and unwieldy failure'. When he then came to the favourable reviewer in the *Westminster*, he let himself go. 'It is a perfect specimen of the super-hyperbolical ultra-extravagance of outrageous Cockney eulogistic foolishness . . . the purest matter of moonshine ever mouthed by an idiot lunatic, slavering in the palsied dotage of the extremest superannuation ever inflicted on a being, long ago perhaps in some slight respect and in a low degree human, but now sensibly and audibly reduced below the level of the Pongos.' After all this, 'having shown by gentle chastisement that we love Alfred Tennyson', he went on to praise him, and to assure readers that 'Alfred Tennyson is a poet.' The articles made Alfred careful in 1832, but the verses 'To Christopher North' provoked Wilson's friend, John Wilson Croker, a principal assassin of Keats and as sneering and filthy a fellow as Wilson himself, to act on his behalf. The main attack on Keats had been by Croker in the *Quarterly*: Lockhart was now above reviewing, being the editor of the *Quarterly*, so he commissioned the ghoul Croker to finish Tennyson in a review of the 1832 *Poems*, in April 1833.

The review began by situating this battle as just another round of the fight against the 'Cockney School'. Croker first mentioned his own fifteen-year-old review of 'Endymion', at which he sneered. His artillery was malevolent sarcasm and the heavy jokes of one who should have been a schoolmaster, indeed the patron saint of those teachers one so well remembers. Christopher North foamed at the mouth, but he was a professor by comparison, indeed the true patron of much modern academic criticism, and he did hold the chair of Moral Philosophy at Edinburgh, but only because he was a Tory. It is incredible that he minded Tennyson's mildly stinging reply, but it looks as if he did. The Cockney School (spoken of only by its enemies) was a matter of political loyalty. It is possible that Hallam was spotted as the son of his father, a Whig whose career as a reviewer had been somewhat blighted when he attacked some Greek verse in Payne Knight's book on Taste, which turned out to be by Pindar. Byron had noticed him in *English Bards and Scotch Reviewers*. Croker's review was a lamentable performance. It ended with two pages of attack on the slight verses to 'Crusty Christopher'. Incredible as it may sound, this review had influence. A Lincolnshire squire of the older generation told old Mr Tennyson the *Quarterly* was next to the Bible, and two years later only 300 copies of the 1832 *Poems* had sold. There is no doubt the poet was crushed, but one should note that after Arthur Hallam's death he hated all publicity for a time: when John Lake, a nobody, wrote a satire on his side against Christopher North, he sent an appeasing letter to Wilson that drew no reply, and when Spedding told him J. S. Mill was going to praise his poems he answered that it was the last thing he wanted. 'I do not wish to be dragged forward in any shape before the reading public at present, particularly on the score of my old poems.' He was, after all, at work on *In Memoriam*, and that I believe is what silenced him.

It was certainly not the egregious Bulwer, who was now a crony of Uncle Charles and a constant guest at Bayons. Uncle Charles, on hearing his nephew had made a book of poems, wished he had made something useful, like a wheelbarrow. He felt the *Quarterly* had hardly been too severe. Bulwer was editor of the *New Monthly* in which he (presumably it was he) wrote anonymously on Tennyson, of the rhapsodies of insanity, the prattle of childhood, Wordsworthian pap, poets who gloat without being voluptuous, and drivel without tenderness. When one considers his own published poetry, written at the age of fifteen, or any of his later verses, one is struck speechless by its awfulness and by the miserable vinegar of this malicious criticism. He must have hated Tennyson because he felt supplanted by him at Cambridge, and perhaps because of an ill-based sense of social superiority and an impulse to sneer that derived from Bayons. At this time Alfred Tennyson does not appear to have noticed him or bothered about him. In ten years' time his day was to come. In the mean time we have the evidence of letters and of manuscripts that Alfred simply went on working at his poems.

His happiness and high spirits might have seemed invincible. Even the poem Croker singled out for his most wounding sneers was a slight and happy vignette of the poet getting back to Somersby from the Rhine in 1832, and delighting in his room there, 'O darling room'. Arthur Hallam was visiting Emily and exchanging letters. Brookfield and Tennant, then Monteith and Garden had visited Somersby; Alfred had been happy in London, where Fanny Kemble and her sister were raving over him, and happy with Hallam up the Rhine: when they got home they seem to have done an excited cross-talk act about their adventures which was the purest high spirits. Henry Hallam and the Old Man of the Wolds continued in frosty financial negotiation admittedly, and Arthur Hallam was put for a time into a conveyancing office which he hated, but it was after the Rhine, at just that time, that Alfred got his book together. When Croker's attack came, Spedding and Hallam both assured him (surely rightly) that it was a sign of his importance, and Moxon was reassuring too, though a few years later he took the gloomier line to Robert Browning that Alfred Tennyson was popular only in Cambridge.[17] Yet Alfred's poetry is an index of his comparative happiness: we must set the enchanting 'The Ruined Kiln' (1832) and 'The Progress of Spring' (1833) against the apocalyptic gloom of his mythological poem 'Pierced through with knotted thorns of barren pain' about 'scummy sulphur seething far below', which represents a strain that goes back through 'Timbuctoo' and 'Armageddon' to the adolescent 'The Coach of Death'. The poem was not finished:

> The fountain pulses high in sunniest jets,
> The blackcap warbles, and the turtle purrs,
> The starling claps his tiny castanets.
>
> ('The Progress of Spring', 54–6)

In the spring of 1833 he went off on his own, as was his habit, to Mablethorpe. His lilac-coloured new books were still in Moxon's Bond Street window, and 'Oriana' was being set to music by a popular composer. His poetry was occasionally about politics (with a stern, Miltonic beat) or about religious awe, a wonder that opened out of the thought of himself as an individual soul observing the evolution and multiplicity of the world. But he also wrote 'Lines', or 'Mablethorpe', a poem that fixes Mablethorpe as it was in the 1830s for ever. Here as a child 'I took delight in this locality', and imagined the Trojan war was here:

> And here again I come, and only find
>   The drain-cut levels of the marshy lea, –
> Gray sandbanks, and pale sunsets, – dreary wind,
>   Dim shores, dense rains, and heavy-clouded sea!

> Yet though perchance no tract of earth have more
>   Unlikeness to the fair Ionian plain,
> I love the place that I have loved before,
>   I love the rolling cloud, the flying rain,
> The brown sea lapsing back with sullen roar
>   To travel leagues before he comes again,
> The misty desert of the houseless shore,
>   The phantom-circle of the moaning main.
>
> (5–8, 9–16)

He did of course think about his critics, but defiantly. The mood is expressed in 'What Thor Said to the Bard Before Dinner', a fine piece of invective verse perhaps modelled on the Icelandic translations of William Herbert, which Byron apparently knew. It is interesting that Byron refers to Herbert in *English Bards and Scotch Reviewers*: 'Herbert shall wield Thor's hammer, and sometimes/In gratitude thou'lt praise his rugged rhymes.' Moore's edition of Byron (Vol. 7, 1832) was then fresh, though the copy at Lincoln reached Tennyson only at Christmas 1838. The Tennysons are not known to have possessed the Hon W. Herbert's Icelandic translations, but a footnote in Moore's edition (1832) says he was a translator:

> The principal piece is a Song on the Recovery of Thor's Hammer: the translation is a pleasant chant in the vulgar tongue, and endeth thus:

> > Instead of money and rings, I wot,
> > The hammer's bruises were her lot,
> > Thus Odin's son his hammer got.

If the ringing, beating rhythm, which might derive from the Icelandic original, came to Tennyson through this footnote (and nothing is likelier), then he was reading Byron's fierce attack on his critics at a significant moment. If this is right, Tennyson was deliberately planning a satirical attack on his own critics, which is at least a much healthier reaction than brooding or dithering. Byron was an excellent and likely source. He repented of his poem as Tennyson did of 'Crusty Christopher', and no doubt his lightness and weight in attack are unique to him and belong to an earlier age: *English Bards and Scotch Reviewers* appeared a few months before Alfred Tennyson was born. If he really did consult Byron for practical reasons in 1833, that would explain why Greece was so much in his thoughts: the next volume of Moore's Byron contains *Childe Harold*.

There is another strangely important matter attached to 1833. Alfred Tennyson owned a copy of the *Post Homerica* of Quintus of Smyrna, called in those days Quintus Calaber, a long, very full and tedious, late classical epic, a sequel to Homer.[18] The text is in Greek hexameters with a Latin version. This book is inscribed on the inside board:

A. Tennyson
MDCCCXXXIII, 1833, Feb. 23.

On the flyleaf opposite is a Greek dedication, written by an amateur, saying 'Αλφρήδῳ [for Alfred] for friendship and the golden days he longs for' and then (still in Greek letters) d.d. (*donat dedicat*, the conventional Latin form of dedicating books) but no signature. This must be a present from Arthur Hallam, who was understandably floored by the problem of writing AHH in Greek, there being no Greek letter H. The reference to golden days is a moving one. It may allude to a gloomy poem of Tennyson's but it surely directly refers to his own coming marriage, and possibly to Alfred's coming visit to London. It must be the last present he sent his friend. Many years later, this book was the chief source of Tennyson's sequel to 'Œnone', whose death it describes. It is the only ancient poem that does so.

He took his sister Mary for an Easter visit to the Hallams. Arthur had been suffering from severe headaches, which were probably put down to the law. Blakesley told Trench that Alfred was 'in town with the professed purpose of studying the Elgin Marbles'. Emily stayed at home feeling liverish and, whether or not this was a diplomatic ploy, it worked like one, because the Hallams fell for Mary, the first Tennyson sister they had ever seen. Ellen decided she was a new sister, and Mrs Hallam was struck by her beauty. Arthur took them both to the Tower and the Zoo and on the river; they went to the Abbey and they drove in the Park. There appeared the usual retinue of Cambridge friends, including John Heath who was apparently falling in love with Mary. At the Gallery of Practical Science they 'saw the wonderful Magnets and heard the Steam Gun', and looked at creatures in a drop of water through a microscope, not a new invention but no doubt a specially powerful example, and new to them. Alfred was at his most Johnsonian about the tiny beasties. 'Strange that these wonders should draw some men to God and repel others – no more reason in one than the other.' Everyone led lives of their own: Alfred at the Marbles presumably, and out to dinner with Moxon, where he stayed until three in the morning talking to Leigh Hunt. This was the first time (so far as I know) that Alfred had talked to any member of that generation of poets, or to any personal friend of Byron or of Shelley or of Keats.

He does not seem to have had any appetite for the low life which London (in this far worse than Cambridge) so richly offered.

Thackeray and Brookfield and other friends went off to 'a divan where a female – of course naked – danced' for them, but Alfred and Arthur Hallam stayed at home. They were serious young men. Henry was pleased with Alfred, everybody liked Mary, and it looked as if Arthur Hallam could now marry Emily Tennyson. All the young people tried hard to find some anemones for Mrs Burton of Spilsby, the old lady whose husband was patron of the living of Somersby.[19]

Arthur Hallam now fell ill with serious flu, which he was unable to shake off for a month. That is probably why his father decided to take him abroad, to Vienna and Budapest. In the early 1830s the Turkish empire was making its 'melancholy, long, withdrawing roar' from Eastern Europe, and the Austrian (Habsburg) empire[20] must have seemed a fascinating area to study; a journey as far as Budapest when the age of railways was barely dawning was as wild as anything in Europe a Whig gentleman would undertake. Arthur, being attached to Emily, did not want to leave England, but having gained his great object of permission to marry he felt he should humour his father in any lesser matter of dispute. Meanwhile Alfred was restless. In May he thought of going to Jersey, early in June he darted over to Mablethorpe again, in late June he was in Cambridge at a meeting of the British Association for the Advancement of Science, where Whewell presided. He lost a suitcase 'full of Dantes and dressing-gowns' and suddenly adventured off to Scotland with Monteith. It is probable that he was tactfully leaving the way clear for Hallam to visit Somersby alone. His other Scottish friend Garden complained that 'Alfred Tennyson was here before I came down, and like a rascal would not wait for me. He saw this part of the world in the worst of weather, which was very provoking, especially as he had previously formed a theory that Scotland had no colour.'[21]

By this time he had written a version of 'The Gardener's Daughter', which critics have suggested is about Alfred and Arthur and Emily and a girl called Rose Baring: the likeness is too tenuous to be sustained. The poem is static and almost plotless; it is also over-written and was kept too long in his head, its varying versions often have equal merit. Probably it suffered from the shock that hit Tennyson later in the year, since it was not completed before Arthur's death. But it is a charming construction, though its characters are static or statuesque, and it should be seen as the climax of his English nature poetry of the previous spring. FitzGerald cleverly noticed a few lines based on some autumnal colouring in a famous Titian, which turned out to be where they came from. But the poem also contains some sharp nineteenth-century detail: bell-glasses or cloches in a garden, and a paddle-steamer (in a rejected variant). It is a poem similar to 'The Miller's Daughter'. A year before there should have been an 'Innkeeper's Daughter' (unless this is it under another name): Alfred went to Richmond, to the Star and Garter, to write it, but then came racing back to London to dine with the Hallams instead.

> From the woods
> Came voices of the well-contented doves.
> The lark could scarce get out his notes for joy,
> But shook his song together as he neared
> His happy home, the ground. To left and right,
> The cuckoo told his name to all the hills;
> The mellow ouzel fluted in the elm;[22]
> The redcap whistled; and the nightingale
> Sang loud, as though he were the bird of day.
>
> (87–95)

Pieces of 'The Gardener's Daughter' were cannibalized to make *In Memoriam*. The Poem is all lilacs and mellow pears, it is a happy picture of heterosexual love, not at all like Theocritus. Among its almost innumerable fresh and beautiful phrases, I am personally very fond of

> the bustling quay
> At eve, when, new-arrived, the packet stilled
> Her splashing paddle wheels, and overhead
> The snoring funnel whizzed with silver steam.[23]
>
> (10–13 *var.*)

He went to London with his friend Tennant to say goodbye to Hallam before the journey to Vienna: they all had supper together at Alfred's rooms, with Moxon and Leigh Hunt, 'and we did not separate until half-past four o'clock: Alfred repeated glorious fragments of "The Gardener's Daughter", which seemed to produce proper effect upon Leigh Hunt. Yesterday we went in a troop to see Rogers' [the poet's] gallery of paintings – In the library we found Charles' volume but *not* Alfred's.' It was the end of June or early in

July; when the goodbyes were over they never met again. Arthur enjoyed himself normally abroad; he was particularly pleased with the paintings in Vienna, and Budapest excited him. On the way back into Austria he caught a slight fever, and then on 15 September he was suddenly dead. It was three years almost to the day since the two boys had taken the train from Liverpool on the way home from Cauterets.

On an evening at Somersby just before his death, Mary saw a tall figure dressed in white pass through a hedge where there was no gap; it so upset her that when she reached home she burst into tears. One day in early October she went to Spilsby for her dancing lesson, and brought home the letters, including one for Alfred. 'She gave it to him as he sat down at dinner and went to take off her bonnet, but she heard afterwards that he had suddenly left the table, and that poor Emily had been summoned to have the dreadful news.' Emily fainted, and he caught her as she fell.[24]

The letter was from Captain Henry Elton RN, Arthur's uncle, written from Bristol on 1 October. Henry Hallam wrote from the same address in Princes Buildings, Clifton, on the 10th: it was probably where Henry Elton lived and where Henry Hallam had gone as soon as he landed. (The Rev Sir Abraham still ruled at Clevedon, and Charles was presumably reinstalled there after his reconciliation of 1827.) This is the first letter:

My dear Sir,

At the desire of a most afflicted family, I write to you, because they are unequal from the Abyss of grief into which they have fallen to do it themselves.

Your friend, Sir, and my much loved nephew, Arthur Hallam, is no more – it has pleased God, to remove him from this his first scene of Existence, to that better world, for which he was created.

He died at Vienna on his return from Buda, by Apoplexy, and I believe his Remains come by Sea from Trieste.

Mr Hallam arrived this morning in 3 Princes Buildings. May that Great Being, in whose hands are the Destinies of Man and who has promised to comfort all that Mourn, pour the Balm of Consolation on all the Families who are bowed down by this unexpected dispensation!

I have just seen Mr Hallam, who begs I will tell you, that he will write himself as soon as his Heart will let him. Poor Arthur had a slight attack of Ague – which he had often had – order'd his fire to be lighted and talked with as much cheerfulness as usual. He suddenly became insensible and his Spirit departed without Pain. The Physician endeavour'd to get any Blood from him – and on Examination it was the General Opinion, that he could not have lived long. This was also Dr Holland's opinion. The account I have endeavour'd to give you is merely what I have been able to gather, but the family of course are in too great distress to enter into details. I am, Dear Sir,

       Your obedient Servant,

       Henry Elton.

Henry Hallam settled £300 a year on Emily, who for a time became very close to the Eltons, as if she had been a widow. She lived long enough to marry again, quite happily, and died in 1887. Arthur Hallam's body was slow in leaving Trieste and the ship was delayed by storms in the English Channel. She was headed for London but put in at Dover, and since there was no rail connection then the body travelled by coach, with three mourning coaches and sixteen black horses, from Dover to Clevedon, where it was buried early in January. The Elton tenants carried the coffin to the family vault under the small, lonely church overlooking the sea. There were no flowers, and the service was very plain. Alfred Tennyson was too upset to attend: he did not visit Clevedon at all until after his marriage. Henry Hallam wrote him a heart-broken letter from Wimpole Street:[25]

I leave town tomorrow. My first thought was not to write to you until it was over. But you may have been apprehensive for the safety of the vessel. I did not expect her arrival so soon. Use your own discretion about telling your sister. Mrs Hallam is very anxious to hear about her. If not too painful to her Miss Tennyson will have the kindness to write. Do your utmost, my dear young friend, to support her and yourself. Give as little way to grief as you may. But I feel that my own rather increases with time. Yet I find also that both occupation and conversation are very serviceable. I fear the solitary life you both lead in the country is sadly unpropitious. We are all here well, though my boy is not so vigorous as he should be. God help you all.

Affectionately yours,

H. H.

CHAPTER FOUR

The Great Poet

MANY YEARS afterwards, Alfred Tennyson used to maintain the critics had hurt him so badly that when Arthur Hallam died he might well have ceased to write if it had not been for the support of his friends. That is a dramatic illusion: the evidence is quite clear that there was no such likelihood. Almost immediately he began to write *In Memoriam*, and in very swift succession some other poems of great power, some of them begun in Arthur Hallam's lifetime.

About the time of Hallam's death Alfred was just producing 'Sir Launcelot and Queen Guinevere', a ballad in 'The Lady of Shalott' stanza form, nearly finished by the end of June; it belongs really with the exultant poems of the spring. It was published in 1842, and yet never really finished; fragments have survived in manuscript that suggest a longer conclusion delving deeper into the Arthurian cycle. What he published is no more than a beautiful vignette, but in the fragments there is a touch of embarrassment and the chastity is not automatic:

> They trampling through the woodland lone
> In clanging armour flashed and shone
> Like those three suns that flame alone
> Chased in the airy giant's zone,
>   And burnished by the frosty dark;
> And as the dogstar changes hue,
> And bickers into green and blue,
> Each glittered laved in lucid dew
>   That washed the grassy park.[1]

'The Two Voices' was begun in June, and that and 'St Simeon Stylites' appear to span Hallam's death. W. H. Thompson noticed in a letter of November 1833 that Alfred 'seemed less overcome than one would have expected.' Since both these poems deal with rather deep spiritual problems, this may be the place to quote Lawrence Durrell in the introduction to a selection from Wordsworth, who puts as succinctly as anyone what I have long supposed to be true of Tennyson's poetry:[2]

> The poetic work, in interpreting these terrors through art, helps him to surmount them in his life. Indeed the lifework of a great poet – a Valéry, Rilke, Yeats – should be considered as a long process of triumphantly surmounting his anxieties, his complexes, the wounds which his infantile psyche bears, by the act of exteriorizing them, of giving them form. We, his readers, profit vicariously from the transaction of reading and studying such work.

His poetry is extremely personal, however indirectly so, and however little it may profit us at this late date to speculate about what exactly his wounds or complexes were.

'The Two Voices' as we have it is 462 lines long; in June 1833 it was called 'Thoughts of a Suicide', but the notebooks of those days suggest the poem Kemble and Spedding first admired was only 309 lines long plus a brief formal closure. It must be said the metre, which is a series of three-line tetrameter stanzas each with a triple rhyme, runs along too briskly, and the poem is now too long for easy reading. Many of the alternate, discarded verses are as good as those printed in 1842. He worked on it too long, and his borrowings from Lucretius, from Spenser, and from Wordsworth are too various to be digested. The metre seemed to be adapted from Charles Tennyson on the death of Byron (1827) and his *Stanzas* (1833), but the best bits are those that recall *In Memoriam*. The temptation to suicide was probably Hallam's: the two of them had propped one another up. Tennyson had rescued Hallam from his depressions and Hallam had conspired with Emily to 'try to restore Alfred to a better state of mind'. Alfred's arguments in the poem are on the whole mystical, from the birth of a dragonfly to mysterious personal intuitions. He interpreted the days of creation in Genesis as eras in evolution, a view he took as a boy from Buffon, though it existed in the days of Thomas Browne, and Shakespeare was conscious of it:

'He dried his wings: like gauze they grew;
Through crofts and pastures wet with dew
A living flash of light he flew.'

I said, 'Where first the world began,
Young Nature through five cycles ran,
And in the sixth she moulded man.'

(13–18)

'St Simeon Stylites' is in its way an even more morbid study
than that of suicide. It is typical of the 1830s to be appalled by the
idea that a man should live alone on top of a pillar and then be
canonized for it, but equally typical of Alfred Tennyson to choose
the subject (of which he had only vague knowledge) for treatment in
a poem. He used to read the most ghastly lines with ferocious
grimness and roars of laughter:

Thrice multiplied by superhuman pangs,
In hungers and in thirsts, fevers and cold,
In coughs, aches, stitches, ulcerous throes and cramps,
A sign betwixt the meadow and the cloud,
Patient on this tall pillar I have borne
Rain, wind, frost, heat, hail, damp, and sleet, and snow

(11–16)

W. H. Thompson and his Cambridge friends thought it was all 'a
wonderful disclosure of that mixture of self-loathing, self-complac-
ence and self-sacrifice which caused our forefathers to do penance
when alive and to be canonized when dead', and Leigh Hunt thought
it a graphic and appalling satire; I am by no means so sure. Self-
punishment was shifting in that generation from being only a
distasteful extreme of the erotic, as it was for de Sade and for
Swinburne, to being a special instrument of what one might call neo-
Christians of more than one denomination. Somewhere in Tennyson's make-up, this had touched a nerve: Newman after all was his
contemporary. The poem was certainly not intended as a joke, even
if he read it laughing (how much of it?) to Edward FitzGerald. Even
the mad old hermit's assurance of salvation and his prediction of the
day and time of his death are not quite a joke. As a side of Alfred

Tennyson this poem has no further offspring, but it remains both surprising and interesting.

He did spread himself very fully in *In Memoriam*, but not at first, and always with reservations. That great work took a long time growing, and fully grown it was still incoherent. The order of poems was changeable, and there was no logical overall plan, so he could treat or reserve any area of feeling as he chose. In the course of its long composition, the main crisis was a change of notebooks, from one tall narrow volume like a butcher's account book to another, just after his sister Cecilia's wedding to Edmund Lushington in October 1842. By 1843 he was already arranging the poems or sections of poem into groups: IX, XVII and XVIII (originally II and III) grew into a long series about the ship, and XXVIII and XXX grew into a series about three different Christmases, which were supposed to mark the inner divisions of the complete work. At least that is how Tennyson looked back on them in 1883. Poems XXXI and XXXII were originally two drafts of the same poem. One must remember what he said to his friend Knowles in about 1870: 'The general way of its being was so queer that if there were a blank space, I would put in a poem.'[3] This peculiarity of composition, which allows generously for half-consciousness and multiple consciousness in the poet over a long period of time, and for weird variations between public and private poetry, is the essential strategy of *In Memoriam*. He had a plan, but more than one, successively or together; he hovered above plans, he shaped the work as it emerged.

This is not the place to discuss the entire book, which he began on 6 October 1833, and which publication in 1850 did not finish, since he added to it and revised it in 1851, and reviewed the diction until 1870, when he added a new piece (poem XXXIX) written in 1868, but lost since then behind or underneath a drawer in his desk. He never stopped reconsidering words: even in 1884 he made eleven verbal changes. In 1870 he was still considering an entirely new piece or section, 'a speculative one bringing out the thoughts of the higher Pantheism, and showing that all the arguments are about as good on one side as the other – and thus throw man back more and more on the primitive impulses and feelings.'[4]

We have seen that he already had the habit of writing poems in contrasting couples, and ten out of fifteen bits of *In Memoriam* written between 1834 and 1838 were arranged in that way, including two at the graveside (XVIII and XXI). The first poem he wrote about

Arthur Hallam's death was 'Fair ship, that from the Italian shore'
(IX), one of the most perfect, which reflects the letter from Captain
Elton; he then wrote two more, early in 1834 – 'Thou comest, much
wept for' (XVII), and ''Tis well; 'tis something' (XVIII) – which
reflect Henry Hallam's letter, though he persisted in imagining a
grave, not a vault, and supposing that the ship had docked at Bristol.
These first three poems, and all the others in the ship sequence unless
you count XIX, each have five stanzas, and sometimes only a single
sentence. What he intended was a monument of the purest neo-
classic, graveyard perfection, based on severe classical models, but
expressed in utterly English terms, intimate only by force of grief,
consoling itself without consolation in the traditional pagan way.
The only mention of God is 'the chalice of the grapes of God' (X,
16) and the only reference to religion is 'come, whatever loves to
weep,/And hear the ritual of the dead' (XVIII, 11–12). These poems
are movingly controlled, they are even august, yet they can express
wild flights of emotion. The later poems are the best, but among
these marvellous earliest, let one stand for many:

> Fair ship, that from the Italian shore
>   Sailest the placid ocean-plains
>   With my lost Arthur's loved remains,
> Spread thy full wings, and waft him o'er.
>
> So draw him home to those that mourn
>   In vain; a favourable speed
>   Ruffle thy mirrored mast, and lead
> Through prosperous floods his holy urn.
>
> All night no ruder air perplex
>   Thy sliding keel, till Phosphor, bright
>   As our pure love, through early light
> Shall glimmer on the dewy decks.
>
> Sphere all your lights, around, above;
>   Sleep, gentle heavens, before the prow;
>   Sleep, gentle winds, as he sleeps now,
> My friend, the brother of my love;

> My Arthur, whom I shall not see
>> Till all my widowed race be run;
>> Dear as the mother to the son,
> More than my brothers are to me.

The form is classical until the last stanza; indeed until that point the poem might almost be by Thomson or by Collins. Yet that stanza does make the reviewer's mistake almost forgivable, who supposed *In Memoriam* was by the affectionate widow of a military man. Alfred apparently had no intention until the last moment of ever publishing these poems, and his language could be as unguarded as that of Hopkins. Elsewhere in rejected versions of the sequence he wrote, 'Stoop soul and touch me: wed me' and 'Long married souls, dear friend, are we' and 'With breast to breast in early years/They met with Passion and with tears'.[5] The images are Shakespearean and the language touching rather than excessive. In its context it offers no foothold to a biographer disposed to pry deeper. Even Fred in a letter to John Frere refers to Hallam as 'he who was more than Brother to us'.[6]

Whether or not the shadow of his friend's death fell as heavily as Alfred Tennyson thought it did on 'Ulysses' and its companion pieces, there is no doubt that he had read classical texts at Cambridge with Arthur Hallam. They came back now into his mind. The difference is that he deserts Ovid and digs deeper in his own soul for what he wants to say. The first stutterings of *In Memoriam* had been in metres and tones that could not carry the poem: 'Hark! the dogs howl!' and 'On a Mourner'[7] became merely curiosities when he had written, or when he had well begun it. But 'Ulysses' dropped out of heaven like a thunderbolt, 'Tithonus' was a pendant to it, and 'Tiresias' completed the group. He wrote 'Ulysses' in October 1833, and 'Tithon' which became 'Tithonus' in 1860 in revision, the same early winter. In grim contrast, 'Tiresias' was started before Hallam died, but filled out with the other two poems, to be finished at last only fifty years later.

'Ulysses' is a stunning poem, memorable and awe-inspiring. There is no better poem in English of its kind, and it differs essentially from the powerful originals in the *Odyssey* (XI, 100–37) and in Dante's *Inferno* (XXVI, 90f.) which it does not demean. It has been taken at the crudest level as a statement of the spirit of European man, and perhaps it has a right to be taken as that. Historians might consider that in 1833 after the failure of the Thames tunnel, Brunel became the engineer of the Great Western Railway (and of the ship *Great Britain* which sailed between Bristol and New York). But it is also vehement self-expression, it is about the survivor and what role is left to him, and Tennyson told Knowles that it stated his own feeling better, more fully or more directly than anything in *In Memoriam* 'about the need of going forward and braving the struggle of life'. Ricks and B. J. Leggett have suggested a source in Byron, in *Childe Harold's Pilgrimage*, but the lines are only distantly similar, and Tennyson would have seen them as allusions to Homer and Dante: the spirit of what he had to say was in the air of the age, that is all. Matthew Arnold felt the lines 'experience is an arch wherethrough/ Gleams that untravelled world, whose margin fades/For ever and for ever when I move' have a rhythm awfully slow compared to Homer: they certainly express what Homer could not feel or say, because the sluggish word 'experience' is not in his language, but it is cardinal to what Tennyson has to say, and apart maybe from this particular line, his rhythm is majestic.[8] The improvements are small between versions, but they are real. The lines 'To follow knowledge like a sinking star,/Beyond the utmost bound of human thought' were taken from the rejected first lines of 'Tiresias', where they represent his youth and what he wanted then.[9] It touches of course only distantly on 'the ringing plains of windy Troy', and on Greek epic: it is essentially a poem about courage, about resolution in moral and philosophic enterprises.

'Tithon' is brief and light compared to the 'Tithonus' of 1860. He was a beautiful boy raped by the Dawn to whom Apollo granted immortality, but not perpetual youth, so that he withered away with age until he was a cricket or a grasshopper:

> Me only fatal immortality
> Consumes: I wither slowly in thine arms,
> Here at the quiet limit of the world,
> A white-haired shadow roaming like a dream
> The ever-silent spaces of the East,
> Far-folded mists, and gleaming halls of morn.
>
> (5–10)

Not unnaturally he begs for death, but pretty and fanciful as the verses are, as he recalls lying 'dewy-warm/With kisses balmier than opening buds', they are fantastical and forgettable, though one may faintly recall their beauty: the poem dies away in the mind as Tithonus died away. His withering has become a fantasy about love. 'Tiresias' is more extraordinary: although it owes a lot to Euripides (the *Phoenissae*), it has more immediate roots in an epic poem as long as a book of Virgil which Tennyson wrote in Greek before going up to Cambridge, and it adapts the fifth hymn of Callimachus on Pallas surprised bathing, a political axiom of Aristotle, a Pindaric phrase from Cowley, and heaven knows what else. The most important thing about the poem is that in writing it he learnt that hammered-out, resonant and hollow sound he used in narrative blank verse for the other poems. 'Tiresias' is the workshop in which he created the tone and rhythms of the best of his narrative blank verse, and of lines like 'So all day long the noise of battle rolled/Among the mountains by the winter sea' from 'Morte d'Arthur', which was also written in this same autumn of 1833 or in the next year. Of all his blank verse, Tennyson liked to quote the end of 'Tiresias' as an example, and though the poem as a whole appears exemplary only as a study in adapting the classics, this ending has a certain ease and mastery which should detain us:

> But for me,
> I would that I were gathered to my rest,
> And mingled with the famous kings of old,
> On whom about their ocean-islets flash
> The faces of the Gods – the wise man's word,
> Here trampled by the populace underfoot,
> There crowned with worship – and these eyes will find
> The men I knew, and watch the chariot whirl
> About the goal again, and hunters race
> The shadowy lion, and the warrior-kings,
> In height and prowess more than human, strive
> Again for glory, while the golden lyre
> Is ever sounding in heroic ears
> Heroic hymns, and every way the vales
> Wind, clouded with the grateful incense-fume
> Of those who mix all odour to the Gods
> On one far height in one far-shining fire.

(161–77)

They are well written, and he has learnt to sway the rhythm within the line by his syntax. He is like a man who has learnt to speak but has nothing yet to say, as if he could belie the true saying that poets learn to use forms only by the necessity to say something. These lines surely boiled down to the two or three in 'Ulysses' about the great Achilles in the Happy Isles which were not in the first version of the poem. But he loves their long, variable sonority. Inside his poetry then, a year after Hallam's death, Alfred Tennyson was in a perfectly healthy state, and the omens for the future could not have been better.

Externally he did not appear so. He wrote to Mrs Rawnsley just before Christmas:

> I am well aware how much I lose by not joining your party today, and it is only myself who have to regret that my state of health and spirits will not permit me that gratification. It would be of no use to come among you with an uncheerful mind – and old remembrances sometimes come upon me most powerfully in the midst of society. I have felt this so often to be the case that I am unwilling to go out when I feel any tendency to depression of spirits.

In that same December 1833 and again in February 1834 Fred wrote in letters that 'Alfred will probably publish again in Spring, but his health is very indifferent and his spirits very variable.' Charles was sipping drops of laudanum twenty miles away and Fred feared Alfred might go down the same road:[10] the fact that he expresses the fear is a sound piece of evidence that Alfred had not done so. As for the spring publication, all that materialized was a letter written in an anguish of embarrassment to the critic Wilson, apologizing for the poem against him: quite unnecessarily as it appears to the modern reader. R. J. Tennant was now wishing to court Cecilia, who was only sixteen, and it seems to have fallen to Alfred to fend him off. Fred had talked of 'bolting to Greece', but went to Italy instead, and from there invited himself to stay with his cousin George on Corfu, so Alfred was left in charge, a duty he fulfilled with honour, to judge from a pathetic letter of gratitude for his help from poor Tennant.[11] In the summer of 1834, Emily was due to go to the Hallams at Molesey Hall but could not face it, and Mary was due to go with Alfred to the Heaths but she could not face it either. Alfred went alone to the Heaths, and gloomily visited the Hallams alone. The only happy excursion appears to have been to Hastings with J. M. Heath, who remembered some boys bathing in the bay, and some distant fishing boats under a magnificent sunset. He stayed with the Heaths near Dorking; they took him to Worthing and offered Brighton, but he preferred the wooded valleys near Leith Hill.

In August he was back at Somersby, 'so unwell as to be almost a prisoner in the house'. He was reading Racine, Molière and Victor Hugo. He was also pouring out a swarm of minor poems, grave warnings to the state about demagogues and ruination. His own politics since 1832 had been Aristotelian but became gradually more patriotic and traditionalist and opposed to the mob. The poems were in ballad metre, and there were flirtatious lyrics that appear to have cost him no effort of heart or of mind, addressed to girls like Rose Baring and Sophie Rawnsley. In July 1834 with the Heaths he tossed off a brilliant vignette of an inn-keeper, entitled 'Mine Host'. It is a sketch from life that confounds those critics who said of Tennyson that he was unable to delineate character. The grey-bearded, fat-faced inn-keeper had mellowed 'like some old cucumber/That curves and fattens on its bed' and filled his glass up 'sometimes with a twinkling drop/For those who will not taste it more': a tear for the dead rather than a drop of gin I take it. In the mean time, nestling like a wild bird among the minor poems, appears 'Break, break, break', of which we know only that it was written suddenly in Lincolnshire in spring, in 1834 or '35 or '36. It is not surprising that he had such moods of intense sadness.

In the autumn of 1834 he went to the Wye Valley and Tintern Abbey, which stands on the banks of the Wye, a few miles from where it runs out into the Severn, at a place which is nearly within sight of Arthur Hallam's grave on the southern side of the Bristol Channel.[12] He did not seek to cross over, but the same mood overtook him, and he wrote 'Tears, idle tears', a sad and perfect lyric which he issued as a song in *The Princess*:

> 'Ah, sad and strange as in dark summer dawns
> The earliest pipe of half-awakened birds
> To dying ears, when unto dying eyes
> The casement slowly grows a glimmering square;
> So sad, so strange, the days that are no more.'

(31–5)

He did not know why he felt like that. It was an emotion he had known at times all his life, particularly strongly in boyhood when it had no object; he used to call it the passion of the past. 'And it is so always with me now, it is the distance which charms me in the landscape, the picture and the past, and not the immediate today in which I move.' The observation is common enough, and a poem by Southey gave him a hint for his. The mysterious fit of quite pure grief with tears is attested in literature and well known to psychology, but Tennyson's is one of its classic statements.

His inner sense of loss and ruin did find an objective correlative in one great narrative poem that was finished by about September, his 'Morte d'Arthur'.[13] Those first 272 lines are Virgilian, classic and almost epic. They are deadly serious, clear, crisp and deeply sonorous. They are the true culmination of all the narrative subjects he had perfected since Hallam's death, and finished before his friend had been a year in his grave. Milton had pondered the subject of the 'Morte d'Arthur', and at least this first fragment of its treatment by Tennyson is admirable. He reveals in the framing poem ('The Epic') that he wrote for it later his unease about modern epic verse (as well he may) and doubts the propriety of his own archaism of style; Edward FitzGerald remembered his intention to pre-empt criticism of him for writing a fairy tale. His sense that it was preposterous must later have been increased by the folly of Bayons and of the famous Eglinton Tournament, the final crazy attempt to restore ancient chivalry in the form of jousting, which took place in 1839, and is clearly revealed by the uncertainty of touch or tone in his numerous ballad treatments of the Arthurian cycle, nearly all written, by the way, before Victoria became Queen. 'The Tourney', a rejected song for *The Princess*, is pure slapstick, and 'Sir Galahad' treats the virginal visionary as St Simeon Stylites in fancy dress. The success of the Pre-Raphaelites twenty years later should not blind us to the real difficulty of using these ridiculous stories, from a parody of a heroic age, as a basis for epic. The answer to the difficulty lies in the extraordinary consciousness not of Tennyson but of Malory, and in style. With that vigorous basis of the 1485 English of 'Morte d'Arthur', Tennyson came as close to Homer as Virgil had ever been. There is a gospel seriousness about the poems, and the lines, 'And wheresoever I am sung or told/In aftertime, this also shall be known' echo St John's gospel. The modern, wonderfully dated early Victor-

ian scene (1838) that frames it is enchanting to this day, and fills one
with longing for such an evening:

> 'For nature brings not back the Mastodon,
> Nor we those times; and why should any man
> Remodel models? these twelve books of mine
> Were faint Homeric echoes, nothing-worth,
> Mere chaff and draff, much better burnt.' 'But I,'
> Said Francis, 'picked the eleventh from this hearth
> And have it . . .'
>   and the poet little urged,
> But with some prelude of disparagement,
> Read, mouthing out his hollow oes and aes,
> Deep-chested music, and to this result.
>
> 'So all day long the noise of battle rolled
> Among the mountains by the winter sea;'
>
> ('The Epic', 35–42, 48–51; 'Morte d'Arthur', 1–2)

Admittedly, Tennyson (like Auden) is one of the most brilliant
beginners of poems, as Larkin is one of the most brilliant enders, but
even given this strange power, he has you gripped by the second line
of this epic as few poems grip. The narrative is level and smoothly
running: how sensible he was to cut out the intrusive Merlin at lines
13/14, and how tactfully he has absorbed the touches of colouring
from Faber's *Origin of Pagan Idolatry* (1816), which at first glance one
would have thought a fatal influence. Think what a mournful Byron
would have made of the moonlit chapel and the graves:

> So saying, from the ruined shrine he stept
> And in the moon athwart the place of tombs,
> Where lay the mighty bones of ancient men,
> Old knights, and over them the sea-wind sang
> Shrill, chill, with flakes of foam.
>
> (45–50)

One can almost hear the hollow oes and aes. One can hear him in the
not negligible repertory of sounds, the 'many-knotted waterflags,/
That whistled stiff and dry about the marge', and 'sitting in the

deeps/Upon the hidden bases of the hills', and 'the water lapping on
the crag,/And the long ripple washing in the reeds'. Tennyson is at
least consummately skilful in this poem. The poetry is almost too
objectively perfect to permit analysis, but of course if we peer
between the images we can observe and reason about it. He makes
Gray's idea of the epic look pitiful, and Pope's Homer wrong in
tone. There had been nothing in English to touch 'Morte d'Arthur'
since Milton:

> Dry clashed his harness in the icy caves
> And barren chasms, and all to left and right
> The bare black cliff clanged round him
>
> (186–8)

Of all this grim and echoing music the origin was not only in Homer
but further back in childhood imagination in the stone figure of the
dead crusader in Bag Enderby church. The Knight walking 'larger
than human on the frozen hills' is *humano maior* like the ghost of
Romulus in Ovid, and like the ghosts *humano maiores* of which Alfred
had intended to speak to the Apostles. The three Queens were
pregnant with meaning for him: Faith, Hope and Charity or the
three Graces 'but they are much more', yet the drawing of them is
clear and fine, straight from the mysterious Malory. If Tennyson
fails at all, it is in moralizing, in giving a heavy significance, and in
deserting Malory to do so, from line 239 to 264, in Arthur's answer
from the barge. Malory just says: '"Comfort thyself," said King
Arthur, "and do as well as thou mayest, for in me is no trust for to
trust in, for I will into the vale of Avilion, for to heal me of my
grievous wound. And if thou never hear more of me, pray for my
soul."' But to make up for that momentary lapse, Avilion itself in
Tennyson is a transformation scene into Homer and the swan is both
real and imaginary; in other words it is wholly Tennysonian:

> So said he, and the barge with oar and sail
> Moved from the brink, like some full-breasted swan
> That, fluting a wild carol ere her death,
> Ruffles her pure cold plume, and takes the flood
> With swarthy webs. . . .
> And on the mere the wailing died away.
>
> (265–9, 272)

F. R. Leavis says of bad Victorian poetry that 'The inferiority, in rigour and force, of the intellectual content is compensated for by nobility, sonority and finish of phrasing.' But I doubt whether intellectual content is at all relevant to this spell-binding narrative, or inferior in rigour and force, and there is nothing hollow about the sonority, though there is about, for example, the end of 'Tiresias'. Whitman was in two minds about the old man's 'finest verbalism', the sheer 'charm in mere words, cunning collocutions, and in the voice ringing them.' That is nearer the mark, and he instances the memorable line 'And hollow, hollow, hollow all delight', from 'The Passing of Arthur'. In so far as this note is a criticism, the only defence I can offer against it is that I find 'Morte d'Arthur' a moving poem, and one that repays study.

There can be no doubt that in 1834 and the next year Alfred Tennyson's mind was full of his mighty creations, yet he also deliberately designed to keep himself busy. He drew up a scheme of work of which Whewell would have been proud, with hardly a mention of poetry at all. It is the kind of scheme young men do write, and then ignore, but it is worth remembering how widely read and seriously informed he was. He did in the end read French, Italian, Latin, Greek, German, apparently Hebrew and possibly Welsh.

Monday:	History. German.
Tuesday:	Chemistry. German.
Wednesday:	Botany. German.
Thursday:	Electricity. German.
Friday:	Animal Psychology. German.
Saturday:	Mechanics.
Sunday:	Theology.

Next week, Italian in the afternoons. Third week, Greek. Evenings, Poetry and Racine, Molière, etc.

This gruelling programme opens one's eyes to how seriously he took the sciences, and how seriously he aspired to a universal culture such as today is hardly to be found, since even within science the specialists of different branches no longer trouble to communicate with one another.

Henry Hallam's grim little memorial volume to Arthur was now out – he was determined not to print anything 'that would too much reveal the secrets of his mind'. There was no obituary by Alfred because he could not write it. Trinity had refused to allow a tablet in the Chapel, on the grounds that Arthur had not been a scholar of the college. (Colleges are like that.) Alfred had promised the Hallams in July to bring Emily to see them later, but they were both ill when the moment came, and the visit did not happen until October. Then Mrs Hallam was kindness itself, and Ellen liked Emily. It must have been a relief that Emily could not bear to talk about Arthur, because Alfred on his July visit seems to have done little else, and Ellen noted the awfulness of that evening in her diary. On 25 October the Hallams gave a dinner party for Emily's birthday, and it was there that she met Mr Jesse, a naval officer whom eight years later she married. (The Hallams claimed to have always hated him.) She stayed with the Hallams all that autumn, and over Christmas and the New Year; she even went with Ellen and Julia Hallam to a London ball, she learnt to waltz and brought waltzing home with her to Somersby.[14]

By the end of 1834, spirits were lifting. Emily had appeared in the drawing room in summer with one white rose in her black hair because Hallam had liked it, but dressed otherwise in complete black; now she hardly seemed the same girl. Edward was gone, Fred and Charles away, and Alfred better. It has been claimed that the Old Man of the Wolds was beginning to mellow, but I cannot believe that, though it is true he was reconciled with two daughters and must have foreseen his imminent death. In Alfred's life James Spedding was in the ascendant. The poet wrote him long and most earnest letters, quoting ancient critics in Greek to define his ambitions for the English political lyric, although it seems to me the ballad metre undid him. The Apostles revelled cheerfully. R. J. Tennant wrote to Tennyson:

Last Saturday, we had an apostolic dinner, when we had the honour among other things of drinking your health as having *once been* one of us. Edmund Lushington and I went away tolerably early, but most of them stayed till past two: John Heath volunteered a song, Kemble got into a passion about nothing but quickly jumped out again, Blakesley was afraid the Proctors might come in, and Thompson poured huge quantities of salt upon Douglas Heath's head. Kemble has just received a Diploma from the Royal Society of Antiquities at Copenhagen,

which is one of the highest marks of distinction that could have
been conferred upon him.

A few days later he was writing again, about his own despair and
desolation, as if Alfred understood such things: and probably Alfred
did; he had after all had plenty of opportunity to study them.

By February 1835 he was writing to Spedding about a promise
broken (to write or more likely to come and see him at Somersby)
which was made between two cigars at Gliddon's cigar divan in
Covent Garden, corroborated in Holborn, and repeated in the
archway of the Bell and Crown (where the coach departed). J. M.
Heath said Spedding was coming, but 'now waiting till he should
grow wiser'. Thompson, Lushington and Alford had all become
Fellows of Trinity in 1834. Alford was now an ordained priest into
the bargain, on the brink of marrying his first cousin and publishing
his second book of poems, *The School of the Heart*. Alfred's brother
Charles had also been ordained, in 1834, but he found himself
extremely lonely and miserable at Tealby as a curate under his
grandfather's eyes. In March 1835 his hard-drinking Great-Uncle
Sam luckily died and left him a fine house in Caistor and the job[15] of
Rector of Grasby, which was five miles away.

In March Alfred's visit to Spedding was postponed, presumably
for lack of money. When Emily read out a letter from Ellen Hallam
about a breakfast with Rogers and Wordsworth, Alfred growled and
complained he was cut off from all society worth living for; he
vented his wrath on the hunting squires of Lincolnshire. Then he
took Matilda and Cecilia, who were eighteen and seventeen, off to
the sea to Mablethorpe to observe the high tides that always thrilled
him. One night in April they gave a dinner and danced. Sophie
Rawnsley came, 'the lightest and most indefatigable dancer I ever
saw', said Emily. 'She is a very nice amiable girl and so cheerful and
happy . . . Alfred is delighted with her.' She was seventeen then. By
mid-May he was at last in Cumberland, having sold his Chancellor's
Medal, which was made of gold, for £15 to get there.

There was no railway yet, so he went by the coach to Kendal,
the southern edge or the beginning of the Lakes. From Kendal to
Keswick at the northern edge was a journey of five hours and some
excitement, passing mountain after mountain and lake after lake. The
Speddings lived at Mirehouse on Bassenthwaite Water, a fine house
in the shadow of Skiddaw Fell which is still standing, to which they

moved from the head of the lake, which Gray calls '*Armathwaite*, in a thick grove of Scotch firs, commanding a noble view directly up the lake . . . a modern fabrick, not large, and built of dark red stone';[16] it was five or ten miles distant from Keswick. At Mirehouse James Spedding amused himself with archery and billiards and the walking of puppies. He had decided against the Church, and shunned public life, which his father favoured for him. The father was a retired soldier, and a breeder of short-horned cattle. He was at school with Wordsworth at Cockermouth, and had given him money; he was also acquainted with Coleridge, so it is hardly surprising that he did not view poetry favourably as a way of life. The other guest that spring (early summer in the Lakes does not come until later) was Edward FitzGerald, who had been at school with James Spedding and admired Alfred Tennyson (though Fred was more his friend). He was a poet too, and a fine one in a minor key: his *Omar Khayyám* was hidden in the future (indeed it would have been hidden altogether had the Pre-Raphaelites not stumbled on a stray copy for sale on a book-barrow). His charm was interfused in his verse with obvious weaknesses:

Tis a dull sight
To see the year dying,
When winter winds
Set the yellow woods sighing:
    Sighing, oh sighing.

When such a time cometh
I do retire
Into an old room
Beside a bright fire:
    Oh, pile a bright fire!

And there I sit
Reading old things,
Of knights and lorn damsels
    While the wind sings[17]

And so on for thirteen stanzas, like a fragile, easily dismissed pastiche of Tennyson at his most easily dismissed. FitzGerald's victory is elsewhere, in the irresistible personal style of his letters. Face to face he was a complex being and not easy; he led a private, eccentric, homosexual life, and as he grew older he became more prickly. Spedding said of him with a certain brilliance that he was the Prince of Quietists. 'Half the self-sacrifice, the self-denial, the moral resolution, which he exercises to keep himself easy, would amply furnish forth a martyr or a missionary. His tranquillity is like a pirated copy of the peace of God.'

It rained a good deal at Mirehouse and it was cold, but the ground and trees were very green with great drifts of daffodils between the house and the lake: those would not have been wild daffodils but naturalized ones, and perhaps beautiful enough. The young men rowed and scrambled, they all dined at two and ate 'a serious tea' about dusk. That was when serious talking took place, but conversation was not perfectly easy in the household and the opinions of the new generation did not pass without remark. Poetry was not broached until the elders were safely in bed. Mostly it was Alfred who read, out of a crimson notebook he had with him. FitzGerald noticed his queer vowels, and Alfred noticed Spedding's prissy way of reading, 'as if bees were about his mouth'. James drew Alfred several times, and the drawings recapture the young Tennyson with a wonderful immediacy, as amateur sketches like amateur snapshots sometimes can. They heard his 'Morte d'Arthur', which he altered a little under the influence of the Lakes, and they heard Dora, a story in 167 lines based on Mary Russell Mitford which he told in simplified, Wordsworthian language (he had been reading Wordsworth's 'Michael'); they heard 'The Lord of Burleigh' which is based on a prose account by Hazlitt of a true story of the 1790s (and which Moore also set in verse), and they heard 'The Day-Dream', which is some 280 lines in stanzas about the Sleeping Beauty. This last is a nothing. It is charming, a little childish but a little sexy too; it is really a sorbet: there is no point in criticizing it. The disturbing thing about the little party in the Lakes is that they do not seem to have distinguished what was nice or very nice from what was genuinely great poetry. James Spedding's criticisms exist in manuscript for *In Memoriam*;[18] they are acute but never important. Edward FitzGerald babbled with pleasure about 'The Lord of Burleigh'. If Tennyson had relied really and fully on his friends or his sisters or his mother for criticism, he would have got lost, but he relied deeply on himself.

We have only the briefest record of when Tennyson and Fitz-

Gerald were first in a room together, at tea in 1831, on 7 December
in Francis Garden's[19] rooms at Cambridge, but by 1832, FitzGerald
and his friend Allen were circulating manuscripts of 'A Dream of
Fair Women'; in 1833 he wrote:

> Tennyson has been in town for some time: he has been making
> fresh poems, which are finer, they say, than any he has done.
> But I believe he is chiefly meditating on the purging and
> subliming of what he has alread done: and repents that he has
> published at all yet. It is fine to see how in each succeeding
> poem the smaller ornaments and fancies drop away, and leave
> the grand ideas single.

This criticism sounds like hearsay or group opinion, but it is surely
just. Tennyson was worried now about the dense richness of 'The
Gardener's Daughter', and discussed with his friends his reasons for
not pruning it. The truth is that he had come up against a rock for
which he had never allowed and which he must now cope with: he
had come up against the authority of the bare style of Wordsworth.
In conversation, Tennyson called him 'the dear old fellow', but Fitz
called him 'the Daddy' (with an animus carried over from college
one supposes) and would not cease to mock him. They agreed that
the prize for bad lines in Wordsworth should go to 'A Mr Wilkinson,
a clergyman', and yet the last line of Tennyson's 'Dora' is 'But Dora
lived unmarried till her death', which is much the same kind of line.
      They now moved down the Lakes to Ambleside, which was just
a few miles from Wordsworth's house. They put up for a week at
the Salutation Inn. James Spedding, who might have smoothed over
this difference of view, had to go home in the middle of it, but the
other two stayed on. They played around, imagined a play called
Gimblet, Prince of Dunkirk, boated and caught crabs on Windermere,
discussed Shakespeare's sonnets (sometimes Alfred thought they
were better than the plays, but then it was only knowing the plays
that made them so fine), and so on. Fitz bought Alfred a copy of
Yarrow Revisited,[20] which had just appeared, and Alfred quoted from
'Morte d'Arthur': 'Nine years she wrought it, sitting in the deeps/
Upon the hidden bases of the hills,' adding 'That is not bad, I think.'
When James Spedding came back he suggested a call on Wordsworth:
Tennyson dithered.[21] Yet he and Spedding did call, and signed their
names, so it appears he was unwilling to go with giggling FitzGerald:

it was to him too serious a matter. We know Fitz did not go, because he said so years afterwards, but he left before the other two, so they may have called when he was gone. The names are not signatures, and not in Wordsworth's writing, but they are in the Visitors' Book under May 1835: Mr J. Spedding, Mirehouse, and Mr A. Tennyson, London. (London is probably a guess.) He did make an enormous impression with 'the fourth bottle of gin' on another visit, to Hartley Coleridge.

There was another visit they neither made nor thought of making: not far away at a house called Fox How,[22] Matthew Arnold, who was thirteen in 1835, was just beginning to write poems, under the influence of Byron and Pope as Alfred had been at his age fourteen years before. But Matthew Arnold never got over Wordsworth.

This holiday in the Lakes generated a number of letters, several of them from the Spedding family, and some later reminiscences. Alfred enjoyed himself, though Spedding's banter grated on him and so did FitzGerald's jokes. Spedding found Alfred lacking in self-confidence, 'accusing the baseness of his lot in life and looking to outward circumstances for more than a great man ought to want of them, and certainly more than they will ever bring.' That was wise no doubt, but unimaginative about a poet from a squire's son. Fitz wrote, 'I will say no more of Tennyson, than that the more I have seen of him, the more cause I have to think him great. His little humours and grumpiness were so droll, that I was always laughing . . . [with] a sense of depression at times from the overshadowing of an intellect so much more lofty than my own.'[23]

The holiday trailed away into letters as holidays when one is that age so often do. Spedding told Thompson Alfred had been 'very gruff and unmanageable'. Alfred was more loyal, but he wrote to Fitz, 'I may have been sometimes grumpy in the North, for I was out of health, and the climate Arctic, and Spedding had a quiet trick of banter that sometimes deranged one's equilibrium, but grumpy to *you* – never, as I hope to be saved.'[24] This is one of the most loving and affectionate letters he ever wrote; its purpose was to assure Fitz he was pleased to be written to, and its news that he was moving to London, because of the dearth of books and people in Lincolnshire (though in fact nothing came of this intention).[25] Fitz replied with equal warmth, assuring him among other things that he could easily let him have the odd ten or twelve pounds if ever he needed it. It seems likely that Fitz knew about the sale of the Chancellor's Medal. Tennyson said later to Carlyle that Fitz was one of the few human beings from whom one could ever accept money, but there is no truth in the persistent story that FitzGerald gave Tennyson a pension or allowance.

On 4 July 1835, immediately after this exchange, the Old Man of the Wolds went to meet his Maker. He was eighty-five and suffered every agony of gout (he was a teetotaller), of maddening itch, and of his own violent rages. He denounced and cursed his son Charles for neglecting him, he raved with fury for an hour at a time, to the consternation of his grandson. 'I never saw him in such a rage.' But the rages did not last, and he died clutching Charles by the hand with the words, 'Charles, I am dying, help me.' Charles gave him an amazing funeral (it was the sort of thing Charles was good at), a cross between a pageant and a political rally, with a procession of 2000 people, and the church bell tolling for fourteen hours. As the body travelled to Bayons, which the old man had disliked (he had lived at Usselby since 1833), sixty mounted mourners joined it at Market Rasen, and blinds were drawn there all that day. The entire affair cost £300. Neither the Bournes nor the Somersby Tennysons were represented, though they were invited, and a lowly place was arranged for Alfred.

Fred was abroad, living off his cousin George in Corfu; he came racing home to receive his inheritance, but did not attend the funeral. Charles and his family were affronted at Fred's non-appearance, and they wrote one another letters of overweening bloodiness about it, like an entire family of Ugly Sisters: it was at this stage that their change of name to d'Eyncourt came through by licence. It annoyed Charles that otherwise he would always have to be Mr Charles Tennyson, while his nephew Fred (eldest son of an eldest son) would be Mr Tennyson. He had his sons instructed that his and their letters should now be addressed to d'Eyncourt. 'It will keep us in a great measure clear of the Somersby family who really are quite hogs,' wrote one to another. 'Not one of them came to the funeral . . . What a blessing for you! You will now get rid of Frederick.' Eustace was in the army, but had six weeks leave in September and early October for the shooting season; they were all glad that Fred had left Corfu. 'It will be a great relief to your mind as well as *purse*.' As their father takes up this same subject one can sense his savage tone. 'The Somersby family were of course disappointed in the old man's will, never satisfied!' Charles then wrote, 'Alfred I find has been so very violent (though he gets the Manor of Grasby and an estate there) that Mr and Mrs Bourne sent him away from Margate where he was with them.' Aunt Russell wrote, 'I believe Alfred incapable of that which has been attributed to him,' but one of his cousins wrote to his father about 'what a *hog* Alfred is and what can you expect from a pig but a grunt . . . I would rather be excused meeting a bloated ploughman.'[26]

The terms of the will were that Somersby got only what the old monster had retained by entail or by inheritance, while Bayons got the rest, a huge fortune. Mrs Tennyson got nothing, though Fred was required to give her £200 a year, and a capital sum in trust for poor mad Edward. Fred got the Clayton money from Grimsby: about £800 a year. That was more than enough to have musicians summoned to his villa in Florence to play him Mozart every morning. Charles got nothing because Sam Turner had looked after him, and Alfred got some Grasby money (because Fred had wrangled over it on his behalf with the old man), amounting possibly to as much as £500 a year, less various expenses. Scholars today tend to be governessy about Alfred's constant claim to be poor, about his unbusinesslike temperament (because he invested unwisely) and about his lifelong resentment of his family's disinheritance. These same scholars are salaried, they are fat cats, but Alfred was in a bad way financially and the will did not rescue him; as for business acumen, he showed it to a remarkable degree in sticking to what he was good at (poetry) in spite of all, and in screwing a large income and two handsome houses out of it. Somersby was treated with hauteur and contempt by Bayons. The affront over the funeral should be compared with that wicked old man's behaviour over the death of his eldest son.

A new hall was going up at Bayons, 'in the old College Hall style . . . like the Hall of a manor house of yore, and I think the very thing to your taste.' It was something like the size of Arundel Castle, and had a drawbridge, vast towers, and other embellishments. Pevsner in *The Buildings of England* was mad about it, but it was dynamited in 1963, and only Harlaxton Manor near Grantham survives as a lesser example of its appalling weight and lavishness.

Alfred's brother Charles the poet was seriously ill at Caistor in July when his grandfather died; his mother went to him there.[27] He was not happy and he was taking laudanum. Alfred wrote to

Brookfield about him in May. 'You ask after Charles: he lives at Caistor (a wretched market town which looks more like the limit of the civilized world than Johnny Groat's house – about nine miles from Tealby): he is however the first man in the place, an owner of books and pictures, a water-closet with a recumbent Venus in it, and a house with a stone front. The country about him is dreadful – barren, rolling chalk-wolds without a tree: he talks of travelling for three years and then taking a wife.'[28] Alfred says he thought of leaving England too at that time, and settling in Italy or in Jersey. It cannot be irrelevant that it was precisely in those places that Fred settled in the end. It is not clear when Charles fell in love, because the Sellwoods were in and out of the lives of the young Tennysons without always leaving a written record, but he finally shook off his opium and became engaged to Louisa Sellwood in September 1835. We do know that Alfred saw Emily again: they sat on an iron bench in the garden at Somersby under budding elm trees that spring and he remembered her dress years afterwards.

Something must be said about Rose Baring (born about 1813, d. 1898). Scholars have come to accept that Tennyson had an affair with her, aspired to marry her, and in the end wrote *Maud* about her. It will be clear to readers that the usual inspiration for his idyllic narratives was not life but magazine fiction, and the strongest argument against this fantastic theory about Rose Baring is simply that no evidence exists to support it: it is a conjecture based on other conjectures, and that is all. Willingham Rawnsley, a young member of the Rector's family who was not old enough to remember what happened, produced some mildly flirtatious poems to Rose in a memoir,[29] and exaggerated their importance, but they are as light as air, and as empty of serious meaning.

Arthur Eden (1793–1860), of Wimbledon, the second husband of Mrs (Frances) Baring, Rose's mother, rented Harrington Hall, the local grand house, from Robert Cracroft (1783–1862), who had acquired it by marriage. It was a country house of palatial size and attractive looks, made of red brick in the classic Queen Anne taste (sadly, it burnt down in November 1991). The Cracrofts moved to his father's house when his father died, and Harrington Hall was therefore rented out from 1826 as a sporting estate. Eden inspected it in March 1831, signed a lease in May, and arrived for the shooting season with his wife and three Baring daughters that autumn. Rose was then aged about eighteen. The rent was £150 a year, and the lease was for three years with an option for five, but the Edens were still there in 1837 when the Tennysons left. T. H. Rawnsley introduced them, and Henry Sellwood, Emily's father, acted as agent.[30] Eden was on dining terms with the Massingberds, General Eden was his brother, Lord Brougham his brother-in-law, and Lord Auckland, the Viceroy of India, a kinsman. Rose tranquilly married her cousin in 1838, and became Mrs Robert Shafto, and when she was a very old lady, sweetly smiling, she met Lord Tennyson again with no touch of rancour or embarrassment on either side. It is inconceivable that *Maud* had anything to do with her. The only record of her being with Alfred as a girl, apart from his poems, is at a ball in Horncastle in October 1837, and again at the same ball in 1838, in which year she married. Alfred's first Rose poem was in 1834, but he is supposed to have been disillusioned by the end of 1836.[31]

On her twenty-first birthday in September 1834, 'Thy rosy lips are soft and sweet . . . pierce what heart thou wilt for ever' does not show Tennyson as seriously interested. In another she is 'Rose of roses, bliss of blisses,/Rosebud-lips for honey-kisses . . . /Comes there no such rose as this is.' This piece of nonsense is in its silly way successful; he recited it to F. T. Palgrave in 1854 and Palgrave wrote it down. If it were about a love affair, he would not have felt so guiltless as to recite it. Then there is 'The Rosebud' from E. V. Boyle's *Ros Rosarum* (1885).[32] Alfred (unusually for him) had liked her illustrations of 'The May Queen'. Once again, he is utterly unlikely to have offered the debris of a fifty-year-old love affair to the public, particularly since Mrs Shafto was alive and his friends Lord and Lady Ashburton were her uncle and aunt. It must also be remembered that he wrote equally light, sweet, meaningless album rhymes for Sophie Rawnsley and Georgina Baring, Georgina's (like Rose's) on a birthday in 1834. They are no more to be taken seriously than 'The Skipping-Rope', in which all the rhymes come from a rhyming dictionary, on the back page of which it was written. Christopher Ricks has linked various poems of disenchantment about mercenary marriages and mercenary obstacles to marriage with the end of Alfred's designs on Rose Baring; they are more clearly to be connected with his grandfather's will, and his own feeling of being an outsider without money or the prospect of getting any, a feeling with which one may reasonably sympathize. The first of the poems is 'The Flight', and Ricks cites 'Locksley Hall' and 'Edwin Morris' in addition. They do form a group, but the theme is not rare or necessarily personal.

Something personal does surface in spring 1836, when Charles married Louisa on 24 May, and Emily was bridesmaid. His sonnet 'The Bridesmaid' is in quite another style: as usual he lets out whatever comes into his head, starting conventionally, then admitting that as best man and bridesmaid they clutched hands during the ceremony, and ending like this:

> I loved thee for the tear thou couldst not hide,
> And prest thy hand, and knew the press returned,
> And thought, 'My life is sick of single sleep:
> O happy bridesmaid, make a happy bride!'

In all the world no one but Alfred Tennyson could fall in love precisely like that, and no one would say it so open-heartedly, but that is exactly what happened. It may be that the brief, probably fragmentary marriage poem ('Move eastward, happy earth, and leave') that he published in 1842 was his own lovesong (or it is just possible it was for Charles). It has rather a complicated image: the sun is to roll eastwards[33] 'from fringes of the faded eve' (that is, into the dark) until the moon rises 'To glass herself in dewy eyes/That watch me from the glen below.' It is to 'move me to my marriage-morn,/And round again to happy night.' The four first and four last lines rhyme abab, but the central four rhyme in the stanza form of *In Memoriam*, and it recalls the diction of that poem. He had not ceased to work at *In Memoriam*, holding in his head many poems that had not been written down, and adding to poems ten years or more after he first composed them. Poem LXXXV of *In Memoriam*, for example, was written as ten stanzas by 1834, to ask himself 'whether love for him have drained/My capabilities of love'.

One would have wished that falling in love with Louisa's sister Emily might have been the answer to that problem, but many obstacles intervened, and he was still unmarried in 1841, when he added twenty more stanzas to the existing ten, going as deeply as Shakespeare went into the nature of friendship, though with less confidence of course and less power than Shakespeare, and addressing himself to Edmund Lushington on the subject.[34] Throughout these restless and not always happy years, one must bear in mind that the poems of *In Memoriam* were being distilled. For example, in

LXXXV, whenever it was written (let us say 1841), he opens himself deeply, but as usual it is the earth and its seasons that make his passion touch us:

> But Summer on the steaming floods
>   And Spring that swells the narrow brooks,
>   And Autumn, with a noise of rooks,
> That gather in the waning woods,
>
> And every pulse of wind and wave
>   Recalls, in change of light or gloom,
>   My old affection of the tomb,
> And my prime passion in the grave
>
> (69–76)

Apart from the slow, steady accretions in *In Memoriam*, in which the original idea had now lost its formality like a wreck underwater covered in marine growth, Tennyson entered a stage of his poetry when he did not cease to be prolific, but ceased to improve. In 'Dora', his 'English Idyls' had attained their style: they were clean, modern narratives with clear plots, with every virtue that one could desire in their prose equivalent. He had abandoned classical myth, at least for the moment, and he hedged 'Morte d'Arthur' with excuses not for the modern treatment but for the antique subject. He had strayed far from Ovid, and further than scholars believe from Theocritus. His preoccupation with longish verse narratives, out of which in 1839 would gradually evolve *The Princess* (1847) was wonderfully productive, and in poems like 'Walking to the Mail' reached a perfection in which art conceals art, but he would not seem quite so refreshing and original to us in this strain if we read more of the inferior poetry of the period, which aims at the same object and misses. Crabbe and Wordsworth are not minor writers and Tennyson esteemed them very highly. But Scott, Moore, Campbell, and even Archbishop Trench were at the same game. Bishop Heber of Calcutta left two and a bit cantos of a 'Morte d'Arthur' unfinished when he died in 1823. The Irish poet Allingham in the early 1860s, who was a Pre-Raphaelite hanger-on before he was Tennyson's, wrote a long, interesting narrative poem, 'Laurence Bloomfield in Ireland', Elizabeth Browning published her brilliant *Aurora Leigh* in 1857,[35] and there is Robert Browning: but we have strayed again from the

marshy territory of minor poets. None of them has Tennyson's
verbal precision or his developed narrative force. If one should expect
greater things of him than he was now producing, the fault is either
that he was searching for subject matter or searching for a form. The
latter seems likelier; it seems a recurring truth about his life. His
greatest poem probably is that entangled shipwreck, that many times
started and incoherent lament, *In Memoriam*. The form of *In Memoriam* is totally original and inimitable. In inventing that, he tapped
his own deepest emotions, fused the intimate with the monumental,
and set them free.

Charles's wedding was a happy occasion for Alfred, but Charles
himself was so nervous on his wedding morning that he took opium
again, and it was many unhappy years before he was free of the
habit. (The unfortunate man was categorized by his cousin Eustace
as the most good-natured of men, certain to kill himself soon, when
he left Tealby.) His wife suffered a breakdown when he did recover,
and it was not until late in the 1840s that they could live together.
Yet at last they became devoted and devout servants of their very
primitive parish; they moved out to Grasby, built a Rectory and a
school, loved their parishioners and worshipped one another. Their
life was tragic, and yet without the extremism that dogged Fred. It
is clear that in their parish they were an adorable couple. Having no
children they adopted everyone in their village. Charles had wanted
to be a priest for years, and there appears no doubt he was devout
and well fitted to his priestly vocation. Louisa went about in clogs,
and a sort of moving tower of petticoats and wraps. They were both
very shabby and both had a strong local accent. Alfred in later life
preferred them to anyone else in the world apart from his own wife
and brood. When Charles died Louisa survived him for just a month.

By now the Tennyson d'Eyncourts of Bayons were caught in
the trap of their own ostentation. Laughter about them in the county
was so unkind that they did not dare to attend the Stuff Ball at
Lincoln in 1836. The air was thick with abusive and anonymous
letters. It was said that Cousin George had announced he was refusing
to be responsible for his father's debts (some £15,000 a year on the
house alone), and a particularly enjoyable bit of gossip put about by
Mr Anderson at Lea said that some fox-hunters riding home had
rung the bell at Bayons, only to be told by a footman that 'The Right
Honourable gentleman is walking upon the Barbican.' Being deeply
like his father and in the merely offensive sense a peasant, the Rt Hon

Charles, PC, began to believe his servants were cheating him, his family neglecting him, and so on. Cousin Edwin came to hate Lincolnshire and longed to leave, but he needed a rich wife. In the end his father threw him out for a period.

A fortnight or so after Charles was married, Fred took Alfred and Mary over to dine in Horncastle with the Sellwoods, to meet Sir John Franklin, or rather to say goodbye to him, as he was off to Tasmania as Governor. Sir John had a dark, shy orphan niece Catherine who was there, whom Alfred alarmed by sitting beside her as she played the piano. She was impressed by the two tall, long-haired men, 'more than distinguished, I should say noble in appearance', but more so by Mary, the most beautiful woman she had ever seen. Mary was in her flower at that time, and engaged to John Heath. Catherine was terrified by Alfred, who sat opposite her, fixed her with his monocle, and asked his neighbour in what was meant to be a whisper, 'Is she a Hindoo?' After dinner, Alfred got a bad mark from Sir John by flinging himself across three chairs as his habit was, and lighting a pipe. (Dining with Thackeray at the Reform Club, he put his feet on the table.) He said he wanted to watch the jewels flashing on her fingers as she played, and he nicknamed her Zobeida. She thought the three of them remarkable to look at, but 'certainly formidable in their unconventional manner'.

John Heath believed Alfred was about to publish two volumes, presumably those that appeared in 1842, and he was at this time revising the 1832 poems, as well as adding to them. Wilson still alternately whined and growled, but J. S. Mill's review, which appeared in 1835, had done something to even the critical score. It was not content to praise him, which it did, but also it disposed of those prancing poseurs of criticism, Wilson and Croker. In praising Alfred it put a finger on one of his most remarkable features, and to contemporary eyes the most appealing: his invention of landscapes to fit moods, 'and to summon up the state of feeling itself, with a force not to be surpassed by anything but reality.' Alfred gave Brookfield his old 'St Agnes' Eve' for an album called *The Keepsake*: he sent it in June 1836 and it appeared in November. In December Milnes wanted a poem for *The Tribute*, another album. Brookfield's was edited by Lady Emmeline Stuart Wortley, daughter of the Duke of Rutland, one of Clare's patrons, and a poet, while Milnes's had Lord Northampton for a figurehead. Milnes had assured the Marquis he could get a poem out of Tennyson, but Tennyson refused. He did

so at first in the friendliest way, and they were on the friendliest
terms, as their letters show, but his refusal to be paraded caused
offence.[36] What followed reveals something:

> Three summers back, provoked by the incivility of editors, I
> swore an oath, that I would never again have to do with their
> vapid books . . . To write for people with prefixes to their
> names . . . is neither honour nor profit . . . And how should
> such a modest man as I see my small name in collocation with
> the great ones of Southey, Wordsworth, R. M. M. etc. and not
> feel like a barn-door fowl among peacocks?

The sharp dig at R. M. M. (Monckton Milnes) is perhaps a justified
rebuke. Richard still had his pretensions to be a poet (he published
his verse in *The Times*, for example),[37] and was on nodding and
smiling terms with those (like Wordsworth) who to Tennyson
seemed godlike. Tennyson was proud enough to insist on making
his own way among them, he scorned the amateurish titled editors
and the lavish albums, he would not in short be anyone's drawing-
room poet. He was a bit abrupt, uncivilized maybe, provincial no
doubt, but at least he knew precisely who he thought he was. The
row went on over the New Year of 1837, the year of Queen
Victoria's becoming Queen. Alfred dashed off a poem about that
('The Queen of the Isles') and tried to get Spedding to get it into *The
Times*, but with no success. It was eleven stanzas in the form of a
toast, worse as light verse than almost any of his later laureate poems
(where at least a pressure to perform created a certain tension). He
patched over the quarrel with Monckton Milnes and there is little
more to be said about it, except that he revealed in one of his letters
utter contempt for Bulwer, the MP for Lincoln (1832–41) and crony
of his Uncle Charles, and was alarmed that Milnes threatened to
print 'Anacaona' from manuscript unless he gave him something
newer. They ended friends again.

He was in London for a long time during that spring of 1837,
house-hunting, though there were still occasional rumours that he
might go abroad. The time itself was unsettled for the Tennysons,
because they knew from late 1836 that young Mr Barton, the new
Rector, was to be married and they must leave home. In London he
would use Spedding's rooms at 60 Lincoln's Inn Fields as a head-
quarters, or sometimes a lodging at 12 Mornington Crescent, perhaps

because it had been Kemble's rooms. Everyone said he smoked too much, mostly shag tobacco in a pipe, but sometimes cigars, and he drank at least as much as was good for him, though he never seemed the worse for it. He used to dine at The Cock near Temple Bar, and at such other London taverns as Bertolini's, Leicester Square. In the autumn of 1835 he had a jolly dinner at The Cock with Spedding, Thackeray and FitzGerald. Later they all got on to a horse-bus. 'Are you full inside?' asked the conductor. 'Yes,' said Alfred. 'The last glass did for me.' In April 1837, Spedding gives the typical menu: 'We had two chops, one pickle, two cheeses, one pint of Stout, one pint of Port, and three cigars.' After that mild blow-out, Alfred refused to go round to the Kembles 'because he had influenza'.

Alfred read some poems in Lushington's rooms, met his long-standing admirer, that leather-faced, elegant old man of taste, the famous survivor Samuel Rogers, and dashed off some fine light verse: the plaintive 'A Farewell' is like a song by Moore, one can hear the harp twanging, but 'The tenth of April' is splendid about the weather:

> So frosty-hard the pavements sound,
> One almost thinks the dome of Paul's
> Should keep his snow the whole year round
>
> (6–8)

'Will Waterproof' is the monument to many dinners at The Cock. It is well sustained, and almost too good to be light verse, but it is also too long alas, however enjoyable; had he stuck closer to his Horation model it could have been a fine poem. He tells of vintages of port that

> elbow-deep in sawdust, slept,
> As old as Waterloo;
> Or stowed, when classic Canning died,
> In musty bins and chambers,
> Had cast upon its crusty side
> The gloom of ten Decembers.
>
> (99–104)

Taken all in all, the poem conveys the quality of an old London tavern, and conveys Tennyson the young Londoner, better than any

other poem in his lifetime. He talks about his worries: critics, politics
(he wants national unity), and want of money. He was probably
spending that rather fast. But he is as remarkably truthful as ever: the
Muse is his only constant girlfriend, he knows his fault is half-
forgetting the poems in his head, or adding and altering over and
over 'till all be ripe and rotten'. And when he considers his own past
life he is touching:

> I kiss the lips I once have kissed;
>   The gas-light wavers dimmer;
> And softly, through a vinous mist,
>   My college friendships glimmer.
>
> (36–40)

The Somersby Tennysons left Lincolnshire in 1837. From
autumn 1835, Alfred had begun to travel more freely: there had been
trips to London and Boulogne and in spring Yorkshire to see
Monckton Milnes. That was a sign that at last he had some money;
still, his taproot was deep in Lincolnshire, where he was loved. 'Most
everybody knowed Master Alfred round these parts.' The loss of
Lincolnshire is one of the more important sources of *In Memoriam*.

CHAPTER FIVE

1842

IN LINCOLNSHIRE, the Tennyson boys always moved restlessly and unpredictably about, but when the time came to go away they were like dead leaves in a whirlwind. All the children were grown up by 1837; the youngest, Horatio, was eighteen. Early in 1837 Ellen Hallam had died, and soon afterwards John Heath broke off his engagement to Mary Tennyson, the eldest sister and Alfred's companion. By that disaster he lost a close friend. There was an idea that Alfred and Mary should go abroad together, but their mother could not face that; he must manage the family move. In June 1837 he was at Charles's fine town house at Caistor. There he and Charles walked over to Bayons, and finally he appeared at his Aunt Bourne's at Dalby at ten at night with Charles and Cecilia. The old lady was fond of them fortunately, and thought them 'the dearest and most interesting of my connections'. After supper they went on to the Rawnsleys at Halton Holgate. The night before they left the county, Alfred dreamed, as he tells us in *In Memoriam* CIII. He was in a hall where young women were singing to a veiled statue, and:

> distant hills
> From hidden summits fed with rills
> A river sliding by the wall.
>
> (6–8)

They put him into a small boat and took him out to see where Arthur Hallam stood on the deck of a big ship: 'Up the side I went,/ And fell in silence on his neck.' The young women wailed more than ever, but Arthur let them come on board as well, so the ship sailed away towards a red cloud looming like the land. Alfred woke up happy. He interpreted his own dream with an innocent high-mindedness by which the girls were muses. It could not occur to him so long before Freud that the water and the climbing indicated sex.

The main record of the move from Lincolnshire is a letter from Cecilia to Susan Haddelsey,[1] a solicitor's daughter in Caistor. She was twenty, but she wrote headlong, without full stops or capital letters. In her father's last years he could not teach her properly, though he believed in women's education. She wrote from the new house, Beech Hill, which was leased from Serjeant Arabin,[2] a kinsman of the Massingberds and therefore a remote connection of Mrs Tennyson. The house was rebuilt in 1850, but Beech Hill Park was and is in a rustic suburb near Epping Forest. The letter is worth quoting in full:[3]

My dearest Susan

We arrived here last Saturday morning, cold and wretched, for I had not slept once during the night. We stopped at Waltham Cross, about five and then took a chaise on to Beech Hill. We were some time before we found our house. Beech Hill is only three miles from Waltham Cross, but we got wrong and went some five or six miles about. Moreover we stopped at a house which was not our own, and disturbed some poor Miss Ma[c]kenzies from their beds who looked out of the window at the sound of the Bell which we rung several times in a little alarm, I thought, but they were very polite, and told us that our best plan would be to inquire at the Inn at some little distance, but we thought that our best plan would be to inquire at Sergeant Arabin's, the person to whom the house belongs, and we accordingly did. When we arrived there, after ringing and calling for some time, a boy ran out to us, and we heard the Postboy say, Is there a family by the name of Towndown or Trendown (some such name he called ours) living here though we had told him repeatedly Tennyson. Then he said Dennyson. At last we shouted out ourselves Tennyson. 'Ay that's the name' said the boy (and directed us right) 'you've just taken the wrong turn. This is High Beech, the new comers are at Beech Hill about half a mile from here where Mr Such a one use to live.' Upon which the Postboy said he [k]new where the house was. All this was owing to the stupidity or something else of Spinks our servant who had been told by Mamma to go to Waltham Cross that morning to direct us to our new home but we never saw anything of him so I suppose he never went for when he was asked about it he made up a long tale of which we could make out nothing. Our neighbours the Arabins are very nice people, really kind amiable goodhearted people. It is very pleasant to us to meet with such people after coming from all those that we love. They are just like old friends to us. The Sergeant is a merry little man. I saw him for the first time yesterday and was much amused by his broad compliments. His son is as happy as the day is long and owns that he never reads a book that does not end happily. Our house is very prettily situated on a Hill. We have a very nice garden with a great deal of wall fruit, all of which had been eaten before we came, but we are in time for the Grapes of which we have abundance in a small Green-house. We have also a verandah which ornaments the house very much. I do not mean to say that the verandah itself does but the creepers which twine about it do. The Lodge too I like. It is pretty and simple and thatched which I like much. Mrs Arabin's house is opposite us and situated also upon a hill. It looks very cheerful from our windows. From thence too our house looks remarkably well. Mrs Neville our prime Husk is now with us. She is much better in health than she was and as charming as ever. My sister Mary is also as fond of her as ever. It will be a long time before I shall know people and things here. Every thing appears so strange to me. How delightful it was to me to see the dear old family faces again. You can enter into my feelings and would know exactly what they were, when I stopped at the door of my new home. Like you when you saw Mrs Haddelsey in France, I actually wept for joy. What hast thou been doing lately? How is Mrs Haddelsey and Mr Haddelsey and all the children, dear little Sam too. How is he? Has Charley learned the Cork leg off? Write soon and tell me about every thing. How are Charles and Louisa? give my best love to them and to Sep and Arthur. I was terribly afraid when I set off from Spilsby by the Mail that Ariel would not be admitted but no objection was made. I met with a woman also in the coach who was fond of Dogs. I was very fortunate was I not? She was very talkative and open, told us where she lived nay even pointed out her house to us, which was a neat looking shop in Spalding. She also said that she had a little child at the interesting age of between two and three. Frederick is in London at present. I am going there soon to spend a few days with him. Mrs Neville, Mary and Alfred also dine at Captain Southeby's on Tuesday. They are friends [of] the Hallams' and seem nice people. I walked with Matilda to Waltham yesterday. It is a melancholy looking Town and it was so strange to me not to meet a single face that I knew. It is very pleasant being so near London is it not? and when we get a horse and vehicle we shall be often going there. Write soon and tell me every thing you do. I have never had any nice rides since I left Caistor. Do you like the Brown Horse as much as ever. I have written horribly but I have the headache and am writing on a sofa so you must excuse it, and now I must bid thee adieu, as I have not been well lately and am rather tired. All desire kindest remembrances to thee and thine. Kiss little Sam for me and tell him not to forget me.

Ever thy very affectionate
Cecilia Tennyson

Will you come and see us in the Summer. How does the Summer-house look?

I walked with Alfred in Epping Forest yesterday. The Trees are very much spoiled there. In many places there are only stumps left shooting out here and there a little green. By moonlight they would look like so many Ghosts for many of the stumps are quite white. Many parts of the Forest are high, from which parts between the Trees the country looks very well and though rather flat still there is a grandeur about it. Adieu. Write soon.

'Mrs Neville our prime Husk' throws light on the social world in which the Tennyson family lived, because the Husks were quasi-sisters who wrote and studied poetry: the 'husks' presumably because they are the rough left-overs that the prodigal son longs for in the parable, as opposed to published poets like Alfred and Charles. Mimosa Neville was a daughter of some Massingberds who was separated from her husband, a penniless and all too adventurous officer. She had gone out to Australia with him and a baby and her father and her sister in 1832, but the officer was accused of forgery; then in 1835[4] or 1836 they tried America, but the pioneering work was too hard for her; she broke down and he abandoned her with three tiny children. She contrived to get home again, and her father took her to Guernsey, since by now she had tuberculosis, and it was there she came across Louisa Lanesborough, an intense, romantic

Methodist girl of twenty-five, ten years or so younger than Mimosa was. Louisa was crazy about poetry of all kinds, but particularly about Alfred Tennyson's. She also had a passion for Mimosa, and the two of them spent hours on Guernsey talking about the Tennyson family and the poems of Alfred. The Tennyson move to Epping Forest was their opportunity because Mimosa was due to be seen by a London doctor, and also invited to stay with the Tennysons at Beech Hill, so Louisa went with her, disguised as her maid or nurse:

> I could not resist the exquisite fun it would be for us to be together, and I unknown to see and speak to those creatures of my imagination, Alfred Tennyson, Mary, Frederick, Mrs Tennyson, all of them, they who are talked of and dreamed of, but scarcely realized, whose notes are read, whose minds are unfolded, whose strange wild thoughts are followed out by my soul, in its love wanderings. To see them, to be in the same house and unknown, quite unknown.

On 11 March 1838 she arrived disguised as 'Marion' in the clothes of a Guernsey countrywoman and a large black wig (the reader will not be surprised to hear that Louisa later became a romantic novelist). As Marion she was shown to the servants' hall, which contained three maids and a footman called John, but the drawing room contained only Mary and Cecilia: Alfred, Fred, Emily and Mrs Tennyson were in London. On the last evening, the pair of them dined upstairs, and Cecilia came up and read them 'Break, break, break' from Alfred's manuscript.

They then moved to Mornington Crescent, for Mimosa to see her doctor, and there Louisa waited at table. Fred and Septimus lived on a floor of their own, where they dined at six, but Mrs Tennyson and the rest of her brood dined at four. Alfred always had an apple pie or an apple pudding with his dinner; indeed, he went on doing so for fifty-five years. He was very civil to Louisa, though when he asked her to fetch a German book from another room as he lay in bed smoking, he was surprised that she found it at once. That night a cork was hard to draw. 'Where's your Marion?' asked Alfred. 'She could do it – she can do anything.' Later on the two went to Italy with Mary and Fred; Mimosa kissed her at Como, so the truth came out. Louisa stayed at Beech Hill without her wig, and none of the servants recognized her. The sharpest impression we get from the whole charade is of Alfred on the coach home from London, murmuring poems and abusing Mrs Hemans. Louisa remembered the household as magical, all the sons dreaming and writing and endlessly talking, Alfred padding about in the small hours muttering poems, the proud, appreciative sisters, and what she called 'the tender mother's spirit brooding over all'.

This curious prank throws some light on the family life, and on the supportiveness they showed to Alfred. They took it for granted he was a genius. A little later Mrs Tennyson would take to addressing perfect strangers, on an omnibus for instance, to let them know she was the mother of the laureate, 'and my other sons also have written beautiful verses'.

New friends as well as old made him welcome to London. In July 1837 he was arranging to see Carlyle (who was away) and Leigh Hunt. Volume three of an anthology called *The Book of Gems, Modern Poets and Artists of Great Britain*, carried six of his poems.[5] In December a lot of his family were in the big house at Caistor. Septimus was writing poems to his mother, Horatio (Rashe) was with him, Cecilia was staying with Fred, and Arthur had a touch of smallpox. In 1837 Septimus and Horatio had thought of emigrating to Demarara, but in the end Horatio went off alone to Tasmania. Charles and Louisa had moved out of Caistor to Grasby, and Alfred was beginning to expect some rent for his fields. But he wrote to Emily, 'I have been at this place all the year, with nothing but that muddy pond in prospect, and those two little sharp-barking dogs. Perhaps I am coming to the Lincolnshire coast, but I scarcely know. The journey is so expensive and I am so poor.' His mother thanked Mrs Rawnsley for a Christmas hamper that included a pork pie. 'It was gratifying to our palates to taste again good, wholesome, dear old Lincolnshire Pork.'[6]

Alfred's correspondence with Emily has been severely censored and mostly destroyed, both by himself and after his death. Nearly every reference to his brother Charles and his troubles has been erased even where a letter has survived. It is therefore almost impossible to trace the story of Alfred's engagement or of its being put off. It is clear that by 1839 he and Emily were regarded as engaged, but Mr Sellwood seems to have put a stop to Alfred's plans in 1840. That is scarcely surprising when it is considered that the marriage of Charles and his other daughter Louisa was so ill-fated for so long: certainly this was reason enough for any father of the day to worry about entrusting a second daughter to Charles's brother. Emily in a note to her children hints that his motive was that one. Money, as we shall see, was a further obstacle, but if Alfred inclined to believe that Mr Sellwood rejected him as a penniless poet without prospects, then I suspect that money was only Mr Sellwood's excuse. The letters that have been destroyed must surely have contained full details of Charles's and Louisa's ups and downs.

Instead of taking opium, Alfred was a most determined smoker. His friend Blakesley wrote of him to Monckton Milnes, 'he smokes the strongest and most stinking tobacco out of a small, blackened clay pipe on an average nine hours every day.'[7] Mr Sellwood was shocked at his smoking cigars, a habit that did not persist into his children's memory. Mr Sellwood thought it a symptom of lightness and luxury and financial unseriousness, perhaps rightly. It is not easy for a poet to marry a lawyer's daughter. The family friendship was inextricable all the same. While Horatio went to visit a Lincolnshire cousin, Mary went to Guernsey for six months with Ann Sellwood in 1838 for the sea-bathing, and 'One of the Miss Rawnsleys, one of the Miss Sellwoods, and now we have our cousin Louis Fytche with us.' Louis went off with Horatio to Chelmsford, a walk of twenty-five miles, to see some Fytche tombs.[8]

Charles's bad period with opium was over by 1838, and it was then or in 1840 that Louisa, having cured him, suffered her nervous breakdown and was taken away by the authority of doctors until 1849. It was some time in 1840 that Mr Sellwood insisted Alfred and Emily should cease to correspond. It is therefore intelligible that Alfred should put such weight on the marriage of Cecilia to Edmund Lushington in 1842. Fred's marriage to Maria Guiliotti, daughter of a judge at Siena, took place in Italy in 1839 and Alfred did not know the girl, but he was particularly fond of Cecilia and of Edmund: they gave him hope. Fred's last folly before he left for Italy had been to fall in love with his cousin Julia, who was his grandfather's companion; he declared himself in a passionate letter but without success. After his marriage Fred never lived in England again. Alfred was left in charge of the rest of the family whether he liked it or not.

His literary life at this time reads as almost more of a whirlwind than his family life. He paced and brooded in the forest in his great cloak, and in winter he skated a great deal. He led his mother round the lanes in a kind of wheelchair drawn by a Shetland pony. But London and his friends drew him: Thackeray in Coram Street and

that certain kinds of landscape still seem to belong to them, and to be haunted by the ghost or the shreds of their philosophy. But Alfred Tennyson, brilliant as he was in detail, and sportive in mythology, was really more mystical than metaphysical: at times he comes close to Belloc and 'The Four Men'. He wrote to Emily, 'I have dim sympathies with tree and hill reaching far back into childhood. A known landskip is to me an old friend, that continually talks to me of my own youth and half-forgotten things, and does more for me than many an old friend that I know. An old park is my delight and I could tumble about it for ever.'[11] While he was in Torquay he appears to have written 'Audley Court', and perhaps 'The Talking Oak'. 'Amphion' is merely bookish light verse, parading his love of the green earth more formally. It is a pity he scrapped in 1859 the four lines printed in 1842:

> The birch-tree swang her fragrant hair,
>   The bramble cast her berry,
> The gin within the juniper
>   Began to make him merry.[12]
>
> (33–6)

There is no lack of weight in the finished poems of this period; indeed it is their ease that is surprising, and may lull the reader into missing something serious. 'Locksley Hall' (1837–8), like 'The Talking Oak' moves effortlessly between light, ornamental tale-telling from an oriental model by Sir William Jones, and deeper, more impressive feelings. But I do not think 'honest Nature's rule' is the point of it: its burden is the still inchoate, somehow painful sense of the future, and as usual 'the hollow ocean-ridges roaring into cataracts'. The poem is too long, and often prosaic or banal, yet it is something to have Tennysonian nature in the same poem as the oriental paradise and 'the light of London flaring like a dreary dawn'. The poem has been much quoted and its prophecies are deadly serious, and yet they are all riddles: probably that is why they are compelling to this day. Nothing that Tennyson prophesied so very early in Victoria's reign had failed to take place within ten years of his death or hers. What seems dated today is his sense of freedom, of scarcely tapped resources. Henry Hallam (of all people) suggested the metre, and some of the lines go back as far as 1830, so it should really rank as a pre-Victorian poem.

'Audley Court' and its cousins rank among Alfred's 'English Idyls', which are transitional poems leading towards *The Princess*. The blank verse is smooth and delightful, then suddenly thrilling for a few lines. The whole poem is agreeably brief and varied, like the seventh idyll of Theocritus, with unlikely songs; the picnic is particularly appetizing. The text is a careful improvement on earlier versions, only the conversation is insubstantial, so that the whole poem is like a wonderful rococo frame with the merest sketch of a picture. In poems like this, Alfred seems to have taken his plot from wherever he found it. 'Walking to the Mail' has a splendid story about Eton boys, which Alfred probably obtained from Fred, since it was often told, but a memoir dates it to an earlier generation, legendary in Fred's time at school: Alfred is not likely to have got it from a privately printed book, though he was omnivorous.[13] He treats it as a folk tale, with the story of the moonlight flitting, which existed independently of his poem even in our lifetimes.

In 'Edwin Morris', another of these English stories, the poet criticizes his own earlier manner in 'The Gardener's Daughter'. His characters are as charming as ever, but the brushwork is deliberately light, though once again there are a number of drafts of this poem. He seems from them to be feeling for the lightness and fire and grace of Catullus: but that was not within his range, at least in these poems, though he came as close as his Elizabethan models could take him, and uniquely close for his generation, in brief song-like lyrics like 'Come not, when I am dead', which he could throw off at any time and poured like sugar and cream over *The Princess*. The plot of 'Edwin Morris' remains untraced: it is about a Lancashire cotton millionaire and has nothing of course to do with Miss Baring. Her sister Fanny got married about this time to the Rector of Ormsby, a Massingberd cousin.[14] The poem is memorable for 'slight Sir Robert with his watery smile/And educated whiskers', but also for a tiny touch either of Milton or of the same old passage from Ovid's *Fasti*, 'Like Proserpine in Enna, gathering flowers'. The story of the lovers interrupted was one he would use again in *Maud*: his mind churned its material over and over, and constantly reworked old poems.

These English poems are all conversation pieces; they all reflect more or less the conversations of the Apostles, and nothing in Leigh Hunt or Southey, still less in Mary Russell Mitford (a more powerful influence) can explain them. They are like Peacock's conversational novels, if they are like anything, or FitzGerald's *Euphranor*. One of the most remarkable depends on a tour of Wales in 1839: of its characters the most interesting by far is 'old James', who is a mouthpiece for the new friend Carlyle. This poem, 'The Golden Year', has a rejected fragment of striking power that reflects the newest science:[15]

> O grand old sires, who wagged their beards in hall
> And laughed and let the earth go round, nor knew
> The noiseless ether curdling into worlds
> And complicated clockwork of the suns.[16]

This brief and striking poem of 76 lines offers at least a velleity for 'the fair new forms,/That float about the threshold of an age,/Like truths of Science waiting to be caught', but it ends with a dose of reality as sharp as a gunshot:

> He spoke; and, high above, I heard them blast
> The steep slate-quarry, and the great echo flap
> And buffet round the hills, from bluff to bluff.
>
> (74-6)

These are almost all the poems Alfred Tennyson would print in 1842. Of the last handful that require to be mentioned, the queerest is 'The Vision of Sin', of which its author thought extremely highly. At least, he said to Coventry Patmore, and again in a letter, that it was his favourite. It is a somewhat impenetrable theological diatribe that seems to boil down to 'vanity of vanities'. Its setting is a painting by Turner, and its most striking line is the enigmatic one, 'God made Himself an awful rose of dawn'. 'Love and Duty' belongs to the crisis over Emily in 1840; it was published in 1842, but its pain is abstract and its accent not intimately personal. One might not know what it was about if one had not been told. The night sky at midsummer is a confused image, though the dawn scene at the end of the poem is beautiful.

'Godiva' is a more promising theme: the poet went to Coventry in June 1840 and thought of it then, so for some time after his visit he gathered historical material. He gave his poem a modern framework which the critics mysteriously connect with Theocritus, although he starts 'I waited for the train at Coventry;/I hung with

grooms and porters on the bridge', which is scarcely a Greek opening
gambit. Even as a character Godiva, who 'Unclasped the wedding
eagles of her belt,/The grim Earl's gift', is magnificently datable to
about 1840. The poem is written with a fluent brilliancy; it is not
possible now to read any of it without a powerful sensation of its
period, and this works rather for than against it. The whole text, as
with several of these finely made and polished vignettes, is less than
80 lines long. Here Ricks has recovered from manuscript a closing
piece of the modern frame, which Tennyson abandoned. It deserves
to be preserved if only as early railway poetry:

> The murmur of the train
> Began to grow. We listened till at last
> The brazen bellied engine rolling up
> A tract of wheels, with breathless gasp and snort
> And brain-dividing whistle drove them on
> In thunder half beyond the bridge, and then
> Swung clanging backward to the double stairs.[17]

These years of prodigal inspiration produced many small poems
that grew and some that did not. 'Rosamund's Bower', a short,
uninteresting song about a girl in 'Inextricable brickwork maze in
maze' (a wonderful and Dickensian image of the city) sprouted
eventually into his play Becket. He had already touched on the legend
in his 'A Dream of Fair Women', so it may well have been a story he
knew in childhood.

The last poem in the 1842 collection, 'The Poet's Song', is one of
the most surprising. Its only connection seems to be to 'Locksley
Hall' since the poet 'sings of what the world will be/When the years
have died away', but it is undatable and has no manuscript. Yet there
is a remarkable and Blake-like freshness about it which is rare in
Tennyson. The Poet leaves the town after a shower of rain, in
summer in a west wind:

> And he sat him down in a lonely place,
>   And chanted a melody loud and sweet,
> That made the wild-swan pause in her cloud,
>   And the lark drop down at his feet.

(5–8)

If he had written no other poem, this one would still have survived.

How did he spent his new-found freedom in London? In 1837, or soon after, he called on Gladstone, who said: 'This was an unexpected honour, for I had no other tie with him than having been in earlier life the friend of his friend.' As a very old man in 1892, Gladstone remembered the call as something that happened in Carlton Gardens, but at this time he was a former junior minister, a bachelor living in Albany, where he gave large breakfast parties. 'I cannot now remember particulars, but I still retain the liveliest impression of both the freedom and kindness with which he conversed with me during a long interview.' Gladstone was reading hugely in 1837 (the entire works of Augustine, for example) and writing ill-conceived works of a theological cast, which Sir Robert Peel thought would ruin him.[18] It is important to remember that Gladstone was Peel's disciple, and Peel had not yet attained his zenith. Gladstone's father was alive and an MP, and so was one of his elder brothers. Peel founded the modern Conservative Party as a party of reform just at this time, and both Gladstone and Disraeli (MP 1837) belonged to it. The new party took shape in 1838, and Peel became prime minister in 1841. In 1832 he had 150 members, in 1834 he had 250, in Victoria's first parliament late in 1837 nearly 320, though a quarrel over the removal of various Whig ladies of the bedchamber, whose powerful positions were a sort of accumulated sediment of their husbands' former influence, lasted until 1841, when it was solved partly by Prince Albert.

All these shifts in political life must be understood if we are to begin to read Alfred's own mind rightly. What he shared with Gladstone and with Peel was the huge impetus of their generation to reform. Peel as a boy had heard Fox and Pitt, and as home secretary in Alfred's youth had produced a series of smoothly executed reforms, of the currency, of criminal law, of jury law, and a new police force, which made progress seem to Gladstone and Monckton Milnes and Tennyson as automatic as a daydream. Even Disraeli wanted to see England united as one nation, not divided into rich and poor, just as Tennyson did. Of course each of them had his sticking point, but none of them favoured a radical solution. Only Leigh Hunt, for whose needs Alfred subscribed a guinea, wrote sentimentally about a poor Chartist.

From 1834 to 1838 Edmund Lushington had been a Fellow of Trinity, so G. S. Venables advised Tennyson to go and live there.

But in 1838 Lushington took off for the chair of Greek at Glasgow. In 1839 Gladstone and Lord Lyttelton, whom W. H. Brookfield had tutored, married a pair of sisters. In 1840 they went back to Eton, where they examined the entries for the Newcastle Prize. In 1861 they went so far as to publish their own translations into Latin and Greek, and in Gladstone's case mostly into English: of the three of them, Lushington was the most accomplished versifier, at least if we are to judge by his and Lyttelton's Tennyson versions, but they are all extremely good. For Alfred the gilt was wearing off that particular gingerbread: it may be that as he gradually grew out of the first impact and deep impression of the classics, his own poetry lost something, but it was not something irrecoverable. He did not try living in Cambridge, or working in Prague either, which G. S. Venables also suggested. He stuck to his own path, as he would later tell his son Hallam. He liked London, and he joined John Sterling's discussion club almost as soon as it was founded in 1838. His great new friend was Thomas Carlyle, whose house at 5 Cheyne Row stood in the village of Chelsea, separated from London by open fields: perhaps because of that formidable little distance, their friendship did not ripen before the 1842 poems appeared. Later, probably in the late 1850s when the Carlyles were quarrelling, someone complained to Tennyson of the fate that had linked two such incompatible human beings: Tennyson answered that their marriage was ideal, because any other solution would have made four people unhappy.

In 1839 Alfred Tennyson was quite cheerful: he enjoyed his Welsh tour, particularly the 'Mablethorpelike' seawaves breaking on the shore at Barmouth, the estuary and the crags. He thought the most beautiful thing he saw was the lakes at Llanberis, and Edwin Morris commemorated that, but it was at Barmouth that he wrote poem LXXXVI of In Memoriam, a single sentence of four stanzas. He used it to mark one of the three springs that divide the entire sequence as the Christmases do, although we need not take his rearrangements of In Memoriam too seriously. He was not in Barmouth until mid-July though the woods there can be 'dewy-tasselled' at almost any date and showers are all too frequent. The poem has a breathing richness that exactly recalls the Barmouth precipice walk at sunset as some readers may remember it. The railway viaduct which dominates the landscape now and dominates Charles Tennyson Turner's lovely poem about it had not been built in 1839.

'Pleasant on the waste shore', Alfred wrote to Emily, 'to listen to the splash of the spray.'

In autumn he had dinner in London with FitzGerald again, 'soles, two boiled fowls, and an Apple Tart – cheese, etc. After this plenty of smoking.' Fitz and his friends wanted him to issue another volume, but he was 'too lazy and wayward to put his hand to the business'. Moxon had been after him for two years for the revised *Poems*.

But 1840 was to be a year of disasters. Fitz wrote to Fred on 7 June that Alfred had 'not even the ambition to go up to London all this spring to see the Exhibitions etc.' In 1839, Alfred had written that Mrs Tennyson was 'afraid if I go to town even for a night; how could they get on without me for months?' A great fireball passed up the valley from Waltham and exploded with an exciting bang near the house. 'I had just gone into my mother's room: she was grovelling on the floor in an extremity of fear when the clap came; upon which she cried out, Oh! I will leave this house: the storms are very bad here.'[19] That seems to have been the only reason for a move from Epping Forest to Tunbridge Wells, which the doctor recommended because it was high and dry. But the new house was like a mousetrap and had no room for Alfred's books; he hated going there. In February 1840 he was 'nervously ill' in Fitz's London lodgings for a few days: Fitz had come back from the theatre and found Alfred installed. Fitz put it down to heredity and tobacco, rightly perhaps. But the dead Rector cannot be entirely to blame for all that was wrong. Charles was ill, Edward was mad, Septimus still needed watching, and Arthur had to enter an institution early in 1843 as an alcoholic.

When they left Epping Forest

Such a scene of sobbing and weeping was there on Monday morning among the servants at Beech Hill and cottagers' daughters, as that cockney residence has seldom witnessed, perhaps never since its stones were cemented and trowelled. There were poor Milnes wringing her hands and howling, Ann Green swallowing her own tears with exclamations of such pathos as would have moved the heart of a whinstone, and other villagers all joining in the chorus, as if for some great public calamity. Finding that we had human hearts, though we lived in a big house, they thought it all the harder that they were to lose us so soon.[20]

This description by Alfred to Emily tells us something about the Tennyson household at this time. The servants went with them in their migrations, so that Alfred still had Milnes when he married, and mostly Lincolnshire servants at least until he moved to the Isle of Wight.

Early in 1840 he stayed at Park House near Maidstone with the Lushingtons. Their father had died in 1839 so Edmund, now the Professor of Greek in Glasgow, had inherited, but his younger brothers were also to be found there. Alfred had some kind of London rooms in Charlotte Street close to FitzGerald's: Tunbridge he abominated. He managed to sell his bit of land at Grasby for £53 an acre, but he felt poor and expressed to Emily the certainty that unlike Fred he would never see Rome. 'I do not think I would live there if I could, and I have no money for touring.' But of course he did make expeditions, and often used the railways. He had a surgeon physician called Mr Snaith at Boston in Lincolnshire, who said the rubescence on the back of his hand was due to 'an irregularity of the liver'. He visited Brookfield at Southampton (which we are told he and Fred often visited) and met Charles Elton with him. He put his hand on Elton's ageing head and remarked what a lot of silly things he must have done in his life, with such a huge bump of generosity. A coachman on the way to Bath told him what a wicked city it was, full of whores, 'but nothing compared to Winchester'. In June 1840 he was at Warwick: 'A railway carriage in front of the train, entirely open without seats, nothing but a rail or two running across it, something like pens of cattle [this was the third class]. I came from Lincoln and stopt all night at Leicester, and came on here this morning by a slow mail. On driving into Warwick I happened to have my glass in my eye and perceived Edward FitzGerald,' who was walking towards Leamington.[21] Alfred stopped the coach and the two of them spent the evening together. Warwick Castle looked grand and black, a nightingale chanted in the woods and the rooks cawed. They toured the whole area, including Kenilworth and Stratford: the visit produced 'Godiva',[22] and probably the poem 'Love and Duty', but at some time not far distant he was writing in an entangled anguish to Emily. Alfred's engagment to Emily was broken off, and Henry Sellwood forbade them to go on writing to each other.

The two of them had been together comparatively seldom, at least by modern standards, but it is apparent from the fragments of letters that have been copied out and retained that they were warmly, intimately, passionately in love. The letters are widely ranging, often intellectual exchanges, but with vivid moments of description and allusion. It is a tragedy that we have lost them. Yet when they come together again after a gap of nearly ten years, they seem to begin where they left off, as if in a dream. Alfred muses seriously about hell and punishment and the life to come, almost as if he were talking to Arthur Hallam. If his answers to his own questions are wise, they are also vague. 'Let us be silent for we know nothing of these things and we trust there is one who knows all . . . If it were proclaimed as a truth "No man shall perish: all shall live after a certain time have gone by in bliss with God" . . . I dare say my own progress is impeded by holding this hope however dimly.'[23]

Almost at the same time as the break with Emily, Alfred became financially enmeshed in the crazy schemes of Matthew Allen, a controller of lunatics, a man twice imprisoned for debt and formerly in charge of an unsuccessful soda water factory at Leith. Allen (b. 1783) was brought up a Sandemanian, an obscure but virulent sect who tended as the century went on to transmute into Swedenborgians. He met Carlyle in Edinburgh after his second marriage (1811) and published two volumes of sermons which he claimed to have preached to lunatics at York. He had been apothecary to the York asylum in 1819, and acquired a medical degree, which was a formality, in 1821. In 1824 or 1825 he opened a private lunatic asylum at High Beech, close to the Tennysons' house in Epping, where he was in touch with Carlyle and a friend of Arabin. He was not a villain, and not cruel to mad people: Septimus Tennyson was successfully treated by him for a few weeks. Spedding wrote in August 1840 that Tennyson 'has been on a visit to a madhouse for the last fortnight (not as a patient), and has been delighted with the mad people, whom he reports the most agreeable and the most reasonable persons he has met with.'[24] It is possible, though it is the merest gossamer of conjecture, that Allen advised Tennyson he ought not to marry. It appears to me far likelier that Alfred stayed with him because he liked Epping and hated Tunbridge Wells, and so fell under his spell, and thought he might be a financial messiah, who would enable him if Charles was ever cured to marry Emily: to have enough money to do so. Certainly Allen's schemes swallowed up the entire fortunes of the family, as we shall see.

There is a further coincidence even more curious than that of

Alfred's undatable break with Emily and his visit to Allen. In June or July of 1837, John Clare had been certified. 'The attacks of melancholy from which he had suffered occasionally for many years became more frequent and more intense, his language grew wild and incoherent, and at length he failed to recognize his own wife and children and became the subject of all kinds of hallucinations.'[25] His London friends had him sent to High Beech, to Matthew Allen. He remained in Allen's asylum for several years, until he escaped in the summer of 1841. In those years, 'He was kept pretty constantly employed in the garden, and soon grew stout and robust. After a time he was allowed to stroll beyond the grounds of the asylum and to ramble about the forest. He was perfectly harmless, and would sometimes carry on a conversation in a rational manner, always however losing himself in the end in absolute nonsense.' Nothing more can be said, but it appears certain that at this time Alfred Tennyson and John Clare will have met, and highly probable that when Alfred wrote his letter to Spedding which is now lost, one of the lunatics he liked so much was John Clare, though he cannot have been conscious of who Clare was (he believed himself at times to be a prizefighter or Lord Nelson). There is one other strange link between the two poets, which is that a member of the Elton family at Clevedon Court near Bristol was interested in Clare, met him in London, published a light poem to him in the *London Magazine*, and invited him to stay: this was Arthur Hallam's uncle, Charles, who was a fine poet himself, though Tennyson seems unconscious of the fact. Clare was forty-seven, and Tennyson was thirty-one.

Allen intended to become rich through a patented system of carving the components of furniture more or less elaborately by machine instead of by hand. No doubt the cottage industries of Epping Forest seduced him. It sounds as if it would have worked but it did not. The invention was called a Pyroglyph which implies that it was steam operated, and we know Alfred was fascinated by steam. He invested his entire capital, and his mother was persuaded by Allen in Alfred's absence to invest hers also. Alfred later became suspicious of Allen's business methods, and compelled him to allow his mother to withdraw her funds from the scheme. In November 1840 Allen gave Alfred an insurance of his life for £2000 against a debt of £900: two days later in the same month the legal agreement or deed of association was signed and witnessed. Communications were unbusinesslike. Alfred was at Mablethorpe where post came weekly with the muffin man, or on the way to France, or just back,[26] and Allen had no secretary and forty letters to answer every day. In September 1841, Allen was to sign a Warrant of Attorney over 'all my property, the security in the Policy, and the cash in my possession'.

In October and November 1841 Charles Tennyson d'Eyncourt, who controlled capital sums as a trustee, was difficult about disgorging them; but Charles Tennyson Turner, then his mother, and finally three of the sisters, demanded and obtained £2000 to invest in Pyroglyphs on behalf of the sisters. In May 1842 Allen's message was to 'have faith and all things will be more than well'. In later summer Alfred was 'dejected, my nerves shattered, my health affected' by suspicion and doubt and rumour. It is evident from his letters that the affairs of the company were an impenetrable morass. Late in 1842 there were attempts to withdraw, if only because Edmund Lushington was due to marry Cecilia and would then become liable for her debts: this was not a limited liability company, and modern company law had not begun to exist.

Allen tried to borrow £1000 from Septimus in October 1842, in addition to the £8000 of Tennyson capital he already apparently had. No one was getting any interest, no one had made any profit. Alfred was now penniless and (for the first time) in serious debt, and the women of the family were living on his brother Charles. He wrote to the Allens in terms of justifiable fury. By March 1843, Allen was in the throes of hysterical despair, and unhappy Mrs Tennyson had to approach Charles d'Eyncourt again, this time to pay Arthur's expenses as an alcoholic in the Crichton Institution, Dumfries. Finally, in 1844 Edmund Lushington advanced the money (about £80 a year) due for the insurance of Matthew Allen's life. In 1845, Allen considerately died of a heart attack, and then at last Alfred got nearly all his money back. It is a prolonged and chilling story.

In the disastrous alliance with Allen, Alfred was at first good-tempered. He flirted gently with Sophie Rawnsley, saw old friends, met his early American admirers, and stayed now with Lushington, now at 7 Charlotte Street. When he was confused over communications with Allen, he wrote, 'I being somewhat in a stew got up early next morning, hired (the only thing to be got) a fisherman's cart, drove over to Alford (three mortal hours going eight miles) put three letters in the post, talkt to the postman, agitated him a little being an old grayhaired man, then' (after a confusion about retrieving letters from the post), 'All being right, I invited the fisherman that drove me to a glass of gin, poor fellow got drunk, talkt wildly about God and the devil, fell down like a corpse.'

Alfred took Lushington with him to Tunbridge and introduced him to Cecilia, thus bringing about their marriage, which was a turning point in the composition of *In Memoriam*. He was also the first to notice that his friend Drummond Rawnsley was likely to marry Catherine Franklin, which he did on 15 September 1842. His other old flame Sophie Rawnsley (1818–89) married Edward Elmhirst, a country rector educated at Trinity, in October of 1840. Jane Elton married W. H. Brookfield in November 1841.

There were other London meetings, with Fitz in Charlotte Street, with Brookfield in the National Gallery, with boring old Crabb Robinson and Robert Browning ('author of unreadable books') at breakfast with Monckton Milnes. In November 1840 he went back to Trinity, and had supper in Merivale's rooms with Brookfield, Trench, Milnes, and Henry Lushington. Trinity was trying to get in Brookfield's old pupil Lord Lyttelton as High Steward of the University. I had imagined that poem LXXXVII of *In Memoriam* was written at this time, but the two big notebooks in which the whole work accumulated are divided by November of the year 1842, and LXXXVII is not to be found in the first, the Trinity manuscript, but only in the second, the Lincoln manuscript. It may of course have been drifting about in his head for a long time without being committed to paper, but it is about a long, lonely walk through Cambridge which may not have happened when he was with friends. Let it stand here for many visits:

> I past beside the reverend walls
>   In which of old I wore the gown;
>   I roved at random through the town,
> And saw the tumult of the halls;
>
> And heard once more in college fanes
>   The storm their high-built organs make,
>   And thunder-music, rolling, shake
> The prophet blazoned on the panes;
>
> And caught once more the distant shout,
>   The measured pulse of racing oars

> Among the willows; paced the shores
> And many a bridge, and all about
>
> The same gray flats again, and felt
>   The same, but not the same; and last
>   Up that long walk of limes I past
> To see the rooms in which he dwelt.
>
> (1–16)

The rowing like the organ-practice indicates the afternoon and the season is probably summer. The first sentence is sixteen lines long, and two more complete the poem, which is forty lines. Of course, 'Another name was on the door', and the Apostles, who allowed themselves no wine on debate days, have taken wing:

> Where once we held debate, a band
>   Of youthful friends, on mind and art,
>   And labour, and the changing mart,
> And all the framework of the land;
>
> (21–4)

He used to show his new poems to the two Lushingtons, Henry as well as Edmund, but I am not sure that Cecilia's wedding to Edmund in 1842 was really the unique crisis that altered the slow direction of *In Memoriam*. It may have been the publication of his new and revised *Poems*, and their huge success in 1842. There seems to have been an attempt to disperse the gloom of *In Memoriam*, to make it end with some sort of hope, to shape the monotone of grief that underlay nearly ten years of his life into something more various and more inviting. When that failed, as it did quite soon, he put aside *In Memoriam* for a few years in order to write *The Princess*, an idyllic, entertaining narrative with a modern intellectual message. Towards the end of February 1841, after he had been in Mablethorpe gazing at the waves for a month, he told a friend of Emerson in a letter to C. S. Wheeler that he was going to correct his old poems and add some new ones, because the American publishers Little and Brown wanted to print him. There is no doubt that Emerson, who was his first and best American supporter, was behind this American initiative. Little, the American publisher, first wrote to Alfred in 1838 intending a straight reprint. He would have got his material from copies belonging to Emerson and Longfellow, but Tennyson turned down the idea and the letter is lost. All the same, among all his early supporters Emerson's enthusiasm was the most effective.

He spent 1841 brooding over his poems and his manuscripts, and Fitz, who now estimated his smoking hours as twelve a day, found him 'with a little bit of dirty pipe in his mouth and a particularly dirty vellum book of manuscripts on the sofa'. He used to write close into the margins and tear off the edges for spills to relight his pipe. By October his friends were telling one another that he was in London 'busy preparing for the press'. But Spedding went at this time with Lord Ashburton's commission to the United States to fix the Canadian border, so how could Spedding review the new book? This seriously worried Alfred; there was a family move too, to Boxley near Lushington's house at Maidstone in the autumn of 1841. Since the Tennysons had a family propensity to 'come uninvited and to stay unwashed', and since Alfred was already a regular visitor to the Lushingtons and Cecilia about to be lady of the house, some fears were expressed in private whether Emily's fiancé Mr Jesse might not in his turn become a fixture. Henry Lushington with a brother and two sisters spent that winter in Italy. But Richard Jesse was genuinely a professional sailor who served at sea until he retired to Margate in 1870 as a captain. The Jesses were married in London in January 1842, Alfred gave away the bride and two of his sisters attended, so the shadows of hostility or alarm were probably only shadows. Certainly Mr Hallam continued to allow Emily £300 a year, and she called her son Arthur Henry Hallam Tennyson.

In March 1842, Fitz caught him and 'carried him off with violence to Moxon, to agree on terms'. On 14 May Moxon printed 800 copies of the two volumes at twelve shillings. That is not many, but he published in a slump, when John Murray was withdrawing books from the press and sending back the manuscripts to their authors, and when Robert Browning feared to publish at all.[27] Moxon had just published the four-volume 1839 Shelley, and been prosecuted for his pains, for printing *Queen Mab*. His surviving accounts begin only in 1843, when Tennyson earned £156 2s. 6d. for a second edition of 1000 copies, a little over half a crown (12½p) per copy, between 20 and 25 per cent of the published price. For 1500 copies in 1845, the publisher got one-third of the profit and Tennyson got £333 7s. 6d., which is two-thirds of the profit. Yet in 1830, only 600 copies had been printed and in 1832 only 450. This time he sold the first 500 in a month. He had of course become better known meanwhile, and must have seemed less of a whipper-snapper. He had even been asked to write the introduction to a reprinted classic, the works of Fletcher, for £60; he refused. The critical reception of the 1842 offering was adulatory. Fitz grumbled about the old reprinted poems about women, Browning was appalled at all the revisions, and Alfred was disgusted at the sight of his proofs, but Sterling as a reviewer was an improvement on the envenomed croak of Croker in the *Quarterly* (Lockhart arranged for Sterling deliberately and Croker was furious). Sterling's criticism had its fatuous side, as one might expect from so terrible a poet, but he was a friend, and largely complimentary. He felt the volumes 'have hardly as much substance as we would have hoped for after ten years' silence, but his fancy is exquisite'.

I deem the new poems to show the greatest improvement over ten years of any English poet since the juvenilia of Shakespeare, and 'Ulysses' and 'Morte d'Arthur' to be poems of substantial greatness, but these are now probably the received opinions. Tennyson's publication climbed gradually up the popularity charts over a few years, but he had found his audience, which was worldwide. He got $150 for his American 'copyright', and seems to be the first English author ever to be paid such a sum. Yet Sterling disliked 'Morte d'Arthur', and by a typical piece of intellectual's apriorism assured readers that 'the miraculous legend of Excalibur does not come very near to us, and as reproduced by any modern writer must be a mere ingenious exercise of fancy.' This rankled, and Alfred said later he had been ready to write his epic in twelve books, until he read it and put his project on the shelf. For some time all he could do at poetry was to compose his elegies. He never says, but it occurs to one now to say, that although the reviews got better as they went on, the best and most penetrating printed criticism of Tennyson down to 1850 was still that brilliant essay by Hallam that had caused the trouble. Only Spedding is nearly as good. The elderly donkey Leigh Hunt, who had been a fine, lively critic in his youth, attacked the framing devices of 'Godiva' and 'Morte d'Arthur' as having 'a certain air of literary dandyism or fine-gentlemanism' comparable to the fine-ladyism of Miss Seward, who claimed to translate an ode of Horace 'while her hair was curling'.[28] Yet the bits of framework to which Leigh Hunt objected do sharply convey the circumstances of Alfred's life and of how he composed, hanging over the bridge at Coventry, for example, among the grooms and porters. His epics would be the better for more such bits of framing, which perhaps derive rather from the most attractive pages of Plato than they do from the duller lines of Theocritus.

If he had written no other book after 1842, and published only what there then was of *In Memoriam*, it is arguable that his reputation would stand higher than it does today, at least with the small élite of poets and lovers of poetry who would have pursued him through libraries and antiquarian bookshops. But he was both a great and a popular poet, illimitably various, as abundant as Dickens and on occasion as perfectionist as any writer in England or in France. Indeed the only greater poet in Europe who was alive in the early 1840s was Baudelaire, who was two years younger than Horatio, the youngest Tennyson: in 1842 he had just been sent to sea to cure him of poetry, he had venereal disease, he was in love with a negress and taking a lot of hashish, but he was writing *Les Fleurs du Mal*. Monckton Milnes and Thackeray were likelier to come across him than Tennyson was, until Alfred was middle aged. *Les Fleurs du Mal* did not appear as a book until 1857, and the edition was then suppressed. It is partly a matter of temperament, and partly the affair of his brother Charles, that Alfred Tennyson remained a somewhat innocent man: there were Bohemian depths that he did not explore either in London or in Paris. Part of the reason is simply that his head was buzzing and booming and echoing with poems.

1842, if it is possible to judge such a thing, was the moment of Alfred Tennyson's supremacy as a poet, in spite of the trauma of publication. Wordsworth was over seventy and about to be Laureate, and Clare was between two asylums; there was no one else, no Baudelaire. Hardy was a child, Hopkins was not born, Matthew Arnold was twenty and Clough twenty-three but they were unknown. Lewis Carroll was a child of ten and Edward Lear had not yet published. Only Browning (1812–89) published poems in 1842 and later in the 1840s that we still read with relish and consider important landmarks of English poetry. In fact the monologues 'My Last Duchess' and 'The Bishop orders his Tomb' are cousins to Tennyson's smoother style of narrative, though 'A Grammarian's Funeral' (1855) is perhaps supreme among poems of this kind. It was not Tennyson's only kind, nor was it Browning's: they are both wonderful lyric poets. But one may sympathize with Fitz who called the 1842 volumes 'the Last of his Best'. He had been close to Alfred in the difficult years before they saw the light. He was there when

Alfred picked a daisy at Dulwich and claimed it indicated a supreme artificer who liked to ornament, there when he sat for a silhouette at Gravesend, there through all the growlings and mutterings and grumblings. Those days were their closest link, and Fitz valued friendship more perhaps than poetry, about which he had a strange semi-blindness.

Volume one of the 1842 publication could have been improved, just as Fitz remarked, by featuring fewer of those Lilians and Isobels and so on, but it had 'Mariana', the two owl songs, the 'Ode to Memory', 'The Dying Swan', 'The Lady of Shalott', 'The Miller's Daughter', 'Œnone', 'The Lotos-Eaters', 'A Dream of Fair Women', 'Mariana in the South', and 'The Death of the Old Year'. It is a volume that any poet of the 1830s could be proud to be remembered by. Yet by comparison, volume two is overwhelming. It begins with 'Morte d'Arthur' and its frame, it has all the 'English Idyls', 'St Simeon Stylites' which Browning greatly admired and Ricks has put in *The Oxford Book of Victorian Verse*, 'Ulysses', 'Locksley Hall', 'Will Waterproof', 'Sir Lancelot and Queen Guinevere', and 'Break, break, break' and a number of minor poems, and it ends with that extraordinary Blake-like ditty he called 'The Poet's Song':

> The rain had fallen, the Poet arose,
>   He passed by the town and out of the street,
> A light wind blew from the gates of the sun,
>   And waves of shadow went over the wheat,
> And he sat him down in a lonely place,
>   And chanted a melody loud and sweet,
> That made the wild-swan pause in her cloud,
>   And the lark drop down at his feet.
>
>   (1–8)

In summer of 1842 Alfred wrote to Fitz after a visit to Dulwich with him, 'I have not had a good day, a perfect white day, for years; I think I require delicious scenery to make a perfect day as well as friends.' At that time he had neither money nor credit to make any new expedition, though he longed to go to Blenheim with Fitz: 'The great oaks are fresher in my recollection than the Raffaelle.'

Edmund Lushington married Cecilia in October of the same year and in November came the change of notebook for *In Memoriam*.

Alfred had thought of CXXIII as a conclusion: it is weighty but also icy:

> There where the long street roars, hath been
> The stillness of the central sea.
>
> (3-4)

He had thought at first of using LVII, which echoes the poem of Catullus about his brother's death ending *Ave atque Vale*, which he remembered all his life, but that in its turn seemed too gloomy and final. On the leaf following LVII he wrote a copy of 'On a Mourner', composed in October 1833 but not published until 1865, because it is not in the *In Memoriam* metre. When he revised that for publication he depersonalized it and made it less painful, as by then he had done to much of *In Memoriam*. For all this sadness he now required a counterweight, and deliberately constructed one in the Epithalamion for Cecilia and Edmund Lushington which is the conclusion of his work, called by editors its 'Epilogue'.

> Nor have I felt so much of bliss
> Since first he told me that he loved
> A daughter of our house; nor proved
> Since that dark day a day like this.
>
> (5-8)

All the same, perhaps Emily's wedding still cast a certain shadow in his mind: 'Nor count me all to blame if I/Conjecture of a stiller guest'. It is a very long, intimate and moving poem. It moves at a majestic pace through every thought and circumstance of the day, magnetized by the moon and by Alfred's genuine religion of the 'one far-off divine event,/To which the whole creation moves'. It is so long that he cut from it one of his finest verses, rightly because it would delay the magnificent and sublime progression of the poem. He cannibalized these four lines in *The Princess*:[29]

> We pace the stubble bare of sheaves,
> We watch the brimming river steal
> And half the golden woodland reel
> Athwart the smoke of burning leaves.

He did not write that poem, or at least most of it, until two years or more after the wedding. The last words recall the poetry of Dante in *The Divine Comedy*, which I take to be conscious imitation, because Alfred told his friend Knowles that *In Memoriam* 'begins with a funeral and ends with a marriage – begins with death and ends with promise of a new life – a sort of divine comedy – cheerful at the close.'

CHAPTER SIX

In Memoriam

THE EIGHT years from 1842 to 1850, from the age of thirty-one to thirty-nine, were Tennyson's most intense of wandering, of London life, and above all of hard work that he had ever known. The second (1843), fourth (1846) and fifth (1848) editions of his 1842 *Poems* contain wonderful new poems and refinements of the text. In his early twenties he was already a great poet, but self-criticism and the perfecting of a style followed. Different elements in his poetry reached their climax or their perfection at different times, and love poetry or lyric poetry always appears to be born perfect, to be written out in the heat of youth, straight on to particularly clean paper, yet it was only in his thirties, in the songs to *The Princess* added as an afterthought, that Tennyson as a lyricist came to his maturity. As early as 'The Gardener's Daughter' he was a love poet on fire with sexuality and delicious smells, but now he offered more powerful distillations. Yet we know from Mrs Brookfield that he disliked his own 'heavy handling' compared to 'the exquisite lightness of Keats', he would have given all his verse for one melting lyric of Lovelace, he thought the songs of Burns had the perfect shape of berries and the radiant light of dewdrops. His humility was real, and so is his poetry. He valued poets and all great men extremely highly: when an old maiden lady at Tunbridge said Dr Johnson used to stir his lemonade with a finger 'often dirty', he growled, 'The dirt is in her own heart.'

Mrs Brookfield knew him early enough, and as Sir Charles Elton's daughter was brought up grandly enough, to observe to what extent he was a rough diamond. It is she who tells the story of him putting his feet on the table at the Reform Club; they got him to take them off only by saying, 'Be careful Alfred, they will take you for Longfellow.' With strangers he could be gruff or shy; once he would not speak to some fellow-guest at dinner until it was explained she was invited specially for him to be nice to her, but then he went beaming up to her and said, 'I could not find anything to say to you before dinner, but now that I have a bottle of port in me, I can talk as much as you like.' At one time he lived opposite the Brookfields in lodgings in Ebury Street and proposed to give a dinner party there.[1] He was found in the middle of the afternoon dismantling his bedroom to make a retiring room for the ladies since his sitting room would have to be the dining room. It will be seen in all these stories that his bohemianism was not without an aspiration to grandeur.

Alfred was now becoming seriously famous, and records of him begin to proliferate. The Lushingtons' Park House was only two miles or less from his family's house (now destroyed) in Kent. With them he saw Milnes, G. S. Venables, William Thomson (later Lord Kelvin), and apparently Edward Lear, who was a friend of Franklin Lushington even before settling in Corfu, where Franklin later became a judge, and who turned up in the Lakes during Tennyson's honeymoon. Lear's letters are peppered with news of Tennyson's latest poems. Alfred was often in London, where he loved the roar of traffic; he haunted St Paul's and the Abbey, and the bridges over the Thames. The noise grew in his lifetime, but it was already formidable. Yet London was small: one walked there from Hampstead through grassy fields. The last salmon was caught in the Thames when he was fifteen and a filthy smell called 'the great stink' pervaded all London in the early 1850s. He lodged at the last house in Norfolk Street, Strand, at the bottom on the left; 'the name is Edwards, which you will see projecting from the door on a brass plate.' His food was tavern food, a steak and some cheese or cold salt beef and new potatoes. 'The largeness of Alfred's proportions, both physical and poetical, were universally the theme of admiration. Maclise admired him excessively, and fell quite in love with him.'[2] His politics were taking shape: he felt that in Afghanistan (where no one in England understood the terrain or the people), we should act firmly and brook no opposition. In 1842, Henry Lushington was not just depressed, he was actually made ill by news of the catastrophe to the British army there, which firm action combined with infirm purpose had invited. But Alfred was extremely pleased with Lord Durham's constitutional solution for Canada. He was by now a determined imperialist, who in the end became an early proponent of a federal or commonwealth successor to the empire. In home affairs at this period he was a Christian socialist, more or less, but not of course a revolutionary (although he did correspond in courteous and complimentary terms with the one serious English Marxist, Ernest Jones). When they were lounging about on the grass eating 'wall-fruit' at Park House, and Chapman, a young Fellow of Jesus, made a joke about 'the disturbed areas', Alfred interjected at once, 'I can't joke about so grave a matter.'

The conditions of travel were not at all comfortable. Alfred would walk a great deal on the Pilgrims' Road, Chaucer's road to Canterbury, but when the university term began 'Early in October we drove up to London in an open phaeton on the old coach-road, which knew no railways at that time.' Cecilia, who married Edmund Lushington in October 1842, could not stand Glasgow, which was dark and grey, yet perhaps at its most beautiful in those days; it may be surprising to modern taste, but she preferred Edinburgh, and lived there, seeing her husband only at weekends or during vacations. In summer they dived southwards to Park House, and Edmund's early retirement easily explains itself.

The Maidstone Mechanics' Institute held the famous outing recorded in *The Princess* in July 1842. Aubrey de Vere, who knew Alfred probably through James Spedding, since he used to see him in Spedding's chambers and knew none of his brothers at that time, but did know some Apostles, tried to lure him to western Ireland, and in the end Alfred adventurously went there alone. We know of his first Irish exploration only from letters: first Alfred is at Eastbourne, in 1842 a tiny place like Mablethorpe, then in September suddenly at Killarney, having missed his friend in London; he had to clip short his tour because of business, presumably with Allen. 'I have been to your Ballybunion caves but could not get into the finest on account of the weather. I was obliged to give Dingle up for want of time . . . and I am afraid I must forgo Glengarry likewise.' Hallam Tennyson says it was then, inside one of the caves, that his father wrote these lines:

> So dark a forethought roll'd about his brain,
> As on a dull day in an Ocean cave
> The blind wave feeling round his long sea-hall
> In silence.

These gloomy verses are not his best, but they reflect what he so restlessly sought in his endless exploration of natural wonders, at home and abroad, and the kind of poetry that he rolled around in his brain, as if that also were a sea cave, where a blind wave felt around the walls in silence.[3]

He knew Rogers, Wordsworth was conscious of his existence, Thackeray had been at Cambridge with him, and so had Milnes, whose poems had ceased altogether to sell in the 1842 book slump. Rogers (1763–1855) was a wealthy and leather-faced old banker and a much better poet than people now suppose. Tennyson was conscious of his kindness but embarrassed by his assurance. In May 1833 Arthur Hallam had written that 'Rogers defends you publicly as the most promising genius of the time.' In March 1837 he gave Alfred his *Poems*, and Alfred offered his in 1842. But it was now that he became a literary figure among all the others, a grandee of the invisible parliament of unacknowledged legislators, more important in those days than they would be today. He was now a crony of Carlyle, a desired guest of Lady Ashburton's salon, an admired acquaintance of Dickens and many others. The company laughed when an obscure Irishman greeted him as a fellow-poet. When he popped in to see Moxon, that important man had just gone off to Switzerland with two sons of Wordsworth; soon he would be going there with Alfred.

Since both of the Carlyles were voluble on paper, we know all about the growth of that friendship at least. The young Thomas was described as having lustrous black hair, fine eyes and a crucified expression. His conversation was vehement, his anecdotes wide ranging, his opinions unexpected or unpredictable, even in his lectures and printed pamphlets. He had risen the hard way as a superior journalist and lecturer, and a provincial air combined with a European mastery in him to attract Alfred. He was Goethe's correspondent, and it may be important that he was very keen (as Alfred was) on greatness and on the great. Mrs Carlyle sent her sister Helen the autographs of Dickens, Bulwer, and Tennyson: 'A Yankee would give almost a dollar apiece for them.' She called Alfred the greatest genius of the three. 'Get his poems if you can, and read the "Ulysses", "Dora", "The Vision of Sin", and you will find we do not over-rate him. Besides, he is a very handsome man, and a noble-hearted one, with something of the gipsy in his appearance, which for me is perfectly charming.'

In 1845 she met him while her husband, with Moxon, was out to dinner, and he was lion enough to merit exclamation marks. 'He only comes to London rarely and for a few days so that I was overwhelmed with the sense of Carlyle's misfortune in having missed the man he likes best . . . Alfred is dreadfully embarrassed with women alone – for he entertains at one and the same moment a feeling of almost adoration for them and an ineffable contempt!' She produced pipes, tobacco, brandy and water, and 'a deluge of *tea* over and above'. The effect was miraculous: he smoked for three hours, 'talking like an angel – only exactly as if he were talking with a clever man'.[4] That was in January, and the friendship deepened in September at some amateur theatricals got up by Forster and Dickens, when, during an interval, 'Passing through a long dim passage, I came on a tall man leant to the wall, with his head touching the ceiling like a caryatid, to all appearances asleep, or resolutely *trying* it under most unfavourable circumstances.' She said, '*Alfred* Tennyson! *Well*! I did not know you were in town.' He said, 'I should like to know who you are. I *know* that I *know* you, but I cannot tell your name.' The next evening he called on her alone by cab, and stayed with her until eleven.[5]

Carlyle had known him for longer. In conversation they were like parodies of one another; indeed an American doctor Alfred had met in Amsterdam, where he was incognito, assumed at first that he must be Carlyle. Tennyson and Carlyle evidently knew one another in 1839. On 5 September 1840, Carlyle called him 'a fine, large-featured, dim-eyed, bronze-coloured, shaggy-headed man . . . dusty, smoky, free and easy; who swims outwardly and inwardly with great composure in an articulate element of tranquil chaos and tobacco smoke', and later, 'beautiful . . . a true human soul . . . I do not meet in these late decades such company over a pipe.' The first time Alfred ever called, Carlyle was out, so Alfred asked for a pipe and smoked it for an hour in the summerhouse in the garden, to his absent host's considerable amusement. After that a pipe was kept for him in a special nook in the old brick garden wall that runs along the back of the houses on that side of Cheyne Row, which was once Thomas More's garden wall, as Tennyson doubtless knew. The pipe of course was one of those little white clay pipes used by children for blowing bubbles. They used to cost a halfpenny at the village shop, and when they broke or got dirty you threw them away. Carlyle wrote a moving account to FitzGerald of one of his long and smoke-besmirched conversations with the poet:

One day we had Alfred Tennyson with us. He stayed with us till late – forgot his stick. We dismissed him with Macpherson's 'Farewell'. The tale of this tune is that the Macpherson played it on his fiddle on the way to the Gallows. Then, holding up the fiddle, he asked if in all that crowd the Macpherson had any clansman – holding up the fiddle that he might bequeath it to someone – any kinsman or any soul that wished him well. None answered nor durst answer. He crashed his fiddle under his foot and jumped off the cart. The tune is rough as hemp, strong as a lion. I never hear it but with something of emotion. Alfred's face grew darker and I saw his lip slightly quivering.

Moments like these were small oases in his life. What he felt inwardly was darkening gloom and horror. The years of his broken engagement and financial disaster brought him to something like a breakdown. Yet the flashes of light in an inner world which must remain unknown to us did exist, and are often all that is recorded. He chewed over, lived and relived his poems more than most writers with their works, but once they were published they had a life independent of him.

In September 1843 Alfred was on holiday with the Lushingtons at St Leonards, for a while after that at 7 Charlotte Street, and then in Cheltenham with his mother. The house near the Lushingtons had to be given up, and since Fred with Arthur and Septimus, who both seemed to be cured of their ills, had all gone to Italy, and Emily and Cecilia were married, it was a less numerous group that settled as starlings settle on the trees, in a rented house at 6 Belle Vue Place. They hated it, and left it in a year for 10 St James's Square. That was an ordinary town house, about ten years old, with three storeys and three bays, in a central and, in those days, pleasant position in a neat, fresh spa town. Cheltenham had first become fashionable in the 1780s, with 3000 inhabitants in 1801 and 20,000 in 1826. The Queen's Hotel dated from 1838, Montpelier Walk from about 1840, the Promenade, the Pittville pump room and the Montpelier Spa from the 1820s. The water is the best of Cotswold water, and I am sure that Mrs Tennyson, who lived at 10 St James's Square from 1843 to 1853,[6] was well suited. In 1843 Henry Holland's Assembly Rooms were still functioning in the next street. The Roman Catholic church of St Gregory that looks so Victorian Gothic and now uses the

Tennyson house for its clergy was not built until 1854, and St James's station (now demolished) was not built until 1847: Cheltenham was served by the Lansdown station (1840) which had a Doric porch with fluted columns, just as Mrs Tennyson's house did. The railway was a reason for choosing Cheltenham, and every building I have mentioned was neo-classic.

What Alfred thought of Cheltenham was best expressed in a letter not written at once, but a little later, to the Rawnsley family. It is one of the most warmly relaxed, charming and I can only say cosy letters he ever wrote. It is very long and he sent it in mid-October 1845, putting off a suggestion he should visit them because he was going to the Hallams at Wraxall (Bristol). He had a very bad cold.

> I am glad to hear of your quadrilling at Horncastle. There is something pleasant in the notion of your figuring in l'Eté,[7] with all your brood fluttering about you and I respect a man who can keep his heart green when the snows of Time begin to whiten his head, not that I mean to say your head is white but the silver hair may intrude *obiter* though as far as I recollect you had a very stout black crop when I saw you last. I should like to have been amongst you as in old times but *The days are awa' that we hae seen* and I begin to feel an old man myself . . . of all books the most insipid reading is second-rate verse . . . Here is a handsome town of 35,000 inhabitants – a Polka-parson-worshipping place, of which the Revd. Francis Close[8] is Pope – besides pumps and pump-rooms, chalybeates, quadrilles (as you have taken to them again) and one of the prettiest countries in Great Britain.[9]

But in November 1843 Alfred had gone to a hydropathic institution in the suburb of Prestbury, to submit himself to appalling rigours.[10] 'My dear Fitz,' he wrote:

> It is very kind of you to think of such a poor forlorn body as myself. The perpetual panic and horror of the last two years has steeped my nerves in poison: now I am left a beggar but I am or shall be shortly somewhat better off in nerves. I am in a Hydropathy Establishment near Cheltenham, the only one in England conducted on pure Priessnitzan principles. I have had four crisises, one larger than had been seen for two or three

years in Gräfenberg – indeed I believe the largest but one that has been seen. Much poison has come out of me, which no physic would have brought to light. Albert Priessnitz, the nephew of the great man, officiates at this establishment . . . he gives me hope of a cure in March. I have been here already upwards of two months . . . no reading by candlelight, no going near a fire, no tea, no coffee, perpetual wet sheet, and cold bath and alternation from hot to cold: however I have much faith in it.

For the future, being so poor, he thought of moving to Italy where he heard that Fred, Arthur and Septimus lived 'on eight shilling a day and are all very happy'.[11]

This sad and extraordinary letter follows Priessnitz's doctrines in every detail, including 'steeped my nerves in poison'. The idea was that severe cold water treatment with no alcohol or rich food provoked crises of vomiting or of the bowels in which noxious objects steeped in mucus and other nastiness were expelled from the body: one might have ten or a dozen crises before being pronounced cured. One of the German doctors himself vomited up a lump of oakum soaked in rancid linseed oil which tasted as he vomited it of a black sailor's soup he had eaten at sea three years before. The cure was for numerous diseases including catarrh, typhus and cholera, but not (scholars please note) for epilepsy. These and many other details of this odd episode in the history of medicine are to be found in a work by Dr Francke of Alexandersbad in Hesse, a more articulate pupil of Priessnitz, translated by Robert Baikie, a doctor from the Indian service, in 1849 as *Outlines of a new theory of disease applied to Hydropathy* (Baikie gives his own case in detail on pages 273–5). The first Englishman to have recourse to it was Thackeray, who took his wife to Germany to undergo a course at an early stage in her breakdown. It did her no good, but Thackeray may well have alerted Tennyson.

The true believers nourished a deep distrust of medicine, which they spent months vomiting, including any salve or cure put into a wound. Is Tennyson's distrust of laudanum in his brother's and his father's cases not at the bottom of his acceptance of this creed? Also he drank a lot of port, smoked so much shag and had by now swallowed so much London smog that his insides must have needed the equivalent of a chimney-sweep. He is known to have suffered at times from skin rashes, and hydropathy cured all kinds of 'inflam-mation'. He was past the age of thirty-three, which is the beginning of middle age.

As often happens with fashionable medical cults, the true church split up swiftly into groups, sub-groups and splinter-groups. In May 1847 Alfred tried Umberslade Hall, near Birmingham, and then perhaps in the autumn of 1847 and certainly the autumn of 1848, Malvern under Dr J. M. Gully, who had established a milder cure there in 1843.[12] Priessnitz himself lived until 1851; his treatment was first introduced into England, most probaby at Prestbury under his nephew, no earlier than 1840, with steam baths, hot and cold baths, sweatings and compresses, fomentations and poultices, wrapping in wet sheets and swathing in many blankets, and what the *Encyclopaedia Britannica* (eleventh edition) calls 'numerous modifications . . . according to circumstance and detail'.

All the same these adventures of Alfred's do not in themselves constitute evidence for a mental or emotional breakdown. But in February 1844 he writes, 'I am at present in such a deranged state of health that my medical man forbids the excitement of composition, forbids me to read, even to think.'[13] It appears that while he was in the hands of these philistine quacks he became so deranged as for the first time in his life to cease composing poetry. His next serious production was *The Princess* (1847). He had discussed that with his future wife in 1839, and by the summer of 1845 he had written down 200 lines of it, and read the manuscript fresh to Fitz and then to Lushington. In January 1846 he was ill, 'Which does not prevent him writing a new poem – he has finished the second book of it.' He had finished the whole work by 7 May 1847 and put the last touches to it in November. The interruption was not prolonged, therefore, although it was serious. Once his habit of composition was broken late in 1843 (from 1842–3 he was actively revising what he had published) it was not taken up until some time before June 1845, and taken up then only with a distinct break in continuity, and a determined entry into a new work. It will be remembered that Matthew Allen died in 1845 (his heart attack killed him in January). Alfred was genuinely sorry for him, but he went to London at once to see Fitz, who thought he looked better, but like a man who had been ill for years. It distressed him to observe that the bottle of port a day and the continuous smoking had revived too. The cure by hydropathy was to recur in 1847 and 1848, but never again with such violence or with such frightening results.[14] What had suffered worst was *In Memoriam*. Once Alfred had started to compose again in 1845, he would never cease while there was breath in his body. Both for better and for worse of course.

In June of 1844 he was still having doleful recourse to the sitzbath, whenever he was 'unwell with blood in the head' (a headache?). He was writing to his aunt, Elizabeth Russell, who had bad eyes but still sent him his £100 a year. His mother was in Scotland with Cecilia, but the Lushingtons would drop her in Birmingham in a few days, and there Charles would pick her up and bring her to Cheltenham.[15] His letter to his aunt was depressing, carrying news of the death of his mother's cousin, Mr Wheeldon of Market Street, and ending 'my head is so bad that I must conclude'. In July he got to Barmouth again on a Welsh tour. He felt lonely in these years: his letter to Fitz from Prestbury had been pathetically grateful to have his health enquired after, and he wrote to Venables he felt he had 'lived a whole age away from the world in the abominable purlieu of a worse watering-place . . . I trust you have got rid of that nasty hacking coughing you had in autumn; it is only by the strictest temperance I can keep myself tolerably comfortably.' But now suddenly in July 1844 (to Lushington), 'I have walked thrice up Snowdon which I found much easier to accomplish than walking upon level ground.'

When he arrived in London he called first at the Turkish bath in Covent Garden. In the first few days of August he caught a fever 'which, said the Doctor, would have been scarlet if he would have let it'. It was then that Alfred lived on eighteen lemons for three days, a feat he was proud of for the rest of his life, but which left him 'miserably imbecile about the knees'. He was admired by many acquaintances whose names are no longer worth recording: he dined with Thackeray who noted he was full of complaints; he showed a journalist how beautifully Virgil can sound, and got Moxon to pay his tailor.[16] One can see him gradually perking up, letter by letter until the winter. He is still Eeyorish in November, but more shamefacedly so. He offers Aunt Elizabeth his views on the squire-archy: 'But what *do* all English country gentleman talk of? dogs, horses, roads, crops, etc. it is better after all than affecting Art and Feeling: they would make a poor hand of that . . . I wish they would be a little kinder to the poor. I would honour them then and they might talk what they would.' She has asked about 'those poems' (clearly *In Memoriam*), but he feels they are imperfect and he may never print them in his lifetime. He carried them about with him, and in January FitzGerald noticed he had 'near a volume'. The difficulty he was in was partly this: they had become essentially a work about the long and slow passage of time, that could never be perfect, and had and could have no overriding plan. So he turned to *The Princess*.

That is a formidable piece of work: a verse narrative about a women's university (its early title) of 3185 lines plus songs added later, including a prologue of 238 lines and a conclusion of 118, each of them as long as an 'English Idyl'. It has seven books, which originally were intended to represent seven friends each taking up the narrative in turn and making it up as they go along. At one time I suspect it was an adventure of seven days, but if so that idea got lost. Its length is prodigious for a poem, but it is only like a brief novel of say a hundred pages with thirty lines to a page. In the tiny format of a Moxon poetry book, it is just 164 pages of twenty lines, like any of Tennyson's books. The setting is a timeless and romantic age of chivalry with modern features, which he took from Shakespeare's comedies, but the modern framework is the Lushingtons' house in July 1842. In his father's library at Somersby, the cause of women's education was represented by Hannah More (1798) and the *English Encyclopaedia* (1802); it had interested Arthur Hallam. By the 1840s it must have been widely discussed. In a way Tennyson's treatment was only good-tempered fantasy, and yet like Plato he was serious enough at a deeper level. F. D. Maurice's novel *Eustace Conway*, which he had glanced at when it was first published in 1834, may have sown a random seed in him. It is interesting that when Cambridge did first take notice of women, it was an Apostle, Henry Sidgwick who set up the first lectures for them in 1870 (Oxford followed Cambridge in 1873).

While Tennyson was hard at work on *The Princess*, a short, sharp explosion took place, which was caused by the innocent and in the end successful attempt of Henry Hallam to get him a pension from Sir Robert Peel. It is apparent from the date of Hallam's first surviving letter to Tennyson[17] on the subject in February 1845, which enclosed Peel's reply and referred to a letter of Mr Howitt to Lady Peel (sent apparently in December or January, before Allen's death and before the insurance of his life for Alfred's benefit was widely known) that the reason for asking for a pension must have been the news of Alfred's poverty and bad health, combined with the claim he had to some recognition by the state after the success of his 1842 *Poems*. Howitt was a Quaker, a writer and editor, and the early friend of Mrs Gaskell. He was much revered in his suburban village, where Alfred later visited him, as well as writing a charming letter to his younger brother, a poet, in February 1845.[18] Mr Hallam felt Howitt's approach to Lady Peel to be 'too much of a begging letter, beginning with "Honoured Lady" and recommending you, though professedly a stranger, for kind consideration.' I take it they were after a Civil List pension, but the fund was exhausted at the moment. In September Hallam sent Alfred a new letter from Peel: 'nothing can be more flattering or delicate'.[19] Alfred answered Sir Robert on 29 September accepting a pension of £200 a year: 'Believe me, though I am not one who say much, deeply sensible of your kindness, and not ungrateful for that delicacy which doubles an obligation in conferring it.'[20] It was clever of Hallam, sweet of Howitt, and generous of Peel. It was generous of the now old and prickly poet Rogers,[21] too, whose word had carried weight, and it appears Milnes had also been kind on his behalf as usual. The other candidate (who failed) was Sheridan Knowles, who as a writer hardly existed, but was old and needy; he later put in to be custodian of Shakespeare's house at Stratford, since he had a theatrical past. A little later Fitz's provincial friend Bernard Barton, a minor poet, got £100 a year, and Wordsworth was already getting £300 a year, so that Peel's decision, taken on a simple reading of 'Ulysses', seems perfectly just. Tennyson was pleased that he was thought twice as good as Barton.

Mr Hallam was sure Peel's act of patronage would be popular. 'It is not the habit of anyone to find fault with the disposal of public money in reward of literary merit . . . You are besides a great favourite with the young ladies.' Sir Robert's cousin Edmund, a poet of a Christian-patriotic tendency of Bonchurch on the southern shore of the Isle of Wight, wrote to his cousin how pleased everyone was, how Tennyson was grateful, how Wordsworth approved. Alas, not everybody approved. Alfred had been uneasy, but as he said in a letter to T. H. Rawnsley, he did not worry about the spleen of 'small literary men whose letters perhaps I have never answered' or about 'certain old crones in or about Horncastle', only about the *Weekly Dispatch* and a Mr Wakley (the *Dispatch* was a venomous radical denouncing paper, Mr Wakley was an MP who was enraged against the new copyright act of 1838[22]). The bomb exploded closer to home.

It was set off by Edward Bulwer (Bulwer-Lytton since the death of his Lytton mother in 1843, which had brought him estates), the bosom friend of Charles Tennyson d'Eyncourt and a frequent guest at Bayons, where he had apparently been envenomed by his host against Alfred, whom in the past he had wished to know. He lived just a little longer than his host at Bayons, and therefore reaped rewards which poor, sad Charles never attained. By 1857 Charles was a spent force and in 1863 he was dead, but Lytton, a person equally without talent and even more insufferable, re-entered politics and became a minister under Lord Derby in 1858–9, and a peer in 1866. In 1845–6 he was not eminent, not a peer, and nothing in politics: he was ridiculous, even preposterous, and malevolent.

When the news broke, he was staying at Bayons in order to write his 'New Timon'. That was not a happy household: Bulwer-Lytton had been married in 1827 and separated in 1834, legally so in 1836. Now Julia, the Tennyson d'Eyncourt daughter Fred had loved, was in love with him, and he of course rejected her: apart from other considerations, he was still legally married. She promptly discovered religion as a remedy for love; he made her promise not to become a Catholic, but she broke that promise. Her father Charles was plunged into extravagant distress: she must leave Bayons and be cast off for ever; she might stay and he would let her live in his castle as a nun, it would be a use for the domestic chapel; she must retire to France, to Ayncourt where he had bought a villa he called his château, and the town council had let him aggrandize it by enclosing part of the Place des Ormes. In the end she became a Catholic nun in Coventry, where she died.

'The New Timon' was a long, satiric poem in couplets, which has verbal malignancy without intellectual weight or serious satiric edge, but it stung Alfred, who wandered into the book club at Cheltenham and found a paper that reprinted part two of 'The New Timon', folded open so that what met the eye was, 'See how Sir Edward tickles up poetasters and their patrons.'

> Not mine, not mine (O Muse forbid!) the boon
> Of borrowed notes, the mock-bird's modish tune,
> The jingling medley of purloin'd conceits

(left) 1. George Tennyson, the poet's grandfather: an unscrupulous, scheming, raging man, here idealized as far as possible.

(below left) 2. George Clayton Tennyson, the poet's father: a clergyman who felt wronged.

(below right) 3. Charles Tennyson d'Eyncourt, the poet's political uncle. (By John Harrison)

(above) 4. Somersby rectory, about 1889.

(below left) 5. Elizabeth Tennyson, née Fytche, the poet's mother.

(below right) 6. Alfred's nanny, in old age and blind.

7. William Whewell, Alfred's tutor at
Trinity College, Cambridge.
(By J. Rylands)

8. Trinity College Gate.

(top) 9. Charles, Alfred's closest brother and fellow poet. (By I. Mayall)

(left) 10. Alfred idealized by Samuel Lawrence.

(right) 11. Alfred's brother Fred. (By Julia Margaret Cameron)

(right) 12. Arthur Hallam at
Cambridge, by Spedding.

(below) 13. Alfred at Mirehouse,
by his friend James Spedding.

14. James Spedding and F. D. Maurice: tall sweet scholar and short clerical firebrand.
(By O. J. Rejlander)

15. Alfred and Arthur Hallam between Bordeaux and Dublin; 1830.

(left) 16. W. H. Brookfield, an unhappy clergyman. (By Julia Margaret Cameron)

(right) 17. Edward FitzGerald, the most eccentric friend of all. (By Lady Carnac)

18. Edmund Lushington, a scholar who left only a Greek verse translation of Tennyson's *Œnone*. (By Cruttenden)

19. Emily seen with passion and accuracy by G. F. Watts.

20. Farringford as Lear knew it. (15 October 1864).

21. Farringford at its largest.

22. Alfred with Hallam and Lionel. (By O. J. Rejlander)

23. (above left) Tennyson as laureate.

24. (above right) W. E. Gladstone, Arthur Hallam's schoolfriend, who in later life liked reading Tennyson's 'Guinevere' to reformed ladies of the night. (By Thomas Woolner, Ashmolean Museum, Oxford)

25. Benjamin Jowett, the adviser, as bright as a button. (By H. Furniss)

26. The shepherd at Farringford, around 1880.

27. Alfred and Emily with Hallam and Lionel on the brink of school, walking in the garden at Farringford. (By O. J. Rejlander)

(top) 28. The Isle of Wight as it once
was, seen by Richard Doyle from a
Farringford window.

(above) 29. Alfred's sketch for
Aldworth, 1867.

(right) 30. Study window at Aldworth,
looking south and west.

31. Alfred, Emily and Hallam Tennyson: the three adored each other almost mystically.
(1892, the Cameron Studio)

Out-babying Wordsworth, and out-glittering Keates, [*sic*]
Where all the ears of patchwork-pastoral chime
To drowsy ears in Tennysonian rhyme! . . .
Let School-Miss Alfred vent her chaste delight
On 'darling little rooms so warm and bright!'
Chaunt, 'I'm aweary,' in infectious strain,
And catch her 'blue fly singing i' the pane' . . .
Tho' Peel with pudding plump the puling Muse . . .
And pensions Tennyson, while starves a Knowles

In a footnote Lytton added the sneer that Tennyson came from a wealthy family and was in the prime of life and without wife or children, though he was now 'quartered on the public purse'. It is scarcely surprising that Alfred was angry. Most of the offensive verse harked back to the anonymous review it is obvious that its author had written of the 1832 collection. As criticism it was bizarrely silly,[23] merely rehearsing a thirteen-year-old fit of malice, and proposing

> Rather be thou, my poor Pierian maid
> Decent at last, in Hayley's weeds array'd

Why Hayley, one may ask: but then, why Knowles, why Wordsworth and why any of it? Tennyson went to John Forster[24] to ask whether he was right in supposing these anonymous insults were by Bulwer-Lytton, and was shown a letter making it plain that they were without confessing to them. Tennyson wrote his reply at once and showed it to Forster, who gleefully got it published in *Punch*, where Tennyson already had a number of friends. It appeared on the last day of February 1846, signed Alcibiades, which is a reference to Shakepeare's *Timon of Athens*. Alfred repented swiftly, so the piece was not reprinted in his lifetime, and in the very next issue of *Punch* appeared his 'Literary Squabbles', expressing a growling sort of displeasure at himself for having been provoked.[25] The reproof was splendid, and the insults quite as bad as Bulwer-Lytton's: 'The padded man – that wears the stays – /Who killed the girls and thrilled the boys . . . /And shook a mane en papillotes', (which means curling-papers) has 'The old mark of rouge upon your cheek . . . You bandbox'. The second part of this brilliant attack was not printed at the time, but it ends with an echo of *In Memoriam*, about fame:

> This London once was middle sea,
>   Those hills were plains within the past,
> They will be plains again – and we,
>   Poor devils, babble, we shall last.

He knew all about Lady Blessington's salon, where Bulwer-Lytton had figured when Alfred was at Cambridge, and he was still joking about Bulwer-Lytton's three-inch cork heels and the pink chamois-leather tips of his shoes in 1865,[26] so it would appear that he got prolonged pleasure out of the entire affair; he certainly never wrote better in this vein. He accomplished what is often said but seldom really happens: he made Bulwer-Lytton, who would otherwise be a very dusty figure indeed, live for ever in his poem. That is what comes of going about with a dozen French poodles with their hair cut to match your own, and of dyeing your hair and beard bright red. It was brave of the Lytton family not to change their name. In about a year Bulwer-Lytton confessed himself beaten, when Forster advised him not to sign his new great work 'King Arthur' 'by the author of "The New Timon"'. He cut the offending passage from reprints of his verse, though he still thought Alfred's poetry full of vulgarities and conceits, written for schoolgirls and Oxford dons. Charles Tennyson d'Eyncourt loved him more and more.

In April 1846 Alfred stood godfather to the sixth child of Charles Dickens, Alfred d'Orsay Tennyson Dickens, and in May he and Dickens had dinner together. Dickens proposed that Alfred should come to Switzerland with him, for company while he was writing *Dombey and Son*. It is an intriguing thought what influence they might have had on one another: more 'English Idyls' and urban verse from Tennyson perhaps, and a grander, Darwinian aspect to 'What are the wild waves saying?' (the death scene in *Dombey*). What Tennyson said at the time, laughing to Venables about it, and what was reported word for word to Elizabeth Barrett by her brother, was, 'If I went, I would be entreating him to dismiss his sentimentality, and so we should quarrel and part, and never see one other any more. It was better to decline – and I have declined.' Carlyle said at the time that he looked 'haggard, dire and languid', but he drew his pension, he went to Richmond with Fitz, and apparently he went to the Derby with young Hallam.

He dined with Macready and the Moxons, where he saw Browning. Browning in his turn reported to Elizabeth Barrett, 'Moxon's care of him is the charmingest thing imaginable, and he seems to need it all – being in truth but a LONG, hazy kind of a man, at least just after dinner.' He wrote a piece about Somersby to be printed in the third person for William Howitt's *Homes and Haunts of the most eminent British poets* (1846), which is how we know Somersby had about a hundred villagers. 'My father . . . a man of very various talents, something of a poet, a painter, an architect, a mathematician . . . My life contains no facts worth mentioning. My native village is secluded in a pretty, pastoral district of softly sloping hills and large ash trees.' Howitt touched up this paragraph to make him seem the original scholar gipsy, 'in a country inn, with a foot on each hob of the fireplace, a volume of Greek in one hand, his meerschaum in the other', or at 'Hastings, Eastbourne, Cheltenham, the Isle of Wight, and the like places'.[27] That same summer of 1846 we hear of him brooding in the New Forest, posting some self-pitying, lonely verses to a banker's wife, and then in the Isle of Wight, where he met the poet Peel and a friend of his at Bonchurch.[28] The three of them

> Threaded the Needles on a day in June;
> Upon the ocean hung a lucid mist,
> And round the cliffs the seabird's plaintive tune
> Resounded

The other two finished the sonnet.[29] According to Fitz, for the past two months Alfred had been 'trying to spread his wings to Italy or Switzerland', and in August he went with Moxon. For the first time we have his travel journal. At Ramsgate he slept at a fishmonger's, and got up at four to travel by the *Princess Maude*, no less. He had 'the worst breakfast I ever had in my life,' and noted 'inhuman conduct and supererogatory fury of the porters.' Next day 'tea not good . . . musée not good.' He cheered up at Cologne, where he woke to the 'clash and clang of steamboat departure,' but then 'three Hyde Park drawling snobs stinking of perfumed soap . . . horrid row . . . stupid hotel . . . sad recollections.' What he liked best was a Swiss girl near Lucerne to whom he quoted Goethe, and who replied by spouting William Tell, 'sorry to lose her,' and at Lucerne 'jolly old Radical who abused Dr Arnold.' The journal tails off, but as it does so his mind is otherwise occupied, because it was at Lauterbrunnen[30] that he wrote most of the lyric, based on a Hellenistic epigram, not by Theocritus,[31] which is the climax of *The Princess*, and which stands at the summit of Tennyson's impersonal lyric poetry: 'Come down, O maid'.

In that poem, more than in any other, he persuaded the English language to perform perfectly what was not and is not in its nature to perform; he did the language violence as Shakespeare had done, treating English as if it were a perfectly musical instrument. That was not his only tune, any more than it was Shakespeare's, but of all his classic themes magically handled, this one was surely his masterpiece. It is a love poem, a poem to love, calling it down from mountains into the valleys; the murmuring Virgilian noises at the end of it are as if the words melted. All the same, love does not melt. He may of course have calculated exactly where he was going to use it.

On 23 August Moxon and Tennyson went by the lake paddle steamer from Geneva to call on Dickens at Lausanne at the upper end of Lake Leman, but in such a mist they might as well have been at Battersea. They arrived after dinner, a little after seven, to find Dickens walking up and down the small colonnade in his garden, racking his brains over *Dombey*. 'Two travel-stained-looking men approached, of whom one, in a very limp and melancholy straw hat, ducked perpetually to me as he came up the walk.' This was Moxon, whom Dickens seems to have disliked. Alfred produced a terribly ragged and tattered £5 note. 'Oh Lor you know,' said Moxon, 'now really – like Goldsmith you know! – or any of these great men.' Dickens says Moxon's manner of speech had reminded Leigh Hunt of Shakespeare's Cloten. They were royally entertained with Liebfraumilch, better than it is today no doubt, and Bath Olivers, a luxury anywhere outside England, and dismissed in the end with handfuls of cigars. Alfred strolled in through the window from the lawn to find Dickens's daughter Mamie at the piano singing his 'May Queen', which he treated as the most ordinary thing in the world.[32] Dickens was a little shocked that Alfred and Moxon seemed unimpressed by the Mer de Glace: but then Dickens compensated for his short-sightedness by concentrating on distant views, and he loved the fuss of expeditions; Alfred had equally bad sight.[33] Still, the journey forged a real link with Moxon, whom Alfred could now reprimand as 'forgetful of our joint sweats up the Swiss hills and of our mutual mule'.

Mr Howitt introduced him to Bailey's *Festus* in an early edition, and he got hold of it through Moxon. I have read that without dislike, but I am not sure what the attraction was for Tennyson, unless it was simply Bailey's belief in immortality and disbelief in eternal punishment: such a belief was extremely attractive to Alfred, and is the key to a number of his relationships. He took up the German poet and liberal Freiligrath, whom the Howitts liked and whom he met with them. The crisis of 1848 was swiftly approaching and German liberals were in exile everywhere (the great scholar Mommsen lost his chair at Berlin in 1848, and retired to lay the foundations of Roman epigraphy in Switzerland, climbing cliffs on ladders whenever necessary; the poet Freiligrath was found a job in a bank by Monckton Milnes). He is nice about W. R. Dempster, a composer of songs, politely regrets that he missed the thirteen singing children (American) of the Hutchinson family, says Bailey's sublimity is Michael-Angelic, and finally announce himself from 6 Michael's Grove, Brompton, where he was staying with Tom Taylor the lawyer until a certain Mrs Wigan turned up and needed the room.

At the same time, he was all over London. He read the books of strangers, and gave money at the drop of a hat to anyone who asked for it. He saw old friends. In December he dined at Moxon's with Brookfield; Rogers had sent them a leveret and they would have 'a pair of soles and no form'. Whewell invited him to a grand dinner at Trinity for the third centenary of the foundation, and he went. He made time to visit the Howitts in their nest. He sat up until three in the morning and 'hailed all attempts at heralding a grand, more liberal state of public opinion, and consequently sweeter, more noble modes of living.'[34] Alfred's preoccupation with the Howitts and their friends became a kind of love affair for a time. Or is it just that they kept his letters to them and their protegés more carefully than other people? It is easier to feel than to delineate his fellow-feeling with this northern, liberal, Quaker, provincial family. They lived in a substantial four-storey eighteenth-century house at Clapton, with long lawns above the Lea marshes and Epping Forest. Its front was hidden behind a row of huge elm trees like Victorian whiskers (speaking of which, Alfred now became frantic about losing his hair, because Moxon had said nonchalantly he would go bald: for a time he went

regularly to a lady to have it expensively treated). The Howitts were
the intellectual cream of nonconformity, though Mrs Howitt went
as a widow to live in Rome, and died a Catholic. Meanwhile,
Freiligrath translated Tennyson into German and W. R. Dempster
set 'The May Queen' to music (again).

At the beginning of 1847 Alfred told the Rawnsleys his sister
Mary was in Paris, and Matilda and Horatio were in Kent; one
should perhaps note that they have really dropped out of his life. The
large fraternity and sorority of his relations trooped here and there,
wherever they had any claim on a large house: their mother's,
Cecilia's, Charles's at Caistor, Alfred's in the Isle of Wight quite
soon, and Fred's in Italy as long as that lasted. But Alfred was
intensely busy with his *Princess* and with seeing his own friends. He
was not at all best pleased to be asked for an autograph, even by one
of the Rawnsleys. He wrote awkwardly and perhaps falsely to Mrs
Barton about a present of violets from Somersby. He was much
nicer, though a little self-pitying, to old T. H. Rawnsley, and he got
to Park House to say goodbye to Henry Lushington, who had landed
the £1500-a-year job of Secretary to the Maltese Government, 'which
he is clever enough to occupy with credit to himself, but being a
man of feeble stamina he is afraid of the climate, and altogether
down in the mouth about it, so I came to see the last of him before
he went, and do my best to set him up.' Poor Henry Lushington:
that job did kill him in the end. Alfred was not well either: it appears
that London bachelor life was not good for him. He tried the water
cure in a milder form at Umberslade Hall as soon as he had finished
The Princess, about the middle of May 1847.

It is hardly surprising if he was worn out and in low spirits,
because *The Princess* was his first full-scale work. It was both a fantastic
fiction and a serious poem. Its impact is muted by the plot, and its
seriousness does not get beyond that of conception, it does not ramify;
none the less, this is a work of astonishing originality. Its framing
device is so brilliantly well executed as to be the most memorable
thing about it, making the Mechanics' Institute available to this day as
history. So is the house with its busts and flowers and its abbey stones
and ammonites in the hall, its snowshoes and claymores and

> Betwixt the monstrous horns of elk and deer,
> His own forefathers' arms and armour hung.

(23–4)

Very few such houses have survived, and those that have are in the tidy hands of the National Trust, but forty years or so back his description was exactly true to life. The hero reads in a chronicle of a heroic woman who defended her house under arms, and so by way of a feminist sister and a maiden aunt the theme alters by dream-like transmutation to the story of the women's university. The feast of the Mechanics is scarcely fifty lines, a little too long to quote, but in its way perfect. Most of Tennyson's attention goes to the talk at a picnic in the abbey ruins, which will introduce his main story. When that comes it is simple, clear, uncluttered narrative: in the first book, three courtly friends arrive at the women's stronghold, which is Athos reversed, with no male creature admitted. In the second book they are discovered; in the third taken out on a picnic with adventures, but caught; in the fourth imprisoned, and in the fifth they fight a duel with a relieving army of the girls' kinsmen. The sixth book is transformation of characters, and in the seventh love wins. The whole key was supposed to be a baby which draws the women out of their defences, but one does not notice that. The passages added in the fourth edition (1851) about seizures and illusions merely confuse matters.

Lyric poems are embedded in the blank verse text, and the six new songs Tennyson added in the third edition (1850) between the books, which are like chapters, scarcely alter the story though they offer keys to mood. The references to trance, and to the weirdness of the hero, in no way alter what happens: they are just an interesting experiment. The women's college cannot go on for ever of course, in the way he plans it, because it would have to be a convent and therefore without progeny. After the duel it became a hospital, as so many of those great houses did in 1914 (VII,2). But having invented a college he must give it a syllabus, and that is fascinating. Laplace plays a part with his pre-Darwinian evolutionary theory, just as he does in *In Memoriam*.[35] There is more science than Alfred learnt in Cambridge. At first he seems to have planned a more developed society altogether, but he saw that would not fit his poem:

> We crost into a land where mile-high towers
> Pufft out a night of smoke that drowsed the sun;
> Huge pistons rose and fell, and everywhere
> We heard the clank of chains, the creak of cranes,
> Ringing of blocks and throb of hammers mixt

With water split and spilt on groaning wheels[36]

(I, 111–12 *var.*)

Those lines were rejected. The few occasional lines that catch the eye more than a striking phrase in a prose writer would do are closer to that innocent kind of realism which lies at the heart of his poetry:

As bottom agates seen to wave and float
In crystal currents of clear morning seas.

(II, 306–7)

The lectures were wonderful, and his description oddly foretells what in later days is familiar to us.

With scraps of thundrous Epic lilted out
By violet-hooded Doctors . . .
            the state,
The total chronicles of man, the mind,
The morals, something of the frame, the rock,
The star, the bird, the fish, the shell, the flower,
Electric, chemic laws

(II, 353–62)

He makes his ideal lecturer not a don but a humanist, a savant; today he would be lecturing in anthropology in the Collège de France. Some of the story is just brushed by the holiday in Switzerland; Love is 'like an Alpine harebell hung with tears'.(VII, 100) Or else it is touched by the 1842 holiday when he went to Killarney and saw the splendour fall from the castle walls. There are even echoes of his earlier poetry one in particular (VII, 135) of the 'Ida – I die' word-play in 'Œnone' ('Stoop down and seem to kiss me ere I die.'). For what it is worth, he faces up to the real difficulties in his story (how to teach anatomy to pure Victorian girls (III, 290f.) for example) rather as a conscientious thriller-writer would do. But the point of the whole long narrative is the charge of poetry it carries rather than generates; the songs are exquisite and recondite in their music, he even writes a *ghazal*, a form of Persian verse I had thought no Westerner had imitated until this generation.

His book was a success and he was pleased: it annihilated any long poem by Keats or Shelley, even by Byron (*Juan* is an exception) and by any writer then living except Wordsworth. And yet was it not wrong-headed? I cannot help wishing he had written more of a Platonic dialogue, using his lyrics as Plato used myth. I feel that the romantic, timeless, Gothic garden bodes ill for the future, and that in the very poem where he proves himself the poet of the Mechanics' Institute and of the Industrial Revolution, he takes another path. Still, there are some temptations to which he did not succumb. He did attempt an Inauguration Ode for the Prince Consort as Chancellor of Cambridge: he devoted the fourth day of March to considering it, but on the fifth he wrote to Whewell refusing. Wordsworth had begun the ode and his nephew finished it. Alfred Tennyson was not moved by disloyalty or any sense of his own dignity as a poet, 'but the work does not seem to prosper in my hands'.[37]

Yet *The Princess* had not been a blind feeling out of the way ahead, as the lyric collections had been; it was a deliberately large poem, in one way like FitzGerald's *Euphranor* (begun in 1846, published 1857) and a dialogue on beauty by the young Hopkins (later still) or even Digby's 'Godefridus', the first part of *Broad Stone of Honour*, about restoring chivalrous values. Long poems were thudding from the presses; Clough's *Bothie* in 1848 has some of the freshness and reality of *The Princess*, *Aurora Leigh* was to come in all its deadly earnestness in 1857, and Patmore's *Angel in the House* in 1859. Shannon on Tennyson's critics maintains that a big poem was demanded of Alfred, so that *The Princess* (Alfred having lost confidence in the Arthurian cycle over Sterling's review) was a response to criticism. That may be so.

He corrected his proofs at his hydropathic institution, fretting in his usual way. At one stage his proofs were lent to Forster and proved hard to get back. Mary Russell Mitford noted he was 'a great torment to Mr Moxon, keeping proofs a fortnight to alter, and then sending for revises'. The first edition was published on Christmas Day 1847, and the second, dedicated to Henry Lushington, early in 1848. The third followed in 1850, the fourth in 1851, and the fifth, in which he expanded the Prologue, in 1853. The five editions close together all sold very well: the original 1500 copies brought the poet over £100, as did the second and third, and the fourth won him nearly £150, being 2000 copies. The fifth was the first that took a year or more to sell out: he made his £150 in two years, and thereafter

£75 a year for ages. Still, Alfred said he hated *The Princess* and so did
Fitz. Years later he spoke of it sadly as truly original but only a
medley (the word is part of his title).

In July 1847 he wandered about Warwickshire and intended to
go to Italy. He wrote a charming letter from Cheltenham to Mrs
Burton agreeing to be a godfather, 'and so I am sure will Charles: he
is not here but in town.' Charles stayed there at least until December,
with Septimus. They were all a burden to one another. Alfred hoped
the little boy was destined to 'a far happier life than mine has been'.
He introduced Frank Lushington to Macready, he gave dinner to
Leigh Hunt with Forster, James White and others, including Thackeray; he sidestepped a Dickens child's birthday party and took refuge
in November at Mablethorpe, still putting the last touches to his
poem. He tried to see White again, calling him 'the dramatist'. The
earliest dinner had been to pay a social debt to him, but the second
arrangement was perfectly voluntary. By December he had rooms at
48 Ebury Street. He could get no companion to go with him to Italy,
and it did not occur to him to travel alone. So he stayed in London,
dining out until it made him sick. 'A pint of pale ale and a chop are
things yearned after, not achievable except by way of lunch.'[38] In
January 1848 he sold some duplicate books to Charles and gave him
a *Princess* a few days later.[39] Harry Hallam gave him a thirty-shilling
golden pen.

The best news was the approach of Aubrey de Vere, who tried
to catch him at Lord Monteagle's; then, when he wanted to go to
Bude to see the north Devon waves, lured him to Ireland instead,
where he arrived in March 1848, to see Atlantic waves. De Vere
wrote:

> His face . . . full of power, passion and intellect – so strong,
> dark and impressive. I find I am growing very much attached
> to him. He is as simple as a child, and not less interesting for his
> infirmities. He is all in favour of marriage, and indeed will not
> be right until he has someone to love him exclusively . . . He is
> to breakfast alone, and sit alone half the day, musing and
> writing poetry.[40]

This Irish expedition was very fully recorded by Aubrey de Vere,
and the record of it is easily available in the memoir of Tennyson by
his son Hallam,[41] but there are certain highlights that it would be

wrong to omit. Never were ruins and waterfalls so shimmering, never was a moon so huge. Alfred read his friends gloomy poems, saying reproachfully after Crabbe's 'Sorrowful Tale', 'I did not see that any of you are weeping.' Dowagers made him dance with their daughters, which he enjoyed, and he played the prince in a charade of the Sleeping Beauty. He liked the girls at any age; he would growl but if they laughed he would adore them. The country was (in 1848) suffering upheavals, as all Europe was, but Alfred said, 'Don't let them land on England's coast or we will shatter them to pieces,' and he recited Gaunt's dying speech from *King John*. He saw seas and terrific sunsets, fuchsias and tamarisks and 600-foot cliffs. A peasant dogged his steps in the extreme west and crept up to ask him, 'Be you from France?' After dinner, Alfred read aloud 'sundry truculent passages in Daniel O'Connell's *History of Ireland*'. He saw promontories fringed with arbutus, and yew forests that had wild deer in them.

In May he met his benefactor Emerson, in Coventry Patmore's house in London.[42] Once again there is a careful record. Tennyson spoke of Carlyle: 'he said, If Carlyle thinks the Christian religion has lost all vitality, he is wholly mistaken. Tennyson and all Carlyle's friends feel the caprice and incongruity of his opinions. He talked of London as a place to take the nonsense out of a man.' He had told Aubrey de Vere that he thought Carlyle had said all he had to say. It was a condition of his Irish visit that he was not to hear anything about Irish distress, and that he must be allowed to smoke indoors, and much of his London conversation is somehow flavoured with his tobacco smoke. Mrs Moxon even let him smoke in her drawing room, provided she was let take part in the conversation. His social round was wildly diverse: his dinner engagements from 3 May read like this: 'Mrs Daniells, Mrs Boyle, Patmore, Spring Rice, Hallam, Brookfield, Titmarsh's soirée (didn't go), Rev. J. Brackenbury, Lady Duff Gordon, Burnham Beeches, Cooke, Helps, Spring Rice, Reece, Proctor, Rashdall.' Burnham Beeches is a place, Cooke is an actor, Titmarsh may be the Royal Literary Fund, and Rashdall was Vicar of Malvern Priory (1847–56), with whom Alfred stayed for the Malvern water cure that autumn; Mrs Boyle was married to the fifth son of Lord Cork, a country vicar, and a cousin once removed of Audrey Boyle, who was to marry Alfred's son Hallam.

In May and June 1848 he toured Cornwall. Early on, he fell over in the dark, looking for the sea at the Falcon Hotel, Bude, and had to be nursed, which meant he got to know a poorer class of people than usual. He was handed on between small-scale grocers and shopkeepers. They all knew about him and had heard his poems. Indeed a Mr Reece, a Cheltenham lawyer, thought him the greatest and most influential of all poets ('Don't talk such damned nonsense,' said Alfred). He called on R. S. Hawker the poet and vicar at Morwenstow, and noted 'coldest manner of Vicar till I told my name, then all heartiness'. He explored Tintagel,[43] and somewhere on the way to Camelford 'went into a cavern all polished by the waves like dark marble with veins of pink and white'. It is like a bit of *The Princess*, is it not? And one cannot help but claim Alfred Tennyson as the poet of the west of England, for the further west he is the happier he gets; it was a west just barely opened up by the railways. When he fell from the unwalled garden of the Falcon at Bude, he fell on to the unfenced railway. At Camelford, he found King Arthur's stone, then he went by Bodmin to Fowey, having not yet adventured far into Cornwall, and there he nursed his knee. Still, he had walked to the sea through clover, 'large rich crimson clover' and the sea 'purple and green like a peacock's neck'. At Fowey he talked geology, read Greek, read Smollett's *Count Ferdinand Fathom*, saw Restormel castle muffled in ivy (that at least has improved: the bareness has brought great beauty to its ruins).

Now he got to St Austell, Truro, Perranzabuloe, Land's End, St Michael's Mount and the Lizard. Land's End frightened him: 'Mist. Great yellow flare just before sunset. Funeral. Land's End and life's end.' At Kynance Cove on the Lizard, 'Glorious grass-green monsters of waves.' At Asparagus Island, 'sat watching wave-rainbows.' It was on the Lizard he smoked with the workmen quarrying serpentine (Queen Victoria had commissioned a table of solid serpentine in 1846), and now that he was better, he took to swimming wherever he went, and to reading William Penaluna's *Historical Survey of Cornwall* (1838). He explored inland as far as remote Cotehele, run by a 'brutish mannered housekeeper' at that time. It was not only a marvellous holiday, it is not only that Tennyson is a recorder of childlike innocence and freshness, but Cotehele became at a stroke the Earl's hall in 'Geraint and Enid'. It is indeed the most beautiful and unlikely of buildings, and Tennyson is its ideally chosen poet. Byron might have been better at Mount Edgcumbe, Jane Austen at Plymouth, Hardy is better at Tintagel, but Cotehele even today is the strangest, ghostliest, most Tennysonian of places: even more so than Place House at Fowey with its polished porphyry and jasper. Of course not everything went well: there were fleas at Plymouth, and at Tavistock 'Ethiopian serenaders, sole hope of the evening'.

Holidays like that do not end just like that: letters as well as memories continue their gentle fall-out for some time. One of them elicits from Alfred a record we would not have without it:

> You do me wrong by thinking that I have forgotten you and that pleasant day among the ruins of Berry Pomeroy. It was one of the golden days of my life. I remember it all – the voyage up the Dart, my meeting with you in the ruins, the lady who sat serving among the ivy, the little Theocritus which I had in my pocket, and even the rabbit we had to dinner. I did not know your name nor you mine.[44]

Alfred was curiously in love with secrecy and privacy.

In November 1848 Fitz records that Fred turned up, 'just off again to Florence, where he will be absent another five years perhaps. He entreats me much to go with him.' Then, exactly a week later, 'A. Tennyson, having only two days ago set off with his brother to Florence, reappeared in my rooms this day at noon.' Later in the month he was 'residing at 25 Mornington Place, Hampstead Road'. He wrote a charmingly despondent and lonely letter in January complaining of smoking fires, unwanted invitations and broken locks; it was peppered with fairly funny private jokes. And at the end of February he wrote in a panic from Bonchurch to Coventry Patmore that he had lost the manuscript of *In Memoriam*. That was the second time. The first he had hidden it behind some books in a friend's house and it was sent on; this time it might have been lent to Patmore, or it might be in his old lodgings at 2 Mitre Court Buildings. 'It was a long, butcher-ledger-like book'[45] and was found in a cupboard in his rooms. For some time the work had been near to completion, and now the final flurry of activity had begun.

On 22 January 1849 he met Aubrey de Vere, who wrote that, 'he was more full than ever of King Arthur, and promises to print at last his exquisite Elegies, and let his friends have a few copies.' This is momentous news, but something else was going on even more important to him. During the second half of 1849 his brother Charles was finally reconciled with Louisa Sellwood. In November Alfred was consulting Emily Sellwood by letter about alternate versions of the song 'Sweet and low', for the new edition of *The Princess*. Also in November Alfred seems to have sent *In Memoriam* to Emily, but these cannot have been their first communications in all those years. Emily told her sons that 'when your father was supposed to be in Italy' she went to stay with Cecilia Lushington, and there she met Alfred again. 'Again afterwards we met there, and again Edmund came forward with his accustomed generosity and offered to give up his carriage horses that he might help us . . . Then we met at Shiplake where Drummond Rawnsley was Vicar.'[46] It appears to me that the departure for Italy and the immediate change of mind at the end of 1848 must mark Alfred's grasping the chance to see his Emily. All the same, the publication of *In Memoriam* and his marriage were intimately connected. Emily felt some scruples at first about religious differences, and Alfred was now becoming more religious, surely under her influence. 'Christianity is tugging at my heart,' he said in Cheltenham. His mother's intellectual interests were now confined to the Bible and the apocalyptic commentaries of the Rev John Cumming.

Just at the same time he decided to print, which is at least a clearer story:

> Moxon, when on a visit to Alfred, asked him if he had been writing anything of late, with a view to issuing a vol. for him. On which Alfred said emphatically, No. Moxon then said surely you have not been idle? Alfred said he had been writing for his own relief and private satisfaction some things that the public would have no interest in, and would not care to see. Moxon asked to see the ms. It was *In Memoriam*. Moxon was delighted, and to Alfred's utter astonishment offered to publish it and to hand him a cheque to a/c on the spot. If my memory serves me I think the amount was £300.[47]

I do not know when Moxon left London to visit Alfred, or indeed when he was invited to do so, except during one of his water-cures. Late in 1848 he emerged from one with Dr Gully at Malvern.

It was the conclusion of *In Memoriam* that worried Alfred. The Trinity manuscript dissatisfied him from poem LXXXV on, and he was further dissatisfied with his attempt to cheer it up. The Lincoln manuscript is still short of the last verses, except for what is conveniently called the Epilogue. He was showing this manuscript by 1845. Fitz thought it was all fuss and fume, and Alfred should have got on a horse and ridden it out of his system. 'As it is, it is about three years before the Poetic Soul walks itself out of Darkness and Despair into Common Sense.' He wrote three or four of the late sections (most of CXXIV, CXXVII, and CXXX, and the brief CXXXI that stands last, in which 'self-control' crops up again) in Ireland or soon after. When he agreed in 1850 to print a trial edition and then to publish he insisted on anonymity, and the poem remained formally anonymous for his lifetime,[48] though his authorship was known at once. Charles said in the context of discussing Alfred's marriage that Alfred's difficulties were overcome by the success of *In Memoriam*, that is, by the money. Here again Charles is quite clear, but he may not be right, because no one would want to hurt him by explaining it was his opium habit that had spoilt his brother's chances in the past. Nor does the clear explanation he offers account for Mr Sellwood's attitude. Charles said that for some years after 1837 Alfred had no money, and no prospect of any, so he released Emily. His mother offered to share her money but he refused because it would be unfair to the others. Then Moxon gave him £300 out of the blue for *In Memoriam*, so Alfred went to Charles and 'thought the engagement might now be renewed'. This does not hold water, seeing that he was earning well enough already and also had his pension. Why not marry earlier? The only new factor was Charles's reconciliation with his own wife. Charles was now to arrange a meeting, because Alfred could not live without Emily, and 'now all would come right'. They met at Hale Place, Farnham, where Emily had been with her father since 1848. Charles was satisfied by the result; all along he had thought Alfred and Emily were made for each other.

Before we turn to that vast entanglement of meditations and grieving verses that is *In Memoriam*, it must be said that literary life continued, however unbearably trivial it may seem in comparison. In 1849 Thomas Woolner the sculptor and F. T. Palgrave sought Alfred out. He went on being sweet to obscure and poor poets and to girls and nice to Mrs Howitt. He went on muddling his accounts, he lost a book of R. S. Hawker's which he discovered years later; he was gruff at partings. He went on dining out and fleeing to Cheltenham to avoid dining out. He adopted a close-shaven beard for travelling which after his marriage he would let grow.[49] He would travel closely wrapped in a dark cloak, in the folds of which nestled a number of books, often in Greek, bumping along on the, outside of a coach, questioning the driver. In the autumn of 1849 he adventured into Scotland, and wrote to Aubrey de Vere about how he steamed from Oban to Skye up past Knoydart, 'and saw more outlines of hills than ever I saw in my life'. He answered a letter from Patmore only from Cheltenham, because of 'my purpose always being nipt in the bud by the fat finger of sloth, or washed out by the sight of great lochs or crushed by Ben Cruachan.' Patmore was ambitious: Milnes had got him into the Printed Books department of the British Museum, and now he was using Tennyson as a lever to move Mr Hallam senior to get him on to the permanent staff. Alfred's mention of Ben Cruachan indicates a return through Oban; the railway further north through Appin to Fort William did not yet exist, nor did the line from Fort William to Mallaig along the coast. Tennyson was pleased to be approached by Samuel Bamford, a handloom weaver from Lancashire who had known prison at the time of Peterloo, 'a great, gaunt, stalwart man' Forster says.[50] He came at Alfred by way of Forster, by way of Mrs Gaskell. Her letter is one of the most moving in all this long chronicle. Unable to afford books, Bamford had learnt Tennyson's poems by heart whenever he came across them.[51] Alfred replied simply, 'I reckon his admiration as the greatest honour I have yet received.' By October 1849 he was at Skegness, in November at Mablethorpe, then with the Rawnsleys. He was creeping up on Emily.

Alfred had been seeing a great deal of Sophie Rawnsley, now Mrs Elmhirst, and her husband who was a vicar in Leicestershire, and it was Catherine Rawnsley who in the end arranged Alfred's wedding in her husband Drummond's church at Shiplake (where he was Vicar from 1849 to 1861), in what was still a mysterious, unfrequented, lost piece of countryside, only recently ruined by the motor car. Local legend said the Vicar in Leicestershire built Alfred a wooden hut in which to smoke and compose poems. He used to sit alone in the back of the church with his hat on, and they said he had once proposed to Sophie, but when?

The most eccentric feature of his marriage is its secrecy even from, or particularly from, his own family. The Rawnsleys knew all about it on Christmas Day 1849, and perhaps after Charles Tennyson Turner's strong urgings early in 1850 Drummond Rawnsley played the most important role, since fifteen or twenty miles or so from

Shiplake lies Eversley, where the Vicar was Charles Kingsley:[52] Shiplake is south of Henley, and Eversley is south of Wokingham on the heathery heath near Sandhurst. When Charles Kingsley got there in 1844, he found awful dilapidation, large arrears of Poor Law dues, an empty church and a labouring population of which not one was literate. They were broom-gatherers and deer-stealers: luckily F. D. Maurice had been a shining light to him since his youthful doubts, and by 1848 he had taken a dive into the sort of Christian socialism that passed through Kingsley and Tom Hughes into a new element in the Church of England. But he was overworked, and his play about Elizabeth of Hungary and his novel *Yeast* (1848) took their toll of him. In October he retired to Bournemouth, and then in winter to north Devon. For the greater part of 1849–50 he was busy writing *Alton Locke*, which Carlyle got published by Chapman and Hall. It is difficult to place the moment when he met Emily, and encouraged and urged her to marry Alfred, probably at Drummond Rawnsley's.[53] Mrs Rawnsley and Emily and Charles Kingsley corresponded over *In Memoriam* in April 1850. The licence was dated 13 May but the wedding took place after frettings and delays (like the publication of a book) only on 13 June. Why the secrecy? They were both shy over so long and so strained a courtship, Alfred was embarrassed by being now so famous, and there were family cross-currents. Alfred's sister Mary heard they were 'married on Friday and raining, about which I feel very superstitious. I hope they will be happy, but I feel very doubtful about it.' Later, she found it was not Friday, and not raining, so she cheered up a little.

The chaos of Alfred Tennyson's arrangements reached a climax with his marriage. The cake and the dresses arrived late, the white gloves got lost. It is a pleasure to be able to say that utterly quiet as it was, Alfred at least thought 'it was the nicest wedding he had ever been at.' The guests were Mr Sellwood, Edmund and Cecilia Lushington, Charles and Ann Weld (another Sellwood sister) and Mr Greville Phillimore (Charterhouse and Christ Church, the curate). Mary and Margaret Rawnsley were bridesmaids, and Mrs Rawnsley was hostess. At Pangbourne the happy couple caught a train that would take them west; Emily was taking Alfred to Clevedon, which he had never faced visiting on his own, to Arthur Hallam's grave. Far away in the Lake District another event had already occurred which would cast an indirect shadow on their marriage: as the cuckoo clock in the kitchen cuckooed twelve midday on Shake-

speare's birthday, William Wordsworth had breathed his last. Since
1843, when Alfred Tennyson was runner-up on the death of Southey,
Wordsworth had been Poet Laureate, and it must have seemed likely
enough that this time Alfred would be appointed. There had even
been a newspaper rumour that the Queen and Prince Albert had
visited him at Esher in 1847, but that was moonshine.[54]

In Memoriam was printed in six copies early in March 1850, with
its Christian prologue, and its title which Emily had suggested, and
then published late in May; by 1 June Alfred's authorship was
announced by *The Publishers' Circular*: it must have been obvious
anyway. Something must be said about the poem as a whole, although
it is tempting to deny that it has any structure in any important sense,
and although most readers dip into it as if it had none; yet it does offer
certain clues or guides to the reader. At first it deals only with death
and the bringing home and imaginary burial of the body, but at poem
XXVIII we reach Christmas, and this definite day links with a second
Christmas (LXXVII) and a third (CIII) to make the passage of time
precise, and more compressed than the time of composition really was.
The truth is that it took seventeen years to write, and as one reads it,
poem overlapping poem, it feels like seventeen: like a lifework. There
are other dates, a birthday and an anniversary of death, and Charles's
wedding day, and the day of leaving Lincolnshire. There are sudden
flashes of the past: LXXXVI Cambridge and LXXXVIII Somersby,
C–CI Lincolnshire, the spring in CXIV, New Year's bells at CV.
Thoughts tend to last five or six poems, but sensations are swift and
feelings close themselves in every poem often with an epigram. The
turning-point (but the sequence has many turning-points) may be
about XC. From LXXXV onwards Tennyson has brooded on the
past, with the sudden intensity of birdsong (LXXXVIII) and the
marvellous recreation of Somersby in LXXXIX:

> Witch-elms that counterchange the floor
>   Of this flat lawn with dusk and bright;
>   And thou, with all thy breadth and height
> Of foliage, towering sycamore; . . .
>
> The wine-flask lying couch'd in moss,
>
> Or cooled within the glooming wave;
>   And last, returning from afar,

Before the crimson-circled star
Had fallen into her father's grave,

And brushing ankle-deep in flowers,
    We heard behind the woodbine veil
    The milk that bubbled in the pail,
And buzzings of the honied hours.

(1–4, 44–52)

The next poem contains some harsh words about his sister Emily for marrying someone else, and ends in the passionate plea, 'Ah dear, but come thou back to me'. It must be remembered that to Alfred Emily's marriage had been a shock, and Charles's marriage which so swiftly followed it, and which entailed Alfred falling for his own Emily, had reversed the shock and turned shock (for a moment) into pleasure. Now he was prepared to live his life, and to give up his quasi-married relationship with Arthur's ghost. That or something like it is the central thought with which he incoherently wrestles in the last touches of composition. Into the final Prologue there enters enough of his old groaning to drown what would otherwise be intolerable pious resignation. It is in 'these wild and wandering cries,/ Confusions of a wasted youth' that the true voice, the truthful tone of Tennyson lies.[55]

He treats evolution and the prehistory of nature, still five minutes before Darwin, in a most interesting way. He has been brought up on Buffon's *Natural History*; in 1837 he read Lyell's *Principles of Geology*, and apparently Cuvier's book on fossil quadrupeds (1812) which appeared in English as *Essay on the Theory of the Earth* (1813). His doubts on these subjects were shared by many, and have exercised most of us at some time. In 1844, Alfred had sent to Moxon for Robert Chambers's *Vestiges of the Natural History of Creation*, saying, 'It seems to contain many speculations with which I have been familiar for years.' His poem does represent the best that was being thought and felt by the best minds of his generation. The problems of course had long existed: they arose for example in didactic verse about conchology by eighteenth-century Italian and French clergymen. But the history of the discussion is not my subject; I raise the matter only because evolution deepens the seriousness of *In Memoriam* by entering into theology as well as science, as Alfred had done with Arthur Hallam, and it adds to the fascination of what *In Memoriam* inevitably is, the very full portrait of an interesting mind. That is something of the nourishment that one feels, underlying its towering, crumbling, uneven greatness as a poem.

CHAPTER SEVEN

Maud

SHE HAD married a tall, bookish, short-sighted poet with fits of hypochondria and melancholy and a habit of brooding solitariness, who drank a good deal and smoked incessantly. He had married a tall, thin girl with a plain, round face but eyes that lit up and sparkled, as Carlyle said, but she certainly had an expression of great sweetness. She was then thirty-seven, and already an invalid with a bad back which got worse. He was forty-one years old, but the full thunderstorm of being famous for ever after, like royalty or a prime minister, was just about to burst over their heads. He was a rough fellow too, and would never wholly mend his habits. The previous autumn Weston Cracroft Amcott, once of Harrington Hall, had observed him: 'When he lights up his face is almost fine, but his expression coarse when unexcited. On the whole his complexion dirty and sallow – he wears spectacles – conversation agreeable. I was amused when the Poet put his feet up on the sofa and Mrs Rawnsley . . . quietly warned him off.'[1]

Emily did make some inroads on this behaviour, instituting an inspection before dinner for example. Once without thinking he came in and presented his hands to a stray guest for inspection; she told him to go back and wash them. All his life he dined with a fresh apple pie beside him and a bottle of port. When Henry Irving dined with him, Alfred poured him a glass of the port and drank the rest of the bottle. Then he sent for another, and when that was decanted he gave Irving a second glass and again he finished the rest. Next morning Irving was woken by Alfred staring down at his face with a candle and an expression of curiosity: 'Is it your custom,' he enquired, 'always to consume two entire bottles of port every evening?' Alfred was never observed to be at all drunk, and never seems to have had a hangover. When he says 'The peace of God came into my life before the altar when I wedded her,' one cannot but believe him. In his bachelor, flirting days he had rolled over on the carpet to Lucy Duff-Gordon and begged her to use him as a footstool, but now that sort of thing was over. A kind of decorum overcame him little by little. In the past he had suddenly left a party in London to flee to Cheltenham because he was 'gorged with men'; he wanted to flee from Cheltenham by balloon from Montpelier Gardens, though his mother and sisters dissuaded him.

He had married a woman in some ways like his mother, though much more intellectual, a scrupulous Christian who was luckily magnetized by his poetry, and engaged at once in that long and loving wrestle with a personality which every marriage must contain. She took over his accounts, and she wrote his letters for him, until in 1874, when she was past sixty and her children already brought up, her health broke down completely. Her last words (after his death) were, 'I have tried to be a good wife . . . I could have done more.' He was devoted to her, and more so as time went on, while affection grew to its vast size and height in the place of passion. People said she was socially ambitious, but that does not seem to be true. He was suddenly a rich, then quite quickly a very rich man (but his household was never splendid: a rich man on a more serious scale like the Duke of Devonshire spent £60,000 on a ball); a member of the Queen's Court, and a close personal friend of extremely grand, rich people, and of those in great places. Gladstone and the Duke of Argyll and the Dean of Westminster, the head of Balliol, Oxford, and the head of Trinity were his friends rather than hers. Now his life became more regular, and with that change came so to speak regular breathing.

The old habit of crunching up and rolling over lines of poetry in his head seems to have transmuted soon after 1840 into churning over his grief, so that he could do nothing but add to the preposterous accumulation of In Memoriam, about sea shells, about the weather, about the soul and love and dog ends of dead conversations. Now that was a finished book, which he depersonalized a little for publication, helped by the wise Spedding. His inward process was slow to recommence, or rather it stopped and started. Soon he was to begin telling people that he had probably the greatest mastery of the language of any poet since Shakespeare, but had nothing more to say. A greater mas ry than Pope's, or the youthful Milton's? With those possible exce ions it was a truthful boast, but a poet who has perfect ability to express and nothing to say is in a fatal position.

In fact his future position as laureate, which was far higher socially (in those days) than anything Thackeray or Dickens or Browning could aspire to, made him abnormally courteous to other writers, so that after 1850 one seldom knows his true opinion about contemporaries. His view of Wordsworth by contrast is difficult enough, but possible to trace. He called him 'old Wordie'. He genuinely thought him a great man, but probably out of shyness he several times told him stories that got a frosty response. One was about a tropical island covered in flowers that blushed red as the sun rose, so that the whole island seemed to blush: Wordsworth disliked the thought. Another was about hot-air balloons to be available at the foot of every tall mountain so that no one need climb the crags, one could waft over Skiddaw or Mont Blanc. That was not well received either. But then Alfred drew him aside and they made each other private compliments expressive of their genuine and deep mutual regard. The poem of Tennyson's Wordsworth really envied was 'Dora'. Yet Alfred as we have seen, was quite capable of mocking some ridiculous line of Wordsworth.[2] The trouble with Wordsworth, he says in another late letter, lies in an inherited style he could never wholly shake off. All the same at the age of eighty-one he told a visitor the best sonnets in English were by Milton, Shakespeare and Wordsworth, and after those three the sonnets of his brother Charles. One might today interpose the names of Hopkins and maybe Donne after Wordsworth, but scarcely before.

His immediate connection with Wordsworth as laureate was the court dress he borrowed from Samuel Rogers for the Levée at which he was to be introduced to the Queen, a court dress which Wordsworth had also borrowed. Alfred was worried whether the breeches would fit. Rogers was then eighty-seven and hardly able to stagger, but he had the satisfaction of refusing the laureateship in May, when the Prince Consort offered it to him. Lord John Russell, a coarse-witted polemical prime minister as complacently philistine as modern holders of the office, submitted three other names with Tennyson's, those of Taylor, Knowles and Wilson. Luckily the Prince Consort had already read *In Memoriam*, and the official letter was sent on 5 November.[3] The night before it came, Alfred dreamed that the Queen and Prince Albert visited him at his mother's house; they were nice to him and Prince Albert kissed him. Very kind, he thought, but very German.

At the end of the year Charles Tennyson d'Eyncourt produced that monumental piece of bad taste, his 750-line poem 'Eustace',

about his military son who had died in the West Indies: it was
massively lifeless, and even Lord John Russell had not thought of
making him laureate.[4]

Alfred Tennyson's old processes of composition had been dis-
rupted again, unless his inner streams of poetry were still occupied
with his own old poems, which he endlessly adjusted and dithered
over. That is perhaps the likeliest solution, but for whatever reason
he was slow to find any new and fitting theme, and it appears that
his light verses, which arose quite immediately from reading the
newspapers, tended to survive and be published where once he
would have lit his pipe with them had he ever written them down.
All the same he did not lose his lyric grace. The poem 'Go not,
happy day' recurs in *Maud* (XVII) though it was first meant for *The
Princess*, but there are slighter verses still that convey genuine
enchantment and personal happiness. In the middle of some formal
and today unreadable stanzas 'To the Queen'[5] about inheriting 'This
laurel greener from the brows/Of him that uttered nothing base'
there is a sudden touch of the intimate and domestic strain which so
convinces in Tennyson, most of all in those early years of marriage.
It occurs in some lines about Kensington Gardens:

> Then – while a sweeter music wakes,
>   And through wild March the throstle calls,
>   Where all about your palace-walls
> The sun-lit almond-blossom shakes –
>
> (13–16)

A lot of dithering lies behind this poem, which is of some
psychological interest, because in the various versions Tennyson is
attempting to sort out his thoughts about being laureate. He notes
that 'the taskwork ode has ever failed' but longs to survive as a poet
to kindle future ages with admiration for 'fair Victoria's golden age'
an ambition it may be felt that time has fulfilled for him. What
crushes him, one notes in this early version, is the thought of
succession to Wordsworth:

> But he your Laureate who succeeds
>   A master such as all men quote
>   Must feel as one of slender note

And piping low among the reeds.

(37–40)

His lines of thanks to Drummond Rawnsley, the Vicar of
Shiplake who married them, are apparently lightly thrown off,
scribbled in the wedding carriage is what he says, but the large
number of versions demonstrates that this throwaway kind of
perfection was not easily nor immediately attained.[6] The three-stanza
version he finally preferred is to be found as an appendix to the Ricks
three-volume edition; it consists of the first, second and last stanzas
of the longer poem and appears to me much better. In one version
he had 'Undisturbed by tedious Greville' as the second line of the
final stanza, which is better still; Greville Phillimore was the curate,
but we may feel free now to offend him.[7] Taken together the three
stanzas read as lightly as a breath, and perfectly convey the atmosphere of a wedding by the undisturbed Thames a week before
midsummer.

Alfred wrote a note to Mrs Elmhirst, Sophie Rawnsley his old
flame, from Pangbourne on 14 June, the day after the wedding: 'We
seem to get on very well together. I have not beaten her yet.' A tiny
misunderstanding with Sophie drew from him a tiny regrettable
poem: they were both too sensitive. The bride and groom went by
rail to Weston-super-Mare to get to Clevedon; 'It seems a kind of
consecration to go there,' wrote Emily. They toured onwards to
Lynton and back to Glastonbury, where she was pleased to see a fine
monastic hostel used by the inn where they rested was built by Sir
John Selwode, an ancestor doubtless. We should thank our stars that
the Tennysons did not choose to build an imitation of the Abbot's
Kitchen to live in: there is one in Oxford attached to the Science
Museum, but one is enough. From Glastonbury they made for
Clifton, where Alfred was treated by a doctor, 'some injury to a nail
having made a painful little laceration', with chloroform, which
blistered his chin. 'I heard him shout as if hallooing the hounds.'
From Clifton they went to Bath, and from Bath to Cheltenham to
face the family.

On 10 July he was still vaguely wandering; finding himself at
Cheltenham he considered a journey to Italy with a sister, but
thought more seriously of Mrs Marshall's cottage on Coniston
Water. Meanwhile he wrote to his friend Monteith about the prospect
of Scotland: 'I have married a lady four years younger than myself

who has loved me and prayed for my earthly and spiritual welfare
for fourteen years . . . My only fear is that I have lived so long
unmarried that I may have crystallised into bachelorhood beyond
redemption.' Then he was in London in St James's Square, then in
Cheltenham again, and at last with Emily in Patterdale, at a hotel on
Ullswater. They were at Tent Lodge, Coniston, from late July until
October, in a house that had the good luck to be painted by Turner,
whose picture of it is in the Fitzwilliam Museum at Cambridge. It
was there that they met a whole group of old and new friends, who
arrived because they were pleased and curious about his marriage.
The new and nearly new ones define a new epoch in his life, partly
because now that he was so famous he was also no longer the newest
thing on the market, and fans sought him out. Coventry Patmore,
whose wife had copied out *In Memoriam* for the press, came; so did
the Lushingtons, Thomas Woolner, Edward Lear, Aubrey de Vere,
Venables and Carlyle.

Of these Woolner and Lear were both Pre-Raphaelites; Edward
Lear was a painter who had joined the Academy Schools late in life
and was about to take part in Holman Hunt's movement (Hunt was
twenty-three in 1850 but Lear was thirty-eight and had taught the
Queen drawing); and Woolner was a sculptor. He worked several
times on Tennyson, but when he had produced a masterly monument
to Wordsworth at Grasmere church and still failed to get the
Westminster Abbey commission for another he went away to
Australia, not a good career move, although the scene at the quayside
produced Ford's 'Last of England'. He was a masterly story-teller to
children and a loyal friend. Tennyson was always recommending
him; his great work was a monument to Gladstone which included
scenes from the *Iliad*, and was erected by public subscription in the
Bodleian Library at Oxford, but is now alas to be seen only by
arrangement, in the cellars of the Ashmolean Museum. Tennyson's
third youthful Pre-Raphaelite friend was William Allingham the
poet, whose high standing with Tennyson startled Patmore.
Allingham is still readable, his selection of old ballads is the best until
Grigson's, and his journal is warm and brilliant.

It is the poetry of the Pre-Raphaelites that is negligible: it is
nearly all damply aesthetic, and reads like early Tennyson without
the talent. Swinburne's is Pre-Raphaelitism and soda water. There is
something over-excited about him. The reason for this sad judgement is to be found in the anecdote of William Morris at Oxford

swiftly scribbling his first poem, and saying, 'If this is poetry it's easy.' They were amazing decorative artists, but poetry cannot be merely decorative without a fatal sag. Apart from Swinburne, only Morris is just a little better, and then only in his Arthurian verses, but the Arthurian frescoes in the dining room at Buscot are enough to strike a chill into the most earnest admirer.

The other new movement of the time was that of the Spasmodics, led by Dobell, who in their attempt to put more grit and gravel into poetry are clearly on the deserving side, but although Tennyson knew and perhaps admired them, alas they are no good; not even their influence on Tennyson, which in *Maud* is faint but undoubted, was productive of good. Only somewhere beyond them hovers the spirit of Poe, whose works Tennyson possessed in 1852 and 1853 editions. Tennyson met Dobell at Malvern and had his poetry in 1854 and 1856 editions, but no Morris before 1867 and no Arthurian Morris.[8]

It is hard now to see the novelty of the school called the Spasmodics. They were scornfully so named by a Scottish Professor called Aytoun.[9] Dobell was a Gloucester wine merchant's son who suffered from bad health, Smith was a self-educated Scottish working man; they met in Scotland and became allies at the time of the Crimean War (they even issued a book of war poems together). Dobell's poetry makes no deep impression, he is an imitation lyric Tennyson. The Laureate liked the boy, and tried to be polite, and wrote a kind letter about *City Poems*, but Dobell will really not do:

> In vain, in vain, in vain!
> You will never come again.
> There droops upon the dreary hills a mournful fringe of rain . . .
> Round selfish shores forever moans the hurt and wounded sea . . .

His best poems are Tennysonian stories like 'Squire Maurice' and 'A Boy's Poem', but that ends woefully badly. Alexander Smith on the other hand started worse than Dobell but learnt quickly and became far better than his friend. He wrote in the end brilliant pastiches of Tennyson's story poems. But he was ruined by an anonymous review in the *Athenaeum* which accused him of plagiarism. It was written apparently by Allingham;[10] it silenced Smith as a poet, and he took refuge in prose. Dobell died very young. By 1880 Smith was as utterly dismissed as once he had been lauded.

A more serious bud of rivalry, indeed the most serious that Alfred encountered in his whole life, was embodied in a visit from Matthew Arnold 'in the heyday of youth' as Emily recorded. He was twenty-eight in 1850, and although the last ten or twenty years of his life (1822–88) were a descent into gloom, marked by the death of children, he was then in the first rage of publication, which for a poet is something like floating a private company on the stock exchange. His first two books, *The Strayed Reveller* (1849) and *Empedocles on Etna* (1851), were anonymous, but he cannibalized them both to produce the masterly *Poems* of 1853, which included 'The Scholar Gipsy' and 'Sohrab and Rustum'. That volume has a curious preface, passionately inhibited, and skirting the important subject of Tennyson, whom he did not mention but who was evidently central to him both as an example and as a target. The boring poem 'Empedocles' was excluded then, though reinstated later on Browning's bad advice; it has done harm to his reputation because it is intellectually so serious, but as a poem so null (as Browning himself often is). At his best he had no fault but further to essentialize the essence of Tennyson like a bee drowning in very thin honey. In the 1860s he turned to prose, and then to religion, but he and Alfred were intimately aware of one another. 'Tristram and Iseult' is an attempt at an English idyll with an Arthurian theme, and 'Sohrab' and 'Balder' perfectly catch the epic tone. Arnold still lived then at Fox How, and worshipped Wordsworth dead as much as living. Tennyson would later want Arnold to follow him as laureate, but Arnold died first. Arthur Clough was thirty-one in 1850 but less formidable to the new laureate: they greatly liked each other as persons, though not much as versifiers. Clough's first publication, *Bothie* (1848), had luckily not left Alfred feeling challenged.[11]

It was a holiday for happy accidents. Alfred went up a small mountain with Coventry Patmore who says 'we got a bit glorious': it appears that Alfred outclimbed him to the top, outdrank him when they got there, and outraced him running down. Emily Tennyson was impressed by the Speddings, and pleased by the Marshalls, Mrs Marshall being a sister of Stephen Spring-Rice, but she liked the herons and the water lilies best. Carlyle dropped in and alarmed her, but Aubrey de Vere's mother delighted her; Alfred said Aubrey looked 'like a young Seraph', and Aubrey in his turn thought Emily really noble, religious and generous. Edward Lear wrote in 1859 that 'computing moderately, fifteen angels, several hundreds of ordinary women, many philosophers, a heap of truly wise and kind mothers, three or four minor prophets, and a lot of doctors and schoolmistresses fall far short of what Emily Tennyson really is.' He was one of her greatest successes: he was eccentric and unsuccessful and no longer young, always on the move and getting sadder as time went on, but she handled him perfectly, as we shall see.[12]

The person she handled most perfectly was her husband. He wrote a kindly but embarrassed letter to a former fellow-patient abjuring hydrotherapy,[13] and on at least two occasions he tried to give up smoking. He became kinder and very much more relaxed. He did nurse a grudge against Lytton, but that was because Lytton had once told him he felt free to use all arts and wiles in the seduction of women, because they were asking for it. Alfred became more and more chivalrous both in life and in poetry; one might say that he became insufferably high-minded about women were it not that a streak of realism persisted. Patmore noticed Emily's wide and intense reading, so Alfred's increasing seriousness may owe much to her. It became a habit of his not to go to church, or it was one already, but the first of many occasions when he read everyone prayers and a sermon by F. D. Maurice, because it was too wet to go out, occurred that August.[14]

October came, they went to Crewe with Matthew Arnold, and from there to Cheltenham in search of a house. Alfred's mother and sisters had begun to ransack the Cheltenham suburbs for a small one, or else they would all move to a bigger one together on the outskirts of London. Charles Weld, who was now his brother-in-law and Secretary to the Royal Society, helped him in London though he found Alfred difficult: 'He must have all the upper part to himself, for a study and smoking-room, etc., and to avoid noise above his head, and indoor privacy, as he is accustomed while composing to walk up and down his room loudly reciting the flowing thoughts.'[15] The worry about where to settle suddenly became urgent, because his wife was pregnant. She must have conceived towards the end of July about a month after marriage, as soon as they got to the Lake District. Can that be why she sounds so happy, writing about those days so many years later?[16] An eighty-year-old woman who had known Scott[17]

> told of travelling tailors who used to recite the fragments of Ossianic poems before the days of Macpherson. They recited in

Gaelic. The ever-changing aspect of lake and mountain was of course a continual source of delight. Day by day lordly wreaths of storm-clouds across the mountains and sunlit clouds like bright spirits or a rainbow in the lake are recorded or the pleasure of gathering grass of Parnassus or Stags Horn moss or of seeing the Touch-me-not, a balsam with a yellow tube flower whose seed vessels coiled in their spirals burst when touched with rather a loud crack. The interest of hearing that thirteen wild swans . . .

Then they went house-hunting and 'ever hospitable Park House received us meanwhile'. On the way they called at Henry Taylor's at Mortlake and met Mrs Cameron the photographer for the first time, 'having the courtly charm of manner which was one of her many phases', and dressed in dark-green silk with open sleeves and a cord at the waist, which sounds the height of Pre-Raphaelite fashion. Monckton Milnes came and stayed three or four days, and Alfred read most of *Twelfth Night* and *Lear* aloud.

In January 1851 they took their first house of their own, at Warninglid near Crawley on the Sussex border. The rest of the Tennyson family were at this time as near to being settled as they ever would be. Fred was in Florence where he had left the Villa Torregiani and moved into the city. In the late 1840s he had a religious conversion, which made him feel he was 'ever in the presence of God'; as a result he adopted Swedenborgianism, following the example of Mary. Swedenborgianism, which had an influence on William Blake, was not then as *outré* as it sounds. Carlyle was interested in Swedenborg and so was Allingham. One of its doctrines is that of purging by 'vastation', a deep depression that may last for years and certainly sounds like the Tennysons. Alfred's grandson Sir Charles says of Fred, 'About the same time he became a fervent British Israelite and a believer in spiritualism.'[18] But old Fitz, who was in close touch with him, records this as news in a letter to Fanny Kemble in 1872:

He has come to England (from Jersey where his home now is) partly on Business and partly to bring over a deaf old Gentleman who has discovered the Original Mystery of Free-Masonry, by means of Spiritualism. The Freemasons have for Ages been ignorant, it seems, of the very Secret which all their Emblems and Signs refer to: and the question is, if they care enough for their own Mystery to buy it of this ancient Gentleman. If they do not, he will shame them by publishing it . . .[19]

Perhaps this unusual religious history can be reconciled, because in 1852 he could still make jokes about the ghosts, and in 1874 there appeared *Veritas: the Meridian and Persian Laws*, by H. Melville, ed. F. Tennyson and A. Tudor. The obsession is oddly reminiscent of Charles Tennyson d'Eyncourt's attempt to revive the Order of Templars with the backing of the mad old Duke of Sussex. The Brownings, who met Fred early in 1851, shortly after he had spent the night in prison after screaming at the guard on a city gate at which he arrived too late, and calling the Tuscan government '*porcelli*', were deeply impressed by his sincerity, his simplicity and remarkable talents, which only his shyness stopped him from using. They thought he had all Alfred's qualities, but they never came together.[20]

Warninglid was not a success. The birds were thrilling, Alfred had heard nothing like it since Somersby, but they 'were blown out of the dining-room and he was smoked out of his room and the rain came more than half through our bedroom and the storm was so loud we could not sleep.' Emily fails to record that part of the bedroom wall blew down, the wind raved through the room and the rain washed into it. They heard that their dining room and the bedroom which was above it had once been a Catholic chapel, and that a baby was buried there. A gang of murderers had lived in the house, no postmen came near it, the nearest doctor and butcher lived 7 miles away in Horsham. Alfred drew Emily in a Bath chair over rough and smooth to Cuckfield, and they left. But one day she fell over a step in a hotel, and that was what she blamed (wrongly it appears) when their first child was born dead late that April. They took refuge meanwhile first at Shiplake, then at Park House. Early in March, Alfred went to his first Levée, where he met a small politician with flaming red hair, an obsessive ornithologist with all of whose opinions he agreed. This man was the Duke of Argyll,[21] a second son who inherited splendours unexpectedly, but remembered if at all today not because his son Lord Lorne married the Queen's daughter Princess Louise in 1870, but because he was Tennyson's great friend. A few days later, after a saga of difficulties not of their own making, they moved into Chapel House, Twickenham.

The Lushingtons' coachman and Mr Marshall's carriage saw them installed, with butler and groom in attendance at London Bridge Station. Marshall, Taylor, the Welds, Spedding and the Patmores all had dinner. It was the last house at the south end of a quiet road that ended at it, though today it is one of many, distinguished only by a blue plaque. The house had a fine open view at the back, and its staircase was dominated by the life-size statue of a bishop several hundred years old. Near by was Keller Hall where F. T. Palgrave, who had known Alfred a year or two, was working at training teachers. He was at Balliol with Clough and Arnold and had been Gladstone's secretary for a year. Nearer still was the Royal School of Militry Music, then newly founded. What drums, what bugles and trumpets must have sounded. One cannot but imagine they were an influence on Alfred, though they are not mentioned, and he did not notice military music until the 'Ode on the Death of the Duke of Wellington', written before the funeral. Still, after his move to Twickenham his poems do take on a polemical colour. It is possible they owe something to the *coup d'état* of Louis Napoleon in December 1851, and all too evident that they are influenced by the rhetoric of the newspapers in which they were intended to be printed. It is also possible that they were Tennyson's version of Wordsworth's severely worded interventions in public affairs, which he now felt it his duty to continue. His opinions were no doubt thought fairly sound by most people, it is the verse which is deplorable. Yet one cannot help hearing the band going 'pom pom pom' in the background. The poems I refer to are 'The Penny-Wise', with the refrain 'Arm, arm, arm!'; 'Rifle Clubs!!!', with the refrain 'I carry the dead, the dead, the dead,/Killed in the *Coup d'État*!'; 'Britons, Guard Your Own' with the title as refrain, and so on. As poetry they do not exist, as a performance by the laureate they are lamentable. Yet at the same time he wrote for Edward Lear one of his loveliest lyrics, 'To E. L. on His Travels in Greece', thanking him for *Journals of a Landscape Painter in Albania and Illyria* (1851).

In March Mr Sellwood paid his first visit: 'Looking at the Bishop, he fell backward downstairs, and bruised his eye and his legs,' but he stayed eighteen days, until Alfred had seen the first swallows skimming up the Thames. A week after that on Easter Sunday the child, who would have been a hefty boy, was born strangled. It seemed likely that Emily became seriously ill. She was better by the end of June when we have a full account of a visit by Allingham.[22] Alfred 'looked tired, and said he had been asleep and was suffering from hayfever. Mrs Tennyson came in, very sweet and courteous, with low soft voice, and by and by when I rose to take leave she said, Won't you stay for dinner?' Allingham enjoyed his evening. They talked about his own poems, then at dinner about Wordsworth and Meredith who had sent Alfred his poems at the age of twenty-three: Alfred had spotted 'Love in the Valley' at once. Over the port he asserted his belief in immortality. 'I could not eat my dinner without a belief in immortality. If I didn't believe in that, I'd go down immediately and jump off Richmond Bridge. Why do you laugh? In such a case I'd as soon make a comic end as a tragic.' After the port, Allingham recited Poe's 'Raven' which Alfred did not know. Allingham came again in 1853, but this time Mrs Tennyson was not well, so he was warned to 'tread softly and speak low'. He found Fred Tennyson and Fitz, who had both come to see little Hallam. Fitz insisted Tennyson must admire Pope's *Homer*. 'Oh yes you do, Alfred.' 'No I do not.' Fred defended Schiller as supreme, but Allingham defended Goethe. 'If one of you is for Goethe and the other for Schiller, you'll never agree on poetry.' Allingham called Browning a vivid man, and Alfred agreed. 'How he did flourish about when he was here!' Allingham spilt some port on the cloth, so Tennyson put salt on it, remarking imperturbably, 'I believe it never comes out.' They smoked and told stories, 'some of an ammoniacal saltness'. Tennyson said nothing would grow in his garden but stones: however many he removed, there were always as many again.

In the summer of 1851 Alfred and Emily saw the Crystal Palace when it stood in Hyde Park, and the Great Exhibition, then they were off, on 15 July, to Paris and the south. In Paris they saw the Brownings, to whom they were very friendly, and the Lushingtons. There is a story about Professor Lushington in Paris which may be earlier, but let me attach it here. He asked a servant in very English French to keep the fire in, but his friend found himself to his fury locked in his rooms, Lushington having said, 'Ne laissez pas sortir le fou.' In mid-August they got to Genoa and from there to Bagni di Lucca, which the Brownings had recommended. Richard Jesse and the Francis Gardens were there. In Florence they stayed with Fred and were called on by Mrs Trollope, the novelist's mother.[23] They moved in an attendant squadron of all these friends, partly because Alfred was now so famous and great, and certainly seemed greater

by his position, which like other positions in English life is not
enough to make its holder glamorous, but enough to triple or
quadruple his glamour if he has any. Alfred's view of France was by
no means urbane, particularly after the coup in December. He liked
the Mediterranean world, and 'The broad-limbed Gods at random
thrown' which are really the Elgin marbles I think, in spite of the
Roman fountain-urns and the nineteenth-century swimming naiads
in his verse 'To E. L.'. He liked the slopes rich in bloom:

> From him that on the mountain lea
>   By dancing rivulets fed his flocks
>   To him who sat upon the rocks
> And fluted to the morning sea.
>
> (21–4)

It is as well to fix that image in one's mind before one looks at 'The
Daisy', which is named after one he gave his pregnant wife on a
Swiss mountain pass on the way home,[24] which he found again in a
book she lent him. It is in a metre he invented, a version of Horace's
Latin version of the Greek metre of Alkaios, called the alcaeic; this is
full of life and spring-like, and very much more palatable in English
than Clough's correcter adaptation. Tennyson's poem is 108 lines
long. Like Addison he begins at Monaco, 'in lands of palm, of
orange-blossom,/Of olive, aloe, and maize and vine.' The vineyards
and the calm sea, the unfamiliar flowers and the architecture take him
over and he offers no resistance: it is as if he had come home. There
is a good deal about Genoa, a city of more enchantment until about
1918 than it is now easy to imagine. Tennyson gives a magnificent
sketch of the landscape:

>   rosy blossom in hot ravine,
>   Where oleanders flushed the bed
>   Of silent torrents, gravel-spread;
>   And, crossing, oft we saw the glisten
>   Of ice, far up on the mountain head.
>
> (32–6)

It is a very happy poem. The only thing he dislikes is 'the clipt palm
of which they boast'; otherwise even the rain that pursues him from
Palma to Piacenza sounds enjoyable. We are not told they meant to

go to Naples but were put off by bad weather, though it was so.[25] The lines on Milan, and the climax of the Alps deserve their fame. The words melt in the mouth; they indicate pure pleasure, yet they are memorable. It is extraordinary that an English poem about mountains, written in the shadow of Wordsworth, should permit no shade of metaphysics, be completely physical:

> I climbed the roofs at break of day;
> Sun-smitten Alps before me lay.
>   I stood among the silent statues,
> And statued pinnacles, mute as they.
>
> How faintly-flushed, how phantom-fair,
> Was Monte Rosa, hanging there
>   A thousand shadowy-pencilled valleys
> And snowy dells in a golden air.[26]
>
>   (61–8)

This brilliant travel poem was published in 1855, and if that were his only contribution to English poetry, Tennyson would still rank high. He told Frank Lushington he came home for want of English tobacco: however that may be, it was a holiday he never expected to have again, because when it was written in 1853 there was already a baby 'whose crying is a cry for gold'. At least for a moment he forgot the lethal gloom of Edinburgh, and 'My fancy fled to the South again.' He already knew his wife could not stand a longer sea crossing than the Channel.[27]

In the spring of 1852 they house-hunted near Mr Rashdall's, Alfred's old friend the Vicar of Malvern, with whom they stayed and explored Herefordshire, blotting out the sad anniversary. They happily and energetically walked the Welsh Marches. Hallam Tennyson was born on 11 August 1852 after some feverish activity at the last moment, with only the help of a midwife. Mrs Cameron was specially helpful in racing off to London but 'the nurse managed it all' Alfred wrote to friends, 'I never saw anything more beautiful than the mother's face . . . or heard anything sweeter than the little lamblike bleat.' Emily wanted him called Alfred but Alfred insisted on Hallam as a second name, and got Henry Hallam's permission. When it came to the baptism in October there was some confusion

over this, so Alfred shouted out 'Hallam!' This must lie at the root
of Henry's joke that they wouldn't call the boy Alfred in case he
turned out a fool, so they called him Hallam. F. D. Maurice was a
godfather with James Marshall and Mr Hallam, and noted in a letter
to Kingsley, 'It was to please his wife he asked me.' We have a list of
the guests, at least of those who accepted, including all the expected
names, some Peels from Marble Hill near Twickenham, neighbours
called Bolton, and Mr Browning, whose wife was ill.[28] The lunch
was splendid, with the best champagne they could find and the best
venison Mrs Tennyson had ever eaten, provided by Drummond
Rawnsley, Shiplake being well placed in those days to find it. Emily
had been unwell from the birth until the end of September, by which
time the Duke of Wellington was dead, and Richard Monckton
Milnes had already suggested to Alfred what an opportunity for a
poem his death could be. Milnes also appears to have provided most
of the christening lunch.

Wellington died on 14 September; the great public poem to catch
the national mood had to be ready in November; in its way it was a
masterpiece of contrivance, monumental and without intimacy,
hollow like all monuments. But its hollow ring is what convinces
about it and conveys an appropriate grief at an appropriate level of
grandeur. Tennyson had seen the Duke once only, crossing Horse
Guards. They were alone there, but he took his hat off, and the old
man saluted. Alfred liked to tell a story of some gentleman helping
the Duke across the road, being thanked, and bursting into assurances
that it was an honour he would be proud to tell his grandchildren
about. 'Don't make a damn fool of yourself,' said the Duke. Alfred's
poem was published in 10,000 copies at a shilling each, two days
before the funeral on the 18th, which he saw, though he did not see
the burial in the crypt of St Paul's, where Nelson already rested in a
tomb of Egyptian porphyry that had been confiscated from Cardinal
Wolsey and had sat around at Windsor until the battle of Trafalgar
created a use for it.

All the same, Alfred was not happy about the reception of his
poem. He offered to reimburse Moxon his £200 if he made a loss,
which he did not. After the funeral Alfred's family moved to Seaford,
to a house of Lord Howard de Walden's where the drains did not
smell, where there was a mild climate and a garden, and beyond that
a great bank of gravel with the sudden apparition of waves of a
startling size. There in the sea mist he went on fiddling about with

the Ode, and adding to it, until after Christmas. The second edition was three months after the first: the 10,000 copies of the first edition in its slate wrappers had sold out swiftly. Still, there is no doubt he was hurt by its not being critically acclaimed; he remembered this insult or grievance for the rest of his life. The hurt was a little assuaged by the popular enthusiasm for his 'Charge of the Light Brigade' in 1854, the second national poem he issued separately: all the same, he thought his Ode was better, and in this opinion he was surely right.

His relationship with his public as laureate is a complex subject. He was lionized in London, intolerably pestered with books of verse that made him howl with fury, and with demands for money, and later hounded out of the Isle of Wight in the end by the tourists, American as well as English. He had never willingly belonged to a salon; he had evaded Mrs Norton (Sheridan's daughter) and Lady Blessington and Mrs Cornwall (Mrs Procter), and even Lady Ashburton caught only a feather or two of his wing. He was a private poet at his best, and in the long process of its marginalization poetry itself had become a private occupation. Fitz became disgusted by Alfred's grandeur, having chosen himself to live in a cottage, in love with a fisherman; but Alfred's house needed to be a castle, and his wife used its routines to keep him going, to protect him.

Tennyson, Dickens and Kingsley all replied to the awful poems of Mr Realf, the eighteen-year-old son of a Sussex policeman, Dickens first on 3 March 1852: 'I have such a strong sense of the danger of making a bad and unhappy Poet out of a good and happy Something-else.' Kingsley replied on 21 June: 'great promise . . . but in these times such a youth has a sad outlook before him.' He should go to King's, London. 'Pray keep him from Australia . . . why is he to go and become a savage?' The Laureate answered on 9 August, awaiting Hallam's birth. He had long pondered what to say because he longed to encourage: 'There can scarce be a purer pleasure than to foster lowly genius . . . remarkable talent and thought.' But one could not judge from juvenilia, Mr Realf should get a job, 'if it be only mechanical it will be time enough to relinquish it when he has found some great theme that taxes all his time and all his powers.'[29] Realf went to America at twenty, became a journalist in Kansas, an abolitionist and a Civil War soldier. His health broke down and he committed suicide at forty-four.

They seem to have enjoyed Seaford, but it was not a permanent

home. Alfred was overpleased by any praise his Ode got, a letter
from Taylor moved him (Taylor would not notice hollowness). He
went to Shiplake to be a godfather. Emily had not Alfred's love of
Mablethorpe but she was impressed by 'great white-headed waves
leaping up every moment from behind the shingle-bank', though she
did not leave the garden, it was so stormy.[30] She read Hengstenberg's
Christology of the Old Testament, and a book by the Rev D. I. Heath,
The Future Human Kingdom of Christ (1853), which Peel of Bonchurch
sent her, and Dr Gregory on Mesmerism (1851). Heath was the
youngest of the Trinity Heaths, and Vicar of Brading (in the Isle of
Wight), of which living he was deprived later for unorthodoxy. It is
queer that no one has ever called her a blue-stocking; one notes that
she got on well with Mrs Browning and George Eliot, but she was
careful not to obtrude her opinions. At this time Alfred was thrilled
to have a cape named after him in the Arctic by Inglefield, later an
admiral and knighted, but alas it has never been indentified officially.
Fitz called: 'I admire the Baby greatly and sincerely: Alfred nurses
him with humour and majesty.'[31] He wrote this to Mrs Cowell, wife
of his orientalist friend, and urged Alfred to learn Persian as he was
doing, advice which was taken, though never fully carried out. A
woman trickster was discovered collecting money in Tennyson's
name. 'I am told she writes verses on pink paper.' She claimed to be
the elected matron of an emigrant ship; he wanted her thrown
overboard. He had fairly serious tooth trouble, but by mid-February
he was eating dinner with several new teeth. In April he tested a
house at Farnham, which he rejected, but he walked over to Hale to
see the Sellwood house, where Emily had been from 1848 to 1850:
she loved the Surrey hills and always hankered for them. In June he
wrote to Milnes that he was about to retire to utter solitude in some
country house when he found one. The numerous letters of business
and duty make it easy to see why.

At the end of July he got to Edinburgh, a journey he thought
Emily would not have stood, and so to Monteith in Lanarkshire.
Then it was Oban, Staffa and Iona: 'Thou canst not conceive the
stew and bore of this little hotel.' He called on Professor Sellar the
Latinist at Ardtornish on the Sound of Mull, the expeditions were
happy[32] and he improvised some jolly parodies which have been
preserved: 'If he did not see Loch Coruisk,/He ought to be forgiven,/
For though he missed a day in Skye,/He spent a day in Heaven' is
my favourite. He was loosening his limbs for some better effort

obviously, and sure enough when he got back to Edinburgh he wrote 'The Daisy'. He left to get there by boat, 9 miles of rowing to Oban, with F. T. Palgrave, and when Sellar told the Gaelic boatman he was carrying one of the greatest men in England, the boatman said, 'That blackavised Mr Tinsmith that came with Mr Pancake? well, well!' In Edinburgh he was ill and needed surgery, for an ingrowing toenail.[33]

In October he was in the Isle of Wight at Bonchurch, and that was where he heard of Farringford. He would have felt happy in the little terrace of houses at Bonchurch by the sea, were it not for poor Peel. He would have brought his mother too, but where she was the whole family tended to flock. In the end she was given the rest of the lease at Twickenham, and then a house in Hampstead where the aunt lived with her. Alfred thought Farringford rather wretched on first inspection, with its Downs and its wet, unswept dead leaves. His two Lincolnshire servants, when their turn came, burst into tears at the sight of it. The Rev G. T. Seymour (Eton and Oriel, 1792–1880) owned it, and in November Alfred and Emily were both in Plumbly's Hotel at Freshwater, a tiny place in those days, on the edge of making an agreement, the only rival being Lyme Regis, which at that time he never visited:[34] Farringford had enchanted them.

They took it for three years with an option to purchase. He contrived this by getting an advance of £600 from Moxon and £400 which he was already owed, and investing the £1000 in East Lincolnshire Railways. It was a lucky move, because the Crimean War was soon to bring a slump in the book trade, and his next year's royalties were only £500, but in January 1854 before war was declared Moxon promised him £2000 profit for an illustrated edition, which would buy the house outright. Meanwhile he had let himself be proposed after some dithering as Rector of Edinburgh University; he was relieved that he failed to be elected. He told them he was 'essentially not a public man in character'; that was true and he meant it. He would not even sign a protest when F. D. Maurice was flung out of King's, where he taught English, on the grounds that he did not believe in Hell. Admittedly he did better: he wrote him the third of his wonderful new lyrics, 'To the Rev. F. D. Maurice'.

The invitation to Maurice to come and stay at Farringford is another happy poem, and one of his most beautiful. In the poem to Lear and 'The Daisy' he has mastered his new stanza form; the little poem is truly Horatian, because it is based on the same deep need for

home that Horace felt, and the same sense of the earth and landscape;
it breathes the same affection. All three of these poems remarkably
convey personality. The poem to Maurice was dated January 1854, but
interestingly Maurice did not see it until 1855 when it was published:

> Where, if below the milky steep
> Some ship of battle slowly creep,
>   And on through zones of light and shadow
> Glimmer away to the lonely deep,
>
> We might discuss the Northern sin
> Which made a selfish war begin
>
> (25–30)

War was declared in March, though Tennyson had thought it
inevitable for some time, and the first noise that greeted them at
Farringford was gunnery practice. It may be that some deeper and
intangible process or public fit of mass hysteria brought about the
Crimean War. Richard Cobden and the radical John Bright attended
peace meetings, but Alfred despised them, though later he would not
accept he had criticized them or the Quakers in *Maud*. He really
longed to turn his mind to social improvement, as Maurice did in
founding his Working Men's College, and to speak of things 'Dear
to the man that is dear to God': in fact as a Christian socialist poem
his invitation to Maurice is hard to better, it seems more moving
than Clough's lucidity or Matthew Arnold's Rugby murk:

> Come, Maurice, come: the lawn as yet
> Is hoar with rime, or spongy-wet;
>   But when the wreath of March has blossomed,
> Crocus, anemone, violet,
>
> Or later, pay one visit here,
> For those are few we hold as dear;
>   Nor pay but one, but come for many,
> Many and many a happy year.
>
> (41–8)

With this light-looking poem I should mention another of the
early Farringford years, which has roots far back in time: it is a

Lincolnshire 'English idyl', called 'The Brook' where the blank verse, as charming and meaningless as ever and still under the old influence of Mary Russell Mitford, is effectively interspersed with brief patches of four-line stanzas:

> Till last by Philip's farm I flow
>   To join the brimming river,
> For men may come and men may go,
>   But I go on for ever.
>
>   (31–4)

It is nothing more than an enchanting piece; even the hint at seriousness in 'I go on for ever' disappears in the babble of the stream. It appears that Tennyson at this time was dependent on what metre chanced to possess him. The verses called 'Forlorn', for example, are a failure: they are an attempt at ballad rhythm of a kind that always eluded him. He loved fine ballads, recited them and quoted them effectively, but when he came to write ballads his own were usually melodramatic.

Farringford was a white house in the Gothic taste, pleasant but unpretentious, of no particular antiquity being built in 1808 and extended in 1810, and by no great architect: it was a villa not wholly unlike Somersby though with more capacity and more surrounding space. The Tennysons added to it cleverly enough, perhaps with Mirehouse in mind, but in this century it became a hotel, and since about 1980 has been transformed into a motor-oriented eyesore: the tourists from whom Alfred was a refugee have taken over. Yet for those with the hardihood to venture inside, there are rooms and fittings that recall the small scale of Alfred's life, parts of the garden are untouched, and the Downs and the sea are the same. Helen Allingham's watercolour of a border in the kitchen garden vividly conveys what it once was. W. G. Ward's house and Mrs Cameron's Dimbola (named after an Indian estate) are recognizable. The south-western corner of the island is still a fine place to be, and the creeping suburbia that now occupies the west coast and laps against Freshwater Bay is easily enough dreamed away. Alfred and Emily had an illiterate farmer called Merwood for neighbour, and a shepherd who lived to be ninety of whom they were very fond. Tennyson gave him for an epitaph 'The hand of God has touched him and he slept'. (He left seventeen shillings and sixpence to whoever was the poorest man in the parish, but nothing to his two sons in Australia.) Hallam arrived as a babe in arms, and Lionel was born there on 16 March 1854 on the eve of the war, Mars then culminating in the Lion, as observed during Lionel's birth by Alfred from the study downstairs: hence the boy's name. It is one omen among many of the military passion that took over England in the years from the death of Wellington and the coup of Louis Napoleon to the Indian Mutiny (1857–8) and later.

The Volunteers that Tennyson had been lustily yelling for, prodded by Coventry Patmore (whom Emily reprimanded for using the wicked word agitator), were formed in 1859, and in 1860 the rifle clubs met on Wimbledon Common: the Queen fired the first shot. Some lady gave Hallam and Lionel Volunteer hats and epaulettes, and Alfred had them drilled by a real soldier. Emily set the awful songs 'Riflemen Form!' and 'Hands All Round!' to her own music, and presumably played them on the piano to her children. Certainly when Alfred read her Campbell's patriotic verses she was thrilled and determined her children should learn them. When Henry Lushington died in August 1855 in Paris, where Venables met him on the way home but his brother Franklin arrived too late, a slim, sad volume of a few poems was published with an added poem by Franklin and a memoir by Venables: the atmosphere of these poems, of which there is a copy in the London Library, is one of blood-stained militarism and deep gloom, yet the authors can never have heard an angry gunshot. The most memorable poem, 'The Guards are going to the War', is the literary equivalent of the Crimean monument in Lower Regent Street, and like it has an exquisite precision of detail, and yet a certain tragic quality not perhaps intended. The Guards in fact went before the war had officially started. Whenever little Hallam fell over in 1855, he said 'This is how the Russians fall down dead.'

I cannot pretend to be a historian of the Crimean War, but it is fascinating how much of it is now forgotten, and how for most of us it is completely overshadowed by the charge of the Light Brigade, which in reality was a disaster, an abominably wasteful military action on a fortunately small scale.[35] The folly and arrogance and teak-like wooden-headedness of which it was a consequence defy analysis. Lord Cardigan was just too young for Waterloo; he bought his regiment for £25,000 or £30,000 and spent a further £10,000 on its appearance: his income was £40,000 a year. Tennyson's background information for his poem was slightly incorrect; it came from a report in *The Times*, but the important thing about the catastrophic charge as a subject for poetry is that melodrama was its essence, so here at last he wrote a successful ballad.[36] If it is based on anything it is based on Drayton's Agincourt ballad or on Chatterton: the form is an ancient ballad form, perhaps Irish, but the dactyls may in this case derive from Virgil's cavalry verses. Tennyson wrote a poem that was stirring for a hundred years, and has indelibly influenced what we think of the Crimean War. Copies were rushed out to be distributed to the troops, and suddenly, overnight England had a national poet. As usual he went on worrying over details, and he was displeased that it was so well received compared to his 'Ode'. Nearly forty years afterwards at his funeral in Westminster Abbey, the aisle was lined by survivors of Balaclava and representatives of the Gordon Boys' Homes, a charity that he took up.

It was in 1854 that he was working on *Maud*, which he finished by April 1855. He put his last touches to it in the summer and published the same year. *Maud* has been called a monodrama (from 1875 onwards, this meant something like a play though not for the stage and all in one person's voice). The madness, the duel, the overwhelming kinsmen, the love lyrics and even the variation of metre go back to *The Princess*. The new poem, 171 pages of the Ricks edition, arose by extension from 'Oh! that 'twere possible', an enigmatic lyric written in 1834 and rapidly finished off for Milnes to publish in 1837. Sir John Simeon, a neighbour in the Isle of Wight who was a very close friend, almost a second father, begged Alfred to expand it. Tennyson told Aubrey de Vere that the process of expansion was a backwards process. The 'mad scene' was written in twenty minutes. 'See what a lovely shell' was a stray lyric from the 1830s, and 'Go not, happy day' was a song first intended for *The Princess*. Its original title was to have been *Maud or the Madness*. Financially it was a huge success, the first edition of 10,000 copies sold out within a year, though Alfred was displeased with its reception. The denigration of it as a pro-war or anti-war tract was ridiculous and has become uninteresting. The metrical novelty is no longer exciting and one may feel nostalgia for the old iambics, but *Maud* is a powerfully impressive poem. It is a melodrama only in the sense in which Hardy is all melodrama; the only criticism to which it is really vulnerable is that offered by Lady Ormonde to Franklin

Lushington and repeated to Edward Lear: 'Life is not like that!' It enabled Tennyson to buy Farringford. The estate had been offered at £4350 in 1853 but by 1856 it cost £6900.

Maud is a disturbed and a disturbing story, written apparently in the utmost domestic tranquillity. His eyes hurt after reading Persian; indeed it turned out his wife had hidden his Persian books. He negotiated for an illustrated edition to be done by Millais and others. He entertained constantly, but little of the burden of doing it fell on him: his household had settled into being a well-oiled machine. The servants quarrelled but it is scarcely worth noticing, because the life of the small family sailed on its majestic way like some great ship, while he read Theocritus and Shakespeare and Dante and Homer aloud to his wife. They all went out in small boats and on picnics with a donkey and away on minor summer tours. Aubrey de Vere was now a Catholic like Sir John Simeon, but they still got on together: even Emily minded less than she expected to. He sat to Milner and read Poe and met Ruskin; and Temple, the head of Kneller Hall and future archbishop, got him an honorary degree at Oxford with the help of Jowett, not yet Master of Balliol. He was applauded, he smoked in the Master's garden at Balliol, chatted with Gladstone and Montalembert, and observed stars through a tele-scope. In August when *Maud* was in the press, Henry Lushington died.

Patmore hated *Maud*, the Liberal Party hated it, Gladstone and George Eliot disapproved, people could not understand it, and Browning, to whose work of course it has similarities, thought it a great poem. Alfred read it aloud indefatigably and victoriously wherever he got the chance. Journalists said it should be called Mad or Mud; they said, 'If an author pipe of adultery, fornication, murder or suicide, set him down as the practiser of those crimes.' It was no use then, and has been less use since, for Tennyson to declare that poetry was not autobiography, and his poems were not a *catalogue raisonné* of his inner self. *Maud* was, as he said it was, 'a little Hamlet'; it was 'a drama where successive phases of passion in one person take the place of successive passions'; it was 'a drama of the soul'.

It is a passionate work that reads extremely well aloud, and might have opened the way towards modern 'confessional' poetry, but it is not itself confessional. The changes in later editions are small but to the good, and make the work as a whole more clearly logical, though I regret his suppression of a phrase in the penultimate verse, 'the long, long canker of peace,' which is Shakespearean, in view of anti-militarist criticism:[37] 'peace, that I deemed no peace' is a dull substitute. *Maud* must be judged as 'a new form of dramatic composition': it had some wonderful moments but I do not think it is a masterpiece in the same sense as 'Morte d'Arthur'; and *Maud*, being more clearly organized yet just as uneven, is not as great or as valuable as *In Memoriam*. Yet it has not lost its experimental vigour. 'I took a man constitutionally diseased and dipt him into the circumstances of the time and took him out on fire.' Nothing by Smith or Dobell, the Spasmodics, and nothing in verse in the whole nineteenth century is so powerfully embittered as *Maud*. Yet it has lines of extraordinary beauty, rhythms that are unforgettable, and adjustments that are perfect, like 'the shining daffodil dies' instead of 'the sweet Narcissus dies'[38] towards the end of the poem (also at the end of section III: 'The shining daffodil dead, and Orion low in his grave').

It can be said of *In Memoriam* that one may open it anywhere, and of *The Princess* that one forgets the plot, but the power of *Maud* is cumulative. It begins its 113 small Moxon pages 'by Alfred Tennyson DCL' with no dedication, with several pages of furious invective about the state of England and the narrator's father's suicide. But Maud is coming home and she may give him peace, because as children they played on equal terms. Not a hope of course; her family intervene. He broods gloomily on evolution: 'A monstrous eft was of old the Lord and Master'; now man 'is first, but is he the last? is he not too base?' He considers the vanity and poverty of spirit of scientists (Billy Whistle?) and the vice and folly of poets, and worst of all the madness of lovers.

Maud is Tennyson's *Timon of Athens*, and even Maud herself is not spared. All the same she enchants him and weaves more and more of her presence into his gloom. He sees her in church, she waves to him on the shore. Metrically the poem is brilliantly excited. Even the jackdaws call 'Maud, Maud, Maud'. The brother is traced with careful, well-observed contempt, such as Tennyson felt, when he was with Moxon, for the two snobs on the Rhine who smelt of scented soap. The garden is well drawn at the climax of seduction (it is not the garden at Harrington Hall, which was made later). The middle part of the poem hums with happiness, but the excitement ends in a duel. There is 'A grand political dinner/To the men of many acres,/A gathering of the Tory/ . . . I am not invited'. The

end of part I is 'Come into the garden, Maud'. Turn one page, and
the duel is over, the poet has killed the girl's brother, and in the last
thirty pages Tennyson, or rather his character, draws morals and
broods over consequences.

> No more shall commerce be all in all, and Peace
> Pipe on her pastral hillock a languid note,
> And watch her harvest ripen, her herd increase,
> Nor the cannon-bullet rust on a slothful shore,
> And the cobweb woven across the cannon's throat
> Shall shake its threaded tears in the wind no more.
>
> (III, 23–8)

There is something in common between Tennyson's thoughts here
and Tolstoy's *Sevastopol Stories*, which made his name at this time: it
is a pity no one noticed, but then God knows what English critics of
the 1850s would have made of Tolstoy. Turgenev was a hero in
London literary circles, but he was easier, and Tolstoy soon longed
'to kick his fat plebeian bum' (something that Thackeray might have
written of Dickens in some unrestrained moment). Tennyson's *Maud*
ends with resigned acceptance of the war:

> I have felt with my native land, I am one with my kind,
> I embrace the purpose of God, and the doom assigned.
>
> (III, 58–9)

In this poem there is a huge release of sexuality, a very full and
fully sexual expression of love, which as a younger and unmarried
man Tennyson could not have written (there he differs from Tolstoy). Later in life, he often said that *Maud* and 'Guinevere', which
he loved to read aloud, were his best works: they are both about
sexual crisis. Gladstone used to read 'Guinevere' to his wicked ladies
to convert them before he sent them off to repent at Clewer, across
the river from Eton. In order to write *Maud*, Tennyson is said to
have interrupted 'Merlin and Vivien', which is a clear study in the
old bard's deliberate seduction.[39]

Tennyson now turned slowly but more or less whole-heartedly
to composing the great epic poem he had kept it in mind to write for
many years, which Sterling's casual remarks over the 1842 *Poems* had
interrupted. It was often interrupted, and its plan was often modified

as we shall see, but for some thirty years of his life, from the age of forty-six in 1855 to 'Balin and Balan', the twelfth book in 1885 when he was seventy-six, the epic of King Arthur in twelve books was usually his principal concern. Other poems continued to flow, with their quality much the same as usual. They had their ups and downs, and they may not have altered our picture of Tennyson except in making him voluminous, but they were never negligible.

Meanwhile, his social and his domestic life took the course that any retiring man of letters, and any distinguished Victorian would have traced. It will be best to deal with the epic as a single work, compressing the thirty years into a chapter. The *Idylls of the King*, as he called them in the end, are sufficiently one thing to call for a single treatment; they are in some or most ways oddly independent of his life.

He had set out in *Maud* his strong views about the world. He published it in 1855 with 'The Brook', the 'Ode on the Death of the Duke of Wellington', the lines 'To the Rev. F. D. Maurice', 'The Daisy', 'The Charge of the Light Brigade', and a short stern couple of stanzas called 'Will'. All these poems together are his work as laureate, most of them are subversive of conventional views: of social life, of government, of theology and of the army. When he was persuaded to remove 'someone had blundered', from 'The Charge of the Light Brigade', he became extremely anxious to put it in again. Even in the 'Ode', his nationalism is not complacent; but he does set out with an alarming clarity in section VII what he considers the vocation of the English to be:

> That sober freedom out of which there springs
> Our loyal passion for our temperate kings;
> For, saving that, ye help to save mankind
> Till public wrong be crumbled into dust,
> And drill the raw world for the march of mind
>
> (VII, 164–8)

These lines are opposed to revolution, but make no concession to aristocracy. They strangely mingle the title of a Gillray cartoon of George III eating a boiled egg, 'a temperate breakfast', with the younger Pitt on England saving herself by her exertions and Europe by her example. As for the march of mind 'Till crowds at length be sane and crowns be just', that must surely be the ideal of Alfred's own generation, and so also, in the person of explorers like Burton, is the idea that the whole world is raw and must be drilled. *Maud* is an inflammatory collection of poems.

Before we leave the subject, consider an evening in the September after *Maud* was published. Alfred spent five or six evenings in London, two of them with the Brownings since Mrs Browning was unable to travel to Farringford. They had rented a house off Manchester Square, and William and D. G. Rossetti came in after dinner. They were fans, but distinctly quizzical ones. Tennyson drank two bottles of port and told his sorrows about the neglect of him before 1842, and the wheedling letters he had to answer now; indeed he told his stories more than once. 'If I had a heart to spare, certainly he would have won mine,' wrote Mrs Browning afterwards. 'He is captivating with his frankness, confidingness and unexampled *naïveté*.' She asked him to read *Maud*. He sat on a sofa and did so, in his Lincolnshire accent, in his organ-notes of a voice (this can be heard in a recording of the poem Tennyson made as an old man), with the tears trickling down his cheeks, Rossetti drew him secretly as he read. William thought 'his grand, deep voice swayed onward with a long drawn chaunt'; Browning then read 'Fra Lippo Lippi', in something more like an actor's style. It is true about the chanting Lincolnshire organ-notes. 'Tennyson was strong, and aimed to be strong.' They broke up at two thirty in the morning and Alfred walked home with D. G. Rossetti. 'What is that place?' he asked as he saw the cabs outside the Holborn Casino. He would have gone in, too, were it not that he feared being noticed by some journalist. They seem to have parted at his doorway.

CHAPTER EIGHT

Idylls of the King

WITH THE *Idylls of the King*, Tennyson becomes dangerously easy to mock, but they were his lifework in a way, though in another way only as he said 'my hobby'. Not counting the prologue, there are 10,166 lines of blank verse (with a very few songs), woven more or less seamlessly from end to end, like knitting, with few heights and no depths, in twelve books because Virgil had twelve in the *Aeneid*. He began in 1832 with what now appears a stray offshoot, 'The Lady of Shalott', and within the next year or two he left at least two stray sets of prose notes on how to treat the entire epic.[1] At some point he composed a Lancelot idyll in his head but then forgot it. His most serious move towards the complete work was 'Morte d'Arthur' (1842), and if at that time he had plunged into the whole huge undertaking, it is probable we might have been hailing him to this day as Virgil's equal or eminent superior: but Sterling's review in 1843 had stopped him in his tracks with a stray sentence. But his mind was merely wandering over the subject, because some time before 1840 he had made a new plan of the whole thing as a kind of masque or operatic oratorio in five acts.[2]

The first of these is set at the court of Mordred, it includes his 'cringing interview with Guinevere' and his meeting the Lady of the Lake. In the second act the Lady of the Lake meets Arthur and tries to persuade him not to fight Mordred. 'Lamentation of the Lady of the Lake . . . Marriage of Arthur.' The third act opens at the oak tree where Merlin is entombed. This act is full of incident, with Nimuë (who in our version is called Vivien) exercising her wiles, Merlin prophesying from his tomb, and 'Guinevere throws away the diamonds into the river.' In the fourth act Lancelot and Guinevere are discovered, and Arthur and Guinevere meet and part. These last two acts are a little sketchy. The fifth is 'The battle. Chorus of the Ladies of the Lake. The throwing away of Excalibur and departure of Arthur.' It is all very like Wagner, though before 1840 too early to be influenced by him. Still, the same themes mostly persist in the prolonged blank verse books that we have. In 1848, in November, Fitz reported in a letter, 'Not but he meditates new poems, and now *The Princess* is done he returns to King Arthur – a worthy subject indeed – and has consulted some histories of him, and spent some time in visiting his traditionary haunts in Cornwall.' Later Mrs Patmore, who had copied *In Memoriam* for the press, did some devilling for Alfred in the British Museum.

That is the end of the first phase. We know his head was then full of stray lines and rhythms, which are often more effective as verse than the material that comes to surround them. The sea–cave lines composed in Ireland in 1848 are one example,[3] and the lines he brought his wife as a birthday present in 1857 are another:

> But hither shall I never come again,
> Never lie by thy side, see thee no more
>
> (575–6)

But the second phase begins with setting a final shape for the enterprise. This does not survive in prose, but there is no doubt that Tennyson had worked it out fully.[4] The subject haunted him for a long time. In 1854 he wrote to Bodham Donne at the London Library, for books for his wife. 'She thinks I can write about the old King. I don't think books can help me to it, nevertheless oblige her.' He relied rather on landscape and the small nuggets of experience it provided. Still, it would seem that by 1855 he had a scheme. He wrote 'Merlin and Vivien' and 'Geraint and Enid', partly in Wales, and by 1856 he had finished the first of these: but a letter of Emily Tennyson in April 1856 confirms one's suspicions: ' "Merlin" is all written down, quite finished I think, but not much else done. He troubles himself that the *Idylls* do not form themselves into a whole in his mind, and moreover that the subject has not reality enough.' We know from a private letter that Jowett, as good a critic as he ever had, felt the same doubts. It is again important to notice that with Tennyson the process of composition had already taken place before he wrote down his poems. The last minute dithering and polishing was only the visible continuation of a process that had been going on in his head.

It is true that the idylls did not form themselves into a whole, and that is one of their deepest faults. They are episodic, they could be rearranged, they were composed in no particular order. Still, in 1857 the new volume was set up as 'Enid and Nimuë: the True and the False'. The British Library has a copy of this proof or trial edition with Tennyson's corrections in it. F. T. Palgrave added a note that Tennyson had meant to publish these two idylls on their own. Six copies were printed, but when a remark about 'Nimuë' was repeated to him, he recalled them, letting only F. T. Palgrave keep his copy. One can understand that after the hypocritical and ridiculous fuss there had been over *Maud*, he was particularly sensitive. In June he wrote to Lady Argyll about 'a man, a friend it was said, to whom I read or showed the Nimuë, who in lieu of giving his opinion honestly at the moment, appears to have gone brawling about town, saying that such a poem would corrupt the young.' In 1858 he wrote to his American publishers to assure them he was not writing an epic poem about Arthur: 'I should be crazed to attempt such a thing in the heart of the nineteenth century.' But in spring 1859 he had four idylls ready to publish. It was not that he hoped 'Nimuë' might escape notice in the crowd, but that the other idylls might be contrasted with her and set her in context. He wrote to Lady Argyll: 'I could be well content to be silent for ever: however the Poems – there are four of them (Your Grace has already heard two) are finished and, for want of a better name, to be called *The King's Idylls*.'

The person who was rude about 'Nimuë', or more likely made a joke of her wickedness, was apparently Richard Monckton Milnes. He liked the clash of social opposites and had a stronger appetite for the ranker side of life than Alfred Tennyson, whom he both esteemed and enjoyed teasing. He once said calmly to the laureate at dinner that he possessed autograph manuscripts of 'a number of your earliest unpublished poems' and that when Tennyson died he would print them. The threat was real. Jackson of Louth secured blackmail of £1000 from the poet by threatening to reprint his first book. They have never been found; as a great collector Milnes would hardly have destroyed them, so it was probably just a tease. Tennyson said 'You beast!' half humorously, half furiously. All the same their friendship did survive these affronts, as did Milnes's general popularity in society. When Alfred took his seat in the Lords, Richard Monckton Milnes as Lord Houghton was one of the two peers who ceremonially introduced him to the House.

The four poems in the 1859 *Idylls* were entitled 'Enid', 'Vivien',

'Elaine' and 'Guinevere'; 'Vivien' is 'Nimuë', and in the 1869 *Idylls of the King* has its fuller title of 'Merlin and Vivien'; it appeared in 1859 flanked by 'Enid' and 'Elaine', deliberately harmless tales, with 'Guinevere' as the climax. Those who find the high-minded chivalry of all the twelve books insufferable may therefore reasonably complain that it was Tennyson's extreme reaction to Monckton Milnes that set him off on the wrong foot. My copy of 1859 contains advertisements for other Moxon books also, including the works of Wordsworth in six volumes, the works of Shelley in three, and the poetical works of Milnes in four volumes.

'Enid' was disproportionately the largest of the four, so Tennyson eventually cut it in two, calling the whole thing 'Geraint and Enid' in the 1870 ('1869') edition, and splitting it in 1873. The two parts took their titles 'The Marriage of Geraint' and 'Geraint and Enid' only in 1886. Hallam Tennyson tells us 'Enid' was begun on 16 April 1856, and the end of what is now 'Geraint and Enid' was written in July and August of that year in Wales. Alfred's chief source was Lady Charlotte Guest's *Mabinogion*. The point of it all[5] was supposed to be that 'The sin of Lancelot and Guinevere began to breed . . . despair and want of trust in God or man.' I am not clear all the same that the text conveys anything more than unexplained bad temper and jealousy. However that may be, 'Geraint' could not be quite the first episode, and Tennyson always felt its two parts must be separated still further from 'Vivien'. And he felt the need to archaize his text of 1859, to make it less immediate, more dignified and fabulous. That is the end of what I call the second phase.

The third phase began like the others with years of uncertainty. He told Allingham in 1867 the original scheme aborted by Sterling had been that 'the King is the complete man, the Knights are the passions.' It is hard to see which of the Knights would be which, and the allegory is jejune. He told Knowles that at twenty-four, in 1833, he had intended to take twenty years writing it. But in 1862 what he was dithering about was 'fear of failure and time lost'. He could not decide between his 'ghostlike passing away of the King' in 'Guinevere', and 'Morte d'Arthur', which was a natural ending. The Duke of Argyll said the Princess Royal was anxious for him to use his old 'Morte d'Arthur', but he was disinclined. 'Morte d'Arthur' was older in style. He thought about the matter, he arranged the order of all the other idylls (does he not mean rearranged in 1862?) but he still dared not undertake it. But the Duke of Argyll insisted, and Alfred was in the end persuaded. In 1869 he published the expanded 'The Passing of Arthur', with a note that it was 'here connected with the rest in accordance with an early project of the author's'. In 1868 his idea was simply to write 'three or four more and link them as well as I may'. Yet in 1869 he was ready to publish four more poems, rather carefully conceived with a view to linking. The series began with 'The Coming of Arthur' and ending with 'The Passing', and contained 'The Holy Grail', and after that 'Pelleas and Ettare'. These two are both about the break-up of the Round Table: Arthur loses a lot of Knights who wander off in search of the Grail, which he describes with unfortunate clarity, and the rest of the Knights quarrel. The Grail was 'rose-red/With rosy beatings in it, as if alive' and in Lancelot's vision, 'All pall'd in crimson samite, and around/Great angels, awful shapes, and wings and eyes.' Yet the moral, that one ought to get on with ruling the earth (or British Empire) and not be distracted by mysticism, is one that would have appealed to Kipling: one may compare his treatment of the Lama's quest in *Kim*.

The Grail may be hogwash or not; it may possibly suffer from uncertainty of view about the Christian Eucharist, but it is essentially a subject of romance not of epic, though I take both tendencies to be present in the Arthurian legends, and as Alfred Tennyson, under pressure from the royal family, interprets the cycle at the age of sixty, it has a subsidiary position in the story. He seems to have accepted an expanded 'Morte d'Arthur' for his climax, without realizing the crucial importance of the defeat and burial of Hector in the *Iliad*, and the death of Turnus in the *Aeneid*, which is a botched imitation of Homer. Epic poetry belongs essentially to the dead and the defeated: one cannot understand epic poetry without seeing that, and few or no critics in Tennyson's time had really understood it. Arnold in 'Sohrab and Rustum', and in 'Balder Dead', was on the right track, though his passion for resolution in beauty, even in the wonderful image of the Oxus at the end of 'Sohrab', was infected with sentimentality. But Tennyson in 'The Passing of Arthur' ends not at once with the moral colours of 'Morte d'Arthur' but with a further set of pretty diminuendo passages:

> Then from the dawn it seemed there came, but faint
> As from beyond the limit of the world,
> Like the last echo born of a great cry,
> Sounds, as if some fair city were one voice

> Around a king returning from his wars.
>
> (457–61)

In fact all the trumpets sounded for him on the other side, 'And the new sun rose bringing the new year.' Beautiful as that line is, it does not grip and convince as immediately as the end of Guinevere had done, 'To where beyond these voices there is peace' which he had sensed to be the right ending for his romance. For his epic, if it had really been one, the best ending had been written long ago in 'Morte d'Arthur': 'And on the mere the wailing died away.'

These four poems, making eight, were all shorter than usual, and they were not thought long enough by the laureate, or by the new publisher Strahan, for a separate book. They are 158 pages, and shorter poems, which as usual he was still writing, made up 66 more. For once he was pleased with the critics, though they appear to have indulged in amazing allegoric interpretations and a luxuriating search for deeper, secret Christian meanings. 'They have taken my hobby and ridden it too hard,' he said. To the Bishop of Ripon, who enquired whether the three Queens meant Faith, Hope and Charity, he said he hated being tied down to *this* means *that*. Wittgenstein says somewhere the commonest philosophical error is to say *this* is only *that*, and the same may probably be said of criticism. Tennyson thought poetry was 'like shot-silk with many glancing colours'. When he was eighty all the same he came out with, 'My meaning was spiritual . . . I intended Arthur to represent the Ideal Soul of Man coming into contact with the warring elements of the flesh.' This tendency to be spiritual appears to have increased over the years in which he wrote the poem. The last correction he made was to his epilogue in 1891, when he added the line, 'Ideal manhood closed in real man,' to what had been a vaguer but perhaps a more moving conception:

> Rather than that gray king, whose name, a ghost,
> Streams like a cloud, man-shaped, from mountain peak,
> And cleaves to cairn and cromlech[6]

He felt he had written a tale 'shadowing Sense at war with Soul'; indeed his 'Epilogue, To the Queen' in these ten lines or so is quite coherent and consonant with his other beliefs and preoccupations. He offers it to the Queen for the sake of Prince Albert, to whom he had dedicated it at the Prince's death in a prologue; he says its meaning is the few lines I have quoted, 'Sense at war with Soul/ Rather than that gray king' or Geoffrey of Monmouth's or Mallory's Arthur,

> Touched by the adulterous finger of a time
> That hovered between war and wantonness,
> And crownings and dethronements
>
> (43-5)

He then lists the enemies of the state, in a remarkable and amusing effusion of the port and prejudice of age, including 'Labour, with a groan and not a voice,/Or Art, with poisonous honey stolen from France.' It is of course probable that he disapproved of Arthur's incest, to which the industrious mole Furnivall had drawn public attention in 1864. He certainly disapproved of William Rossetti, not only for his admittedly ghastly illustrations to the 'Illustrated Edition' of 1857[7] (Rossetti sulked for a lifetime), but because he felt that Rossetti's gang had corrupted 'that puny boy' Swinburne. By that I take it he meant not the strange but charming Balliol youth of twenty whom he saw and liked at Farringford, but the boy he must have known at least by sight on his numerous visits to Bonchurch where Swinburne lived. The other obvious source of his idea of 'poisonous honey stolen from France' is of course Monckton Milnes, who owned a fine collection of French pornography.

In 1871 he produced 'The Last Tournament', another piece of the jigsaw of the break-up of the Round Table, a bit longer than anything he had written recently, and then in 1872 'Gareth and Lynette' to go with it, an episode of enormous size, 1390 lines. He told his wife with a laugh that it was 'a pattern youth for his boys' in 1869 when they were in their teens. He set it aside for a time, finding it more difficult to deal with than anything that he had ever written, except 'Aylmer's Field'; he hated having to write 'He said', 'She said', or their equivalent. Without this story the golden age of the Round Table would have gone unrepresented. But he was still concerned to take the pressure off the sexual motive of his chosen subject: with disastrous results I fear. With the publication of these two episodes, this third and all but final phase of composition was over, but the need for one more episode, making twelve, still lay at the back of his mind, and thirteen years later, at the age of seventy-four, in 1885, he

produced 'Balin and Balan', 620 lines which he fitted in before
'Merlin and Vivien'. But he had apparently composed it in 1872–4,
so it is really a concluding part of the third phase, and not an
afterthought.

The complete edition of the *Idylls of the King* first appeared in
1889 and was twice reprinted (in 1891 and 1892) before the poet's
death. Macmillan produced it, in an only slightly grander form than
all the other pocket-sized, green-bound volumes.[8] It was illustrated
with a fine engraving of what looks like an early fourth-century BC
white marble goddess, but it is Guinevere by Woolner. The 421
pages of verse are distinctly easy to read; no other English poet is so
readable at comparable length, not even Wordsworth, certainly not
Pope or Milton or Auden, no one at least since Shakespeare or before
him Chaucer, whom Tennyson read intensely at a crucial stage of
composition. If the style seems today a little yellow at the edges, like
a minor Latin poet, the *Idylls* remain all the same an extraordinary
tour de force, because he invented them and sustained them so well
that they never fall to a disastrous level. What lets them down if
anything is the occasional touch of bad taste in the visual arts: there
the taste is always contemporary, it is just what was popular in its
day, and Tennyson's intense realism magnifies it. The moral of
course is absurd, or at least remote from us, and the fundamental
scheme does not work. And yet a certain formidable and beautiful
presence does brood over the entire work, it comes and goes like a
marsh-light.

This is the place to deal with a most interesting controversy. As
he grew older, Tennyson became more certain and more crotchety
about classical metre. He believed he knew the classical length or
sound value of every English word except possibly the word scissors.
It follows that he thought length and shortness were fixed and
immutable in English. He made experiments in classical metres in
English which he thought critics failed to notice. He disapproved
though of any attempt at the classical hexameter in English verse,
and he clashed with Matthew Arnold over the translation of Homer.
Arnold had viciously attacked *Maud*, but that was the only time he
made a public onslaught on the laureate, with whom all the same he
spent much of his career as a poet secretly wrestling. In his lectures
on Homeric translation there were some covert digs at Tennyson's
idea of an epic style, and one open attack. In his 'Specimen of a
Translation of the Iliad in Blank Verse', in December 1863 in the

Cornhill, and in his 'Achilles Over the Trench', which he wrote at the same time but published later (*Nineteenth Century*, August 1877),[9] Tennyson dealt with Arnold in a devastating way, but without ever mentioning his name.

Arnold had said in 1861, 'If blank verse is used in translating Homer . . . it must not be Mr Tennyson's blank verse,' and in 1862 he defended this unnecessary piece of impudence. In doing so, he made the mistake of offering his own version of the end of the eighth book of the *Iliad*.[10] If I may be autobiographical, I recollect as an undergraduate putting Homer into sub-Tennysonian blank verse, because I then thought that was the best English had to offer, but my failure was so abject that I came to think Arnold might be right about blank verse, at least were it not for his own hexameter version, and had I not, years later in time, come upon these brilliant versions of Tennyson's. I had not realized however that Arnold's comparatively innocent-looking hexameters mask his appalling errors in the length and shortness of English syllables. He scans by beat, so he can read 'white' as a short syllable, ending a verse 'champed the white barley', though he can begin a line 'Between that and the ships', pulling a long syllable from somewhere up his sleeve. But the appalling error is his habit in three or four lines of scanning the word 'fire' as two syllables. If the reader does not believe me, let him consult Arnold's 'Tristan and Isolde', where I have observed the same singular habit.

That removed Arnold's positive argument from serious consideration, and to be fair in his 1862 *Last Words* he says we were not meant to take those verses seriously. There had been a scream of outrage from Mr Newman, whom he also attacked, but silence from Tennyson. Tennyson's immediate reply came from Spedding, and Arnold dealt with that by a more general attack,[11] in which he showed Tennyson was not Homer's equivalent (how could he be, and who had said he was?) and made clear his preference for Wordsworth's 'Michael' over Tennyson's 'Dora'. He could not have known at that time that Wordsworth had told Tennyson he had been trying all his life to write a poem like 'Dora' but without success. But I do not wish to stray far from the question of epic verse. Tennyson made in the end the only effective reply that could be made: he produced 22 lines and later another 31 of the *Iliad* in his own iambics, and they annihilate every other translation ever made of these lines. Arnold had quoted some weak and many un-Homeric lines of Tennyson for attack, and two or three in bad taste (for visual reasons as usual), but these he could scarcely fault: they are the proof that Tennyson was technically fit to write epic poetry.

> and heaped
> Their firewood, and the winds from off the plain
> Rolled the rich vapour far into the heaven.
> And these all night upon the bridge of war
> Sat glorying; many a fire before them blazed:
> As when in heaven the stars . . .
>
> ('Specimen of a Translation', 6–11)

Matthew Arnold's addiction to paradox, and perhaps his undergraduate audience, had put him into a false position, because after all his own iambics in 'Sohrab' at least stand up very well to Tennyson's, had he relied on those. We should be grateful to him that he drew from the laureate these verses, which burn like the clear fires they describe. Of his last two lines for 'Specimen of a Translation', Tennyson offered four different versions. The earliest was:

> And champing golden grain, their horses stood
> Hard by the chariots, waiting for the dawn.

In the end, he decided on:

> And eating hoary grain and pulse the steeds,
> Fixt by their cars, waited the golden dawn.

The volume of the *Idylls* that appeared in 1889 is discernibly by the same hand, with the same technical mastery but without the *Iliad* for a guide. The prologue is in the form of a 'Dedication',

> These to His Memory – since he held them dear,
> Perchance as finding there unconsciously
> Some image of himself

Prince Albert had died on 14 December 1861, and the 53 lines were soon written: Tennyson sent them to the Queen in early January 1862. By this time he was on friendly terms with her and of course he had known Prince Albert, who had been just as kind to him and as informal in real life as he had been in the dream in 1850. The verses are private really, and within a month he began to squirm about them. The Argylls smoothed him a little, but to everyone's surprise the news from Spedding and from Alfred's friends was that they were all secretly moved by them, and had not at first dared to confess it. They do not add to the *Idylls* anything but a touch of pomp and pathos, but they contain one at least of the poet's vivid, one might almost say Betjemaniac images: the Prince Consort passed 'through all this tract of years/Wearing the white flower of a blameless life', a line that Arnold might justly have complained is by no means Homeric.

Reading the poems in the order in which they finally came to rest turns out less, not more confusing than attempting to spot development in the order in which they were written. The most remarkable thing about them is their coherence. 'The Coming of Arthur' has a deliberate, archaic ring, but a brisk tone. Guinevere, Leodogran's only daughter, is installed as heroine in the first four lines: the gesture of a romance, not of an epic. She was born in Brecknockshire, which like the whole Welsh border country is thickly covered in ruined castles that might well suggest to Alfred the chaos before Arthur came. It was 'thick with wet woods' and wild beasts rooted in the fields. Arthur was already a crowned king, and arrived there to bring help, while Guinevere watched him (like Helen) from the walls. When he went to his first battle, 'the world/ Was all so clear about him that he saw/The smallest rock far on the faintest hill'. There follow thunders, lightnings, and a fine list of the dead, with resounding names from a variety of sources. It is not the battles but the duels in these stories that are in some way ridiculous. Arthur's birth, his Round Table, and the gift of Excalibur occur only in brief summary of the past, though the fatal attraction of Victorian visual effects crops up with the Lady of the Lake: 'a mist/Of incense curled about her, and her face/Wellnigh was hidden in the minster gloom.' She dwells in the deep and walks on the waters, and she has 'a voice as of the waters'. Indeed the mysteries become more unlikely as the book goes on, and Merlin's riddle is preposterously dotty: better the device of the *Iliad* in which Athene reveals her mysterious nature by transforming into a bird and the prophecies are gruesome and enigmatic. Still, if it read fast the first book is a charming piece of nonsense.

Serious action begins with 'Gareth and Lynette', and at once one of the fundamental faults of the whole work is revealed, because the

focus is off Arthur, who has been too much surrounded by magic
and mystery to have any particular character so far: only in 'Guinevere' will he come to life. In the first 142 lines, which are not to be
found in Malory's story, Gareth is trying to get away from his
mother: a suitable subject for Victorian concern, but not one that
much preoccupies Homer or Virgil. The weather is good (180–8)
and the gate of Camelot is spectacular:

> For barefoot on the keystone, which was lined
> And rippled like an ever-fleeting wave,
> The Lady of the Lake stood: all her dress
> Wept from her sides as water flowing away
>
> (210–13)

The later part of this description is ridiculous: her arms upheld the
cornice, she held a censer and a sword, and 'o'er her breast floated
the sacred fish', but the first few lines seem to be pure Greek. Gareth
meets Merlin, then Arthur, and the first stirrings of the break-up are
heard (376–410). Gareth serves in the kitchen, but merit will rise,
and at last, after nearly 600 lines, we meet Lynette. He puts on his
armour, in which he appears like a flying beetle in beautiful colours
under a dark wing-case; but Tennyson is too obviously fascinated by
the chivalric paraphernalia. Still, the adventure story is well told. It
is loud with lyric feelings, and a song that was rightly rejected has
left traces which work far better. Every so often the long poem is
lightened by details one had no right to expect, such as the Roman
inscription on the river Gelt (1172–5), and one ends reading it
grateful for its pleasures and not displeased with its tedium or
unreality.

'The Marriage of Geraint' is 849 lines, as opposed to 1394, but it
begins in parsonic or Lucretian gloom, 'O purblind race of miserable
men'. The two 'Geraint' poems taken together are more about the
much-tested heroine than her beef-witted husband. Their best passages are always of landscape, the sun flashing on the scythes of the
mowers or the gloom of a great wood, and the names of familiar
places are attractive – Severn side, the White Horse, Caerleon on
Usk,[12] Bala and the Dee. The story unfolds in a never-never land of
beauty and happiness where whatever is bad scarcely counts, though
the wicked Earl is real enough. The jokes are not very funny though.

and he sighed;
There with another humorous ruth remarked
The lusty mowers labouring dinnerless,
And watched the sun blaze on the turning scythe,
And after nodded sleepily in the heat.
But she, remembering her old ruined hall,
And all the windy clamour of the daws
About her hollow turret

('Geraint and Enid', 249–56)

The truth is it is chivalry, the idea of an age of chivalry, which is preposterous, more so than the coal-scuttle arms and armour. It is a strangely boyish dream, and one comes to suspect that Tennyson's boredom shows through even these sparkling tales. The world of Arthur has become a drugged, Pre-Raphaelite world, falling asleep as he works to awaken it, a world of the Sleeping Beauty to which no Prince comes.

Most of 'Balin and Balan' is an original story, though the fight to the death of two brothers is in Malory, and something very similar is in 'Sohrab and Rustum'. The end is well and movingly told by Tennyson, and he was right not to print his long piece about Vivien at court and the funeral arrangements, which would have invited comparison with Arnold's masterly ending. Only the chivalry and the fighting fail to convince. Even the flowers, which are likely enough, sound here strained:

A walk of roses ran from door to door;
A walk of lilies crossed it to the bower

(237–8)

Even in *Maud* Tennyson usually shows a delight in flowers that overcomes all artificiality, but these are symbolic, and it shows:

'Sweeter to me' she said 'this garden rose
Deep-hued and many-folded! sweeter still
The wild-wood hyacinth[13] and the bloom of May

(264–6)

A little later Balin picks up a goblet to fling at someone's head. This object is so Victorian as to be embossed with the story of Joseph of

Arimathea, and 'all of massiest bronze'. One side shows the sea and
a ship 'and angels blowing on it', the other

> was rough with wattling, and the walls
> Of that low church he built at Glastonbury.
>
> (362–3)

The massive pot adds a touch of the ludicrous to the entire quarrel:
yet only a moment before the enemy who provoked has been hissing
with rage like

> The white swan-mother, sitting, when she hears
> A strange knee rustle through her secret reeds
>
> (348–9)

The lines are as well woven together as a dream, but of oddly
discordant elements, and the same is true of this whole poem, and
indeed of most of the entire work. The angry swan is bizarre but
splendid, the pot is absurd. Vivien, the wicked woman, comes
prancing through the woods almost credible, but reciting a foolish
rigmarole to represent sun worship. In 'Merlin and Vivien' she exerts
her powers but they are (because real evil is) beyond Tennyson's
imagination. This is the poem he put on one side to write *Maud*, and
thought in March 1856 promised so well. The anti-heroine could not
believe in anything good or great, but Tennyson cannot believe in
anything else. Even in *Maud* the duellists are improbably chivalrous
with one another. Malory has Merlin put under a stone by 'one of
the damsels of the lake . . . Nimuë' but we are not told how she did
it. In a French romance she is Vivien, they sit under a whitethorn
tree and he falls asleep. She makes nine circles and says nine spells,
and he wakes walled in. When he accuses her, she says, 'I shall often
be here, and you shall hold me in your arms and I shall hold you in
mine.' The world well lost for love, in fact, but this ending does not
suit Alfred Tennyson, so she leaves him in a hollow oak, weeping
admittedly:

> The snake of gold slid from her hair, the braid
> Slipt and uncoiled itself, she wept afresh,
> And the dark wood grew darker toward the storm
> In silence . . .

'There must be now no passages of love
Betwixt us twain henceforward evermore'

(886–912)

Lightning flashed, a thunderbolt hit a tree, she yelled for Merlin to save her, she embraced him, he told her his secrets, she shrieked 'O fool!' and deserted him. What had been a rather real scene, going forward by the force of passion and under the influence of the French story, has become this muddle. 'She put forth the charm/Of woven faces and of waving hands' like Madame Blavatsky. And the thunderbolt though it is not ridiculous is unnecessary, and like the rest of this ending, terribly melodramatic.

'Lancelot and Elaine' at 1415 lines is one of the longer idylls. In 1859 it was simply called 'Elaine'; Lancelot's name was added ten years later. Almost all these poems are about the passions of women, and this is no exception. Its working title was 'The Maid of Astolat' but that had to be abandoned because of confusion with 'The Lady of Shalott'. Tennyson said that in this episode, 'the tenderest of all natures sinks under the blight, that which is of the highest in her working her doom.' The final text begins with Elaine's resounding praises. For a reason we shall be told, she guarded Lancelot's shield. She covered it in silk, embroidered with the same heraldic arms, and I am sorry to say

A border fantasy of branch and flower,
And yellow-throated nestling in the nest.

(11–12)

Arthur found a dead man's crown, and (unlike Victoria one must note) pulled out the diamonds which he thought should be public property, so he made them tournament prizes. Lancelot argued with the Queen, who called Arthur 'a moral child' (145), about whether and how to take part; he wandered off to Astolat to get a blank shield and left his own, so as to appear incognito. There is a list of places and names, but not as resonant as those in book one, and Arthur owns 'Our Lady's Head Carved of one emerald centred in a sun/Of silver rays', which derives remotely from Nennius, though Tennyson had modernized the jewel. Lancelot is wounded in the tournament, so he goes away and hides, in spite of having won. He lies in a poplar grove where Elaine finds him. The story is preposterous and the details which may detain our fancy irrelevant: and yet it reads pleasantly enough. The truth is that Tennyson really loved chivalry because it was so chivalrous. One cannot quarrel with him over that; but a good deal was sacrificed to a kind of homogeneous decorum. Indeed this is the only book where a suppressed passage that has survived does seem a serious loss. It should occur at 1047, where the dead Maid of Astolat arrives in a barge guided by a dumb oarsman:

> And what is Avalon? Avalon is an isle
> All made of apple-blossom in the West,
> And all the waves are fragrant and the winds
> About it and the fairies live upon it
> And there are those have seen it far away
> Shine like a rose upon the summer sea
> And thither goes the king and thence returns
> And reigns: some hold he cannot die.[14]

It is nice to have it put so clearly, or at least to see Tennyson doodling with this idea so late in the day: it is a version of the happy isles, part of ancient folk religion. But small wonder that Carlyle dismissed the entire enterprise as 'superlative lollipops'. He was wrong all the same: Avalon is Welsh for apple trees.

One would expect 'The Holy Grail' to be a climax, but it is not. Tennyson's Lancelot at the end of the previous book, groaning with remorse, 'Not knowing he should die a holy man', is convincing. But Alfred does not honestly believe or cannot make us believe in the Grail. He wrote the poem in less than a fortnight in September 1868, just as he said he wrote 'Guinevere' in a fortnight. It appears probable that however finely polished they were, the episodes were mostly written fast when the mood took him. Macaulay had suggested the subject, so he said in 1859, but he felt misgivings, though Emily (1863) longed for him to write it. It is therefore of some interest that in 1859 he declared he had actually composed a Grail poem 'in as good verse as ever I wrote – no, I did not write, I made it in my head, and it has altogether slipt out of memory.'[15] If that is the case, then it must be part of the mass of poetry lost perhaps in hydrotherapy, when he was forbidden for months to write poetry, or anyway lost soon after 1850, and it may have been written in the style of 'Morte d'Arthur'. What a pity it is lost. There is some evidence that it was a poem of about 300 lines. Tennyson's explanation of what sounds like the very different poem that we have, is 'Faith declines, religion in many turns from practical goodness to the quest after the supernatural and marvellous, and selfish religious excitement . . . I have expressed there my strong feeling of the Reality of the Unseen.' He thought his accounts of Galahad's and Lancelot's quests to be among his best blank verse. But somehow all this, which probably he did think was a climax, will not do. The reasons why are philosophic or religious, rather than critical. The disturbance in Arthur's hall (182f.) is splendid, but the personal visions are too subjective, the more so as five different visions are carefully distinguished. The description of the hall (225f.), and the King supposing from a distance it was on fire, rest uneasily with the theme. The Knights holding a tournament (like a football match) to say goodbye adds farce to absurdity. Yet the verse itself is magical and carries everything. The departure from Camelot (338–60) is touching and almost beautiful, like certain pages of Tolkien by which one is ashamed to be touched. It is genuinely a quest poem unlike anything he had written since 'Ulysses', and it takes on the power of a quest, so long as the Grail itself is not described: even the magnificent scene of the magic mountain (489–535) fails for this reason. This book is a *tour de force* all the same.

'Pelleas and Ettare' brings us down to earth with a thump: it is as Tennyson says 'the breaking of the storm'. It was common in his generation to feel nostalgia for ancient England as well as the classical heroic age, but Alfred felt it more for his own early life. It is part of his nostalgia that he is forced to spend so much of his time telling us why chivalry broke down, why it cannot exist, why it was lost, and spends so little time enjoying his own account of it, yet pleasure does keep breaking in. Pelleas is a knight of barren islands riding across the Forest of Dean. It is a hot day, the bracken burns like emeralds, and for a few lines (24–38) we are as happy as Alfred must have been when he dreamed them up in the New Forest. He shows the way to Caerleon to some girls, 'damsels-errant' strayed out of *The Princess*, and we are off. We have chivalrous adventure, tournaments, dawn stars, a furious boy whom Lancelot brushes off, faint (and few) Shakespearean echoes and more numerous biblical echoes, and the queer word 'lurdane' meaning heavy or torpid ('Red after revel droned her lurdane knights/Slumbering, and their three squires across their feet' (421).

'The Last Tournament' is nearly as short. He was writing it in

November 1870 and it was finished in May. We know that in 1859 he was considering a poem on Tristram and Iseult. Tristram appears here just home for the tournament, with holly for a crest and a green armour 'whereon/There tripped a hundred tiny silver deer'. The ominous signs have been almost too many to mention, Arthur doubting, Lancelot gloomy, yellow leaves, a swineherd nastily cut up, and finally it came on to rain. All the same Tristram won, though he shows up less well in argument with the Fool Dagonet, whom we meet for the first time here, rather late in the day. Tristram wandered off towards Lyonesse through the autumnal woods remembering his wicked past, and complicates the matter by the vividness of his dreams. He meets Isolt who tells him equally strange tales:

> and near me stood,
> In fuming sulphur blue and green, a fiend –
> Mark's way to steal behind one in the dark
>
> (611–13)

One comes to like Tristram ('I am woodman of the woods,/And hear the garnet-headed yaffingale' (the green woodpecker)[16]), but Mark gets him in the end. Arthur comes home, 'All in a death-dumb autumn-dripping gloom' and finds the Fool weeping.

The climax of it all is Guinevere, expected since book one. We are not told much about her happy days, though her guilt is a recurring minor theme, in contrast with the ridiculous idealism which sets the tone of most of the work. Nothing much happens in 'Guinevere' either, because she is old and penitent in a nunnery at 'Almesbury', and the book is largely seen backwards through her remorseful eyes. Large parts of 'The Last Tournament' were in retrospect too, and so was 'The Holy Grail': of the three books, 'Guinevere' was written first and the Tournament last: so it looks as if the technique gets more complex as it goes on. It is a device that is bound to do away with the innocence of his simpler narratives. Even they of course have their melancholy, their 'lords of waste marches, kings of desolate isles'. In the end 'the dry harsh roar of the great horn' is echoed in heaven by a storm:

> then one low roll
> Of Autumn thunder, and the jousts began:

And ever the wind blew, and yellowing leaf
And gloom and gleam, and shower and shorn plume
Went down it

('The Last Tournament', 152–6)

By another of Tennyson's bizarre, successful images, 'Guinevere'
begins on a night when 'The white mist, like a face-cloth to the
face,/Clung to the dead earth'. The Queen remembers the wickedness
of Mordred, which I find it hard to relate to her own guilt, but there
is no doubt she and Lancelot were ashamed: it was then she fled to
Almesbury. She 'heard the Spirits of the waste and weald/Moan as
she fled, or thought she heard them moan', though they did not say
anything. She saw a raven, cousin to the Twa Corbies, and decided
he had spotted a battlefield where the heathen were attacking, 'Lured
by the crimes and frailties of the court', which sounds like an
accusation made by a Marxist mob orator. In her convent she hears
Mordred is King and Arthur is fighting Lancelot, though we are not
told why. A novice sings her a gloomy song, but being in iambic
verse only rhymed, the songs throughout the *Idylls* are only sing-
song. Her account of signs and omens in the past is much more
cheering:

All down the lonely coast of Lyonesse,
Each with a beacon-star upon his head,
And with a wild sea-light about his feet,
He saw them – headland after headland flame
Far on into the rich heart of the west:
And in the light the white mermaidens swam,
And strong man-breasted things stood from the sea,
And sent a deep sea-voice through all the land

(238–45)

The idylls are perhaps best when they touch the sea, 'the thundering
shores of Bude and Bos', and 'the idle-plunging waves' on the sand
dunes. Still, these are only episodes, and in this idyll the Queen after
about 350 lines loses her temper, and falls to recalling the past in a
trance. The King suddenly arrives in person and makes a long, noble
speech over her. This speech is Tennyson at his most Shakespearean,
and I suppose therefore as good a pastiche of the great man as we
shall ever see. If there is a touch of the Boy Scout about Arthur in

this guise, that cannot be helped. He speaks for 156 lines almost
uninterrupted, like a character in a Greek tragedy, and goes off to die
in a battle. When she peers after him he vanishes in the mist. She
makes a speech of about 50 lines, the nuns recognize her, everyone
weeps. She then rather movingly becomes a real nun, and one
believes in her penitence as one never did in her sins or in Arthur's
foolish jealousy:

> Then she, for her good deeds and her pure life,
> And for the power of ministration in her,
> And likewise for the high rank she had borne,
> Was chosen Abbess, there, an Abbess, lived
> For three brief years, and there, an Abbess, past
> To where beyond these voices there is peace.
>
> (687–92)

In 'The Passing of Arthur' the weather is still misty, it is winter.
The lines added to 'Morte d'Arthur' to make it are fine, and they fit
far better than one would surmise. The ghost of Gawain is a powerful
atmospheric effect, little more than an articulate wind prophesying
Arthur's death the next day: he is almost Dantesque:

> Farewell! there is an isle of rest for thee.
> And I am blown along a wandering wind,
> And hollow, hollow, hollow all delight.
>
> (35–7)

The sea was 'the phantom circle of the moaning sea', and in the end
there was silence 'save for some whisper of the seething seas'. The
King speaks a few despairing lines, and suddenly at verse 170 we
come on the poem that we know, which in a true sense engendered
all the others. With the conclusion we have already dealt.

As an epic the poem does not work; however the lost books
might improve it, probably no modern epic could work (for reasons
outside literature) but the *Idylls* represent an extraordinary and brave
attempt. There is not really enough of a thread, enough of a plot, to
furnish the continuous motive force necessary to make an epic, or to
display continuous energy. When it rains, one remembers the Eglinton Tournament: and the blows of Arthur and his men are somehow
languorous.

But it would be unjust to Tennyson to carry over the huge botch of *Idylls of the King* to obscure the rest of his reputation. It does not matter to us that his *Idylls* were so popular with the public, and so derided so soon after. In these same years of churning out his hobby, he remained as brilliant as he had already become, wherever his poetry was not about the Arthurian legends. Meanwhile he was bringing up the two little boys whom he worshipped, and interesting things happened to him. He walked all over the Isle of Wight, to very distant villages now ruined by tourism.[17] He came to know and love it as if he were its familiar spirit. Indeed no poet has ever known England as well: Goodrich Castle on the Wye, Hawes and the Eden valley, the Peaks and the Humber all drew him, and in his poetry it shows.

In October 1855 Edward Lear and Franklin Lushington came to stay. Lear sang his own settings of Tennyson for two or three hours. In the morning they looked eastward towards Blackgang Chine and St Catherine's and counted five capes in the golden morning mist. In the evenings Alfred would read Milton or Shakespeare sonnets or Plato's *Symposium*. In mid-December they made a bonfire of pipes and he burnt his last tobacco 'thinking he would give up smoking'; they went to church together too, because in those years Alfred still went at times with his wife. They were both happy and Emily drew comfort from the peace and quiet even when Alfred was away. She was already (or still) hankering for a house on the mainland all the same. The income from publishers was improving: after a dip in 1855 because of the slump, when he earned only £445, it went up in 1856 to £2058 with *Maud*, and £4542 in 1860 with the *Idylls*, of which 10,000 copies sold in a week. They had bought their house in 1856, and Alfred prepared the ground for rhododendrons. In May, Prince Albert suddenly called. Let Emily record it, though she is in the middle of decorating:

> May 13th. In the midst of all our confusion while all imaginable things strewed the drawing-room and the bookshelves were bare and the chairs and tables dancing, Prince Albert came. We wished things had instead been looking their best to have done him honour. One of the gentlemen with him gathered a great bunch of cowslips which the Prince admired very much and took them himself. One dropt and I kept it for the children as a memorial. A nightingale was singing while he was here I think.

It had been singing delightfully all the morning close to the
house. Afterwards A and I had a very pleasant walk in the fields.
He took me to that field where the great bunches of white
Narcissus grow. The steep sand bank in it is very pretty. After
dinner he came to fetch me that I might see the beautiful view
from the North attic where he was sitting because his own was
piled up with books and other things . . . 17th . . . a message
from Lambert telling us to expect the Queen, for orders for her
reception had been given at Yarmouth and one of the carriages
was to be in readiness to take H M to Freshwater Gate, and the
Prince had said to Captain F. on leaving Farringford, 'It is a
pretty place, it is a pretty place. I shall certainly bring the Queen
to see it.' We dressed our children in their rose-coloured dresses,
and all went into the Farringford garden to receive H M . . .
However the Queen did not come, probably because of the
stormy morning.[18]

It is tempting to gather swathes of this pleasing journal: it makes
an excellent read on its own, and clearly reflects a life in most ways
extremely happy, and also the pleasing personality of its writer,
which won over everyone, even Carlyle. Fitz thought the life at
Farringford too grand, but he was becoming eccentric, and it was
perhaps too like his family's life. There was trouble at times with
maids and nannies: one had to be sent away for favouring Lionel, but
back she came again a little later. The tenant farmer Jeremiah
Merwood was illiterate, but he caused enjoyment by a long wrestling
match over the rent, against which he would set off numerous jobs,
not necessarily wanted, until he could show he had nothing to pay.
This tussle went happily on as long as he lived, though he lost his
position as bailiff, but it was he who told Alfred about the best
building stones, and found him fossils, and made the little lane up on
to the down. Tennyson built himself a hut in the field across the
road, which he bought to forestall developers, and painted it with
dragons and exotic vegetation (it has not survived and was never
properly photographed). His own taste in gardening was for close,
tall cover to protect the house, without stifling the light; he liked
simple spring flowers, and he had some red-hot pokers. His favourite
rose, which he found unprocurable, was the pre-Victorian Provence
rose: his taste in most things was pre-Victorian except in the *Idylls of
the King*. His greatest dread was a railway station near Freshwater.

The pair of them went to Wales for the summer and tried hard to learn the language. Poets and scholars were mobilized to find him texts and he did in the end have some mastery of Welsh literature. Ten years later he made a determined onslaught on Hebrew. He was more scholarly and better read at the age of fifty or sixty than any poet since Milton, though his learning was not donnish. A lot of his time was spent in advising young poets, who by and large were no good at all. It is interesting that his harshest, frankest criticisms were reserved for those in whom he saw real promise, like Allingham. He wrote him one of his severest letters in October 1856:

> The poem seems in part too fine, in the style of the last century, and some of the worst parts of Wordsworth, a style which he inherited and could not quite shake off. For instance your Corinthian bush means currants – why not say 'currant bush' at once. Wordsworth has 'The fragrant beverage drawn from China's herb' for tea.[19] This sort of avoidance of plain speaking is the more ungrateful to me in your poem because other parts of it are quite unadorned and justly simple . . . Mind, I like your poem, and therefore say about it what I have said. It is *worth* correcting.[20]

At Twickenham he was called on by an old Waterloo soldier who had learnt to write in order to write down an epic about that battle which turned out unreadable: to him Tennyson was extremely kind.

It is not possible to chronicle all Alfred's worldly successes: he was an ideal laureate because he so enjoyed it after the initial nerves. He may have been overwhelmed with business, and swept off course as a poet by the public. Indeed I believe it was his public, the people he set out to please and did please, who are responsible for the worst aspects of *Idylls of the King*, for the furious prudery after Milnes had spoken ill of Vivien, and so for much of the absurd idealism, for the false sense that this could be a national epic: that 'chivalry' as perceived in the nineteenth century could be a basis for poetry. Yet he all but overcame every such difficulty. His anger over the illustrated poems should be set off against his warm admiration (with a few exceptions) for what Doré did for him: he was surely right to admire those four tall, stately volumes. His friendship with Jowett, from whom he got excellent advice,[21] and with the admiring Dobell,[22] his visits to Little Holland House, where Mrs Prinsep taught him at last to be a tame literary lion, and to the Duke of Argyll's castle shaped like a clover-leaf at Inverary (the most exciting bit of eighteenth-century town planning and one of the finest castles in Europe), are comparatively unimportant, when one considers the new directions that his muse was taking. His letters make a fascinating study, but as he wrote in December 1858, 'I would as soon kill a pig as write a letter': it is the poetry that counts.

His friendship with Edward Lear is a great pleasure to read about; they are two of the most interesting creatures in their century and they emerge shyly from its forest of inhibitions to come face to face. A book could be written about their relationship, which on Lear's side never declined from fervent and at times jealous admiration of Emily; he once left Farringford 'unable to stand Tennyson's selfishness', he took Emily's side without understanding there was no quarrel between her and Alfred. In 1860 Lear felt he could not bear to visit the Tennysons ever again, Alfred was too gruff and growly and self-absorbed. Lear's private journals, now at Harvard, are vehement in anger. His great projected illustrated edition of Tennyson was involved in the ruin of his eyesight, while on Tennyson's side a fit of suppressed fury at being parodied ended in a silence. Parody was an essential part of Lear's admiration: he could proceed in no other way.[23] He sent to Farringford a parody translation of a Tennyson poem into Italian. No doubt he made many other innocent jokes, but the benefit in poetry all went his way, because at the end of his life he was learning to be a great poet, as he had learnt other arts, always by imitation or parody. He had nothing to teach Tennyson, who at a deep level seriously admired and loved him, not even the limerick.

This had been a problem to me, since I greatly admire Lear's limericks, and also because there was a rumour I heard thirty or forty years ago, and have come across since, that many of the naughty limericks that come to us anonymously from the nineteenth century are by Tennyson. There is even a story of a visitor to Farringford who found him asleep on the lawn surrounded by screwed up bits of paper, which turned out to be limericks. That is quite unlikely, as he did not compose in that way, and in fact it can be disproved through a story told by Harold Macmillan to Lord and Lady Briggs of Worcester College, Oxford. Harold's grandfather Alexander told him as a youth that he had once asked Tennyson if he had ever written any limericks. No, replied Alfred, but I soon will. There was a pause, and then he came out with this one:

There are people who live down in Erith
Whom nobody seeth or heareth,
And there by the marge
Of the river a barge,
Which nobody guideth or steereth.[24]

The limerick has an eerie and quasi-metaphysical quality which I think guarantees its authenticity. At any rate its provenance is impeccable, since as we shall see Alexander Macmillan was his publisher and his friend at the end of his life. But when Tennyson's muse did turn away from mainstream poetry, it turned in another direction.

Enoch Arden (1864) contains what he nearly called 'Homely Idylls', the fine point of what he could do with his verse short stories, and also his experiments in classical metre using quantity: the brilliantly successful poem to Milton in alcaeics, the hendecasyllables to reviewers, and the blank verse Homer; it also contains something potentially more valuable still to English poetry, his first dialect poem. He had known Burns of course since he was a boy, but 'Northern Farmer' is more of a tribute to William Barnes, that great, underestimated poet of Dorset, which you can see from the Isle of Wight. Dialect poetry might have taken off at that time: FitzGerald as a boy had known Major Moore, a Suffolk dialect collector since 1815, and Barnes belonged to a flourishing English Dialect Society which commissioned twenty or more dialect versions of 'The Song of Songs' from all over England. But in poetry the moment passed, the only dialect left alive now is in Scotland, and we have fine Scots and Lallans poetry; in English we have only the lonely monument of Tennyson's wonderfully moving Lincolnshire poetry and the large, neglected lifework of William Barnes.

Barnes was a little older than Tennyson, being born in 1801. In February 1861, Alfred thanked him for his *Poems of Rural Life*, assuring him that he had known them many years. Barnes had sent him the second edition (1847) which he passed on to Hallam, since he already had the same book (1848), and both of these copies survive at Lincoln.[25] The two poets rapidly became friends, but it was in February 1861, when they were still on distantly respectful terms, that Alfred wrote his 'Northern Farmer'; we know from Palgrave's journal that in October of that year it was complete, and we know when he composed it from the *Memoir*:[26] he started on the 17th and finished on the evening of the 18th; it was on the 28th that he wrote to Barnes. I have put some stress on these dates because without question in this case the greater artist followed the lesser, and learnt a valuable lesson from him. Alfred knew his dialect, and also studied it in a number of books, the earliest of which he got from Drummond Rawnsley in 1866, but his transcription has been criticized, and unless one knows the dialect already that makes him hard to read:[27] the same complaint may be made about Barnes. The language is a million miles from that of *Idylls of the King*. But these poems of Tennyson's allow of a sharpness of characterization which goes far beyond comedy. Poetry of this kind is not just meant to be laughed at, as Thomas Hardy in his selected poems of Barnes pointed out. Tennyson's first dialect poem arose from the dying words of an old farm bailiff, which he heard from 'my old great-uncle': 'God A'mighty little knows what He's about a-taking me. An' Squire will be so mad an' all.' Fortunately the poet in old age made a recording of one of these poems in his own voice. Was it putting down roots of his own in the Isle of Wight that made him long for Lincolnshire people of the past? It was not Jeremiah Merwood, the tenant farmer at Farringford, since at least as bailiff he was got rid of in October 1861.[28] It was Barnes who struck the spark.

The main items in the 1864 collection were 'Enoch Arden', 'Aylmer's Field', and the revised 'Tithonus'. Of these the first was written in the winter of 1861–2 and the second between July 1862 and December 1863. Both the stories were supplied by Woolner, one from reading and the other from childhood in Suffolk, but both were altered and sharpened to a degree of which Tennyson only now became capable. He felt 'Enoch Arden' had come out the better, but they both contain extraordinary passages. I admire both these poems greatly, though their plots are melodramatic. 'Enoch Arden' is a love story about village lovers, with a voyage, a desert island, and a sad homecoming. In detail it is often understated, but its story is sound in structure, and it is hard to forget:

> On the nigh-naked tree the robin piped
> Disconsolate, and through the dripping haze
> The dead weight of the dead leaf bore it down:
>
> (672–4)

'Aylmer's Field' was the hardest to write of any of his verse narratives: it is written with burning indignation, and even his son

Hallam observed that the ruin of young lovers and marriages for worldly reasons always produced in him an incandescent rage, and turned him into a minor prophet. Ricks tells us: 'In conception and manner the poem is influenced by the verse tales of Crabbe, whom Tennyson was reading in 1862', and that may be the salt source of some of the bitter feeling.

The action of the poem 'Aylmer's Field' takes place in 1793. When one hears the name of Sir Aylmer Aylmer one knows he is doomed; his heraldic trappings are recorded with glee, as if by Trollope (but for some reason Tennyson never took to the novels of Trollope, which he thought too quotidian and without poetry). The countryside is both beautiful and sinister:

> A land of hops and poppy-mingled corn,
> Little about it stirring save a brook!
> So sleepy was the land.

It is not practicable to follow the plot here, but some well-contrived phrases do need recording. For instance he talks of boyish stories,

> sketches rude and faint,
> But where a passion yet unborn perhaps
> Lay hidden as the music of the moon
> Sleeps in the plain eggs of the nightingale.
>
> (100-3)

He prided himself more on the flower-eaten cottages, yet they are less striking, indeed they are as he says like visions out of Sweden-borg, who was so much the rage that this allusion does not name him, it is only to 'visions in the Northern dreamer's heavens' (161). We get a lusty parody of fox-hunters' conversation (251f.) and a family quarrel. Fox-hunters' conversation always sounds rather envi-able in books, though Surtees does it better, but the point is always missed that these people talk about nothing else at all: that is what is suffocating. Still, he summons up some fine invective, and scorn of 'These old pheasant-lords,/These partridge-breeders of a thousand years'. And the comfort of port, which in this poet calms, rather than inflames, is well done. It is no ordinary port, but 'His richest beeswing from a binn reserved/For banquets'. At the end comes a

really fiery sermon, which is an extreme statement of social scorn:
Vicars against Squires.

> Crown thyself, worm, and worship thine own lusts! –
> No coarse and blockish God of acreage
> Stands at thy gate for thee to grovel to –
> Thy God is far diffused in noble groves
> And princely halls, and farms, and flowing lawns,
> And heaps of living gold that daily grow,
> And title-scrolls and gorgeous heraldries.
> In such a shape dost thou behold thy God.
>
> (650–7)

'Tithonus' was written as 'Tithon' in 1833, but in 1859 Thackeray
was yelling for a new poem for the first issue of the *Cornhill* magazine
the next January. Tennyson rooted about and found this for February; all he had written of serious quality since *Maud* was 'Sea Dreams'
(December 1857) which he had already given to *Macmillan's Magazine*
for January 1860, a lesser, idyllic piece of writing closer than usual to
Theocritus in small touches. It was published with 'Enoch Arden',
but unfortunately it ends with a nauseating lyric to an infant.
Tennyson was entering a stage where his principal poems are better
than ever, but his others are nonsense. Some of them, such as the
idiotic verses to 'Havelock', an Indian Mutiny hero, were not printed
by him and should have been destroyed. There was pressure on him
to produce quantity, and we owe the rediscovery of 'Tithonus', a
wonderful poem and a brilliant revision, to that fact. The 'Tithon' of
1833 was shorter as well as worse.

> Ay me! ay me! the woods decay and fall,
> The vapours weep their substance to the ground,
> Man comes and tills the earth and lies beneath,
> And after many summers dies the rose.
>
> ('Tithon', 1–4)

> The woods decay, the woods decay and fall,
> The vapours weep their burthen to the ground,
> Man comes and tills the field and lies beneath,
> And after many a summer dies the swan.
>
> ('Tithonus', 1–4)

He brooded over this amazing revision, this transformation of his poem, in November and December 1859, before Jowett came as he always did for Christmas. It was worth that length of time.

> Ere yet they blind the stars, and thy wild team,
> Spreading a rapid glow with loosened manes,
> Fly, trampling twilight into flakes of fire.
>
> ('Tithon', 35–7)

> Ere yet they blind the stars, and the wild team
> Which love thee, yearning for thy yoke, arise,
> And shake the darkness from their loosened manes,
> And beat the twilight into flakes of fire.
>
> ('Tithonus', 39–42)

The other poems in this volume are well enough, but neither here nor there in comparison with these great works.[29]

The Tennysons went to Cauterets, and his poem about that is moving as a recollection, although it is frail as poetry. Dakyns, the boys' tutor, held back and let Tennyson rumble silently to himself. I am afraid to say Emily's chief memory of that summer was of the suffocating ripeness of French drains.

CHAPTER NINE

Aldworth

ALFRED TENNYSON changed his publisher, as most writers do in the course of a lifetime, but in his case the series of moves was particularly painful. The ghastly 'Illustrated Edition' by various Pre-Raphaelite hands was already a cause of anxiety, because it was intended as a Christmas book but failed to appear until the following May, and then sold badly. There were 10,000 copies, and halfway through July Moxon had sold 1300 and was still smiling, but six years later, when half the edition was sold off to Routledge, total sales had amounted only to 2210. Tennyson had fumed a good deal over this enterprise, and accepted £2000 from Moxon in July 1857 as full settlement: that after all was the amount Moxon had originally promised him. Then in 1858 Edward Moxon died. His printers were the executors of his will, and his younger brother William, a lawyer of the most niggling kind, inherited the business. William claimed nearly £9000 which he maintained Tennyson owed the firm over the Illustrated Edition. The agreements seem all to have been verbal, and it appears certain Edward Moxon would never have made this preposterous claim: in fact his son Charles, who ran the business for a time, wrote to apologize. Tennyson of course threatened to change publishers, but the printers begged him to reconsider because the firm depended on him. He should consider Mrs Moxon: but he had already given her £1500 or so, and went on paying her (privately) £300 a year, so that horse would not run. In fact although he fought for money with shrewdness and determination, and worried over it, Tennyson was never ungenerous.

It turned out that having produced their luxury version of the 1842 *Poems*, Moxons had embarked on their own account on something similar for *The Princess*. Tennyson therefore let them produce it, though he was certain he had never agreed, and he hated the idea of illustrations in bad taste. At least he got nearly £1000 in the end from Routledge and Kegan Paul, at 4 shillings per volume, now selling for a guinea, and the same again for two further impressions in 1865 and 1869. By his new contract with Moxons when it was hammered out he took 90 and not 66 per cent of the profits of any future books or editions. The first *Idylls* sold 40,000 copies in six months, and seven editions before 1869, so it is clear he was now a best seller. *Enoch Arden* sold 17,000 copies on the first day, and made him more than £8000 in 1865 alone. He refused £10,000 for an American lecture tour in 1863. Alas in 1864 a clerk at Moxons called J. B. Payne was appointed executive manager and then made a partner: Mrs Moxon seems to have liked him, so did her son Arthur.

Under him the volcano erupted. First he pushed Tennyson into a *Selected Poems* (1865) which Alfred thought prettified. Payne ran the firm itself into difficulties, and his accounts seem to have been put together with blithe disregard of propriety. There were rows about the recovery of royalties from other firms: Tennyson had a lot of trouble over these in America and Canada. Now Moxons resorted to law on their own account without telling him, against a religious charity his wife supported, for reprinting poems without their permission. All these grumbles are what led him in 1868 to publish verse in periodicals, but finally his wife advised against this practice: he would earn a lot more by publishing it fresh in new books. Finally Payne issued misleading advertisements for a four-volume 'Standard' edition, before any such publication had even been agreed on.

Alfred took advice from Alexander Macmillan as a friend, and in January 1869 he moved to Strahan whom he met through James Knowles. Moxons were taken over, creditors being paid 15 shillings in the pound. Tennyson roars with fury about Payne in his letters, and it appears that Payne was the source of malicious attacks on him. He seems to have stuck donkey's ears on Tennyson's portrait at Moxons: '*auriculas asini Mida rex habet* . . . King Midas has a donkey's ears' (Midas was proverbially avaricious). Strahan made a profit, which you could hardly fail to do by publishing Tennyson. His popularity had become a kind of public mania. Alexander Macmillan offered £3000 for his old books, but Strahan paid him a regular £5000 a year and still made a profit. Strahan was a decent kind of a man but not businesslike, and in 1873 his business failed. Tennyson was plagued by disputes at that time, Moxon's business was hard to settle, and the law loomed in several directions at once, but Strahan's failure was not his fault. Alfred moved to Henry King, a model publisher and a charming character who began as a bookseller in Brighton: it appears that it was Knowles again who arranged matters. But King's health began to fail, and Alfred was then tormented by King's manager, Charles Kegan Paul, an ex-vicar who had lost his faith and become a prep-school master to whom Hallam and Lionel had been sent. Lionel was bullied at that school and developed a stutter that had to be cured, and Hallam, who by this time was his father's secretary, did not find it at all easy to stand up to his old headmaster.

The contract ended in 1878, and the following November King died; Alfred therefore passed into the hands of Kegan Paul as publisher. Alfred's objection to the popular editions had been to invasions of his privacy for purposes of advertising: Mr Paul had wanted to use pictures of his houses as frontispieces. That would seem a venial sin today, but of course he was right to resist it, because he hated the tribes of tourists who came by bus, and on foot if necessary, to peer over his walls and hedges, and in at his windows. The unpleasantness with publishers, and the pressure on him to conform, increased as he became more and more of a goldmine. The delay in publishing the last Idyll of the King was probably by counter-suggestion, because the publishers were shouting for more.

Paul was a most magisterial figure, a person of strongly held views who from being a vicar became a Conduct or chaplain at Eton, then a mesmerist, a vegetarian, and a disciple of F. D. Maurice. He resigned from Eton under pressure from the Provost, which is why Tennyson chose him as a prep-school master; in the end he became more or less a Unitarian, which was a sure sign of intransigence in the 1870s, then at last in 1890 a Roman Catholic. He was never without views. The Trench of Kegan Paul and Trench was a son of Tennyson's friend the Archbishop of Dublin, but in business Paul was a mean and tricky man, and both envious and contemptuous of Tennyson for his income and for what he called the poet's poses. He was not old enough to remember how genuine these 'poses' were.

Paul's contract ran for five years as the last had done, and during this time (1879–83) he produced the thirteen-volume cheap edition at a shilling a volume a month; within two years he had printed 100,000 and made a profit of £1000. The editions by now had proliferated, and since Maud I have ceased to record each one; there are some I have never seen, and a few I have noticed that no one else appears to refer to: the poems of Alfred Tennyson had become an industry.

Queen Mary, published by King (1875), advertises The Author's Edition, the Cabinet Edition, the Library Edition, the Miniature Edition, the Illustrated Edition, the Original Editions (now first reduced in price), *Selections from*, and *Songs from Tennyson*. The old plain green covers and clear print of the pocket-sized Moxon and scarcely larger later volumes are surely best. Of the collections in numerous volumes, I am fond of Strahan's 1870 Chiswick Press edition in ten tiny volumes bound in gold and white. Macmillan's Eversley edition in nine large volumes with the poet's annotations (1907–8) has been useful to scholars and used to be standard until the Ricks one-volume edition (1969, three volumes in 1987). It was really only yesterday that the honour of publishing Tennyson passed from Macmillan, who took over as Alfred's publishers in 1884 and went on after his death until 1908. Macmillan paid him an advance of £1500 a year, plus a third of the price of every book sold: the contract was for ten years from 1884. Alfred had known Alexander Macmillan as a friend since 1859.

In this brief survey of business troubles, which included serious fears of the collapse of his bank in the early Farringford days, I have brought together what pained or agonized him worst about being a success.[1] He thrashed about desperately in the net, he took to the stage, he insisted on composing the most absurd public poems, he writhed and wriggled over some pretty but alas silly light verses he had written being set to music by Sullivan, and then made public. When he read a piffling popular ode privately to the Princess of Wales, they both laughed aloud. It appears that he eluded both his public and his publishers to an amazing degree. What he enjoyed most in his forty-two years of life as the laureate was his private life with his wife and his adored children. He may have enjoyed being laureate, but he enjoyed bringing up his two boys far more. One day he went with one of his little boys in the trap to meet the ferry: a stranger was amazed to observe that Alfred and his son had swopped hats and then forgotten about it. Visitors from Jowett downwards were conscripted to play football with the children and to every manner of high jinks.

In the background, grandeurs rained down on his head in an inconsequent series. He saw the Queen who was kind to him, but she told Edward Lear later that he 'would not come to see her because he did not know how to bow'. He became a Fellow of the Royal Society, and a member of 'The Club' of which Dr Johnson

had been a member. Its thirty-eight members in 1889 included
Gladstone, Argyll, Derby, Dufferin, Rosebery, Tennyson, J. A.
Froude, Sir Charles Newton, Sir Joseph Hooker, Professor Huxley
and Sir Alfred Lyall.[2] He was a welcome guest at Argyll Lodge in
London where the butler was a kilted Highlander, and at Little
Holland House where the Prinseps held court with easy manners and
a wonderful cook. He was an honorary Fellow of Trinity where he
surprised them by mixing the best port with hot water. He cruised
on yachts, and in the end he entered the House of Lords. He was
President of the London Library when Lord Houghton died, a
Cornish Bard and Vice-President of the Welsh Eisteddfod Society.
These things did not happen to him in any logical order, they just
became more frequent with the passing of time. They really hardly
seem to have altered him at all; by the time he was fifty he had
become a deeply ingrained eccentric, wildly dressed, shaggy-haired,
as swarthy as a gipsy, and liable to say whatever came into his head.
As an old man out walking, he would fling himself on the ground to
inspect a flower. In a yacht full of royalty where he read *Maud*, he
patted the Empress of Russia on the shoulder and called her a good
girl, because he had no idea who anyone was, though the Tsar was
not amused. The children's first tutor Dakyns adored him. Almost
every description of him is the same: people thought him like 'a great
child'.

His most manipulative male friend was James Knowles,[3] who
picked up *In Memoriam* as a new book in 1850, thereby discovering
poetry and Tennyson and geology all at once. He grew up in the
Clapham of the 1840s, with its Clapham Athenaeum and its Literary
and Scientific Society. Charles Kegan Paul had known Tennyson's
poetry since 1842, but each of them discovered him at around the
age of twenty. Swinburne called on him at Farringford with a Balliol
friend younger still, but Swinburne had known Alfred when he was
a boy of twelve at Bonchurch. His real and trusted friends were
closer to his own generation, as Argyll was, and Sir John Simeon,
the Catholic landowner to whom he several times opened his heart,
and who opened his own in return; Simeon was probably his best
friend and closest confidant in these years. Knowles was the son of a
self-made architect. He and his father built the Grosvenor Hotel at
Victoria Station, a heavy monument whose pretensions are now
masked in soot, though his father had shown a lighter talent in his
own Friday Grove, Clapham, and in that wilderness of two-storeyed

pillars, Silverton Park, Devon, both now pulled down alas, while the Grosvenor Hotel still gloomily survives like a monument in a pea-soup fog. James had dedicated a book of Arthurian legends to the laureate in 1861 and called on him five years later.

In June 1867, Tennyson was house-hunting for a secret plot of land where he might build a little lodge, which might be a refuge from the tourists and from his hay-fever.[4] We have his sketch of what he envisaged: at first sight it tends to remind people of his father's Gothic extension at Somersby, but on closer inspection it is more unassuming, and very like the nondescript dons' houses in South Parks Road, Oxford. James Knowles secured the commission by the fluke of being able to offer Tennyson a lift one day from Haslemere station, but what he built was a kind of Camelot, a grander, private version of the Grosvenor Hotel. It was later bought by the Gaekwar of Baroda. It has been further aggrandized since Tennyson's time with a billiard room added at one end for Lord Parker, who rented the house; still, the spirit of the place survives.[5] That day in June Knowles had been on his way to visit a brother-in-law near Chiddingfold.[6] The Tennysons were combing the area because Emily knew and loved it: the house they built was named Aldworth after her family's house in Berkshire, and it is sometimes said the grandeur of Aldworth was due to her, but it is easy enough to see in detail after detail how Alfred was lured into it, little by little, by Mr Knowles, who did not charge for his services because this was his flagship, and he knew how famous it was going to make him, and how it would feature in every 'Haunts and Dwellings of the Poets' for a hundred years.

While the hillside land, which had been a clearing used as a potato field, was secured, Knowles was building Albert Mansions, Victoria Street, where he and Tennyson both took rooms later. From 1868 though, Alfred would stay at The Hollies, the Georgian house overlooking Clapham Common where Knowles lived. Some of the features of the new house that seem to reflect Alfred's personal ideas are a set of ground-floor rooms en suite, for dinner and dessert moving processionally from room to room, bounded by a vast indoor corridor where he could walk, and at the very topmost attic a window giving on to a balcony with a fine southward view, which Alfred wrote about in verse and showed to his friends of both sexes. The bathroom over the porch was his pride and joy. He sat soaking in hot water three or even five times a day 'reading big books about small birds'. He had never had running water before. He used to empty these baths through a window on to a lawn. Details of architectural embellishment for Aldworth were borrowed from Westminster Abbey, and a shield was left without blazon in allusion to one like it in 'The Holy Grail'; there was once a queer, solitary bird statue on the south-east corner of the roof, which was put there by chance but stayed because Alfred happened to like it.

He laid the foundation stone on Shakespeare's birthday, '*Gloria in excelsis*' in carved stone went all round the roof, and a motto in Welsh meaning 'The Truth against the World' in tile mosaic confronted the visitor in the hall. The 'deathwhite mist' that Alfred added to 'Morte d'Arthur' in 1869 was apparently a feature of Aldworth more than Farringford: Emily said 'the cold mist seems to suck the life out of one Vampire like', and you could still hear the gunnery practice out at sea from the direction of Portsmouth. His sundial all the same said *Horas non numero nisi serenas*. His favourite places in the district were Waggoners' Wells near Hindhead (where he wrote '*Flower in the crannied wall*'), which George Eliot thought a good place for a murder, and the Silent Pool near Albury, under Merrow downs. He liked the play of light as water gushed from the chalk over the greensand, the 'mackerel colours' of the water and the currents 'like crystal smoke'. It reminded him of Keats.[7]

To Knowles, it must be stressed that friendship with Tennyson was a step up. With Tennyson's support he conjured into existence the Metaphysical Society, in which the great men of the age addressed themselves to the simplest and most serious questions. Tennyson grew excited about metaphysics as he wrote his 'Holy Grail': Emily doubted if that would ever have been finished but for her 'and the Queen's wish and that of the Crown Princess'. At least through the royal family, Wagner may by now have been an influence. But metaphysics is argument, and the argument (as usual with Alfred) was with anyone who was present, so that the Society arose from discussions with Knowles: Knowles was a ringmaster, that was his forte. When the Society met, Alfred did not say much, and he has been scorned for asking whether the rising of sap does not disprove the universal law of gravity, a question that bewildered Huxley: yet I do not find it a stupid question. The word 'osmosis' first occurs in 1867.

The Education Act was already looming, so Knowles edited a primary-school text of the story of Arthur, with an ideological bias in articles that sprouted from its preface, such as Art for Man's sake instead of Art for Art's sake. He was active in many directions: but the Metaphysical Society was perhaps the oddest.[8]

As far as it touched on Tennyson's interests it was a mighty high-minded organization, but he did not regularly attend all its meetings. He did produce some verses read at its inauguration in 1869, which are disarmingly honest: 'The Higher Pantheism'.[9] After Alfred read his 'Holy Grail' to Mrs Bradley he said there were moments 'when the flesh is nothing to me, when I feel and know the flesh to be the vision, God and the spiritual only the real and true – depend on it the spiritual is the real'. His poem for the Metaphysicians scarcely rises to the condition of poetry, it is a low, growling murmur, yet as a thought expressed, it has an obvious honesty to his experience:

Glory about thee, without thee; and thou fulfillest thy doom,
Making Him broken gleams, and a stifled splendour and gloom.

Speak to Him thou for He hears, and Spirit with Spirit can meet –
Closer is He than breathing, and nearer than hands and feet.

('The Higher Pantheism', 9–10)

As he approached his sixtieth birthday his mind strayed to his earliest natural and innocent mysticism. In his 'Lucretius' he noticed lust as he would never before have expressed it, and death with clearer eyes, 'Poor little life that toddles half an hour/Crowned with a flower or two, and there an end'. The lust, not in a passage tormented by it but in another where he happily draws it, caused trouble with his publishers, though the disputed passage was reinstated:

The mountain quickens into Nymph and Faun;
And here an Oread – how the sun delights
To glance and shift about her slippery sides,
And rosy knees and supple roundedness,
And budded bosom-peaks . . .
        Catch her, goat-foot: nay,
Hide, hide them, million-myrtled wilderness,
And cavern-shadowing laurels, hide! do I wish –

What? – that the bush were leafless?

(187–91, 203–6)

So even in his treatment of the classics[10] Tennyson had at last become a fully sexual and an uninnocent poet. He has not given in to the age all the same, or to Lord Leighton's boredom and display of the nakedness of women, or Swinburne's unappeased excitement at the idea of sex. He proceeds with cool originality to distill from the experience of life his amazing and unexpected poems. Lest it be thought that the oreads and satyrs have pushed him off balance, one should remember that the same poem contains these lines too; he had already imitated the same bit of Lucretius in 'Morte d'Arthur':[11]

> the Gods, who haunt
> The lucid interspace of world and world,
> Where never creeps a cloud, or moves a wind,
> Nor ever falls the least white star of snow,
> Nor ever lowest roll of thunder moans,
> Nor sound of human sorrow mounts to mar
> Their sacred everlasting calm!

(104–10)

Charles Pritchard, the astronomer, was a new metaphysical friend, the only FRS of the old Clapham Athenaeum, who saw his lifework as an Oxford Professor as reconciling science and the Bible. Alfred was even in touch with Darwin himself, some of whose disciples, but not whose books, he viewed with alarm. The new Metaphysical Society was meant to iron out such vast subjects as God, the soul, free will, necessity, matter and spirit, and Knowles was to 'get it up', like any learned society, with the calmness of discussion that learned societies enjoyed. At first it was sensibly called a Theological Society, but once they had decided to invite non-Christians and anti-Christians, Dean Stanley of Westminster suggested 'Metaphysical'.

Knowles had always been interested in magazines and he was now running the *Contemporary Review* as a platform for analogous ideas, just as Dean Stanley ran the Abbey. The members of the Metaphysical Society included Manning, Huxley, Dean Alford of Canterbury, Walter Bagehot, Froude, Gladstone, Martineau, Lubbock, Tyndall, Lushington, Grove the music historian, L. Stephen,

Ruskin, Arthur Balfour and the albino Chancellor, Robert Lowe, supposed at the time to be the shortest-sighted man in England, Alfred being the second. Their Proceedings were not recorded. Knowles plunged happily in, relying on an ability to master any subject in half an hour, though Alfred, who admired that in him, remarked that he did not at first know a hypothesis from a hippopotamus. Although the poet was not a prominent speaker in the debates, the others seem to have enjoyed themselves, and these meetings clearly promoted a new and unexpected tolerance. This was a phenomenon of the 1870s, when Stanley was Dean and Tennyson was Laureate and Gladstone at his height. It lasted just those ten years; the Society represents Alfred's greatest contribution to public life, and also of course it made a wonderful recruiting ground for the *Contemporary*, and after that for the *Nineteenth Century*. Knowles was impertinent enough to suggest to a vice-chancellor[12] a chair of Periodical Literature.

While the boys were young, the Tennysons lived a rather settled life at Farringford. Emily's records are like the most intimate photographs, almost too painful to look at so long afterwards:

A. gathered a rose and gave it to me as we walked thro the kitchen garden . . . A. read me some of 'Enid'. It seems as if we were the people of those old days. A stag's horn beetle came into the room with a harp-like sound . . . Went to Communion and afterwards in the garden heard A's low whistle and found him lying by the strawberry bed under the trees . . . The Cloughs came to dinner. Very taking they are . . . Isaiah one evening and Chaucer the other . . . He burns leaves in Maiden's Croft as he did yesterday and he gets me the long bench to lie down upon and gives me his cloak. Smoke and flames very beautiful when Merwood puts in the brambles. Little feathery tongues of flame.

They took the children to the Zoo where the lions growled at them. Alfred went to Denmark in a storm, and then they all went to the Crystal Palace: that was the pace of life. Lionel saw a column of smoke and said, 'How smoky God will be.' Hallam told him not to talk like that, but 'It's true,' he said. 'His face will be as black as the funny man.'[13]

'Every possible day he takes me out in the little carriage and the boys are delighted if they are allowed to help. Certainly the pleasure of being drawn about our pretty fields by him is greater to me than most drives, much as I love driving . . . After dinner I play merry old dance tunes and the children dance, Lionel nearly flying as usual.' F. D. Maurice stays and impresses them greatly but he loses his hat. Alfred brings home a hedgehog which eats bread and milk and then curls itself up in a ball. 'It is hard to deny kind, good Mrs Cameron anything': she has sent her maid, much to everyone's surprise, to demand the manuscript of 'Guinevere'. Alfred does not care a fig for his old manuscripts but Emily does, so if necessary he copies out the whole poem for people. Mrs Cameron's photography makes her still more demanding, and she insists that if Americans arrive and are found dolefully wandering, Alfred must receive them. When Edward Lear comes, he sings, sometimes for four hours at a time. Mrs Cameron one day spotted his arrival, and sent across her servants at once, carrying her large piano. It arrived at the door with Mr Lear, like his luggage. But in Lear's unpublished journal for 1860, the piano story is different. At Waterloo Station he met Franklin Lushington and a lot of Prinseps, and 'shirked'. At Lymington they got beer and biscuits and crossed over to the Isle of Wight, to find Mrs Cameron on the quayside to welcome the Prinsep party. Not that evening but the next, a grand piano suddenly arrived at Farringford from Mrs Cameron and at nine thirty she came herself with a party, and Lear sang until midnight. There is more than one view to take of this anecdote, but however one looks at it Alfred is unlikely to have been pleased. We know from Edward Lear's diary that as young children Hallam and Lionel were charming and funny; in fact they were normal children: they buried a dead redbreast in the garden with their father to say its liturgy, which was 'God bless all things', and when Emily said the conserved fruits were making Lionel naughty and had better be taken away, he answered that it was sago and tapioca pudding that were to blame and ought to go. These scraps of Victorian nursery news come from a letter of Hallam's to Franklin Lushington, which he showed to Lear in 1856.

At last the day came when Mr Dakyns had to leave and the children had to have their hair cut, on the headmaster's urgent advice, before they were sent over to Mr Kegan Paul's little gang of pupils in Dorset. It was presumably here that they got kicked 'because my father was a poet'. Whenever they came home, the rejoicings, the flags and special banners, and the sense of paradise regained defy description. Hallam went to Marlborough because his father knew and trusted the headmaster, Dr Bradley,[14] but Bradley became Dean of Westminster in 1881, so Lionel was sent to Eton, perhaps for that reason or perhaps to avoid the rigours of the Marlborough winter, which had made Hallam ill. They both appear to have been happy. Whenever Alfred went to London his life was absurdly crowded: just reading Emily's list of the people he met is enough to make one's head reel. But when the boys had gone to boarding school he became freer at home, and William Allingham records some captivating visits.

One day in August 1867, he met Alfred on the quay at Yarmouth (Isle of Wight) with his brother Fred and two daughters. Alfred was off on his own to see Lyme Regis, where he had always wanted to visit the Cobb because of Jane Austen's *Persuasion*. 'Will you come?' Of course Allingham said yes, so off they went to Dorchester in a second class carriage, in a slow train, in a cloud of shag tobacco smoke. 'In our carriage a Cockney clock-winder, who gets out at every station to regulate the Railway Company's clock.' At Dorchester they took rooms ('not good') at The Antelope, and walked among river-meadows. The Antelope produced a pint of port for dinner, and Allingham proposed a twilight visit to William Barnes; he showed the way to Came Vicarage 'in a hollow among trees'. They found it by starlight a little before ten. Barnes cried, 'Here's an honour! Put out something – put out something.' But they could not stay, so Barnes walked back with them the mile or so to Dorchester, 'talking of British antiquities, Wareham, Sun-worship, etc.' The next day they set out to walk to Lyme from Bridport, 'leaving bag to come by carrier', and passing behind the large bulk of Golden Cap, through Chideock with its old church and 'flowery houses', to Charmouth where they had beer and cheese, and Alfred chatted to the girl who served them, and discovered she came from Cowes. 'We see Lyme below us and take a fieldpath.' They stayed at The Cups, where after dinner they talked about marriage. 'I used to rage,' said Alfred, 'against the social conditions that made marriage so difficult.' Was he really thinking of his own personal case? I doubt that: what worried him or had worried him was that money should be such a barrier. Does he imply that he no longer raged? He is fifty-eight, he may well have calmed down a little, and he is talking to a younger man still in search of a wife.[15]

They had a happy few days: one is reluctant to leave them, and

Tennyson was reluctant to let Allingham go home. They talked as one would expect about Swinburne and Morris and Burne-Jones, and then about Scott and Jane Austen, they sauntered along the Cobb and looked out to Portland at the far edge of Lyme Bay, they followed tracks and pathways a mile or two west to the Devon border. Tennyson went on to Dartmoor with Palgrave, whose family were staying in Lyme, and sent a message through him begging Allingham to join them at Moretonhampstead on the west edge of the moor. Palgrave appears to have been less than delighted to transmit this invitation: jealousies were developing among Alfred's fans however Emily tried to smooth them over. Patmore seems to have been so furious that Alfred put his name forward for the Royal Literary Fund and neglected to write about his wife's death (he swiftly married money) that he sulked for twenty years. The permanent monument of Palgrave's friendship is *The Golden Treasury of Songs and Lyrics*, which in the right edition exactly represents Tennyson's choice and range, all but two poems. They must have made a queer couple, Palgrave with his fine, miniature features, small-built, pedantic, Jewish (his father altered the name from Cohen and died reading prayers in Hebrew), and Alfred large and flowing-haired, wearing perhaps his blue-tinted spectacles, his amazing hat and huge cloak.[16]

But Allingham was like an adopted son to him, someone for whom one might decently apply to the government for a pension.[17] By contrast with the lyrical Lyme Regis episode, and with the return match when Barnes visited Farringford, but went sternly to bed when Alfred's late-evening talk veered towards approving of pantheism, a scene not without a certain innocence, after all, it is interesting to observe an evening of Alfred among equals. He was in London, at a dinner with Gladstone, with whom slowly and gingerly he was becoming great friends, and with Holman Hunt and Woolner,[18] whose house it was, and Dr Symonds of Clifton, whose son J. A. Symonds, a recent Balliol first, recorded the evening with more clarity than charity. It was 8 December 1865; young Symonds was invited round after dinner, but in fact he was shown in during dessert. They were discussing Governor Eyre, who had put down a black rebellion in Jamaica with the most savage repression. Gladstone was attacking him, Tennyson defending:[19]

Gladstone had been reading official papers on the business all the morning and said, with an expression of intense gravity, just after I had entered, 'And that evidence wrung from a poor black boy with a revolver at his head!' He said this in an orator's tone, pity mingled with indignation, the pressure of the lips, the inclination of the head, the lifting of the eyes to heaven, all marking the man's moral earnestness . . . Tennyson did not argue. He kept asserting various prejudices and convictions. 'We are more tender to a black than to ourselves.' 'Niggers are tigers; niggers are tigers,' in *obbligato, sotto voce*, to Gladstone's declamation. 'But the Englishman is a cruel man – he is a strong man,' put in Gladstone. My father illustrated this by stories of the Indian Mutiny. 'That's not like Oriental cruelty,' said Tennyson, 'but I could not kill a cat, not the tomcat who scratches and miaowes over his disgusting amours, and keeps me awake . . . I have not got the English courage. I could not wait six hours in a square expecting a battery's fire.'

Palgrave came in at this point, 'a slight cast in his eye, an impatient, unsatisfied look, and some self-assertion in his manner.' Tennyson was drinking glasses of port, and glaring round the room through his spectacles.

They discussed universal franchise, but Gladstone fobbed them off, he would not reveal the provisions of his coming Bill. Tennyson said ' "Oh, I think a state in which every man would have a vote is the ideal. I always thought it might be realized in England, if anywhere, with our constitutional history. But how to do it." This was the mere reflector. The man of practice said nothing.' Over coffee, Alfred was left to smoke a pipe. Woolner was 'agreeably subdued', Palgrave 'rasped a little' and Holman Hunt kept quiet. They met Mrs Woolner and Miss Waugh, Holman Hunt's fiancée, only in the drawing room. Woolner showed Gladstone a manuscript of Tennyson's Homeric versions, but Alfred was very upset, and had to be calmed down by the Doctor, who drew him out on the nature of size and greatness:

'I cannot form the least notion of a brick . . . I cannot penetrate the brick. But I have more distinct ideas of God, of love, and such emotions. I can sympathize with God in my poor way. The human soul seems to me always in some way, how we do not know, identical with God. That's the value of prayer. Prayer is like opening a sluice between the great ocean and our

little channels ... Huxley says we may have come from
monkeys. That makes no difference to me.'

They moved back into the dining room, where they got down to
detailed arguments about Homeric Greek. The most interesting of
the poet's remarks was about *Helkechitones*, the Homeric epithet for
Ionian women.

> 'Ah! there's nothing more romantic than the image of these
> women floating along the streets of Troy with their long dresses
> flying out behind them. Windy Troy! I dare say it was not
> windier than other places, but it stood high, open to the air. As
> a schoolboy, I used to see them. A boy of course imagines
> something like a modern town.' ... Palgrave suggested a
> translation of Homer into Biblical prose.

He had begun it, but Jowett dissuaded him, saying he had not
enough command of English. '"Rather disparaging to you," said
Tennyson. Tennyson said he had read out in Old English to his wife
the *Odyssey*. "And it struck me I did it very well."'

A few months earlier Symonds had heard Woolner chatting to
his father. Tennyson had told Woolner that Browning said he wrote
his poems straight down, and never corrected them. 'Tennyson says
form is immortal, instancing the short poems of Catullus. Browning
hopes to live by force of thought, and is careless about form ...
Tennyson makes mistakes about the poets he admires. He once wrote
to Bailey, and said he [Tennyson] was a wren singing in a hedge,
while the author of 'Festus' was an eagle soaring above him.'[20]

Beyond this, Symonds observed little of interest about the Poet
Laureate beyond an attack of nervous eczema. The extremely pushy
Mrs Cameron took it into her head to bully Alfred into being
vaccinated.[21] This was done, but the injection went wrong (surely
not from a 'gouty baby' as we are told by Symonds, but from a dirty
needle?) and gout was at first diagnosed, though wrongly, it was
decided later. Poor Alfred was not only seriously ill with infected
legs for at least six months, but was stopped from port for two years
(1863–5). Very oddly indeed, he was encouraged to take to sherry
instead, in which he rapidly became an epicurean expert. He drank
Woolner's port with Gladstone though, as we have seen, and in
February 1867 he was drinking Waterloo port,[22] the equivalent of

1930s port today, and no more easily to be found. Symonds knew nothing about the port habit, he just recorded what he saw. He never got close to Alfred personally: he even spoke of 'the nightmare of Tennyson', but he called at Farringford a fortnight after his own wedding and fell in love with the boys; Tennyson never knew this, though Dakyns (by now a classics master at Clifton) was told. Apart from that, he luxuriated in the poem 'Lucretius' at Venice and was gratified in 1891 that Tennyson dying was familiar with his enormous history of the Renaissance.[23] Had Alfred any animus against homosexuals? It is not at all obvious that he had. His brother-in-law Charles Weld, who was mysteriously disgraced, may have been one.[24]

When the Victorians want to cover up anything scandalous, we are lucky if we can pull back the curtain, but Alfred himself is not hard to read. It is not his inner or his private life but only his public and ceremonial role that rings hollow. He liked the hothouses at Chatsworth because they were like his forest scene in 'Enoch Arden'. He fell six feet into a hole his wife had ordered dug in his garden, showing an American home to his hotel, and ten feet down an attic ladder in the dark, and laughed it off. The thought of the dons at Trinity terrified him, though he admitted he would prefer a week there as the Master's guest to a week in Buckingham Palace. When he was invited for a Cambridge degree, he trembled all day before deciding to refuse. The offer was repeated, but he could not face going. He got used to grand visitors, and cheerfully entertained the Ethiopian monarch's princes and the Queen of the Sandwich Isles.[25] When his 'Ode Sung at the Opening of the International Exhibition' was pirated in The Times, he never forgot the ignominious printing errors, but the massive piece of silver plate he was given by the Exhibition Trustees was never mentioned. He never gave up loving London life: he told Palgrave once in Yorkshire that if he could always live in the Dales or always in London, it must be 'all London'. Yet the most official of his duties as laureate became the least official, because he and the Queen got on like a house on fire.

Their relationship has been studied, naturally enough, in a somewhat serious spirit,[26] because its climax was not only Alfred's seat in the Lords, but a strange little episode towards the end of his life, when the Queen could not stand Mr Gladstone a minute longer and wrote to Alfred, asking him to persuade the old man to retire. It was an indiscreet request. Alfred did approach Gladstone, though with small expectation of success, but Gladstone sensibly took no notice; at least no reply of his has survived.[27] That peculiar episode was untypical: Alfred was a member of the Court and thereby excused from jury service, but he had no political duties and no standing.

The Queen had his wife and children over to Osborne where they were shown round (what they saw is much what one sees today), and she and her own children were pleased with their poet and took an interest, not disastrous but normal, in his poetry. They sent one another books: they were familiar. He was more thrilled to be asked by Prince Albert for his autograph in a book to be given to the Queen than he was with the offer of a baronetcy in 1865, and in 1873 and 1874.[28] The turning-point of the friendship had been the death of Albert on 14 December 1861; the Queen was greatly moved by Alfred's new Prologue to the *Idylls*, which he published almost at once, and in the sad years that followed found serious comfort, as so many Victorians did, in *In Memoriam*. Every personal sorrow deepened their friendship: or so it appeared from their letters of condolence. And he made himself useful: small commissions were swiftly and capably executed, epigrams for statues, an extra verse to the national anthem for a royal wedding, and so on.

There were some bizarre episodes all the same. In 1863, the Queen determined to commemorate her mother the Duchess of Kent with a statue and an inscription, in a new mausoleum at Frogmore. She sent through the Dean of Windsor for some verse from the Laureate to be delivered 'as soon as possible'. He produced what was asked for, four lines beginning 'O blessing of thy child as she was thine'. He got back a letter from Katherine Bruce, a lady-in-waiting:

> Beautiful as they are, your tried kindness induces the Queen to let you know honestly that they do not quite express Her idea. The Dean may not have explained that the Mausoleum is divided into two parts – a lower chamber which is approached by a different path, and encircled by a terrace where seats are placed, and flowers grown in ornamental vases, and where if the Duchess had lived it was her intention often to take tea, etc. In the centre of this Gallery, the statue will be placed under a cupola – the statue represents the Duchess standing in full evening costume and the Queen wishes to remember Her

mother as she was in Life. Your lines HM thinks would be most appropriate on the tomb itself.

This time Alfred sent a selection. He had been told to take for theme, 'Her children arise and call her blessed', and he must have written them swiftly, because six days after Katherine Bruce's first letter came a second one:

> I have by Her Majesty's command already sent to the Sculptor a copy of the lines beginning 'Long as the heart beats life etc.' to be engraved on the pedestal of the statue. Her Majesty preferred this verse both from the expression Guardian-Mother mild, which she particularly admired, as so descriptive of the Duchess, and also because the Queen did not quite like Herself putting 'O blessing of thy Child *as she was thine*' under the image of her Mother. HM thought it too presuming.[29]

And thus it is to be hoped that the ashes of the Duchess of Kent rested in peace.

That Christmas Thackeray died, and Mrs Cameron brought his daughters to stay with her at Farringford. Thackeray had been a true friend and an ally, but Tennyson probably saw more of his daughters. Mrs (later Lady) Ritchie is the eldest, and one of his most enchanting memoirists, but she is a full Victorian, and the change from her father's generation to hers is saddening. The 1860s were a decade punctuated by death. Mrs Bourne's in 1864, Elizabeth Russell's in 1865, and Tennyson's mother's the same year, at the age of 84. She died before Alfred could get to Hampstead. 'I dare not see her . . . she did not ask for me specially, which is one comfort.' To the vicar who took the funeral, he said, 'I hope you will not think that I have spoken in exaggerated terms of my beloved mother, but indeed she was the beautifullest thing God almighty ever did make.' To his wife he wrote, 'The departure of so blessed a being almost whose last words were, when asked how she felt, "very quiet" seems to have no sting in it and she declared that she had no pain.'[30] At the end of the decade, Sir John Simeon died (abroad, in June 1870). That death was grievous to Alfred, because Sir John was a neighbour in the Isle of Wight, a genuine and close friend. He was a Catholic convert (1851), and an MP, but for whatever reasons he struck a deep note from the poet. It had been said that Alfred's anti-Catholic prejudices,

which were certainly healthily developed in youth, were abated by
this friendship: perhaps they were equally so by W. G. Ward, whom
he loved and had for a close neighbour in the Elysian fields of West
Wight. Yet the same strong feelings are to be found in his plays. It
cannot be unimportant in their friendship that John Simeon was a
liberal (and a gentleman) just as W. G. Ward had been a Balliol don.
Alfred wrote for Simeon one of the most touching of his personal
poems, 'In the Garden at Swainston'. It is in pesonal poems like this
that he labours at his true vocation, and reappears as the kind of poet
he most truly was. They are often for those he saw most in the Isle
of Wight: Lear, Maurice, Simeon, and the few lines to Jowett. They
have something in common with the happier, nostalgic stanzas of *In
Memoriam*. In this poem indeed he recalls three dead men, Arthur
Hallam, Henry Lushington and Sir John Simeon:[31]

> Nightingales warbled without,
>   Within was weeping for thee;
> Shadows of three dead men
>   Walked in the walks with me,
>   Shadows of three dead men and thou wast one of the three.

> Nightingales sang in his woods:
>   The Master was far away:
> Nightingales warbled and sang
>   Of a passion that lasts but a day;
>   Still in the house in his coffin the Prince of courtesy lay.

> Two dead men have I known
>   In courtesy like to thee:
> Two dead men have I loved
>   With a love that ever will be:
>   Three dead men have I loved and thou art last of the three.

His feelings about Catholics were not reformed overnight,
because the very next month the Vatican declared the Pope to be
infallible (in July 1870), and soon afterwards James Knowles read
him a newspaper story that the Christ of Oberammergau had been
conscripted into the Austrian army. 'Quite impromptu, as he lay
upon his bed, he made and chanted' a ballad of five spirited and
ironic stanzas, which Knowles wrote down. Those who doubt other

examples of the impromptu composition of light verse by Tennyson should remember this one, 'The Christ of Ammergau':

> They made the old Pope God –
>   Which God, if He will, may pardon –
> And Christ stepped down from the cross,
>   Christ came out of the garden.
>
> They made the old Pope God
>   While God was rolling his thunder,
> And Christ came out from Ammergau
>   To massacre, burn, and plunder
>
> (1–8)

The thunderstorm that rattled the Roman rooftops during the vote for infallibility continued to re-echo in his verses. It appears to be true of him as it is of other poets that one poem follows exactly on the heels of the next, disregarding any interval of time. His next poem 'The Voice and the Peak', was not written until September 1873, after much work on the *Idylls*, but it enshrines the 'long roar/ Green-rushing from the rosy thrones of dawn', and a rejected verse asks 'Why dost thou roar, O stream?' The answer is 'I am the voice of the Peak, I roar and rave for I fall'. That period following Sir John Simeon's death was one of intense gloom for him. His epigrams snap and crackle and snarl both on public issues and private ones. Darwin, or rather the public effect of the Darwin controversy, was undoubtedly distressing to him, although he always claimed otherwise, and his best lines written then were his melancholy sonnet in memory of poor Brookfield, who died in 1874, or stray lines like 'And secular perforations of the worm'. Somewhere about his sixtieth birthday (1869) something broke in him or went wrong with the world; he began to be an old man.

In 1860, after all, he had spoken lightly to Woolner and others about going to Constantinople for a few weeks, or the West Indies, or more vaguely the Levant.[32] It may be that 1860 was the true turning-point, but rather for English history than for Tennyson personally. The row over the liberal *Essays and Reviews* assailed Jowett, the British Association for the Advancement of Science suffered convulsions at its Oxford meeting over Huxley's defence of Darwin's views, news of Sir John Franklin's death marked the end of a great age in exploration,[33] and in 1861 the American civil war broke out. But whatever altered in Alfred took time to alter. He still visited the Turkish baths in Covent Garden, and a letter was kept there for him though he was years between visits,[34] and for a large part of 1865 he was obsessed with the question whether a weasel has a hunting cry. The Duke of Argyll thought they might occasionally utter a thin yelp when they hunted in packs (something one would give a good deal to witness). When he moved to Aldworth he engaged in prolonged warfare with an elderly character called Lord Egremont who sounds pleasingly eccentric, over his right to an approach road to the old potato patch where his house stood.[35] These are not signs of creeping gentility, but only of increasing age.

His family filled his mind. The evening readings were still the same: one night Jowett read from Isaiah and Plato, but mostly it was Alfred: the *Hylas* of Theocritus in Greek, Marvell 'To his Coy Mistress', and 'Northern Farmer' were one programme one would like to have heard. Both the children were rather old in years as well as wisdom when they left school, Hallam went rather late to Cambridge. Meanwhile Mrs Tennyson was ageing, and Alfred must have worried about that. When they married someone called her 'a cloud of white muslin out of which would suddenly emerge a small voice', and at every age Alfred was accustomed to pulling or pushing her in wheelchairs and carriages. We are constantly told of the appalling burden correspondence with strangers threw on them both, and one should believe that, though her patience and labour for Alfred may also have been a burden.

In 1874, there came a crisis. Emily was sixty-one. Both the boys were away at Cambridge (together at Trinity to Emily's great relief), when having written no journal since February, she noted under September: 'I had to answer many letters from unknown correspondents, asking advice from Alfred as to religious questions, and desiring criticism of poems, etc. and I became very ill and could do but little, so my Journal ends here.' Hallam added to her manuscript a note saying, 'I did not return to Cambridge after the long vacation of this year, but remained at home as my Father's secretary. Otherwise our life did not undergo much change.' That is an astonishingly bland observation. It appears Emily was ill on and off throughout 1874, and a visit to France with Alfred in August utterly undid her. (It is significant in Emily's life, considering all this, how few letters from 1874 have survived.) Still, she lived on for another twenty years. As for Hallam, he seems to have settled down quite smoothly to his new task. One of his first actions was to fill an old Marlborough exercise book with anecdotes remembered from his father's conversation. The dating of this fascinating but fragmented text, which was plundered by Sir Charles Tennyson but has never been fully published, has eluded all those who mention it, but it can properly be dated from an anecdote about the punishment of adultery among birds, which Alfred first came across in French in the *Revue des Deux Mondes* for 15 August when they were at Cauterets in 1874.[36]

What was it that so filled the old man with gloomy thoughts, and so diverted the streams of his poetry? The advent and new challenge of Swinburne has been suggested: but that should have registered if at all in 1862. Later, Swinburne's output became uneven and dwindled, yet even at the moment when poetry poured out of him like a waterfall it did not distress Alfred or make him pause. As a very old man he sent for Knowles and passionately insisted that his opinion was and had always been that Wordsworth was the greatest poet of the century. He deeply disapproved of Swinburne for his atheism and for his Bohemian style of life, though he admitted his metrical skill. As we have seen he blamed the Pre-Raphaelites.[37] Milnes (Lord Houghton) has at times been blamed, but that is too knowing; it should be noted that Tennyson never blamed him. It is a relief that he never knew how Bertrand Russell's contemporaries used to march around Trinity together, chanting Swinburne's intoxicating verses in the 1890s. All the same it was not Swinburne, and it was not worries about publishers, and it was not Darwinism that so deeply infected him.

His mind was as restless as it had ever been. The Metaphysical Society which Knowles constructed around him in the 1870s, was a retrospective answer to the disturbance over Darwinism, just as his personal answer to the modernist crisis in theology was to learn Hebrew and to pour scorn on any visiting clergyman who did not know it. In poetry, his mind was stirred by a sense of inadequacy in his own lifelong, well-modulated smoothness, to a hunger for the grit and gravel of dialect and the tensions of dramatic verse. He turned that way when he wrote his sonnet 'Show-Day at Battle Abbey' in May 1876: in that he is judgemental; he can scarcely bear for the battle of Hastings to be forgiven. In December of that year he began *Becket*; but in 1874 he had already written his *Queen Mary*

about Mary Tudor, which was almost a play; *Harold* was finished in
1876, and *Becket* in 1879. It will be better to deal with these three
works later; here it is sufficient to notice that when the *Idylls* were
finished in 1874, his mind turned at once to an arena even more
formidably difficult than that of the epic. At the same time, his search
for a growling English noise in poetry led him into one of the most
interesting of all his experiments: his 'Battle of Brunanburh' in 1876.
It was not until the five years of his most intense affair with the stage
were over that his output of lyric poems in all their energy and
variety would begin to pick up again.

Brunanburh is an Anglo-Saxon text in tenth-century Old English
which Hallam had discussed and rendered creditably enough in prose
in the *Contemporary Review* (November 1876), which Knowles
edited. Alfred used that, but he also studied Guest's *History of English
Rhythms* (1838), which printed the text with a translation, as Hallam
did, and he had already gleefully adopted the metre in his *Harold*:
'Heard how the shield-wall rang,/Iron on iron clang,/Anvil on
hammer bang'. One recalls (though Alfred may not have done) the
early poem about Thor's hammer. *Brunanburh* particularly appealed
to him because for once it was an English victory. The battle was in
937; it apparently gave Athelstan some genuine title to be called King
of Britain.

The original poem comes at the end of oral tradition; it is as
Michael Alexander said, 'the first royal panegyric, the first court
poem, the first heroic poem to mention the reading of books, and
the last example of correct versification.'[38] The age when it was
written was still dark enough that no one knows where Brunanburh
is or was; only that there the West Saxons and the Mercians hacked
to pieces the Picts, the Scots, the Welsh, the Strathclyde Celts, and
the Vikings. Tennyson faced a subtle task, because the technique of
the original is not only as musical as he is, but relies on endless,
shimmering variation. Hallam offered some good suggestions, such
as 'the fallow flood', which I take it means coloured like a fallow
deer (*fealo*, yellowish). Elsewhere the colour defeats the poet: 'Many
a livid one, many a sallow-skin' a characteristic Tennysonian grue-
someness over the dead, should really read 'many a dun-feather,
many a dark-feather', since it is about eagles and crows:

> Many a carcase they left to be carrion,
> Many a livid one, many a sallow-skin –

Left for the white tailed eagle to tear it, and
Left for the horny-nibbed raven to rend it, and
Gave to the garbaging war-hawk to gorge it, and
That gray beast, the wolf of the weald.

Never had huger
Slaughter of heroes
Slain by the sword-edge –
Such as old writers
Have writ of in histories –
Hapt in this isle, since
Up from the East hither
Saxon and Angle from
Over the broad billow
Broke into Britain with
Haughty war-workers who
Harried the Welshman, when
Earls that were lured by the
Hunger of glory gat
Hold of the land.

(105–25)

This is not laureate verse, but neither Swinburne, nor G. M. Hopkins himself, a writer Tennyson probably never knew, can improve on that as a study in the rhythms of Old English.[39] Today, Tennyson's achievement looks less because others have followed where he led the way; all the same, nothing from his own or any earlier generation compares for full-blooded experiment with his 'Brunanburh', not even Peacock. We shall find in 'The Voyage of Maeldune' the same degree of originality, though there it is not metrical. He is also the first English poet to make anything of Chinese poetry: Jowett found Lao-Tzu for him and he wrote 'The Ancient Sage', which is a translation of the name. He was right to rank that among the better of his later poems (1885) though it is not a translation, but a wandering and sage-like reflection. Shades of Arnold and even of Rogers pass across it, but its good plain bread-and-butter wisdom is highly unusual in English poetry.[40]

The cleverest of the literary young, such as Hopkins and A. E. Housman, distrusted the *Idylls* and could not accept Tennyson's total yet still increasing sovereignty, a claim after all that he had never

made, but which was made by the new reading public. The middle-
aged, both the intellectuals like Pauline Trevelyan, and the Queen
and Lady Ritchie, to take examples of another kind, stuck fast to *In
Memoriam*, and knew that he was a great poet, however they might
calculate the balance of his by now voluminous works. To the
ordinary, literary, though not necessarily sharp or intellectual, young
in about 1871 he was like a god. That moment of low tide for him
personally and as a poet was the high tide of his reputation.

He was in the British Museum about his normal business one
day when a Senior Assistant in the Library, W. Ralston, came
clattering down a spiral staircase to the bowels of the place (which
are bowels indeed, galleries uncarpeted and unlighted, where the
reader in the 1950s still proceeded with a lamp held over his head) to
a place called the Den, where the young Edmund Gosse worked in
silence. Ralston was a Russian expert and translator, and a close
friend of Turgenev's, who stayed with the Tennysons at Farringford
from 5–10 May that year.[41] He now wanted to introduce Gosse to
the laureate. They found him in a long sculpture gallery, the one
now devoted to postcard-selling I think, chatting to Spedding. Gosse,
who felt by 1912 that Tennyson's fame was over for the time being
and who blamed his silly lyric suite *The Loves of the Wrens*, explains
what happened in *Portraits and Sketches* (1912):

> As we climbed those steep and spiral staircases towards light
> and day, my heart pounded in my chest with agitation. The
> feeling of excitement was almost overwhelming; it was not
> peculiar to myself; such ardours were common in those years.
> Some day a philosopher must analyse it – that enthusiasm of the
> seventies, that intoxicating belief in the 'might of poesy.'

They discussed Norway, where Gosse was going and Alfred had
been, and the tiny carriages you had to drive yourself, which were
the only way of getting about. Alfred could not use them, because
he could not see, and Gosse noticed his extraordinary thick glasses.[42]

Indeed his poor and decreasing sight so worried Emily that in
Cornwall she had entrusted Palgrave with his life. That scholar took
the charge so seriously as to run after Tennyson whenever he escaped,
yelling 'Tennyson! Tennyson!' All the same, Alfred fell into the
Camel in spite of him, looking for Arthur's Stone. He was not
pleased by Palgrave's behaviour, since he hoped to be incognito.

Now he stood by 'the famous black bust of Antinous. Tennyson bent forward a little, and said in his deep slow voice, "Ah! this is the inscrutable Bithynian!" There was a pause, and then he added, gazing into the eyes of the bust, "If we knew what he knew, we should understand the ancient world."' Many years later, when Gosse was in trouble with Churton Collins, the *Quarterly*'s literary hatchet man, he was comforted by Tennyson calling him a jackass,[43] though he elaborated the remark to 'a Louse upon the Locks of Literature', which he must have found in Smollett, in *Humphrey Clinker*.

Still, not everything was gloom and jackassery even in 1871: one must remind oneself again and again of Alfred's absorbing private life. In that same May he was at home in the Isle of Wight; they did not go to Aldworth until June. At the end of April they had their old shepherd in to dinner and sat a long time with him. Then in May they drove about to see some new fossil bones, and to visit 'the old Laburnum under the Fir Trees'. He read Emily his 'Tristram', 'The Last Tournament', and she thought it 'very grand and terrible'. Then on 24 May, when they have been nearly twenty-one years married, she records: 'We drive to the Needles, A. and I. A beautiful day. I enjoy it much. There is the old mystic light on land and sea. He drives with me not infrequently now, and we have together such little walks as I can take.' At the end of March she had written, 'A. returns. Lionel and I go to the boat to meet him. A day never to be forgotten. Surely love as one grows older has the tenderness of the eve of parting – the long parting. A. never seemed to me so beautiful and touching, and I never had moments of the same sort of happiness. Thank God for ever for this time alone with him and our boys.'

Hallam was growing into a poet; not only with school prizes and essay prizes but on the evidence of a sonnet he wrote later to Edward Lear.[44] Of all the family of Tennyson poets, he is the only one never mentioned, yet he is as good as any but Charles and his father. He must have intensely adored the father to whom he sacrificed so much of his life and marriage. His poem to Lear is thanks for the loan of a house for his honeymoon, though he took only a week off even for that. Perhaps the poem would not stand up among poems of the first rank, maybe it is just personal poetry, written to be kept in a drawer, but it is touching. In 1862 Lionel (aged nine) negotiated an exchange of his verses with Lewis Carroll, but alas those are not preserved.[45]

The story of the rest of Alfred's tattered family is touching also. In 1870 Fred was suffering from his great obsession with Masonic imagery: *Veritas*, the book he helped edit about it, appeared in 1874 and he spent a year or two trying to interest the Duke of Leinster, an Irish Mason of high status. In 1859 he had moved to Jersey, but between 1854 and 1890 he published no more of his poetry. He confined himself to such activities as landscape paintings on the bottom of his plate after breakfast, and to explosions of rage such as 'Where are my trousers? Where are my trousers? I have forty pairs and I can only find thirty-five!' His son was known as the strongest man in the British army, but could be quelled by his father with 'Enough! To your room Sir!'

Charles had a relapse when he took to opium again in 1859, but he settled after that to a humble, only mildly eccentric life in the Victorian clerical manner. Grasby was a backward place, where you cut a sheep in half and walked between the two halves as a charm against witchcraft. Charles offered a therapy of spelling bees and poetic bees, but he was not always cleanly shaven, and his wife wore clogs. Back in 1850 he had been forced to sue an agent; he recovered a large sum from the man, all of which he used to build a church and a school. In 1864 his cousin Lewis Fytche offered to make him Sheriff's Chaplain, but he said the position was 'too public and prominent for my rural habits'. He published his poems in the 1860s,[46] and when he died there were 342 collected sonnets, some very beautiful:

> The bells awake the Sabbath's choral prime;
> By breezes soften'd to a harp-like tone; . . .
>
> . . . While the sick ewe, in the next pasture ground
> Lifts her white eyelash, points her languid ear,
> And turns her pensive face towards the sound . . .
>
> . . . I listen'd, while that multitudinous sound
> Peel'd from the highway, through the twilight air . . .

His at least was by no human standard a wasted life. He exuded simplicity and warmth; both he and his wife sank back into their native roots and there found nourishment. But Edward died mad in 1877. Septimus, despite the £3000 inheritance from his grandfather in 1835, could do nothing; until 1843 he lived with his mother: he clung to her or to Fred or to Arthur, and in 1866 he died at 51. Arthur drank; he was cured in 1842, and then lived thirteen years with Fred, but never got over Fred's coldness to him. He came to England about 1859, got a deep fit of religion, and married in 1860. His wife died in 1881 and he was thought to be inconsolable, wandering about weeping over one of her gloves, but in 1882 he married again. They went to Malvern, where he used to give spirited readings of Alfred's poems. Horatio lived fourteen years with his mother or Alfred or Charles. He married Charlotte Elwes of the Isle of Wight in 1857; she died in 1868 and he remarried, this time a sister of Arthur's wife. He was fervently religious and built the Freshwater local library. He died in 1899. One of the brothers built a cottage in Alfred's grounds, another settled at Freshwater Bay. From 1865 when their mother died, the visits to Alfred greatly increased, and his sister Tilly, whom Longfellow noticed as 'an angular, dyspeptic woman', came to live with him.

Mary had married a barrister, who was the brother of a Cheltenham doctor. She had led Fred and her sister Emily into the Swedenborgian church. Her husband worked in the West Indies, where he was not felt to have been as successful as he deserved. 'The whizz, the whirr, and the metallic ring' of mosquitoes tormented her, and finally in 1884 she died; her husband died a year later. They are an interesting couple, and their son was a scholar, but they are outside the immediate circle of Alfred's life. Tilly was inside it when her mother and aunt died in 1865, but there is less to say about her. She luckily took to Alfred's house, and when he died in 1892 she moved on to the Lushington house with her sister Cecilia. Unluckily, Professor Lushington died the next year. Cecilia had been a spirited, ballad-singing girl, and she had four children, but one after the other they died: the first a boy of thirteen in 1856, a girl of nineteen in 1868, and one of twenty-one in 1872. Only her daughter Zilly lived on, and the three of them lapsed into extreme oddity. Cecilia died at 92 in 1909 and Tilly at 97 in 1913. Emily Jesse died formidably but more cheerfully eccentric, accompanied everywhere by a raven that ate raw meat. Alfred bought her a house in Flask Walk near her mother's. 'I have known everything,' she told one of Thackeray's daughters in her strong Lincolnshire accent. 'I have known what it is to feel like a stoän.' These brothers and sisters went with Alfred Tennyson through life like a swarm of flies.

But his bitterest feelings were not about them. They were neatly stated in one of those growled-out epigrams of his, of which Rawnsley remembered a version:

> In my youth the growls,
> In mine age the owls,
> After death the ghouls.

He felt he would be ripped open like a pig by biographers (a recurring theme in his conversation); he was appalled by Froude's book on Carlyle, and must have known plenty about the case of Thackeray, whose life was never written until his letters were collected in our lifetime. That is why he relied on Hallam to see him protected, why he outwitted Knowles who intended to be his biographer, and why he was so lucky that his wife outlived him. He was not really old at sixty but he could no longer plan any vast programme of work: he no longer knew how long a poem he could hope to finish.

CHAPTER TEN

The Curtain Falls

THERE IS one more phase of Alfred Tennyson's activity that should be treated as a whole, like the *Idylls of the King*, if only to get it out of the way, even though it is entangled with the annual chronicle of his life, just as the long fever of the *Idylls* is. I mean his passion for the theatre, which exactly follows on the end of the *Idylls*, so that one might choose, as critics have tended to do, to treat it as an old man's weakness, a folly piled on a folly. It is possible he was manoeuvred into the theatre by his friends; it is certain that, because of his worries over publishers, money became very important to him. The theatre for that reason if for no other occupied much of his attention until the time of his death, and yet it did not prevent the extraordinary flowering of lyric poetry at the end of his life, nor did it prevent his remarkable verse experiments, or his still more remarkable simple achievements in old age.

He had a deep-rooted, personal ambition to succeed in the theatre. He had always liked to see acting at home, and as a boy had some talent for it. He did not do so, though his failure was not as catastrophic or obvious to the public as it might have been. The truth is that the English theatre was in a very low state, the public taste was by no means enlightened, and the actors and managers he met were often charlatans and blockheads:[1] he could hardly have overcome these obstacles as a very young man might have done. An ageing poet coming fresh to the theatre will seldom have anything very exciting to offer it. As for the deeper problem of the revival of an English verse theatre, one can only say after a hundred years more of attempts since Tennyson's, and now since T. S. Eliot's, Christopher Fry's, Ezra Pound's, Tony Harrison's and Seamus Heaney's, let alone the masterly dramatic verse of Yeats, that the more the verse theatre is revived the more obviously it is dead.

Alfred's first serious assault on the heights of dramatic fame in the theatre had been in association with the actor/manager Irving,

who both flattered and despised his efforts. Irving had taken the
Lyceum in 1871, he liked historical plays, and Alfred saw his
opportunity. In 1874 he began his *Queen Mary*, a work of liberal
Protestant history with forty-four characters and some attempts at
period humour. Alas the speeches are at times too long, the history
absurd, and the structure broken-backed. But there are pleasing lines,
like 'It was never merry world in England since the Bible came
among us', and a remarkable study in what should be Oxfordshire
dialect, which would seem to be carefully based on the publications
of the English Dialect Society, but in fact derives from some notes
on Wessex dialect he got from Tom Hughes of Uffington. The result
is very peculiar. Sometimes a touch of real poetry lights the play up:
'like sungilt breathings on a frosty dawn'. The play was published in
1875, and produced in 1876. Alfred wanted Irving to play the
Cardinal, but Sabine Greville, an aesthete of ridiculous and socially
appalling intensity who was managing Tennyson's stage career,
made Irving play the minor part of Philip. Stanford, who was a
friend of Hallam's, wrote the music. But the cutting was drastic, and
anyway the play shut down after five weeks.

Still, his friends of the time supported him, he appears to have
trusted their opinions, and he got on at once with another play, *King
Harold*, which he dedicated in 1876 to Lord Lytton, his old enemy's
son, with a graceful reference to Bulwer-Lytton's novel, *Harold*. To
my mind this was his best play, or his nearest to a good play, though
it is still stuck in the rut of costume drama. It has no real origin in
the open day at Battle Abbey, about which he wrote a poem, because
by then he had finished it. It does contain moving allusions to
'Brunanburh' and uses its metre. But the conversation of its fisher-
men is absurd and overdone. It is a million miles from the Lincolnshire dialect poems, which are quite unpatronizing. Even the stars in
this play are grotesque. But Edward's vision is well written, and
stray lines touch a nerve of poetry; 'in cold white cells beneath an icy
moon' promises better things. The epic part is fine, but what is
lacking is the conception of a whole play, which is almost there,
almost on paper. The fault may be the absurdity of the Laureate's
ideas of medieval religion.

The trilogy of Tennyson's three full-length plays was supposed
to show three stages of the battle of the English people against the
Papacy: the third play was his *Becket*, which was published only in
1884. Irving was sure in the late 1870s that it would fail financially: it

would cost £2000 and £135 a night before Alfred made a penny, it would not run long or draw more than £150 a night. He asked for a shorter work fitter for the modern stage, and that is when Alfred wrote *The Cup*. But in spite of everything his heart swelled at the thought of great projects, and as late as 1889 when he was eighty and trying to get his *Foresters* produced, he wanted to embark on a full-scale play about Tristan.[2] *Becket* is once again deplorable. Fair Rosamund is ridiculous, but wicked Eleanor is worse. She is far less convincing than Vivien in *Idylls of the King*.

His shortest play, *The Falcon*, was in a way the most absurd, though in 1879 it ran sixty-seven nights, Alfred thought it 'stately and tender', and the Prince and Princess of Wales thought it 'one of the prettiest pieces they had ever seen'. It was a one-act play based on a story by Boccaccio, which Coventry Patmore had rendered into negligible verse. The laureate is supposed to have begun work on it as early as 1870. FitzGerald objected to the scene of reconciliation over a dinner of roast hawk, an unpalatable bird he believed. There is an extravagance and a preciousness about it, as the laureate's grandson has noted, that make it unacceptable on the stage, and unreadable at the desk. Had we been assured that it was a piece of pastiche written at the time of *The Devil and the Lady* when he was fourteen, no one would have been surprised.

In fact it raises the curious problem of whether his dramatic style does not go right back to his boyhood, in just the same way as his lyric style and for similar reasons. In him the memory and the composition of verse were strangely intermingled. But his idea of the theatre was fed meanwhile by such works as Lytton's *Richelieu*, in which Irving is said to have done well. A critic who attempts to solve this problem will have to cover a Siberian wasteland of Victorian dramatic verse from Browning and Byron through Swinburne's *Chastelard* and the Spasmodics to de Vere's *Alexander the Great*. *The Cup*, which was published with *The Falcon* in 1884, was presented by Irving and Ellen Terry at the Lyceum in 1881. *The Cup* is more ambitious in that it has two acts, but really no better, because its status as costume drama adds to the unreality of the plot, which is from Plutarch, and the flatness of the verse is unredeemable. It was played with *The Corsican Brothers*, which was very popular, and everyone apparently thought *The Cup* part of that success.

Late the same year, Alfred wrote a Lincolnshire village tragedy in three acts in prose. In a way it was a foretaste of moral realism fifty years before its time, but the story is as melodramatic as anything by Hardy, and improbable in a way that even Hardy's stories never were. It was called *The Promise of May*; it failed badly, and although it was already in print ready to be published, Tennyson had the print broken up. Irving had refused it, and the production was not good.

Its brief run was enlivened by an intervention of Lord Queensberry, one night in November 1882, backed by what sounds like a chorus of hired ruffians. This is not the only time that this eccentric nobleman figures in the history of the theatre, because it was the same Lord Queensberry who provoked Oscar Wilde a few years later into suing him over one of his sons, Lord Alfred Douglas. He was an associate of the radical politician Charles Bradlaugh, and a strong secularist (he was a strong everything), as well as being the promoter of the modern rules of boxing, and the author of a poem called 'The Spirit of the Matterhorn' (1881), which was no doubt intended to overshadow Tennyson's 'The Voice and the Peak' (1874). He leapt to his feet to protest at what he thought a monstrous caricature of an agnostic. It does not appear that anyone took him seriously, but in view of his later outbursts of rage against Wilde and against his son, this incident has some interest.[3]

After *The Cup*, Irving had suggested a Robin Hood play, and the laureate dashed one off, but as his grandson noticed it was really too trifling, like a light opera libretto. It was not improved by the addition of a fairy scene, which Irving suggested and Alfred dutifully cobbled into the text. He never gave up hoping about his plays, and in March 1892 *The Foresters* was a success in New York. And *Becket* was staged at last: Irving presented it in London in 1893 when the poet was dead. It ran a long time, indeed Irving revived it again and again, always successfully, until his death in 1905. He said it had changed his whole view of life, and that no other dramatic poetry and no other character had so influenced him.[4]

Irving had suggested a number of cuts, which Tennyson allowed, but his emissary Bram Stoker was alarmed to discover that the old man, who was then very close to death, knew his entire play by heart, and noticed every alteration. It would be a pleasure to leave him on the happy note of these late successes, and it is very tempting to suppose that even in the theatre he was magnificent, and not wholly a failure. Only a convincing modern production could set one's fears at rest about that. He had a certain largeness, and a spiritual quality that appealed to his contemporaries. Maybe his shyness undid him; certainly he was not at ease in the theatre. There is a gruesome tale told by a friend of Lionel's of being taken as a boy to sit in a box during one of Tennyson's plays with the author, who applauded loudly when the audience was silent, was silent during applause, and generally showed off in a most embarrassing way. It was an awful evening. Indeed, the entire episode of Tennyson and the theatre is awful.

Henry James criticized him as a dramatist with marvellously implacable gloom. But James was a social animal, he responded more to Browning, and Tennyson had always thrown him off balance, from the days when he craned across his neighbour to hear the great man chatting to Schliemann, and was disconcerted to hear him burbling about port and tobacco, an act that he often put on in public. James was comparatively crisp about Queen Mary: 'It is simply a dramatized chronicle, without any internal structure . . . It has no shape; it is cast in no mould; it has neither beginning, middle, nor end, save the chronological ones.' The two men came to like one another all the same, though nothing came of that, because by then Tennyson was wrapped in a world of his own. His encounter with Thomas Hardy, who says that Emily rose up for lunch as if from a coffin, was equally null. Alfred wrote Kipling a complimentary letter about a patriotic poem about the Flag and got a ridiculously grovelling reply, but there was no real contact there either. It was as if women and children had stolen his heart away. Or was it the worldly glamour and immediate contact of the theatre and theatrical people? He wrote The Promise of May for Mrs Beere and her theatre, only because she got so excited when he read her a Lincolnshire dialect poem. He was manipulated by women. To the dreadful Mrs Cameron, his friend and bear-leader, who would arrive with anything from two legs of mutton to half a dozen Americans, to 'bathe herself in his peace and light', succeeded Sabine Greville, almost his puppet-mistress, a vast lady draped in amazing colours who sent him queer-coloured notelets that began 'Dear Heart, dear Master'.

He had begun to like awful Mrs Cameron because he thought her funny, and genuine, and warm-hearted. He let her embark on her preposterous photographic illustrations of the Idylls, and often sat for her. When she paraded a whole gang of local officers to meet him in line, he offered them his stables and let them put a sergeant in the attic. But why he tolerated Sabine Greville is beyond conjecture.

Henry James heard him growling at her on a doorstep, 'You can do what you like, but don't kiss me in front of the cabman.' On one occasion, with Alfred standing there, she flung herself on her knees to read a sonnet on the Rev Mr Brookfield to his widow; she was wearing a long violet dress which she overflowed. Mrs Brookfield, who was Arthur Hallam's sister and Thackeray's mistress, particularly relished this scene. Had Alfred created it? There was something deeply comic buried within him.

A young lady at a garden party was horrified when he rushed away from her, complaining of the creaking of her stays; but then he came and apologized, having discovered that his own braces were to blame.[5] Farce flourished around him, because of his vast ungainly presence, but also because he relished farce, not because he was spoilt or had his head turned. It is Irving and Bram Stoker and their like, and maybe Mrs Beere, who are to blame for his theatrical disasters, and perhaps he was led on by such daft women as Sabine Greville; she used to kiss his hand in public on meeting, as his little grandchildren did when he came downstairs in the morning, too old to stoop. No doubt she represents his weakness for the theatrical: he paid for it by being pelted with verse plays, Gosse's *King Erik*, Martia Tupper's *Washington*, and heaven knows what else.[6]

His own poetry was as bright and often as successful as ever. In 1877 he wrote 'The Revenge', after much pondering. Victor Hugo's ballads had excited him in 1873 and his opening line was jotted down in 1871, but the whole poem was composed in a day or two in 1877. Scholars have cleverly adduced likenesses in the anti-Russian poetry of 1878, and Ricks fancies a ballad by Browning (March 1871) but neither Campbell nor Macaulay, nor even Browning is quite as intoxicating as Tennyson. His rhythmic experimentation is the victorious factor. It is curious that Arber's reprint of the Elizabethan account, which was sent to him and which he lost and then rediscovered, goes much more easily into blank verse then into the metre he used. He took the rhythm of 'The Charge of the Light Brigade' from a phrase in *The Times*, but this later poem is maturely pondered: it is the resurrection of his powers, and the two ballads together are the best of his or anyone else's 'national' poetry. It was Sir Clements Markham who first told Tennyson the story, after dinner with Knowles at Clapham Common (8 March 1873), drinking hot gin and Liebfraumilch 'steamed in large tumblers'. Hallam tells us the line 'At Flores in the Azores Sir Richard Grenville lay' lay for years on his father's desk. Where Tennyson in the end has 'Sink me the ship, Master Gunner – sink her, split her in twain!' Sir Clements Markham notes in his copy of *Ballads and Other Poems* (1880) that his ancestor records 'Sweet Maister-gunner, split our keel in twain'[7] which is a pure iambic. But the rhythm of Tennyson's version runs through the poem from the first line to the last like the breath of life.

In 1878 he wrote 'Rizpah', which at first he called 'Bones'. It was the story of a man executed in 1793, found in a magazine article about Brighton and told to Tennyson by Mary Brotherton. Metrically it reverts to *Maud*. 'Rizpah' seems a strange title now, but it is a biblical allusion (2 Samuel 21, 8–10), which no doubt lent dignity in its day, however much one may now prefer 'Bones'. This has been called one of Tennyson's cries of furious protest against society, which he disguises as mad monologues.[8] A poor old woman has to gather her son's bones from the gallows; she must go when the moon is hidden. But she is rather prophetic than mad, indeed she is quite sane, and her monologue is devastating: of all Tennyson's poems it is in this one that he comes nearest to his true successor, Thomas Hardy. 'Rizpah' has the same gruesome melodrama and horror at the tragedies of the poor that Hardy relished. It has the same stern arguments about God, and the same rejection of middle-class comfort. Further, it has the same disregard of the more obvious charms of poetry while it keeps a grip on the real core of what it touches. His minor poems at this time begin again to have fine lines, but they do not rise to this height. All the same, the lines to the Montenegrins recall Milton's to the Waldensians: 'Great Tsernogora! never since thine own/Black ridges drew the cloud and brake the storm'. The lines 'To Victor Hugo', whom Lionel had visited in Paris, and the ones (unused) to be inscribed on the base of Cleopatra's Needle, are equally lapidary.

But he had settled for a time into old metrical skills, like a wheel settling into a rut, and that is why 'The Defence of Lucknow' is less effective than 'The Revenge'. Lucknow was relieved in September 1857 and Jowett, whose brother was killed, suggested 'an *In Memoriam* for the dead in India' the next year. It was perhaps the only bad advice he ever gave to Tennyson. The poem was written in March 1879. Its refrain 'And ever upon the topmost roof our banner of England flew' is as high as it rises. At times it sinks to absurdity. 'Mine? yes, a mine! Countermine! down, down! and creep through the hole!/Keep the revolver in hand! you can hear him – the murderous mole!' All the same, Tennyson is boldly specific: 'Click with the pick'. This poem, with its dedication to Princess Alice, who died in 1878 from kissing her child who had diphtheria, must rank as an honourable failure. It is over-heroic about the heroes, over-grandiose about the tawdry grandeurs. Tennyson unlike Tolstoy lacked the experience of war, and it shows. 'The First Quarrel' is a good plain narrative from a story told him by Dabbs, the local doctor. It is a moving tale, yet it might be even better without the dramatic emphases of verse. Still, in February 1879 he was back in his true form with another Lincolnshire dialect poem, 'The Northern Cobbler'. I will not discuss this brilliant piece of verse, because everything I said about its predecessor applies again. The story is well known, but he had heard it in his youth. The beautiful plainness and the prosaic poetry of the language are a proof of that. Lincolnshire in the ten years after Waterloo had become to him a country that was clear and distant.

In 1875, Alfred was still playing games with his sons as if they were all in the Somersby vicarage together: he sent them his epitaph for Sir John Franklin for the Abbey, inviting them and their friends to try putting it into Latin or Greek verse, as Lord Lyttelton had already done and as Gladstone did.[9] But by the end of the year Lionel, still an undergraduate, had got engaged to Eleanor Locker whose uncle was Dean Stanley of Westminster Abbey. He was a lively lad: it was he of them all who knew Oscar Wilde and Henry James, and called on Victor Hugo in Paris. His father always seems a bit startled by him, not I think guilty as scholars suggest, but just surprised. As a boy, Lionel used to gallop his pony up and down Kensington High Street, and even as a married man he raced about the hilltops alone on his horse; the original Russian wolfhound was his. Now he took his degree, and he and his father worked hard to find him a niche in the establishment: the Foreign Office or a clerkship in the Lords or the Commons. A lot of letters were written, but the only ones of 1876 written with real pleasure and warmth by Tennyson are to Browning. One in particular deserves to be reproduced, from July 1875:

Aldworth, Haslemere.

After dinner talk between husband and wife.

W.   Why don't you write and thank Mr Browning for his
      letter?

H.   Why should I? I sent him my book and he acknowledged it.

W.   But such a great and generous acknowledgement.

H.   That's true.

W.   Then you should write: he has given you your crown of violets.

H.   He is the greatest-brained poet in England. Violets fade: he has given me a crown of gold.

W.   Well I meant the Troubadour crown of golden violets: pray write: you know I would if I could; but I am lying here helpless and horizontal and can neither write nor read.

H.   Then I'll go up and smoke my pipe and write to him.

W.   You'll go up and concoct an imaginary letter over your pipe, which you'll never send.

H.   Yes I will. I'll report our talk.

He goes up and smokes, and spite of pipe writes and signs himself

A. Tennyson.

Maybe it was just ageing poets for whom he felt a deepening sympathy. He had given a huge garden-party for Longfellow once, though he sometimes expressed reservations about him, as he did about all Americans but Poe (and later Whitman); still, in January 1877 he wrote him the most genial letter of thanks for congratulations over *Harold*. His social life outside the house continued to have intervals of farce. In 1871, rather by chance in pursuit of architecture, he had got to know the Stanleys and the Howards, amazing all concerned by his hypochondria over burning his mouth with hot porridge at Castle Howard. It is always loosely true that the upper class are all one another's cousins, and Tennyson knew these grand families through their habit of frequenting one another's houses.[10] Lionel was marrying into the kinship and cousinship.[11] Tennyson now found himself in Upper Wimpole Street, where he took a house to support Lionel in his successive applications for jobs. He drifted in the grandest circles at this time because he was determined to find a place for Lionel. Many of the letters the Laureate wrote were to fend off the importunate, such as Ellen Tennyson D'Eyncourt Bunbury, or to limit invasions of his privacy: to the Governor of Witley Hospital for Convalescent Lunatics for example, asking him to restrain his patients from visiting Aldworth. One of his neighbours there was Lady Ashburton's niece, Mrs Stanley, one of Dean Stanley's numerous cousins. So the Stanleys had the Tennysons in for Scotch songs or Irish melodies, which he loved. The Tennysons had them back to a concert in Eaton Square, where John Herschel sang his Tennyson songs. When 'Break, break, break' was over, the audience hung breathless for the poet's verdict. Alfred covered his face in his handkerchief, so the entire audience showed its sympathy by doing the same.[12] It must be quite hard to go on being a good poet in those circumstances.

A man came up to him in the street and said 'Mr Tennyson, I've been dead drunk half a dozen times this week; if you'll only shake hands with me, I'll never get drunk again.' His more general response to fame, at least during the London season,[13] was to forget everybody and growl at them, 'Haven't an idea who you are.' People like the Secretary of the Shakespeare Memorial Association were lucky if his letter refusing their invitations was barely civil.

His fatherly anxiety for Lionel was rewarded, because Lord Salisbury was a fellow-member of The Club, and happened to be Secretary of State for India; it was Lord Salisbury who nominated Lionel in June 1877. As soon as Lionel had won his position (which was by examination) and an assured career, he was married in February 1878 in splendour at Westminster Abbey. The elder Tennysons themselves found a door locked, and got lost in the Abbey precincts, but they arrived before the ceremony was over. Gladstone and the Duke of Argyll were witnesses, and Alfred failed to recognize his friend George Eliot. Lionel and Eleanor are said to have been on the cheerful side as a married couple, and not perfectly faithful, but their children were devoted to them.

Tennyson was still exercising what influence he had for far lesser writers: in 1878 it was for R. H. Horne, the writer of an epic allegory on the senses and the intellect called *Orion*; in 1879 it was for Fanny Keats, and the flow of demands on him was steady.[14] In May 1878 the Duchess of Argyll died at fifty-three after bearing eleven children: the Duke hoped for a monument in verse, because she had loved Tennyson, but it was not forthcoming. In April 1878 he had written for Matthew Arnold's sister's album the one line from 'Tithonus', 'Alas for this grey shadow once a man.' In April 1879 his brother Charles died, and then he did write a monumental poem.

The poem was not written at once. Charles died on 25 April, and Alfred scribbled a touching line to Louisa, but on 20 May she died too. Edmund Lushington had sent an immediate reaction in 58 lines of his own verse entitled 'May 1, 1879',[15] but he had first written (on 27 April) about the collection of the sonnets, which it is clear Charles had planned or at least desired. Alfred's poem, whose title is again a date, 'Midnight, June 30, 1879', was printed as a prologue to the *Collected Sonnets* the following year:

> Midnight – in no midsummer tune
> The breakers lash the shores:
> The cuckoo of a joyless June
> Is calling out of doors:
>
> (1–4)

The poem is very sparely written, so that its words hardly scratch the paper. What it says is utterly simple, yet it is as moving as anything that Tennyson ever wrote. If the lines recall anything, it is Housman.

> Midnight – and joyless June gone by,
> And from the deluged park
> The cuckoo of a worse July
> Is calling through the dark:
>
> But thou art silent underground,
> And o'er thee streams the rain,
> True poet, surely to be found
> When Truth is found again.
>
> (9–16)

There lurks somewhere at the back of certain poems by Tennyson the ghost of the distillation of a hymn tune: the same is true of Housman of course. But no ghost can explain away these bare, considered verses. He says only what he has got to say.

> Far off a phantom cuckoo cries
> From out a phantom hill
>
> (19–20)

It is unbearable because it is predictable, and yet true, down to the last fumbled embrace:

When all my griefs were shared with thee,
As all my hopes were thine –
As all thou wert was one with me,
May all thou art be mine!

(25–8)

After this, he fell back into the old habits and gestures of his poetry like an automatic language, with 'Emmie (In the Children's Hospital)', a sentimental story from a religious magazine told him by one of Gladstone's daughters, then 'Columbus', an attempt at the Great American Epic (on request) which has a few fine lines and passages, but it raves and wanders, and his heart is not in it as it was in 'The Revenge'. One may take comfort (as one suspects that he did) in 'The Village Wife', a fine life study in Lincolnshire dialect. This is as deeply pleasing and warming as the other dialect poems; it is in its sleepy provincial way as conscious of social change as a poem by Philip Larkin. And late that year he began 'The Voyage of Maeldune', which he finished in 1880.

That is based on *The Book of the Dun Cow*, a twelfth-century Irish manuscript, which Tennyson knew through Joyce's *Old Celtic Romances*, but to every island encountered on the voyage Tennyson added an opposite kind of island: he added silence to shouting, flowers to fruits, a fire island to a drowned island, and he added gloomy and violent moral colouring to the adventurers. He told Allingham, 'At first I made half the men kill the other half in every fray, and Maeldune himself return *alone*.'[16] The poem itself is a marvellous piece of virtuoso story-telling, the verse falls naturally from Tennyson's lips and he sways it to climax without one noticing.

And we came to the Silent Isle that we never had touched at
   before,
Where a silent ocean always broke on a silent shore,
And the brooks glittered on in the light without sound, and the
   long waterfalls
Poured in a thunderless plunge to the base of the mountain walls,
And the poplar and cypress unshaken by storm flourished up
   beyond sight,
And the pine shot aloft from the crag to an unbelievable height,
And high in the heaven above it there flickered a songless lark,

And the cock couldn't crow, and the bull couldn't low, and the
dog couldn't bark.

(11–19)

The extraordinary thing about this poem is his complete mastery of
his hearers, his perfect mastery of his metre, which in no other hands
would be acceptable. One is somehow restrained by its unpreten-
tiousness from calling it a great poem, but how extremely memorable
it is. 'And the warm melon lay like a little sun on the tawny sand.'
At the end of the poem, the Odysseus figure meets the man who had
murdered his father and lets him be. This is written with a feeling
that may go deep, though Tennyson had considered a grimmer
ending. It is apparent from numerous anecdotes and remarks that at
the end of his life he was given to dire prophecies; his political aim
was to turn the British empire into a commonwealth, but he feared
and foresaw an Armageddon: he came close to foreseeing 1914. I
think he intended the moral of this poem very seriously. In 1880, he
finished '*De Profundis*', begun at Hallam's birth in 1852. The poem is
written to a child born from darkness and mystery:

> Out of the deep, my child, out of the deep . . .
> And last in kindly curves, with gentlest fall,
> By quiet fields, a slowly-dying power,
> To that last deep where we and thou are still.

(1, 23–5)

There are three parts to the poem, or two parts with the second
subdivided. What it says is both mysterious and clear: the *profundis*
of the title do not really refer to the famous psalm, but to 'The
Passing of Arthur', 'From the great deep to the great deep he goes'.
There is some suggestion it was an anti-secularist statement or
concerned with his still-born child, or the Metaphysical Society, but
I do not really believe that, because in explaining poems Tennyson
too easily took on a colour from the people he was with or something
he read yesterday. Yet he has an ability to translate deep thoughts
into simple words, and the text as we have it is a lucid document:

> Out of the deep, Spirit, out of the deep,
> With this ninth moon, that sends the hidden sun
> Down yon dark sea, thou comest, darling boy . . .

O dear Spirit half-lost
In thine own shadow and this fleshly sign
That thou art thou – who wailest being born
And banished into mystery

                                        (32–4, 39–42)

It may be the 'Hallelujah!' poem 'The Human Cry', and the
sweet few lines of welcome to his grandson Alfred should be taken
as a complement to it, but *'De Profundis'* as it stands is one of his
weightiest declarations. The child Alfred was born on 20 November
1878 (the wedding had been on 25 February, so no time was lost),
and the lines of welcome were written in May 1880, but in June he
was in Italy, and Sirmio brought back, through its memory of
Catullus, a flood of grief over his brother Charles, and that brought
forth one of the most famous and most moving of all his poems,
'Frater Ave atque Vale'.

These dashes abroad of his had started again soon after his
marriage and had never ceased: when he went to Ireland with his
two grown sons, Alfred went off to the Turkish baths in Dublin
while the two young men more soberly visited St Patrick's and
Christchurch. From Farringford, he stole two days with Lecky the
historian to visit Stonehenge and Salisbury, and the Abbey at
Malmesbury, and Wilton and George Herbert's church at Bemerton.
The Italian journey was on doctor's advice, because he had not been
really well since Charles died. Hallam took him to Munich and
Venice. They stayed for a while with Lord Acton, who liked
Tennyson better than before, and came home by Sirmio. Alfred
draws first on the famous local poem, *'O quid solutis est beatius curis'*,
and on that saddest and most unforgettable poem Catullus ever
wrote, to his dead brother. But as Alfred wrote in a letter to
Gladstone, 'nor can any modern elegy, so long as men retain the
least hope in the afterlife of those whom they loved, equal in pathos
the desolation of that everlasting farewell, *Atque in perpetuum, frater
Ave atque Vale.'* The undertow of his thoughts even on a happy day
was grievous, and the glittering sea and the thrill and poetry of
Venice had not obliterated his mourning.[17]

It was in 1880 that Allingham, who had married in 1874, stayed
with his wife in Haslemere: the next year the Allinghams took their
house at Witley, which is almost equally close to Aldworth. They
have left us many pages of fragments of the Laureate's conversation,

his quirks and grumbles and enthusaisms. Helen Allingham began to make the drawings which appear in her 1905 book on Tennyson's houses. William Allingham died in 1889 in Hampstead, and his ashes were taken back to Ireland where he had not been for twenty years, but Helen's drawings are so fresh and attractive and fragile that one feels as if he was a failure by comparison. That is an unfair estimate, though this is not the place to unravel it. In 1881, Allingham's other great hero, Carlyle, died. He was still in touch with Alfred, and he liked 'The Revenge'; 'Eh, he has got a grip of it.' Thackeray had died in 1863 and Dickens in 1870. No doubt seventy-two is an age when one's friends are bound to die, but Alfred mourned for his, even though in Allingham's pages he is like an *enfant terrible* in the Elysian fields.

They had tea under apple trees in August, and he said, 'If the pronunciation of the English language were forgotten, Browning would be held the greatest of modern poets, having treated the greatest variety of subjects in a powerful manner.' The future Sir Charles Tennyson was a baby, rolling about with his brother in the grass. Frederick might be there, or Edward Lear. Alfred had been reading a paper by William Crookes of the Royal Society which aroused him to an old theme: 'I believe we never see Matter: what we count the material world is only an appearance.' One day he hated the English withdrawal from Afghanistan, on another (October 1886) he thought England should leave India. Another day his visitors might be the Bradleys and Aubrey de Vere. Alfred told them he thought the long, unreadable parts of Wordsworth were caused by cheap printing: Horace and Catullus let out only their best work. He talked with reminiscent love of Shelley and of Keats (whom he had come to prefer), or he spoke wistfully of living all the year round on Chelsea Embankment. 'He always gets tired of London in a fortnight,' muttered Hallam. Another day Alfred boasted, 'I can run uphill, I can waltz – but when I said this to Fanny Kemble she replied in a ghastly voice, "I hope I shall never see you do it."' As he got older his party trick was how many times he could leap up out of a low chair, and when Mrs Brookfield visited him on his death-bed he asked her to dance a quadrille with him. When she demurred, he got up and danced one for her down the room on his own. On the night he told the story about Fanny Kemble, the Allinghams 'went home in Tennyson's carriage, happy with the good company and friendly kindness'.[18]

Once in 1876, he and Hallam turned up suddenly out of the blue to see FitzGerald, and all was immediately as it once had been between them. Leslie Stephen claimed Alfred had copied FitzGerald's *Omar* in his *In Memoriam*; that was nonsense of course and produced a furious Laureate grumble. *Omar* had appeared in 1859 and was famously slow in becoming famous. It is clear that Tennyson liked it very much, but he was not part of the network by which it made its way. Fitz disapproved of Emily, who answered his private letters to his friend. He thought Alfred 'would have done better to remain single in Lincolnshire, or married a jolly Woman who would have laughed and cried without any reason why.' What he really felt was the simplest, most childish jealousy. When Alfred went to Venice, Fitz wrote to Frederick about how Alfred suddenly seemed well enough for a jaunt, but how Venice stank in summer. Perhaps that was the truth, because Alfred only stayed there three days. In 1882 he heard Alfred was 'in some grand locality of Eaton Square', and refused to go near him.[19]

But in June 1883 Hallam found a copy of the fifty-year-old poem 'Tiresias', from just the period that Fitz loved, and Alfred set to work on it again, and on a graceful prologue to go with it, when suddenly he heard his friend was dead.[20] He turned the prologue into an elegy, for which added gravity the poem is the better: but in human terms it is only this late poem that reveals how heavily the loss was felt. And in 1881 the adorable, scholarly James Spedding had died, run over by a London bus. Alfred was not let in to see him as he lay dying, but kept in an outer room, and Spedding asked at once was it Alfred Tennyson who had called.

The poem 'To E. FitzGerald' is intimate and loving, and its opening is really funny, but the end has a gloom touched with pre-Victorian magnificence. The playfulness is pre-Victorian too, taking its tone from some verses by Peacock to Lord Broughton. The compliment to *Omar* restores the entire balance of criticism on that poem,

> Than which I know no version done
> In English more divinely well; . . .
>   your Omar drew
> Full-handed plaudits from our best
> In modern letters, and from two,
>   Old friends outvaluing all the rest,
> Two voices heard on earth no more
>
>   (33–4, 37–41)

The two were Spedding and Brookfield (d. 1874). The Laureate
sends this poem to recall old times,

> When, in our younger London days,
> You found some merit in my rhymes,
> And I more pleasure in your praise.
>
> (54–6)

Even the little reminiscences in this first part of the poem are
charming: the pigeons perching on Fitz's head, Alfred's attempt to
be a vegetarian, and then the *Omar*. They are exactly planned, as
Horace would have planned them. The second part is dignified, even
beautiful, it has a sunset quality. FitzGerald was no believer, and
Tennyson enters into his mind, so that his only prayer is

> when I from hence
> Shall fade with him into the unknown,
> My close of life's experience
> May prove as peaceful as his own.
>
> (85–8)

The other poems of this time are lesser creations. 'Sir John
Oldcastle' is as readable as 'Godiva', but it is only a Protestant tract, a
piece that would have fitted into one of the plays, were it not 196 lines
long. 'The Sisters' is one of his magazine tales, redeemed only by some
fine landscape. Two sisters love the same man, though one sister is the
other's bridesmaid: it shows a remarkable innocence in Tennyson that
he never thought of Emily and Louisa. The poem has lovely phrases,
like 'watching overhead/The aërial poplar wave, an amber spire', and
in a rejected line, 'Your photographing sun' (one must think of the
flash of Mrs Cameron's old-fashioned camera). I also like 'Beneath a
pitiless rush of Autumn rain', and 'the mother's garrulous wail', but
the story somehow fails to impress, and it lasts 288 lines.

Tennyson addressed some lines 'To the Duke of Argyll', who
resigned as Lord Privy Seal in 1881 over Gladstone's Irish bill, a
subject that roused Alfred more than once to his most vehement.
What he really wished, as he told Allingham, was for Ireland to be
towed away into mid-ocean and there dynamited and its pieces
drowned. Ireland was the *memento mori* of his political ideas, he found
it deeply irritating. What was worse, he liked the Irish. He was not
of course alone in this state of mind. In the poem he attempted to

ring a Miltonic chime of bells for his friend, but the subject was somehow not susceptible of the treatment.

Most of this new work had been in magazines, but in 1880 Tennyson issued *Ballads and Other Poems*, his first new book since *Gareth and Lynette* (1872) and his first collection since 1864. After it came *Tiresias and Other Poems* in 1885, and then *Locksley Hall Sixty Years After* (1886), which contains mainly *The Promise of May*. In 1889 came *Demeter and Other Poems*, and on his death-bed in 1892 he was preparing 'The Death of Œnone'. That makes over four collections of verse in the last twelve years of his life: one cannot help suspecting that Hallam as his secretary was an important influence on the number. They were all interesting, and taken together they represent one of the most surprising of his achievements. We know that poets do sometimes flower again in old age. Yeats certainly did and so did Roy Fuller, but it is still not the usual pattern, and if you judge him entirely by his printed works, Tennyson had seemed exhausted. The first signs of his recovery, or rather his robust continuing life, are in *Ballads and Other Poems*, a book which includes 'Rizpah', 'The Northern Cobbler', 'The Revenge', 'Maeldune', 'Brunanburh', some Homeric translation and '*De Profundis*'. This strong collection may possibly be weaker than the high points of the 1842 collection, but it is more experimental, and if old men should be explorers, then Tennyson was one. Maybe that happens to poets whose lifework and self-criticism have left them with the art or courage of exploration as their principal skill.

He met James Russell Lowell, the American Minister in London, to whom his memorable first question at lunch was 'Do you know anything about Lowell?' They exchanged concerned letters about the state of copyright laws and even about poems. Alfred tried and failed to get a 'grace and favour' residence at Hampton Court for the widowed Mrs Brookfield, whose husband was a Queen's Chaplain, and exchanged further letters with Gladstone in which affection is not quite drowned out by the rumble of power. The old man was pleased with Charles's sonnets in his impossibly high-minded way.[20] Gladstone in 1880 was still pressing a baronetcy on the poet: 'such an honour coming through you, I need not say, would be more acceptable than through any of your successors,' replied Tennyson, but he wanted it to go to Hallam in his own lifetime, which discloses an interesting point of view.

To visitors at Aldworth Tennyson presented a bizarre figure. He did not always notice them at all. Winny Seebohm went with a family party to lunch there in 1882, having been introduced by the Locker Lampsons, and reports the day with some asperity.[21] They were met at Haslemere station by a carriage with a footman in scarlet coat and cockaded hat. This was conventional enough but, inside, the carriage was the shabbiest thing she had ever seen, and both its windows were malfunctioning. The journey was very difficult (everyone says that) and the footman had to jump down and run behind, so that he arrived panting to open the front door. Emily was a pile of silken quilts on a sofa from which emerged a quavering voice, and the poet did not address a word to Winny. It was Hallam who greeted them, but the introductions were incompetent. Alfred did take them up to see the view from his study, but then 'wasted the time' by looking up a word in *Skeat's Dictionary*.

At Christmas 1881 Tennyson tried to get Hallam an independent foothold as secretary to Gladstone. Something must underlie this: Hallam was married in spring 1884 to Audrey Boyle whom he met in 1883 when her aunt, Mary Boyle, took her to Farringford.[22] It is possible that the prospect of his thirtieth birthday, still living at home as his father's private secretary, may have stirred his father to those family discussions which must have preceded the unsuccessful application to Gladstone.

Alfred went doggedly on with his pursuit of dialect studies, sending away for books, and triumphant at meeting A. J. Ellis, an expert on Shakespeare's and Chaucer's pronunciation, which he achieved through Furnivall. One may feel that dialect and pronunciation is what every poet should have been interested in, but no other poet was. Of all English poets since Milton, Tennyson was closest to a philologist. When he dined out, it was only when his pipe was sent for that 'he began to unroll (a hedgehog simile)'; he would read mostly the same poems, *Maud* or 'Morte d'Arthur'.[23] One feels that his intellectual and inner life were in reserve. In August 1881 he excited the scientist Lockyer by reporting a pink rainbow. Alexander Macmillan saw it as pink, and so did Hallam, but by the time Tennyson looked, its colours had gone back to normal.[24]

The deep tide of Tennyson's feelings was still, to judge from his poetry, very dark. In November he published 'Despair', written in June. It is about loss of faith and a suicide pact, a grim subject even for him:

And the suns of the limitless Universe sparkled and shone in the
  sky,
Flashing with fires as of God, but we knew that their light was a
  lie . . .
And the stake and the cross-road, fool, if you will, does it matter
  to me?

                                                    (15–16, 116)

The subject came from a newspaper as one might expect. Some
colouring of James Thomson's 'City of Dreadful Night' has been
suggested, since that appeared in a volume in 1880, but it is not in
the Lincoln collection. It was first produced in 1870–74, and Thomson, who is not only a dark genius but one of a pure black, to which
neither Clough nor Tennyson attained, must remain on his own, too
terrible to own to predecessors or to followers. He was an urban
poet, which Tennyson no longer was. He complained that he could
no longer bear to walk in London at night because of the brightness
of the lights, which were now I take it electric.

   In March 1882, Tennyson wrote his 'The Charge of the Heavy
Brigade', to even the score so to speak, but it lacks the fire of the old
poem. The epilogue he wrote to it in 1883 for Laura Tennant, with
his true feelings about war and about fame, is a period piece, and an
interesting exercise in the manner of Clough, but it is not of any
startling greatness. It is however conscious of Horace, who had been
his best influence since he had welcomed F. D. Maurice to the Isle of
Wight so long ago. Its fault is that he uses too many words. Yet
his neo-classic vein still ran fresh. His poem 'To Virgil', written
on request for a centenary at Mantua (June 1882) is a dazzling
achievement. The poem consists of ten couplets of trochaic verse
in very long lines (always wrongly printed cut in half to make ten
four-line stanzas). The Mantuans asked for a scribble and got a
masterpiece:

Thou that singest wheat and woodland, tilth and vineyard, hive
  and horse and herd;
All the charm of all the Muses often flowering in a lonely word;

Poet of the happy Tityrus piping underneath his beechen bowers;
Poet of the poet-satyr whom the laughing shepherd bound with
  flowers;

Chanter of the Pollio, glorying in the blissful years again to be,
Summers of the smokeless meadow, unlaborious earth and oarless
    sea; . . .

Wielder of the stateliest measure ever moulded by the lips of man.

(5–10, 20)

This poem is one long sentence of long lines, it is one long trumpet-blast, and its length of breath, and its sustained rhythms, somehow constitute its message. It is remarkably glorious, and if there is a touch of Swinburne that is all to the good. It seemed nothing could stop Tennyson: he adapted a youthful spring poem of 1833 with such verve that he seems no older than twenty-four. He wrote Farrar a fine tribute to Caxton for a stained glass window at St Margaret's, Westminster, he wrote his tribute to Fitz, and he wrote 'The Throstle', which is a cheerful little bit of nothing from an old man. It was Hallam who was making his father retouch old, unpublished poems at this time.

'The Dead Prophet' was a blow against Froude's life of Carlyle, who died in 1881, though the poem is headed '182–', and 'Poets and their Bibliographies' is against rakers up of fragments: Southey had apparently declared that quantity was important in estimating poets. But it was Hallam who turned him back to Lincolnshire dialect, to write about an old woman talking to her cats. Hallam must have been a God-given companion for the old man. The poem was called 'The Spinster's Sweet-Arts'. Among the curiosities thrown up by his restless temperament and insistent interest in dialect, there is another poem, close in date to this, but in Irish dialect, which I find literally unreadable. His friends encouraged him, Aubrey de Vere gave him the story, he corrected his Irish from Carleton's *Traits of the Irish Peasantry*, and Allingham worked through the result, 'Tomorrow'.[25] No one knows Hallam's opinion. Tennyson would have done better to write a tribute to Penn, for which Lowell approached him with a tribute of tobacco, but who knows why that did not spur him? He said he had the gout (arthritis?) in his right hand and 'you have your noble old Longfellow still among you'. He loved Penn, and certainly toyed with writing about him.[26]

He became great friends at this time with Sir Henry Parkes, an Australian who wanted to federate the Australian states, who had first written to Tennyson in 1876. This ebullient character luckily kept a full journal. Parkes found Woolner at Farringford, and describes a jolly outing to a sea cave, a reading, and some walks, but he is too reverential, however amiable. He was at least preferable to Mr C. O. Groom, who was a vegetarian, teetotal, anti-Darwinist, British Israelite confidence trickster, who collected autographs by offering a 'gold' medal from the Duke of Mantua, though he was caught at last raising money 'for a Welsh university'. Tennyson was quite nice to him. Cardinal Newman would have been a more rewarding guest; he was invited, but too old to come, and both sides had to be content with elaborate and very friendly courtesies. Alfred said: 'I feel that some day or other I ought to go to you, for though, I daresay, there are a hundred things on which we might differ, there is no man on this side of the grave, more worthy of honour and affection than yourself; and therefore though I have never shaken you by the hand, let me subscribe myself Affectionately yours.'[27]

In the background to all these letters, and to the steady building up of the *Tiresias* volume (1885), the drama of his theatrical activities went on absorbing him. Sabine begged him to desert 'that *ungentlemanly* old woman' Queen Elizabeth for pastoral comedy; Sandringham assured him his *Promise of May* was 'only too pure and good for the taste of the present day'. In spite of the fiasco he was happy enough, though in August 1883 the Queen thought him shaky. In September he was Gladstone's guest on the *Pembroke Castle*, for the first cruise of Sir Donald Currie's new ship. They went all over the North Sea, saw royalties, were cheered by battle fleets, and heaven knows what. The Queen was cross about Gladstone's jaunt abroad without her permission, but Alfred was to blame. His disposition was to sail on for ever, like Ulysses. Gladstone offered him a peerage. Later that year Hallam's engagement was announced.

The peerage was certainly the Queen's design and wish, as Lear wrote to his friends, though Hallam thought he had suggested it, and Gladstone felt it was his own idea. The precedent was that old Grote the historian was offered a peerage which he refused. It was an unusual honour for a poet, and has remained one. Gladstone was worried whether Tennyson had enough money to carry off a peerage, but Hallam said he had. The worry was real at the time: the Governor of the Bank of England in the late 1880s was made a Privy Councillor but not a Baronet, because he was not rich enough. Certain fees were remitted in Tennyson's case, as they normally were for soldiers. I do not know whether some impoverished nobleman had recently embarrassed the Queen or the government, but the fees are certainly not great: only a few hundred pounds payable to the College of Heralds. It is queer that money should have mattered so much, but it definitely did. Tennyson dithered over the title Tennyson d'Eyncourt, to which name he clearly had a right if his juniors had one, but luckily on Gladstone's advice he stuck to Tennyson. In 1884, he moved at last to Macmillan as publishers, and worked very hard at a *Complete Poems*. His son was married in June, and perhaps for the first time in his life at the age of seventy-five Alfred appeared in public perfectly normally dressed. He was introduced to the Lords by Argyll and Kenmare, who was deputizing for Houghton.[28] A snowdrift of letters settled on him, but what moved him most was news of Susan Epton, an old servant who had nursed him once and was now blind and ninety. But Lord Houghton died abroad the next year, and in the autumn Lionel went to India.

Alfred wrote a picturesque shipwreck poem with a strange feeling of Hopkins, 'The Wreck', about the *Rosino*, a Sicilian immigrant ship bound for New York. He took some lines on a stormy sea from his memories of the *Pembroke Castle*. He wrote a poem about 'Vastness' too; a little elegy of a few moving lines on W. G. Ward, and his 'The Ancient Sage'. These are works in which the poetry almost bursts through the very serious thoughts. The peerage drove him both to distance himself from Gladstone in severe political verses, and to these grand utterances about life. If 'The Ancient Sage' had been by a lesser poet it would be famous, or if it were a touch more Chinese it would be a great poem. As it is, 'The kernel of the shrivelled fruit is jutting through the rind.' And yet it has magical lines and moments, like 'The first gray streak of earliest summer-dawn,/The last long stripe of waning crimson gloom'. It is a substantial poem of 285 lines. It was Jowett's idea, and a good one, to write about the classic poet of Taoism.[29]

Alfred also wrote a poem at the Prince of Wales' request, on an Indian and Colonial Exhibition, which has associations of unquenchable laughter, because 'Britons, Guard Your Own' has been adapted as the slogan of school football teams (Britons! Hold your own!) and carved on wooden games shields. *Tiresias and Other Poems* appeared in December 1885, and by 1886 he had written the name poem of *Locksley Hall Sixty Years After*. He still seriously believed that 'poetry should be the flower and fruit of a man's life.'[30]

By 1884, when with much heaving and groaning he had gone to

London and voted Liberal, he was sure that England had attained her zenith and was going downhill, and he said so freely to visitors. Both Lionel and Hallam were called on to support his new role as a political grandee. He loved the Empire, or thought he did, but hated politics: he knew what the Prussians thought of English imperial success, and he resented them. He loved Gladstone as a friend, but he could not really follow the currents and backwaters of affairs, though he thought he could. He was perhaps a typical reader of the serious journals, in fact a typical, intelligent member of the House of Lords, somewhat fuddled and confused about complex issues, but deeply patriotic and not badly informed. In April 1885, Jowett reported that 'Tennyson says, O Lord Bismarck, come and govern us; we will give you a million a year.' Meanwhile, Alfred was on a committee to set up a training scheme at Aldershot called the Gordon Boys, and wrote for Gordon one of his numerous epitaphs; it touched the mood of the moment. This training scheme had arisen from a conversation Lord Tennyson had with that curious General.[31] The laureate spent August 1885 like any retired officer, on an island in the river Test, and in November he wrote a brief note to back F. T. Palgrave for the chair of Poetry at Oxford.[32]

For 'Locksley Hall Sixty Years After' the influences suggested have been many and amazing, indeed so much so as to indicate that critics have been at a loss. We know that Lord Tennyson's son died while he was writing it, but that has left little mark on the poem. The description of a son who dies saving others and loved the good and the true is the merest feint towards a gesture of memory.[33] Lionel caught a fever in Assam in January 1886, he seemed unable to shake it off so his host, Lord Dufferin, sent him home: he died on the ship that April. 'Loxsley Hall Sixty Years After' is a passionate explosion, and it may be that grief set it off in the direction it took. I do not recollect any indictment of the Victorian age that is more terrible. Gladstone felt bound to reply to it. The dangerous pages are few, and of course it is only a poem, though it drops the mask of fiction: it has not the slow, awful, judgemental pace of *London Labour and the London Poor*. But it is stronger than anything by Dickens, or Thackeray, or Engels. 'Cold upon the dead volcano sleeps the gleam of dying day' but there the volcano erupts. A train has been derailed.

> Is it well that while we range with Science, glorying in the Time,
> City children soak and blacken soul and sense in city slime?

There among the glooming alleys Progress halts on palsied feet,
Crime and hunger cast our maidens by the thousand on the
   street.

There the Master scrimps his haggard sempstress of her daily
   bread,
There a single sordid attic holds the living and the dead.

There the smouldering fire of fever creeps across the rotted floor,
And the crowded couch of incest in the warrens of the poor . . .

Poor old Heraldry, poor old History, poor old Poetry, passing
   hence,
In the common deluge drowning old political common-sense!

Poor old voice of eighty crying after voices that have fled!

                              (217-23, 249-57)

The poem is devastating, and a million miles away from the tribute
to Virgil in the same metre, in which he had stood among his own
generation. He did not like the England he was leaving, and it
appears that with his barony he was conscious (whether falsely or
not does not matter) of a duty to speak out. This one poem, which
is 282 lines long, with one or two negligible political pieces of verse
and The Promise of May, make up his 1886 volume. In his whole earlier
life, he does not give evidence of great bitterness, except increasingly
about scandalous revelations following the death of great writers like
Carlyle, and the sale of letters like the love letters of Keats.[34]
   But he kept up his reading, knew Amiel's virtues two years
before Matthew Arnold's essay, read Les Fleurs du Mal and thought
Baudelaire a moralist, though he disapproved of Zola and grumbled
even at the low-life element in Thackeray. His memory was prodigious: he recalled how his father had admired Dryden the more as he
grew older, and how they acted Dryden's plays as children, and he
recalled pointing out a couple of lines in Moschus's lament for Bion
(never a prominent element in the curriculum) to Arthur Hallam
more than fifty years ago. Politically he was in despair, 'never so
many lies told in the world as now.' He was deeply grieved over the
Irish question.
   Yet he could enjoy places and landscapes, and even the theatre.

He seems to have suppressed his grief over Lionel's death in such a way that it could never heal. He sent for Venables, who came for the last time in October 1888, and for Palgrave, whom he assured that Wordsworth was the greatest poet of his century. He carefully explained to Elizabeth Chapman, a blue-stocking writer who shared his detestation of Comte and wrote about *In Memoriam* (1888), his views about free will and immortality. 'You know *there is* Free Will. It is limited, of course. We are like birds in a cage; but we can hop from perch to perch – till the roof is taken off.' His poem 'On the Jubilee of Queen Victoria' has a valedictory tone, like that of a minor prophet signing off. He was glad to hear of his old preoccupations. Professor Jebb delighted him by sending a Pindaric Ode in Greek (no easy task) to the University of Bologna. Jebb suggested to Hallam that his father should look at the Homeric hymn to Demeter, with the result that Alfred produced 'Demeter and Persephone', 150 classic English lines, with a tiny Horatian dedication: but the old spirit did not come when it was called, the lines are all about the mourning of Demeter for a dead child:

> I climbed on all the cliffs of all the seas,
> And asked the waves that moan about the world
> 'Where? do ye make your moaning for my child?'
> And round from all the world the voices came
> 'We know not, and we know not why we moan.'
>
> (62–6)

His last Lincolnshire poem, 'Owd Roä', is about a dying dog that rescued a child from a fire. In 1887 he wrote a long piece called 'The Ring' for Mrs Lowell. It is a story Lowell had also told to Henry James,[35] but neither version is distinguished. Lord Tennyson's reads as if it were by a skilled apprentice, an imitator. His poem is continually musical but never bold. His poem 'To Ulysses' to Palgrave's brother the adventurer in early 1888 is better, because it is about his own trees, in a Horatian mode hovering between alcaeics and the *In Memoriam* rhythm, one enormous sentence of 48 lines (Horace likes these long lyric sentences). He counts his trees in the Isle of Wight with a passion of particularity, leafless elm, naked lime, green cedar and evergreen ilex, and Garibaldi's memorial pine,[36] with a whole stanza for that ugly duckling of southern English gardens, the yucca:

My yucca, which no winter quells,
   Although the months have scarce begun,
   Has pushed towards our faintest sun
A spike of half-accomplished bells

                   (21–4)

In February he found an old poem of his, 'The Progress of Spring' from the 1830s, and sent it with another charming set of Horatian lyrics as an invitation to Mary Boyle, his illustrator and Hallam's wife's aunt. He recalls the days of the rick-fires and the bucket-line, but he seeks really to console for a death. In the end his consolation is only,

The silver year should cease to mourn and sigh –
   Not long to wait –
So close are we, dear Mary, you and I,
   To that dim gate.

In September 1888, Lord Tennyson became seriously ill; as he recovered, he wrote a few lyrics, including 'the mellow lin-lan-lone of evening bells' in 'Far-Far-Away', a poem of mysterious, apparently almost chance beauty, over which he worked very carefully, and a poem 'To the Marquis of Dufferin and Ava' giving direct expression at last to his grief for Lionel. The words he chose are terribly public and marmoreal, until the ninth stanza:

But ere he left your fatal shore,
And lay on that funereal boat,
Dying, 'Unspeakable' he wrote
'Their kindness,' and he wrote no more . . .
Not there to bid my boy farewell,
When that within the coffin fell,
Fell – and flashed into the Red Sea

              (32–6, 42–5)

It is not quite certain whether this sad poem was written in 1888 or the next year. Lord Dufferin, the Viceroy, was a grandson of Sheridan; Tennyson's relations with him were formal until his son's death. But there is no doubt that in all these deaths, even in the private cry 'I have had no friend like Fitz,' he was contemplating his own. In October 1889, at the age of eighty, after he had crossed the Solent to the Isle of Wight for what might have been the last time, there blossomed an idea planted by his nurse, a lady called Nurse Durham, who told him in April or May to stop grumbling; she said he might better offer a hymn of praises to God. Suddenly, in about twenty minutes, he wrote his poem 'Crossing the Bar'. When he said it to her, with 'Is that good enough for you, old woman?' she burst out crying, and ran away out of the room. When he read it out that evening to Hallam, Hallam said, 'It is one of the most beautiful poems ever written.' Later, he altered his record of what he said to 'It is the crown of your life's work.'

> Sunset and evening star,
>   And one clear call for me!
> And may there be no moaning of the bar,
>   When I put out to sea,
>
> But such a tide as moving seems asleep,
>   Too full for sound and foam,
> When that which drew from out the boundless deep
>   Turns again home.
>
>   (1–8)

He insisted that this poem should be treated as his last, as his epitaph, and always printed at the end of his poems. So it always has been, but he went on living. He even recovered from his serious illness. In 1887 he had taken Sir Allen Young's yacht, the *Stella*, and steamed round the south-west peninsula, calling on Fred at Jersey. Alfred and Hallam went to Cambridge in November to see some Sophocles in Greek, and some Shakespeare. In August 1888 he drove about the New Forest, 'to the two great Beeches in the Queen's Bower through the long Rhododendron drive', but soon he could hardly be persuaded to leave rainy, misty Aldworth to go as far as Horsham. In the same year, 1888, Lear died and Tennyson agreed to a signed, limited edition of the best twenty-two of his Tennyson illustrations.[37] With some difficulty he was transported to the Isle of Wight at the end of November, but there he got worse.

It is hard to understand much about the illness, since Hallam talks of gout and fever in vague terms: but we are told that gout and rheumatic fever afflicted him, and clearly that is what the doctors said. He was in bed more or less from December to March 1889, but by April he could resort to his summerhouse in the field opposite, called Maiden's Croft, and in May he was off for a cruise in Lord Brassey's *Sunbeam*, a famous yacht which had been round the world. It brought back the skeleton of a whale from the Faroe Islands still to be seen in a grotto at Heythrop. In July there was an appalling detonation, when Browning read in a private letter of FitzGerald, most idiotically published by Aldis Wright of Trinity, a bad remark about Elizabeth Browning. He not unnaturally responded with an attack on Fitz, and Alfred was left vainly attempting to placate him. The remark was 'Mrs Browning's death is rather a relief . . . no more *Aurora Leigh*s thank God.' About the time of his eightieth birthday, someone spotted the poet at a quarter past eight in the morning, running in the August sunshine. That November, Hallam's son Lionel was born. He grew up to be a dashing diner out and a famous cricketer. In December 'Demeter' was published in its remarkable volume, and Browning died. Tennyson was asked by the Dean if Browning should be buried in the Abbey; he replied 'Of course.' Hallam acted as his father's deputy as pall-bearer.

Apart from minor poems and those we have already noticed, *Demeter* contained a death-bed monologue about the FitzGerald letter where gloom overshadows the brilliance, called 'Romney's Remorse', the lovely 'Progress of Spring', and a curious piece interesting to a biographer but not a success as a poem, called 'Merlin and the Gleam' (written August 1889):

> And so to the land's
> Last limit I came –
> And can no longer,
> But die rejoicing,
> For through the Magic
> Of Him the Mighty,
> Who taught me in childhood,
> There on the border
> Of boundless Ocean,
> And all but in Heaven
> Hovers The Gleam.
>
> (109–19)

By the gleam he intended something mystical but the final effect of his refreshing directness is absurd. The metre has a sound that recalls old Welsh, and it appears that this gleam pops up here and there in old Welsh sources, which he often quoted. Here I cannot follow him, but it does look as if the poet is Merlin, and the gleam in his vision. The poem is like a mysterious tinkling of harp-strings. Perhaps the gleam ends in 'The king who loved me,/And cannot die', but who disappears, yet it flies on again, singing through the world. As an allegory, it is impenetrable.

One of the minor poems in *Demeter* was an elegant little epigram about having flirted fifty years ago with Rosa Baring that turns on blushes and roses ('Rose, on this terrace fifty years ago'). Her husband had died in March that year, but it is obscure whether Lord Tennyson knew, and obscure when he wrote his little poem. It was the payment of a small debt, something due to the past.

In the July of 1890 he completed his 'Death of Œnone', and offered it with a warm Horatian lyric to Jowett. It may be thought odd he had never written directly for Jowett before, but these things cannot be forced. He had known Jowett nearly forty years, and now he was paying his debts to humanity, and his special tributes to individuals. Jowett was by eight years the younger man, but there was a reverential grandeur about him now. The only recorded rebellion of Tennyson against his authority was once, years ago, when Jowett advised him not to print a certain poem. Alas, we do not know which one, though we do know from private letters Alfred never saw, that Jowett deprecated and disliked the *Idylls of the King*. Still, he was a pillar of support, and this occasion may have been Tennyson's only squeak of defiance. 'Come to that, Master,' said Alfred, 'the sherry you gave us at lunch was filthy.' It is one of the most endearing anecdotes about Tennyson.

He offers a late Greek tale to the Master of Balliol, who was busy revising his Plato for a third edition; the first had been twenty years ago. This tale, remarks Alfred offhandedly, 'Quintus Calaber somewhat lazily handled of old'; he adapted the last 236 lines of the tenth book.[38] But if one thing is certain about Tennyson's classical sources, one would have said it was that he did not just happen to be reading Quintus Calaber. This is the obscurest, dustiest of authors, whom not even scholars read, and whose text most of them do not possess. Matthew Arnold says somewhere that the Greek hexameter is still, even in Quintus Calaber, the hexameter. This is a superior joke, because he was a fourth-century writer (AD). But Tennyson had a 1734 edition, dated 'Feb. 23, 1833', and inscribed to him in Greek by Arthur Hallam. That was the time long ago when he went to London to study the Elgin Marbles, but otherwise the book remains a mystery. It is the kind of volume one might easily give to any classical scholar if one found it cheap or had it knocking about. If Hallam Tennyson had looked up Œnone in a classical dictionary, he might have put his father on the trail, but Tennyson would tell us so, and there is no reference to Quintus in Lemprière. It appears then that Tennyson was simply rooting about among his books.

The new poem is a pendant to the old, Ovidian poem about Œnone,[39] and may have been begun at the same time. The death of Œnone was transformed by Tennyson into the form of a classical tragedy: we do not really know why or when.

> Today, before you turn again
> To thoughts that lift the soul of men,
> > Hear my cataract's
> Downward thunder in hollow and glen,
>
> Till, led by dream and vague desire,
> The woman, gliding toward the pyre,
> > Find her warrior
> Stark and dark in his funeral fire.
> > ('To the Master of Balliol', 13-20)

The landscape and background are the same as ever, and as beautiful as ever, even though he tells us they had changed: he cannot resist dwelling on their former beauty.[40] Paris comes to Œnone to be cured of an arrow wound:

> > Thou knowest,
> Taught by some God, whatever herb or balm
> May clear the blood from poison, and thy fame
> Is blown through all the Troad, and to thee
> The shepherd brings his adder-bitten lamb

She refuses, because of his adultery with Helen, and he dies. The shepherds find him, and gather wood:[41]

And, while the star of eve was drawing light
From the dead sun, kindled the pyre, and all
Stood round it, hushed, or calling on his name.
   But when the white fog vanished like a ghost
Before the day, and every topmost pine
Spired into bluest heaven

(64–9)

Œnone sat in her cave in despair, until in the end she slept, and Paris came to call her in a dream. She woke at night and saw the funeral pyre, and found that it was his,

           and all at once
The morning light of happy marriage broke
Through all the crowded years of widowhood,
And muffling up her comely head, and crying
'Husband!' she leapt upon the funeral pile,
And mixt herself with *him* and past in fire.[42]

(101–6)

This whole poem is not 110 lines long, but in its neo–classic 1830s way, it is perfect.[43] One cannot help wondering what he really thought about widows. Obviously he was deeply linked to his wife and grateful that she was to him: he showed every day that he adored her. He told Audrey that no man could have had two better sons, and Hallam that no man could have had a truer or better wife. But was she to leap on a pyre when he died? Evidently not, because Œnone was guilty of refusing to heal Paris. All the same, when Eleanor proposed to marry again after Lionel's death, Alfred was extremely shocked and grumbly. Emily and Alfred did not like second marriages; perhaps that was because of the precision of their belief in personal immortality. When Mr Birrell, who was going to take poor widowed Eleanor off the household's hands, was brought for his interview with Tennyson, he was greeted with 'Why do you wish to intrude yourself into our family?'[44] Behind many of the old man's quirks and foibles lay passionate stories like the death of Œnone: or is it that they found expression in those stories, just as suppressed passions are filtered into dreams? He wondered at the modernity of Euripides in *Iphigenia in Aulis*, and he was fascinated by the idea of Tolstoy's version of Christianity.

He was so old, and so eminent, that poems which would once have been thrown away were carefully hoarded, and bits of his conversation were written down by practically everybody who met him. When he gave a Mr McCabe a sprig of white heather, McCabe pressed it and had it framed. Many of his stories were now twenty years old at least, or they go back to Lincolnshire. There was one about an old fellow who prayed for rain only on his own field, 'and if you don't know it O God, it has a little thorn tree in it'. Lord Brassey's yacht in 1889 was the fulfilment of a lifetime's ambition, because he had always longed to have a steam yacht and go round the world. It was too late of course: it had always been too late, because Emily did not like these sea adventures. But he said what he thought of the *Sunbeam* to Gladstone: 'Lord Brassey did all for me in his floating palace, beautiful as a dream, that princely munificence and friendly kindness could do.'[45]

In June 1891, old as he was, he borrowed Colonel Crozier's yacht *Assegai* for another odyssey.[46] Colonel Crozier casts a sidelight on Isle of Wight society at the end of the last century, because his daughter was a founder-member of a secret society or club consisting entirely of Tennyson's neighbours, who conspired together to effect the anonymous salvation of ruined, beautiful buildings, and in later years, after it was founded, to give money to the National Trust. The last of them is still remembered at Queen Anne's Gate by the Trust. They called themselves 'The Larky Lot'.[47] No doubt they were young women with nothing else to occupy them, but it is curious that Canon Rawnsley, son of Drummond Rawnsley, and an intimate of the Tennysons, was a founder of the National Trust. The Larky Lot venerated Tennyson.

Tennyson on *Assegai* with Hallam was working at his Akbar poem, which Jowett suggested. Jowett seems to have picked on this big subject in order to keep the old man busy; he advised him to work at poetry on every day left to him. The poet could still walk his three miles a day, and climb over gates, and run downhill, and read *Maud* aloud with passion, from beginning to end. But a stranger who had come to lunch encountered him out for his walk, and was met with a waving stick, and 'What's that? Who are you? Go away. I don't know who you are. What do you mean by coming here to annoy me?' The poor fellow went straight back to London. I am even fonder of the tale of the American artisan who worked his way to England in a cattle boat in order to go and read *Maud* aloud to its author. Lord Tennyson listened in agony, and then hastily paid his fare home by the swiftest ship available.[48]

It is possible of course that in suggesting Akbar Jowett under-estimated the Laureate. Jowett had by now lost two brothers dead in India, and still hankered after some memorial for the Indian dead. But Lord Tennyson got to work seriously on Moghul intellectual history, a subject that opens floodgates in the mind. That may have happened to Jowett too in his old age, as he pondered over Plato; at least it fits his earlier suggestion of Lao-Tzu, the Ancient Sage. What Lord Tennyson wrote in the end was by no means shallow, it was even rather impressive, but the long notes are far more thrilling than the rather ordinary iambic text, and it is in the notes, not in the monologue, that Akbar is a hero: all the same he is a credible figure even in the poem, and its opening and its beautiful closing hymn really are impressive. It is a poem about religious tolerance and enlightenment: today it may seem old-fashioned and woolly, and even prejudiced, but it seems to me moving and innocent and liberal.

Tennyson worked hard to get one last new book ready for the press, but it was published late in October 1892, just a fortnight after the stones of the Abbey had closed over him. The first poem in it paid a debt to his wife. He had dedicated his *Locksley Hall* volume to her, and others to Browning, to his first grandson and (by implica-tion in his poem to Lord Dufferin) to the memory of Lionel, but this is the first verse to Emily in old age, and it was worth waiting for. It is all the more touching because it has an inconsequent, almost throwaway quality as most poems in this book do. Their themes are solemn, but brevity or a light twist of the fingers reveal them as an old man's poems. He was shy about his most private emotions, and this poem, which stands first in the book as Lord Dufferin's poem had done, is titled 'June Bracken and Heather':

> There on the top of the down,
> The wild heather round me and over me June's high blue,
> When I looked at the bracken so bright and the heather so
>   brown,
> I thought to myself I would offer this book to you,
> This, and my love together,
> To you that are seventy-seven,
> With a faith as clear as the heights of the June-blue heaven,

And a fancy as summer-new
As the green of the bracken amid the gloom of the heather.

With 'The Death of Œnone' it makes as fine a beginning as any of his books ever had; the studied casualness of the fourth line gives particular pleasure, and flings an emphasis on to the ending.

'St Telemachus' is a minor poem that copes with a great theme by merely stating it: it is hardly more than an anecdote, the sketch of a pendant to his old poem about the Stylite. It is sandwiched between 'The Death of Œnone' and 'Akbar's Dream'. What follows that is sketchy, an absurd tribute to the verse of old Sir Walter Scott, 'The Bandit's Death'. It is perhaps of some interest that Gladstone had to argue against the analogy of Scott in promoting Tennyson's peerage: his argument had been that Scott had not been rich enough, and Tennyson was. I do not believe it occurred to Tennyson that this analogy had been raised: he was just placating a ghost from his childhood, as he did in an epigram as well. Perhaps one should add the note that when he said Thackeray was a finer writer but 'Dickens was more affluent', he was not talking about money: he meant more generous, more abundant as a writer, which is exactly true. There is no doubt of course that Tennyson had some worldly sense. He included here the funniest of his Lincolnshire poems, 'The Church-Warden and the Curate'. Attempts to track this old man down have always ended in uncertainty, but at least his advice is clear:

But Parson 'e *will* speäk out, saw, now 'e be sixty-seven,
He'll niver swap Owlby an' Scratby for owt but the Kingdom o'
   Heaven;
An' thou'll be 'is Curate 'ere, but if iver thou meäns to git 'igher,
Tha mun tackle the sins o' the Wo'ld, an' not the faults o' the
   Squire.
An' I reckons thou'll light of a livin' somewheers i' the Wowd or
   the Fen,
If tha cottons down to thy betters, an' keeäps thysen to thysen.
But niver not speäk plain out, if tha wants to git forrards a bit,
But creeäp along the hedge-bottoms, an' thou'll be a Bishop yit.

                                     (43–50)

He adds a note that the dialect 'was current in my youth at Spilsby', because there had been some annoying suggestions that his dialect was supposed to be north Lincolnshire. That is the sort of thing poets worry about on their death-beds.

Anecdotes flare up into poems, but they do not amount to much. The very last poem he published, 'The Dreamer', was little more than a gesture towards his mystical view of life, with the refrain 'Whirl, and follow the sun'. 'God and the Universe', 'Faith' and 'The Silent Voices', which is annoyed that his dreams are all about the past and not about his future state, are the merest guttering candle flames. Of all these last verses, the one with a curiosity value is 'Kapiolani', which he said was in a metre based on the Hawaiian chanting of the Queen of the Sandwich Isles at Farringford in 1865. The story comes from Charlotte Yonge's *Book of Golden Deeds* (1864); Kapiolani was a Queen in 1825, when the story happened. The poem combines his themes of the defiance of priestcraft, the victory of calm and reason, and the woman who climbed a fiery mountain. He had read an account of his heroine in this poem recently in the *Nineteenth Century*. The long, swaying dactylic lines remotely recall the prologue to 'Akbar's Dream', but the last word of alternate verses, which is given four syllables, surely does remember Queen Emma of the Sandwich Isles. It is Hawa–i–ee. The last poem is a formal funeral tribute to a dead prince, but apart from that, the final word is not the zany 'The Dreamer', but the solemn 'God and the Universe':

> Will my tiny spark of being wholly vanish in your deeps and
>   heights?
> Must my day be dark by reason, O ye Heavens, of your
>   boundless nights,
> Rush of Suns, and roll of systems, and your fiery clash of
>   meteorites?
>
> 'Spirit, nearing yon dark portal at the limit of thy human state,
> Fear not thou the hidden purpose of that Power which alone is
>   great,
> Nor the myriad world, His shadow, nor the silent Opener of the
>   Gate.'

The solemnity of these words is common to Victorian death-bed scenes, and those born late enough to have digested the 1914 war, let alone the 1939 war, have a distaste for it.[49] At Tennyson's own death-bed one must choose between fine memorable utterances and poetic touches, and the fact that he was not wearing his teeth, so that his last mutterings were unintelligible.

But death did not remove him the moment his last book was ready. In 1891, after cruising with Hallam on the *Assegai* – the June bracken and heather were on Exmoor – he went to London, and then had numerous guests at Aldworth, though Jowett was too ill to come. He was as active in September as he had always been, and when the mist closed in he retired to Farringford, though he had to hire a special train to get to Lymington. He climbed a gate and ran down a hill on Christmas Day. Louise Ward who was there said Alfred and Emily enjoyed Christmas just as much as their smallest grandchild. He wrote kind letters to poets and an angry one about Russian persecution of the Jews, and he was apparently pleased when the Queen sent him photos of *tableaux vivants* of the *Idylls of the King*. But in January 1892, he found himself unable to read aloud. He was attempting 'The Lotos-Eaters' and the Wellington ode, for the musician Parry.[50]

Hallam's second son had been born in April 1891. His arrival was a relief to his grandmother, who disliked the idea of only sons; the little boy's name was Alfred. He went through Eton and Trinity, but was killed as a Captain in the Rifle Brigade in March 1918. In the last few years of his life, and always excluding Emily, about whose conversation we know too little at this time, Tennyson was at his best with small children. He would take them for walks and look at simple flowers with them, or watch the gulls planing in from the sea. His sister Matilda continued safely in love with an opera singer who had died in 1877. Emily Jesse was dead. Alfred's thoughts were troubled. He sometimes felt when he prayed that God was not listening. But he did not believe in hell, and said so to the Bishop of Ripon, who whispered in his ear that he agreed with him. He read new books, such as the early volumes of *The Golden Bough*, Lockyer's *Meteoritic Hypothesis* (whence the rush of suns and roll of systems), and Pritchard's *Thoughts of an Astronomer*, which thrilled and delighted him.

He scarcely complained, except that he had to drink whisky instead of port, and about what he called Hallam's 'soft invincibility' over this rule. He suspiciously tried out a number of kinds of brandy. He was extremely pleased when Jowett told him that the philosophic element in his poems was of more use than any philosophy there was in England. Burne-Jones wrote him a very generous letter saying the same thing from his different point of view.[51] But the laureate was still capable of disputing furiously the distinction between a rook and a crow; he remembered settling it 'some years ago in Derbyshire' (with Palgrave?) by asking the driver.[52] He refused an honorary degree from Cambridge in May: perhaps it may be true as Hallam maintains that in 1861 he had actually set out for Cambridge to collect one, when 'a bad attack of palpitation of the heart' made him turn back. Now he said that if he were twenty years younger, that is in 1872 if we take him literally, he would have said yes.

Meanwhile, he reprinted 'Riflemen Form!' because he was excited that summer by an organization called the Artillery Volunteers: one feels that was closer to his heart now than any university. He found time for another little jaunt on the Assegai,[53] and Jowett was drumming up material for him on Chinese Buddhist pilgrims to India, with a view to a new poem, but Max Müller, whom he approached, was no use to him, and the Assegai set off without its load of learned books.[54] Müller was made Professor of Philology at Oxford, at a time when that science was not well understood; the great Mommsen, who came to Oxford for an honorary degree, said of him 'Have you not charlatans of your own, that you appoint German charlatans?' He was thought respectable all the same, and I have found him useful, as Jowett did. He may well be remotely responsible for 'Akbar's Dream' and 'The Ancient Sage'.

One of Lord Tennyson's last new friends came as the sister of a Canadian called A. H. Lee, an officer at the Isle of Wight school of artillery. 'He was so entirely the reverse of formidable that day, so winning, simple and sincere.' He read to her, and they wandered off for a walk, chatting easily about his usual subjects. In London he visited his old friends the Sloth and the Ichthyosaurus at the Science Museum. On 30 June 1892 The Times printed his last letter to the papers. It reads: 'Sir, I love Mr Gladstone but hate his present Irish policy. I am Yours faithfully Tennyson.' That year he stayed on at Aldworth after the summer.

As the autumn came on, he sank back into illness and fatigue, and after half past one in the morning of 6 October, he died. He had been delirious on the 4th; in the evening he said to Hallam, 'Have I not been walking with Gladstone in the garden, and showing him my trees?' Hallam said no. 'Are you sure?' Alfred asked. The Abbey authorities having asked his advice before burying Browning, he knew by what entrance he would soon enter the underworld. His final illness began with a cold, then turned to neuralgia, which he attributed to a bad wind, and then 'gout'. It is possible his doctor gently murdered him, since he calmed the old man's spasms with chloroform.[55] Alfred wanted *Cymbeline*, from the Steevens edition of Shakespeare,[56] and it was found for him, though he was beyond reading. It kept being tidied away, but he insisted on keeping it. At least he could open it, at a moment in the play that had always made him weep, in act V, scene v, where Imogen says to Posthumus:

> Why did you throw your wedded lady from you?
> Think that you are upon a rock, and now
> Throw me again.

She embraces Posthumus, and he says:

> Hang there like fruit, my soul,
> Till the tree die.

We do not know his last words to Emily or to Hallam; Audrey says only that he muttered inaudibly. Then quite quietly he died. The full moon was streaming into the room.

The old horse they had took the farm cart to the station. Lord Tennyson was given some laurel from Virgil's tomb, and an old *Cymbeline* of Audrey's. At the Abbey there had been some trouble about assembling the pall-bearers: Gladstone could not come, and wrote to the Queen to apologize, and the Queen herself did not come to London. Watts the painter was too old to come. The aisle was lined by survivors of the Light Brigade, and by the Gordon Boys, and the pall-bearers were Argyll, Dufferin, the Earl of Selborne (Lord Chancellor to whom *Becket* was dedicated[57]) and Rosebery (Foreign Secretary and a friend[58]), Jowett, J. A. Froude the historian, Lord Salisbury, H. M. Butler the Master of Trinity, H. White the American Minister, Sir James Paget Surgeon to the Prince and Princess of Wales, London Vice-Chancellor and Tennyson's doctor,[59] and Lord Kelvin the Trinity scientist. What writers England could boast were in the Abbey: the best of them were Hardy, James and Meredith. There is no mention of Kipling or Swinburne, though there is of Conan Doyle. The Pre-Raphaelites were all there except for William Morris. But everyone present who recorded their feelings was disappointed.

Lord Selborne wrote later that the wish of Wordsworth that his days should be 'bound each to each in natural piety' had come true in Tennyson. Froude, with whom Tennyson was reconciled after his life of Carlyle, and whom he used as a Protestant historian, said he had been an inspiration for fifty years. Tyndall described deep excitement about the poet, including the day when 'he filled a pipe for me, lit it himself, and transferred it to my lips'. The Duke of Argyll spoke with something like veneration of his humility and his truthfulness. But the most useful recollections were Jowett's. He was at work on his brief memoir of less than ten pages until a fortnight before he died. He says Alfred told him one day that Emily had once remarked to him quite simply, 'When I pray I see the face of God smiling at me.' Jowett loved Emily with an amazing intensity, as Lear had done, another unmarried man. He was perceptive about Tennyson too. Incredible as it is, no one else has recorded that in any room he would choose the tallest, most uncomfortable, upright chair. Tennyson's quiet life at home was his greatest pleasure, but he was genial, and loved to fill the place. 'He was not a man of the world in the ordinary sense, but a man who had the greatest insight into the world.' In 1842 he had shot up like a rocket, and after the death of Wordsworth there was no living poet who could be compared with him. Jowett was as awed at meeting him as Boswell was at meeting Samuel Johnson. From all this and from very much more, Hallam settled down with his mother Emily's help to write his father's large *Memoir*. When it appeared at last in 1897, she was already under the earth. She died on 10 August 1896, and was buried at Freshwater. When Hallam's literary work was done he went off to be Governor of South Australia. When his wife died he married again, a Miss Prinsep, a young kinswoman of Mrs Cameron's whom he must have known for most of his life.[60]

NOTES AND REFERENCES

ALL QUOTATIONS from Tennyson's poetry are, unless otherwise stated, from Christopher Ricks' three-volume edition (second edition), 1987. Two major sources of information about Tennyson and his family are his son Hallam's *Alfred Lord Tennyson, a Memoir* (1897, revised 1899) and Sir Charles Tennyson and Hope Dyson's *Tennyson: Background to Genius* (1974), to which I shall not give detailed references.

INTRODUCTION

1. ed. James Hoge 1981. Hoge also edited her letters in 1974. For the Farringford part of her journal there are better notes in Hutchings and Hinton, 1986.
2. ed. Kolb, 1981.
3. I came late to exploit the recent companion edition of *Maud*, but with the help of Ricks I hope to have avoided pitfalls.
4. John Collins in *The Two Forgers*, 1992, has thrown much light on their activities, but their crimes have still not all been discovered.
5. Alexander Smith (1829–67), *Collected Poems*, 1909 and Sidney Dobell (1824–75), *Collected Poems*, 1875.

CHAPTER ONE

1. When he died one of the King's daughters, Sophia, sent money to his widow, though she returned it.
2. One of the prose fragments of John Clare confirms Byron's genuine popularity. It was strongest in the Nonconformist cities that supported Greek independence. Clare's prose ed. Tibble, 1957, pp. 99 and 258.
3. At Cambridge he would recite real ballads that had been printed, and he copied out a late version of 'Tom of Bedlam's Song' that exists also in his father's hand.
4. A. de Vere records this, and so does Louisa Ward, in *Tennyson, Interviews and Recollections*, ed. N. Page, 1983, p. 15 and p. 40.
5. The best brief discussion of Thomson is by J. W. Mackail in 'The Poet of *The Seasons*', 1920, printed in his *Studies of English Poets*, 1926.
6. H. D. Rawnsley, *Memories of the Tennysons*, 1900. cf. *Tennyson, Interviews and Recollections*, ed. N. Page, 1983, p. 64.
7. This mistake was first spotted by John Betjeman, and the solution recorded in a footnote to the introduction to his and Charles Tennyson's edition of a selection of sonnets by Alfred's brother, Charles Tennyson Turner.

8. It first occurs in Tennyson in 'New Year's Eve', in *Unpublished Early Poems* (in the section 1830–42), ed. Charles Tennyson, 1931.

9. James Spedding's Introductory Essay to Charles Tennyson Turner's collected *Sonnets*, 1880.

10. Roger Lonsdale does devote two pages of his wonderful *Oxford Book of Eighteenth Century Verse* to 'The Minstrel'.

11. The poet's uncle John inherited Thorpe Hall from his wife's brother, and altered his name to ffytche; his grandson was a major-general in India who pronounced it to rhyme with *fight*(ch). He wrote a book about Burma with the Fytche arms prominently displayed on the cover, dedicated to the Laureate. I mention these bizarre details only to set off others.

12. Bishop Maltby (1770–1859) of Chichester (1831) and later of Durham (1836) was married to another of Mrs Tennyson's cousins. He was the son of a presbyterian weaver in Norwich, was at the grammar school under S. Parr, and then Winchester.

13. It is possible to construe the old man's financial arrangements for his grandchildren as not unjust (*Tennyson Research Bulletin*, Vol. 3, no. 2, pp. 41–54, Sir F. Hill), but bad feeling was inextinguishably rampant and it is only within the last forty years that a reconciliation has gingerly taken place. All the same Alfred and his brothers can be glimpsed in letters getting on well with their first cousin George.

14. The evidence is in his own library, the remains of which are now at Lincoln. It includes a lot of Voltaire. He owned about 2500 volumes, 1300 titles, many from the library of Dr Johnson's friend Bennet Langton, who succeeded the great lexicographer as Professor of Ancient Languages to the Royal Academy. Bennet Langton was a Lincolnshire neighbour, who died in 1801. His house was Elizabethan but it was burnt down about 1822. George seems to have veered from classical towards oriental studies.

15. We know this from the letter of a ship's officer which says George had planned to wait for the Tsar on 15 October at St Petersburg and take this route home. He arrived in Cambridge in February very ill.

16. Harold Nicolson describes it as painted brown but he seems to be referring to the Vanbrugh house, which does indeed contain a brown-painted dining-room mantelpiece.

17. Ricks (Vol. 3, App. B, p. 605) prefers *infantile*, from a Lincoln notebook, but *difficilior lectio potior*, at least in dreams.

18. Ricks, Vol. 3, App. B, p. 605.

19. Hallam Tennyson, repeating a note written by the poet in 1890.

20. *Tennyson, Interviews and Recollections*, ed. N. Page, pp. 3–4. I suspect the influence of Potter's verse version of Aeschylus.

21. Quoted by Joanna Richardson in *The Pre-eminent Victorian*, 1962.

22. Note written for Hallam Tennyson, 1890.

23. Dyce's Introduction to the 1831 edition.

24. For a sexual explanation of ecstatic emotions less early in life than Tenny-

son's and not associated with pseudo-epilepsy or guilt, cf. my *Frontiers of Paradise*, 1990, p. 202–3.

25. Gifford Lectures, published 1902, pp. 383–4, in two lectures on Mysticism. For Tennyson's letter and a note on B. P. Blood with full bibliographical information cf. Lang and Shannon, *Tennyson's Letters*, Vol. 3, p. 78. Tennyson also refers to trances in passages added to *The Princess*.

26. Ricks, Vol. 1, no. 2, p. 13.

27. One child was stillborn, so Fred was the eldest (June 1807). Charles was the next (July 1808), followed by Alfred (August 1809), Mary (September 1810), Emilia (October 1811), Edward (January 1813), Arthur (May 1814), Septimus (September 1815), Matilda (September 1816), Cecilia (October 1817), and Horatio (September 1819): ten children in twelve years.

28. When Stephen Fytche left the Vicarage he moved two houses away to what is now The Limes, a boarding house of Louth King Edward VI School, that is the grammar school.

29. Fred went to school at Louth in 1814, Charles in 1815 and Alfred in 1816. Fred left in 1818, and Alfred in 1820, but Charles stayed on until 1821. I owe this information to an article in *The Leader* by Christopher Sturman.

30. In a manuscript notebook at Lincoln of his conversation recorded by Hallam.

31. The combination in one building of care for the old and the young was a Renaissance idea which survived in England at the London Charterhouse, at Kirkby Green in Yorkshire, and at Ewelme in Oxfordshire until the nineteenth century.

32. It is small wonder Alfred had to have special coaching in mathematics, at the village school in Holywell Wood, but it was ineffective. A lot of boys had this problem as R. B. Martin shows in *With Friends Possessed*, a life of E. FitzGerald, pp. 48 and 56. When Fred took the Trinity scholarship exam he was very highly commended, but awarded nothing for lack of mathematics.

33. December 1892 (not the Christmas issue) p. 562. The Victoria County History of Lincolnshire, which is utterly incomplete, draws on this useful article, and Hallam Tennyson in his one-volume edition reprints part of the article. Hales wrote it in about 1868 and it dealt with the school in about 1828, when the younger Tennysons were there.

34. Also in his 'Elegiacs', written at Cambridge and first printed by Sir Charles Tennyson in *Unpublished Early Poems* (1931): 'Loudly he sang from the thicket, and nigher the shrilly balm-cricket'. He revised this poem as 'Leonine Elegiacs' (1830), and called it a grasshopper. Immediately after 'A Dirge' (1830) where the balm-cricket has a position of climax, comes 'The Grasshopper' which is based on a famous poem of Anacreon about the cicada; Ricks (Vol. 1, p. 257) discusses existing translations, but the Anacreon is in Dalzel, and Charles also wrote a poem based on it (*Sonnets, Lyrics and Translations*, 1873).

35. Before 1885, when Part 2 of the dictionary (Ant–Batten) was printed, presumably therefore in 1884. Murray also wrote about 'bowl'd' (intransitive) in *The Princess*, Prologue, 81, about May 1886 (Lang and Shannon, *Letters*, Vol. 3, p. 337).

36. Andrew Dalzel edited a textbook for schools, later re-edited by George Dunbar, both in turn Professors of Greek in an Edinburgh school. The title occurs in Greek type as *Analecta Hellenica (Hessona)* and in Latin as *Analecta Minora* and *Maiora*, the latter meaning either a fatter selection or possibly part two for senior boys. This good old workhorse of a textbook had several forms and varying contents. My own copy (Edinburgh, 1832, prize book bound by Robert Seton and awarded by Dunbar) is entitled *Dunbar's Excerpta* on the cover and title page, but it begins at p. 215 with Theocritus. Theocritus may have been recently added to the old anthology, because his text follows Kiessling 1819. The Rector of Somersby had a copy in two volumes. Lincoln no. 93, *Analecta maiora*, London 1820–1. It carries Alfred Tennyson's signature, one volume 'Trin Coll Cambridge' and the other '*Somersby in agro Lincolniensi*', and contains numerous notes and translations in his handwriting.

37. He came to prefer Blomfield. It may be worth recording that in the 1830 volume in the poem before 'A Dirge' he uses the queer word 'coronach', probably from Blackie on the *Persae* of Aeschylus. That whole poem, 'The Dying Swan', is at least remotely based on Ovid's *Heroides*. Potter's *Aeschylus* is a book he outgrew early.

38. Sir Charles Tennyson points to old George's new worldly ambitions while young George was at Cambridge and fearing disinheritance. He prints a grim letter from son to father, August 1820, in *The Tennysons*, Tennyson and Dyson, 1974, p. 39–40.

39. At this time, for part of the eighteenth and most of the nineteenth century, the MP for Lincoln generally came from the Sibthorp family, on which the *Dictionary of National Biography* is particularly useful.

40. Charles distinguished himself in 1830 by getting himself sent to prison for fighting a duel with Lord Thomas Cecil, over a libellously insulting election speech. He was let out, however.

41. John Fytche was a St John's, Cambridge man who served in the 6th Inniskillen Dragoons and married Anne Willson of Lincoln in 1811. The Tennyson boys remembered her head nodding like a rose in the wind from Parkinson's disease.

42. C. Tennyson, *Alfred Tennyson*, 1949.

43. The library did not always do good. He read *Othello* as a little boy in a haystack, and hated it (ibid. p. 347).

44. There is a good succinct account of the accent in G. Edward Campion's *Tennyson Dialect Glossary* (1969, third edition 1976), in the Introduction by Sir Charles Tennyson. *So, road, gone, ale*, become *soä, roäd, goän, aäle, knowledge* becomes *knŏwledge* (like rollage) which he taught to Jowett. The slightly accented pronunciation affects the sound of the whole of his poetry.

More is said in Charles Tennyson, *Six Tennyson Essays*, 1954, essay 6, 'On Reading Tennyson', e.g. he said shaäkes, laäkes, woodbīne and dänce.

45. Not true. The local clergy and gentry founded Skegness soon after 1800 as a cheap summer resort to take their children. The house was built for them and rented.

46. He left some youthful translations, but not of great merit (Ricks, Vol. 1, 1A.). The versions were printed from his boyhood copy of Horace, 1822, in the *Tennyson Research Bulletin* in 1982.

47. I am not clear when, but he is said to have debauched a servant girl at home. It does explain why his family was so cross with him.

48. Tennyson and Dyson, *The Tennysons*, 1974, p. 50.

49. Ibid., p. 45-7.

50. The needy knife-grinder appeared in the *Antijacobin* which began in November 1797; these gleeful parodies set the tone of much satire for a generation.

51. Preface to the 1893 facsimile edition. Fred, who was still alive, was surprised to find the poems so good (which shows how greatly his critical powers had declined).

52. Notebook 9, 1824-7.

53. At the age of about eleven he wrote to his aunt Mary Anne Fytche a mannered critical letter about *Samson Agonistes*, mostly about the first few pages and commentaries on them. Naturally he singles out 'O dark, dark, dark, amid the blaze of Noon'. (Lang and Shannon, *Letters*, Vol. 1, p. 1-2.)

54. Many of them were long-lived. Old George the grandfather lived to be 85, his wife to be 102, and their daughter Elizabeth 89. The poet died at 83, Edward in the asylum 77, Arthur 85, Matilda 97, Cecilia 92 and Horatio 80.

55. This amount is certain; the other versions are wrong (cf. Hagen, *Tennyson and His Publishers*, 1979, p. 7).

56. Daughter of Rev Edward Walls of Boothby Hall, Welton-le-Marsh, managed by Dame Hildred, who made delicious curd cheese-cakes.

57. Mr and Mrs Wildman, 'old friends' in a letter to Emily. Quoted in H. Tennyson's *Alfred Lord Tennyson*, 1905, p. 141.

58. Shannon in *Modern Language Notes* 64, 1949, p. 107-10.

59. It is likely that the carrier did not pass by Somersby, but went regularly by Tetford on his way to Horncastle. It need hardly be underlined that parcels are not so easily delivered, nor anonymous first books so punctiliously reviewed, in the 1990s.

CHAPTER TWO

1. Porson was sent to Eton by his patrons only because Charterhouse refused to take him, reserving all the places for their relatives. Byron says the undergraduates despised him for his rudeness.

2. 1774–1846; BA 1796, Master 1820. He resigned in 1841, while the prime ministership of Peel ensured a conservative succession, the mastership of Trinity being a royal appointment.

3. Edward Bulwer (1803–73), later Bulwer-Lytton, later Lord Lytton, wrote awful verse but won the Chancellor's Medal in 1825 for a poem on Sculpture. He was a dandy, who advocated black evening dress (his first novel, *Falkland*, came out in March 1827, followed by *Pelham*, his great success – much to his old tutor's surprise – in 1828). He cultivated Alfred Tennyson's rich uncle, Charles. Nothing he wrote is of any merit and the man was a pretentious charlatan. Even his *Last Days of Pompeii* (1835) owes a good deal to an opera of 1827.

4. The Dean was H. P. Hamilton, later Dean of Salisbury. Trinity was exceptional even in 1840 in setting tests (on book one of the *Iliad* and *Aeneid*, some prose, arithmetic, algebra, Euclid, and Paley's *Natural Theology*) but the examiners were lenient, and only four or five candidates were failed out of 130 or more even as late as 1840. Tennyson's test was clearly less formal. cf. C. A. Bristed, *Five Years in an English University*, 1851², p. 11–12, quoted by Lang and Shannon, Vol. 1, p. 20.

5. Ricks (Vol. 1, no. 58A, p. 177f.) admirably summarizes the arguments about this piece.

6. It was called the Stuff Ball, annual since 1785 for the promotion of cloth, the year's patroness choosing the year's colour; a party of Tennysons always went. Whig families and Tory families sat as far apart as they could, though their children danced together. Alfred was an excellent dancer and a popular partner. When he was over eighty he got up and danced a lonely quadrille for Jane Brookfield in memory of old days.

7. The poet Aubrey de Vere, who does figure, was this man's younger brother, but Aubrey was born in 1814 and was not yet at Trinity.

8. His friend and college ally Julius Hare was keen on Fichte.

9. Lincoln MS and *Memoir*. It is not certain who the vicar was.

10. Lang and Shannon, Vol. 1, p. 14. The cousin was Mr Wheeldon of Market Street, died 1844. 'He was like her, for he had not a touch of gall in his whole nature.' (p. 224)

11. It should be remembered that when Eton boys of this period got girls into trouble in the village, the row was comparatively slight, because the girls were simply paid off. What the boys' fathers really feared was clandestine marriage.

12. What the cook said in real life was 'If yore raäked out hell wi' a small-tooth coämb you wouldn't find their likes.'

13. Lang and Shannon, Vol. 1, p. 23–4.

14. The first curacy of Fred's Eton friend, John Frere, was unpaid, and simple living cost him £60 a year, but in 1840 half the 4000 curates in England made less than that. The Rector's curate's £35 was not always easy to find (Alfred said his boyhood resounded with the detestation of curates).

15. He knew the father of this Rector who was Thomas Rawnsley, born in

1790, twelve years younger than George. He got a Lincolnshire living in 1814 and Halton in 1825. Thomas Rawnsley's son, Drummond (1817–82), later officiated at Alfred's marriage. Drummond's second son became Canon of Carlisle and a founder of the National Trust (1815–20).

16. Lang and Shannon, Vol. 1, p. 45.

17. Tennyson and Dyson, *The Tennysons*, 1974, p. 80.

18. It was said at Bayons of Alfred's brother Charles that he 'dressed in rabbit skin and went about looking like the dog's meat man'.

19. Lang and Shannon, Vol. 1, p. 39.

20. See *Richard Monckton Milnes*, by James Pope-Hennessy. His papers contain numerous anecdotes and sayings of Alfred Tennyson. They are now at Trinity (the Houghton papers) waiting to be worked over.

21. Sir Charles (1778–53) was 64 and a widower when he inherited. He is mentioned and quoted in J. L. Cherry's *Life and Remains of John Clare*, 1873, and must have known Wordsworth and Coleridge at Nether Stowey. His two young sons were drowned together in 1819, and in 1820 he published 'The Brothers', which is a moving elegy to them, and some other fine poems. There is a copy at Northampton which he sent Clare.

22. Abraham Elton V (1755–1842), a curate of West Bromwich who blew up his church with gunpowder and rebuilt it. Meanwhile his father splendidly Gothicized Clevedon Court.

23. Henry Hallam was a historian with inherited money, mostly a medievalist, but popular enough to be read by John Bright to his wife and commended by F. D. Maurice to the workers (1866). He wrote for the *Edinburgh Review* (1804–9) but later deserted. He thought 'the dignity of history' lay in subjects not noble families, but disapproved of the 1832 reform, preferring the level progression of 1688 to 1830. His voluminous papers are of as great or greater interest as his son's; they are now in the library of Christ Church, Oxford, his old college. They include a few letters and school exercises of Arthur's. Henry behaved like tutor as well as a heavy-handed parent. He married Julia Elton in 1807, she bore him eight children and died in 1846. He survived her and all his children, to die at 82 in 1859.

24. Probably a boy called Farr.

25. There is an excellent short account of the Apostles in its later history by Noel Annan in his *Our Age*, 1980, p. 317–20.

26. It gives a corrective pleasure to record A. C. Benson's view of A. H. Hallam (*Fasti Etonenses*, p. 345) as 'a rubicund, good-humoured, almost beery-looking young man, with a sly and sensual cast of the eye', but that is only based on his ruddy-faced Eton leaving portrait.

27. Gaskell failed too in the end but his daughter married a Wintour in 1855. Anne Wintour had been at Miss Starke's Roman ball (January 1828) where she was Thalia in a tableau of Parnassus. Miss Starke was a guide writer of 65. Miss Wintour married a Colonel Healey (1834) but her ten children all died.

28. It was not only offered for sale by Ollier in August 1821 in London (sent

from Pisa) but pirated in December by the *Literary Chronicle*. For details cf. Shelley's *Adonais*. ed. Rossetti and Prickard, 1903, p. 38–40.

29. He loved *Euphranor*, FitzGerald's pastiche of Plato, with its ending about the crowd of young men scattering homewards in the dusk, past the flowering chesnuts (sic) of Jesus, and he loved a passage from De Quincey of the same deep and glamorous colouring.

30. 1841, Vol. 2, *Letters*, ed. Gordon Ray, 1955. For the cachet of a great man, see Vol. 1, p. 284.

31. Lang and Shannon, Vol. 1, p. 43. The list was supplied by H. Sidgwick (1839–1900) towards the end of the nineteenth century. All the following notes on Apostolic debates come from him. They continue to December 1831, but with no further mention of Alfred. Perhaps he became an honorary member like Hallam in 1832.

32. Hallam Tennyson's *Tennyson²*, p. 861–2; cf. *Harvard Library Bulletin*, X, 1956, p. 255.

33. All this and much more detail about The Literati of the Eton Society is in 'Unpublished Letters of Arthur Hallam from Eton', ed. M Zamick. *Bulletin of John Rylands Library*, Vol. 18, January 1939.

34. Letter to Blakesley. Donne was at Cambridge and an Apostle by 1828; he withdrew later without a degree because of religious scruples. He was a kinsman of the poet Cowper.

35. Amy Cruse, *The Englishman and his Books in the early 19th century*, 1930, p. 117–18.

36. Lincoln MS, and Tennyson and Dyson, *The Tennysons*, 1974, p. 197f. Monckton Milnes was a friend of the explorer R. F. Burton whose *Mission to Dahomey* (1864) was among Tennyson's books (no 676).

37. Essay on *In Memoriam*, 1936.

38. Henry Hallam at first suppressed this essay which appeared only in 1869. Alfred Tennyson had always pleaded for it.

39. Did he know *Alastor* was written at Bishopsgate on the edge of Windsor Park, within his and Gladstone's walking range of Eton?

40. Alfred thought Blakesley an honest man and a subtle, powerful reasoner who should be Lord Chancellor, but he became Dean of Lincoln.

41. I do not think the refrain 'I would that I were dead', which falls with a truthful flatness, has anything to do with the idiot Bulwer's 'O God! O God! would that I were dead', in his *Falkland* (1827).

42. Later on, in 'The Gardener's Daughter', he referred continually to the flowers as 'hollyoaks', presumably a Lincolnshire pronunciation. Turner calls them Holyoakes in 1548.

43. Whatever his business ethics, Wilson lived on till 1868, and his firm survived into the 1890s. (Hagen, *Tennyson and His Publishers*, 1979.)

44. He impressed an exceptionally dim poet, a baronet called Sir Francis Doyle, an Etonian neighbour of 67 Wimpole Street, whose country house was in Holderness. Doyle became Oxford Poetry professor later and was a Fellow

of All Souls. He wrote *A Private of the Buffs* and lectured against Shelley, but he did publish an excellent volume of memoirs.

45. He had eleven brothers, two of whom were distinguished in the Indian service. In 1829 he got an honorary doctorate at Oxford, then surveyed the coast of Greece (August 1830). He has a statue at Spilsby.

46. It is dated from *Materials*, Vol. 1, p. 246, and the watermark (1835) of its manuscript. FitzGerald connects a reference in the poem to Queen Anne with a letter from Alfred written in April 1837.

47. The Victorian baby-cult was at full blast by 1840, as can be seen in Marina Warner's *Queen Victoria's Sketchbook*, 1979, p. 101. When Tennyson admired the fine wedding hymn of Catullus he singled out the untypically sweet lines about a baby. See also the end of 'The Gardener's Daughter'.

48. Lang and Shannon, Vol. 1, p. 45.

49. 1851 or Vol. 11 of the thirty-volume centenary edition. It embodies Carlyle's contempt for the biography of Sterling by his old tutor Archdeacon Julius Hare of Lewes.

50. The European context was studied by Clive Church in *Europe in 1830*, (1983).

51. The innumerable private debating societies at Cambridge were not intended for political action, but they were equally a sign of the times. So were the Reading Clubs where newspapers were available: they acted as a network for volunteers for the Greek War of Independence, for example.

52. Ricks, Vol. 1, p. 419f. gives both.

53. The 1832 version is close to Ovid, *Fasti* IV, 432f.

54. It is also worth recording that Charles Weld, Tennyson's friend and neighbour, gave Emily Sellwood (to whose sister Ann he was married) his own extra illustrated and enriched copy of his book *The Pyrenees*, 1851, which treats Cauterets (Lincoln 3405).

55. Lincoln MS.

56. Lang and Shannon, Vol. 1, p. 46–7. R. J. Tennant (1809–42), Christ's Hospital with John Sterling and Trinity, was in love with Cecilia Tennyson. Became a schoolmaster, Hare's curate at Herstmonceux, Horatio Tennyson's tutor, Chaplain to the British Embassy in Tuscany, and died in Florence.

57. He did quote and adapt the urbane Praed in his unpublished 'Lines to the Picture of a young Lady of Fashion'. *Unpublished Early Poems*, ed. Tennyson 1931, p. 56.

58. Ibid. p. 67 and Ricks, Vol. 1, n. 135, p. 305.

59. The metre recalls the '*Pervigilium Veneris*'. It is vigorously taken up in 'What Thor Said to the Bard Before Dinner', which is against critics and surely written for a dinner of the Apostles?

CHAPTER THREE

1. Charles had the habit by 1834. It is R. B. Martin's conjecture that he must have begun as an undergraduate: it is not unlikely. Family tradition has always been that he was prescribed it. The illness for which he took it remains obscure. The symptoms of his father, and those which Alfred describes as 'gout' and Charles late in life as 'like having gout all over', have a disturbing similarity to the case of Charles Lloyd, another opium addict, in Thomas De Quincey's *Recollections of the Lakes and the Lake Poets*.

2. The elder brothers £235 each and Alfred £180 is apparently the true figure.

3. Her grandfather advanced the money for this trip out of her mother's allowance.

4. For 1832, which appeared in October 1831; the letters are in Lang and Shannon, Vol. 1, p. 64.

5. Ricks, Vol. 1, p. 322, no. 150. Hallam sent it to Moxon. Tennyson had not meant to print it, and he never reprinted it.

6. Ricks, Vol. 1, p. 325–8 unfolds the history of the poem.

7. Not in Ricks, but *Tennyson Research Bulletin*, 1971, p. 147. R. Adicks. This was not the only poem they wrote together.

8. 'The Queen of the Meadow', in which the story of the miller's daughter occurs, was one of those collected in *Our Village* (1828) but is not in the usual modern selection published by Everyman, and edited by J. C. Squire. The influence is only that of an impression. Mary Russell Mitford was earlier than Tennyson both in generation and in taste.

9. Ricks, Vol. 1, p. 479, no. 173.

10. Hallam's letters, pp. 522 and 537.

11. Lang and Shannon, Letters, Vol. 1, p. 74.

12. Lang and Shannon, Vol. 1, p. 109.

13. *Memoir²*, p. 80–81.

14. He had been a poet, Newdigate Prize 1806, *Isle of Palms* (1812), *City of the Plague* (1816). His verse was dull but his prose frenzied.

15. Quoted in Moore's edition of Byron, at *Childe Harold* canto IV, stanzas 26, 51 and the end.

16. He had known Wilson in the Lakes and mentions him in his *Recollections*.

17. Moxon was offered *Paracelsus* in April 1835: his reaction was to groan that Henry Taylor's verse play *Philip Van Artevelde* had failed by £30 to meet its expenses, and Tennyson was not selling. He was doubtful if he would do anything as precarious as publishing poetry ever again.

18. Lincoln 1845, Pauw's edition (1734).

19. We might never have known, though we ought to have guessed, that Alfred was on friendly terms with the Burtons. William Burton was a farm labourer (d. 1849) who inherited from his mother's uncle, Robert Burton, and adopted his name in 1815. Old Robert Burton had given the Rector his

living, and William continued that, reserving the succession to his own son, the Rev Langhorne Burton (1808–78) of Trinity.

20. The Habsburgs still ruled Austria, Venetia, Lombardy, Bohemia, Moravia, Galicia, the enormous Hungarian lands, Slovenia and Croatia, which made theirs a maritime empire.

21. Lang and Shannon, Vol. 1, p. 91–2, notes.

22. Ricks notes one original that this line echoes. There are some other interesting suggestions in W. Watkins, *The Birds of Tennyson*, 1903, p. 72.

23. Variant in Ricks, Vol. 1, p. 563. The details prefigure *The Princess*; there was once going to be a celebration of a naval victory (p. 565).

24. Mrs Tennyson's journal, 28 November 1869 is the only record.

25. Lang and Shannon, Vol. 1, p. 105.

CHAPTER FOUR

1. Ricks, Vol. 1, p. 548, footnote.

2. Penguin, 1973, p. 13.

3. *In Memoriam*, ed. Shatto and Shaw, 1982, p. 8–25.

4. Ibid. The last new poem was added to the series (CXXXIX) in the small, white multi-volume Strahan Chiswick Press edition.

5. Mostly in XCVII, 'My love has talked with rocks and trees'. Shatto and Shaw on line 18 of this poem, p. 173 and rejected versions p. 114–5.

6. Lang and Shannon, Vol. 1, p. 107.

7. See also 'Youth' of which the same may probably be said.

8. Arnold grossly misquoted. See Ricks, *Force of Poetry*, 1987, p. 412–3.

9. Dante, 177–9. But the source (in 'Tiresias') may be Shelley.

10. Lang and Shannon, Vol. 1, p. 107–8.

11. He married Mariquita, a sister of Maria Edgeworth and daughter of Don Antonio Eroles in 1838: when he died she edited his sermons and was Keeper of the House of Mercy at Clewer, which is where Gladstone used to send reformed prostitutes.

12. *In Memoriam*, XIX.

13. Ellen Hallam speaks in October of Emily reciting to her 'a little poem of Alfred's – a kind of ballad upon the death of King Arthur', which I take to be a forerunner (now lost) like the idiotic 'Sir Galahad', written about then. James Spedding greatly admired 'Sir Galahad'. It was intended as a pendant to 'St Agnes' Eve'.

14. Moore published in *Miscellaneous Poems* about 1825 (*Works*, ed. A. D. Godley, Oxford, 1910, p. 563) a poem called 'Country Dance and Quadrille' remembering a time before Waltz laid hands 'on virtuous English backs and shoulders'.

15. He left him the advowson, the perpetual right to appoint a Rector. These advowsons of small places were costly when they were bought; Lord Bath sold the advowson of Marston Bigot to the Earl of Cork in 1805 for over £2600: probably ten times what the tithes brought in to the Rector.

16. Quoted in Thomas West's *Guide to the Lakes*, 1784, p. 116 (Facsimile 1989).

17. *Letters*, in two vols. ed. W. Aldis Wright, 1901, p. 7–9.

18. *Tennyson Research Bulletin*, November 1984, p. 110.

19. 1810–84, theologian, friend of F. D. Maurice and E. Lushington, at one time a Newmanite.

20. Inscribed and now in the Tennyson Research Centre at Lincoln.

21. Spedding wrote to Thompson of Tennyson, 'He would and would not (sulky one) although Wordsworth was hospitably minded towards him,' but he may have been careful because Thompson was a friend of FitzGerald.

22. The Arnolds moved into Fox How in 1834. Matthew's youngest sister was still living there after the First World War.

23. Aldis Wright, *Letters*, Vol. 1, p. 33.

24. Lang and Shannon, Vol. 1, p. 132.

25. In a fragmentary, undated letter about this time we learn that Alfred wandered across to Boulogne for two days. Lang and Shannon, Vol. 1, p. 139 (and note on date).

26. Lang and Shannon, Vol. 1, p. 135–141.

27. Ibid., cousinly letter, p. 138.

28. Ibid., p. 131.

29. Part of H. D. Rawnsley's *Memories of the Tennysons* (1900).

30. The best article on this tenancy is by Christopher Sturman in *Tennyson Research Bulletin*, November 1989, p. 130–143, which contains full references.

31. Ricks, Vol. 2, p. 59 note on 242.

32. E. V. Boyle was the widow of the Rector of Marston Bigot, near Frome, who was a son of the Earl of Cork. Alfred knew her as a friend of her kinswoman, Mary Boyle.

33. Surely not the way it does roll, or does he imagine it as the Greeks did, reaching the west and then crossing over behind the world to the east, where it rises again?

34. *In Memoriam*, ed. Shatto and Shaw, (1982), p. 239. Professor Lushington married Alfred's sister Cecilia in 1842.

35. Tennyson was an influence on *Aurora Leigh*, as he was on 'Laurence Bloomfield', which was published as a serial in *Fraser's Magazine* by Froude. Allingham appears among the Pre-Raphaelites in Mary Howitt's memoirs.

36. Lang and Shannon, Vol. 1, p. 144 to W. H. Brookfield and p. 145–9 to R. Monckton Milnes.

37. There is a hint of Tennyson's mixed feelings about this in 'An Idle Rhyme'.

CHAPTER FIVE

1. They were long-established friends. C. R. Haddelsey acted for Alfred over a bit of land he owned up there. Susan exchanged letters with Alfred on his deathbed.
2. William St Julien Arabin, who appears as Serjeant Snubbins in *Pickwick Papers*. A Serjeant is a superior barrister, abolished in 1880; Judges called them 'my learned brother'.
3. Lang and Shannon, Vol. 1, p. 151–3.
4. In May 1835 Mimosa went with the Tennysons to the Sellwood party to say goodbye to Sir John Franklin, *Tennyson Research Bulletin*, 1975, p. 156.
5. Edited by S. C. Hall who seems to have approached Tennyson in 1831, but then in vain. His critical introduction is acerbic.
6. Lang and Shannon, Vol. 1, p. 158.
7. Reid, *R. M. Milnes*, Vol. 1, p. 221.
8. Lang and Shannon, Vol. 1, p. 159–61.
9. Monckton Milnes published his *Poems of Many Years* privately and experimentally, but later in 1838 Moxon published it properly. This device of a private edition to test the water for a public one became very dear to Tennyson. Lang and Shannon, Vol. 1, p. 162.
10. Henry Lushington (Trinity College), admitted to the Inner Temple 1834, called to the Bar 1840, Chief Secretary to government of Malta 1847–55, was a critic Tennyson greatly respected.
11. Date conjectural. Lang and Shannon, Vol. 1, p. 166.
12. Ricks, Vol. 2, p. 116.
13. John Chandos identified this in *Boys Together* (1985), p. 128–9. The memoir that enshrines it is *Reminiscences of Eton*, by Sir H. Crickitt Blake, privately printed at Chichester in 1831. He entered Eton at eight in 1799. The sow is p. 76f. The boys were hungry for meat because the school was served roast meat but its dripping was the cook's perquisite, so meat was always 'roasted to a chip'. Boys dependent on school catering were called 'Tug-muttons'.
14. *Tennyson Research Bulletin*, 1975, p. 158.
15. Babbage, *Ninth Bridgewater Treatise*, 1837.
16. Ricks, Vol. 2, p. 151, no. 276.
17. Ricks, Vol. 2, p. 176, no. 280.
18. Tennyson also breakfasted with Gladstone, it appears, at Monckton Milnes's rooms at 26 Pall Mall. It was Monckton Milnes who recorded Peel's view of Gladstone's early writing.
19. Lang and Shannon, Vol. 1, p. 171.
20. Ibid., p. 177.
21. Ibid., p. 182.
22. I do not think 'Godiva' has more than the remotest or most tenuous connection with the end of Tennyson's engagement.

23. Lang and Shannon, Vol. 1, p. 175.

24. Ibid., p. 183 note.

25. J. L. Cherry, *Life and Remains of John Clare, the Northamptonshire Peasant Poet*, 1873.

26. In 1840 a hint to Charles Elton and perhaps in 1841 a note of Alfred to Allen and a letter from Fitz to Fred suggest two unrecorded visits. A stray American met him incognito in Amsterdam (Lang and Shannon, Vol. 1, pp. 182 and 192).

27. Hagen, *Tennyson and His Publishers*, Chap. 3.

28. *C of E Quarterly Review*, October 1842. For an example of his early criticism, see the notes to *Feast of the Poets*, 1814 (reprinted 1989).

29. VII, 335–7, cf. Ricks, *Proceedings of the British Academy*, 1966, p. 225.

CHAPTER SIX

1. Thackeray's daughter called Anne Ritchie says this feast was for Jane Brookfield and Lady Duff Gordon (Ruskin and Browning, *Records of Tennyson*, 1892, p. 57).

2. 1905 edition of H. Tennyson's *Memoir*, p. 153, footnote, quoting a letter from a journalist.

3. They were intended clearly for an epic; used in 'Merlin and Vivien'. Of all the critics only Spedding (*Edinburgh Review* April 1843) was to say he had the power to produce such a 'very great work'. The editor cut out 'very'.

4. *Letters*, ed. Trudy Bliss, p. 157–8. Charles Tennyson dates this to 1839 or 1840, wrongly I believe.

5. G. Craik (Professor in Belfast, 1849) was also there and outsat him. Ibid., p. 166.

6. D. Verey in Pevsner is wrong about the Tennyson dates, cf. Lang and Shannon, Vol. 1, p. 230, and *Tennyson Research Bulletin*, 84, p. 127.

7. The five figures of the quadrille are Le Pantalon, L'Eté, La Poule, La Trénitz, La Pastourelle.

8. Was Mrs Tennyson keen on the Rector? Rev F. Close (1797–1882, Rector from 1826) was a St John's man and strongly evangelical, who followed Tait as Dean of Carlisle in 1856. In Cheltenham he built five churches and schools, opposed racing, the theatre, alcohol, tobacco and Papism. In 1844 he wrote 'Church architecture scripturally considered'. and 'The restoration of churches is the restoration of popery', and in 1853 'Table turning not diabolical'.

9. Lang and Shannon, Vol. 1, p. 246–50.

10. Prestbury has fine spring water. Fred Archer the jockey (1857–86) used to

train there on Prestbury water and black coffee; today it is marketed in
Westminster as House of Commons' Water.

11. Lang and Shannon, Vol. 1, p. 222–3. (I have slightly altered punctuation.)

12. E. Jenkins, *Tennyson and Dr Gully*, Tennyson Society Paper no. 3, 1974, is
    particularly strong on Gully's later history.

13. Lang and Shannon, Vol. 1, p. 223.

14. It is mentioned in the early years of his marriage, and Franklin Lushington
    tries it, but Alfred never went back.

15. Birmingham has always been a staging post. Gladstone had to change there
    as a little boy travelling between Liverpool and Eton.

16. We already know his Cambridge contemporaries, but he now sees a lot of
    younger Hallams, Lushingtons and their friends. It is impossible to define a
    'circle' in London, because it ebbs and flows: for example he knew Mrs
    Norton (Sheridan's daughter, b. 1808), but no one knows if her feminism
    influenced him. There was a more definable circle of lawyers based on the
    Inner Temple: B. L. Chapman, Fellow of Jesus, who helped sort out Allen,
    and whom the Brookfields and F. Pollock (who wrote memoirs) knew, G.
    Venables, E., F. and H. Lushington, G. Barrett, T. Taylor, J. Sterling, J.
    Kemble and young Harry Hallam.

17. Lang and Shannon, Vol. 1, p. 234, note.

18. Ibid. p. 234.

19. Ibid. p. 242.

20. Ibid. p. 242–3.

21. 'The old man and I fell out one wet day in Pall Mall about half a year ago
    when I said something that offended him and his face flushed and he plucked
    his arm out of mine and told me I was "affecting the smart" and since then
    I haven't seen him.' Lang and Shannon, Vol. 1, p. 248–9.

22. Also against lawyers, the corn laws, the Irish union, Wordsworth (who
    rapped him over the knuckles) and the adulteration of food.

23. Even Stephen in the *Dictionary of National Biography*, who is at pains to take
    this buffoon seriously, admits to his 'coxcombry'.

24. John Forster was a lawyer, who became Bulwer-Lytton's financial
    agent later, and in the 1860s lent him money. Bulwer-Lytton had taken
    to him when Forster was running an appeal for Leigh Hunt, but had
    then got furious when Forster (19 when he was 28) fell asleep while
    he was reading his works; now they quarrelled even worse, and later
    they parted over politics. He does defend his friend all the same. Lang
    and Shannon, Vol. 2, p. 251. Two questions remain: had Tennyson read
    Chevely (1839), a satirizing novel about Bulwer-Lytton by his wife
    Rosina? Did he ever read his *Confessions of a Water-Patient* (1845) about
    hydropathy?

25. Tennyson's poems are in Ricks, Vol. 2, nos. 283–5, p. 178–83.

26. Lang and Shannon, Vol. 2, p. 406.

27. Lang and Shannon, Vol. 1, p. 254–5.

28. Ibid., p. 257–8.

29. The friend was the Rev James White, retired and specializing in Scottish historical plays. Friend of Dickens.

30. He wrote to Fitz that Lauterbrunnen and the pass were 'the stateliest bits of landscape I ever saw . . . I was so satisfied by the size of crags that I *laughed by myself.*'

31. There are a number of these, cf. my 'Theocritus', in *Papers of Hellenistic Conference at Austin, Texas*, 1993, (Univ. Calif. Press).

32. Ackroyd, *Dickens*, p. 500.

33. What he says later about seeing Shelley's birthplace from the Surrey hills sounds more like information than eyesight.

34. Mary Howitt's memoirs, 1889, edited by her daughter. Vo!. 2, p. 27f. The Howitts' house at Clapton is illustrated on p. 27; connoisseurs should also consult p. 56 for Belsize Lane, St John's Wood.

35. II, 101f. and IV, 1–2. *In Memoriam* CXVIII, 9 and LXXXIX, 45.

36. Ricks, Vol. 2, p. 200 note.

37. Lang and Shannon, Vol. 1, p. 272–3.

38. Ibid., p. 281.

39. Theocritus, Lincoln 2595, and *The Princess*, Lincoln 4227. Both books are dated.

40. Lang and Shannon, Vol. 1, p. 283.

41. Tennyson², Vol. 1, p. 287–93.

42. He is supposed to have said of very early Patmore that he feared he might be surpassed by him. It seems an odd remark, maybe just politeness, but Champneys recorded it, Patmore himself being his likely source.

43. Hawker called it Dundagel, and Matthew Arnold called it Tintagyl, to rhyme with Print a pill.

44. Lang and Shannon, Vol. 1, p. 295. To C. F. Williams(?).

45. Ibid., p. 297.

46. Ibid., p. 323 note.

47. Shatto and Shaw, *In Memoriam*, p. 18, deriving from Charles Tennyson's account.

48. Ibid., p. 13–19.

49. Lang and Shannon, Vol. 1, p. 300.

50. Ibid., p. 307.

51. Chapple and Pollard, *Letters of Mrs Gaskell*, p. 84–5.

52. Kingsley's father had been a vicar in the Fens and now had St Luke's, Chelsea. Charles Kingsley (1819–75) was at Helston grammar school, at Clifton, at King's, London and at Magdalene, Cambridge. There (how unlike Alfred) he attended Sedgwick's equestrian geology lectures, learnt boxing from a Negro prize-fighter, and scraped a first in 1842.

53. We know they were close friends from Sir C. Tennyson (p. 242). In his note on *In Memoriam* (Letters, p. 323) Kingsley trumpets like a minor prophet.

54. He was at Umberslade then. Lang and Shannon, Vol. 3, p. 454 note.

55. Something similar may be said of the gloom about his own generation,

most clearly expressed a few lines before the end of Clough's *Amours de Voyage*.

CHAPTER SEVEN

1. Tennyson Research Bulletin, November 1977. Amcott (1815–83), Lieutenant Colonel, and Deputy Lieutenant of the county, was at Eton with a Rawnsley, and his great-uncle had married Emily Sellwood's aunt.
2. Lang and Shannon, Vol. 1, p. 305, (to Aubrey de Vere about Scotland). Wordsworth is constantly criticized in fine detail in the letters; see for example Lang and Shannon, Vol. 2, p. 162 and note.
3. Lang and Shannon, Vol. 1, p. 342 (from C. B. Phipps, Keeper of HM Privy Purse).
4. This publication is remarkable for its engravings of Bayons.
5. Ricks, Vol. 2, no. 299, p. 462 and Vol. 3, App. A, p. 599–600.
6. Ricks, Vol. 2, no. 297, p. 459 and Vol. 3, p. 601 (which I prefer).
7. His undistinguished career is charted in the *Dictionary of National Biography*, for no clear reason. Drummond Rawnsley was about to get rid of him.
8. The books are at Lincoln. The second of three Poe editions was a present from an American publisher. Dobell and Morris presented books.
9. He published a parody, 'Firmilian, a Spasmodic Tragedy by Percy T. Jones' in 1855.
10. A. Waugh is the source for this in his life of Tennyson, 1892.
11. Published his *Amborvalia* in 1849. In 1850 he had just written *Amours de Voyage* and was at work on *Dipsychus* in Venice.
12. Lear is supposed to have met Alfred through the Lushingtons in 1849; that is likely enough but I do not recall the evidence. He was Franklin Lushington's friend.
13. Lang and Shannon, Vol. 1, p. 329 (to L. Colquhoun).
14. Quoted in Lang and Shannon, Vol. 1, p. 336 from Champney's *Memoirs and Correspondence of C. Patmore*.
15. Note by Walter White, Weld's Assistant, quoted by Lang and Shannon, p. 340 note.
16. *Journal*, ed. James Hoge (1981) p. 20.
17. Eliza Fletcher (1770–1858) (Autobiography, 1875, ed. Lady Richardson her daughter.)
18. C. Tennyson, *The Tennysons*, p. 100–1.
19. W. A. Wright ed., *Letters to F. Kemble*, 1902, p. 16.
20. The Lilly Library of Indiana University has a haystack of his papers. In 1853 he published poems privately and in 1854 publicly, in England.
21. (1823–1900), Lord Privy Seal 1852, Secretary of State for India 1868. The flaming red hair was hereditary. Princess Louise brought him a dowry of

£30,000 and an annuity of £6000 a year voted by the House of Commons by 350 votes to one.

22. *Journal*, ed. Grigson, 1967, p. 60f.

23. She was a voluminous novelist whose prose style was at times indistinguishable from her son's.

24. The Aplügen. Clough shows in *Amours* that it was the normal nineteenth-century route.

25. Lang and Shannon, Vol. 2, p. 26. Probably Emily could not face the stormy sea journey, and Alfred was tactful about that.

26. This must be the only occurrence of rose in Tennyson no one has yet thought of referring to Rose Baring.

27. Lang and Shannon, Vol. 2, p. 20 (to Brookfield going to Madeira).

28. Ibid., p. 47–8 gives a full list including excuses.

29. In the London market in about 1989, Tennyson's letter for £450.

30. Lang and Shannon, Vol. 2, p. 53–5 (to Fred).

31. Ibid., p. 56.

32. Memoir by his son, p. 304–7.

33. He called it 'A matter which seemed trifling enough but I had two surgical operations to undergo which have left me horizontal.' Lang and Shannon, Vol. 2, p. 71. One discovers years later that it was his ingrowing toenail that had to be treated surgically twice.

34. Which house at Lyme Regis? The Regency house that became a hotel, opposite Umbrella Cottage? It is about the right size and date.

35. The interested reader should consult Cecil Woodham-Smith's *The Reason Why* (1953). The British aim was to take Sebastopol: the campaign did produce a great writer, an artillery officer on one of the towers of the city, who was so bored by the siege that he composed the memoirs of his childhood while the guns were in action there: Tolstoy.

36. We have a recording of Tennyson reciting this poem, in which *hundred* duly rhymes with *blundered* as it would in Lincolnshire.

37. Ricks, Vol. 2, p. 584.

38. Noticed by Roy Fuller in a perceptive review of the new fuller edition of *Maud* to match *In Memoriam*.

39. Said by Sir Charles Tennyson, p. 282, cited by Ricks, Vol. 3, p. 393.

CHAPTER EIGHT

1. Ricks, Vol. 3, p. 255–6 and see p. 262.

2. Ibid., pp. 256–7.

3. 'Merlin and Vivien', 229–31.

4. Ricks, Vol. 3, p. 260, where the relevant letters are also all conveniently cited.

5. Ricks, Vol. 3, p. 349.

6. Cf. Ricks, Vol. 3, p. 259.

7. There is little to record about this edition but Tennyson's justifiable fury over it. It is a Bible-sized sugar plum of a book bound in Cambridge blue and gold with embossed Pre-Raphaelite flowers and Gothic lettering front and back, gold edges, and mad, gloomy, black and white pictures.

8. Blackwood's used the same Moxon green and the same size for the four-volume *Middlemarch*, and Macmillan continued using it for Tennyson.

9. Ricks, Vol. 2, p. 653–7. His other bits of *Iliad* are in Vol. 3, App. A, p. 603.

10. P. 95 of the 1896 'Popular Edition', 'On translating Homer'.

11. Ibid., p. 161f.

12. Caerleon, it is said, may offer in its circular amphitheatre an origin for the legend of the round table: there is a round one at Winchester supposed to date from Edward III, but by his time the legend was old.

13. Bluebell.

14. Ricks, Vol. 3, App. A, p. 602.

15. Ricks, Vol. 3, p. 463. Was this the Lancelot poem or another?

16. My only worry is, what is the ptarmigan (picked up from his friend Argyll) doing so far south (692–5)?

17. Tourism had been virtually unknown in Britain until the late eighteenth century. It can be traced through early watercolourists, and through visitors to Scotland and the Lakes, but by the time of the earliest railways it was flourishing. In 1840 Mr Cook invented his tours and in 1844 Thackeray took his pioneer journey by paddle-steamer, horse and camel from Cornhill to Cairo, so that even foreign tours had a rosy future before Tennyson settled in the Isle of Wight.

18. *Farringford Journal of Emily Tennyson 1853–64*, ed. R. J. Hutchings and B. Hinton, 1986. There is a longer, funnier account in her letter to C. S. Venables on 21 May (Lang and Shannon, Vol. 2, p. 150). It turned out Prince Albert wanted the cowslips to brew cowslip tea for the Queen. Alfred offered him a drink but not a chair.

19. Wordsworth (*Excursion* IX, 570, altered it in 1828, for the 1837 edition). Tennyson had the five-volume 1827 edition.

20. Lang and Shannon, Vol. 2, p. 162.

21. Lang and Shannon, Vol. 2, p. 197.

22. Ibid., p. 270.

23. See my lecture on Lear in *The Art of Poetry* (1990). It is curious that Lewis Carroll, who adored Tennyson and whose first published work was a word-list from *In Memoriam*, offended in the same way.

24. Lady Briggs noted this version; 'Down there live the people of Erith' is what Lord Briggs remembered. But down where? Was he writing it at a station? Or by the Thames?

25. Numbers 495, Alfred Tennyson from Adelaide Sutor, and 3494, with the Author's kind respects. The first edition was only a very few years earlier.

26. Vol. 1, p. 471.

27. Readers in difficulty should use G. E. Campion's *Tennyson Dialect Glossary* (with the dialect poems), Lincolnshire and Humberside Arts, 1969 (third edition 1976).

28. I know rather little about Tennyson's farm, but he liked to hear no sheep could rival his but the Duke of Richmond's (at Goodwood which is just across the Solent). Emily felt they had not lost by it financially but not gained, and that Alfred soon lost his first passionate enthusiasm.

29. The last 1833 poem to see print was 'On a Mourner', in 1865.

CHAPTER NINE

1. There is a full account in Hagen, *Tennyson and His Publishers*, p. 100–161.

2. For a full list see M. E. Grant Duff, *A Victorian Vintage*, 1930, p. 112–3. The Club was founded by Reynolds, Johnson, Burke and Goldsmith in 1764.

3. For all information about Knowles, see Priscilla Metcalf's *James Knowles, Victorian Editor and Architect*, 1980.

4. In October 1864 Edward Lear 'found all that quiet part of the Island fast spoiling, and how they can stay there I can't imagine' with a big hotel, an estate of 300 new houses, and a railway (not built) (Lear's *Letters*, ed. Lady Strachey, Vol. 2, p. 47). The railway still threatened in 1888 (Lang and Shannon, Vol. 3, p. 385). It had then reached Freshwater, and proposed to extend to Totland Bay.

5. On detailed arrangements and changes, see Sir Charles Tennyson's pamphlet, *Aldworth*, 1977 (Tennyson Research Centre, Lincoln).

6. James Stilwell of Killinghurst. In 1871 Emily recorded a visit there: 'A. asked to be allowed to go into the hayfield. He misses the haymaking and the harvest here at Aldworth very much.'

7. Hallam's *Memoir*, Vol. 2, p. 209.

8. A. W. Brown, *The Metaphysical Society*, 1947, and Metcalf, *James Knowles*, p. 208–27.

9. Ricks (Vol. 2, p. 705) believes 'The Higher Pantheism' took its spark from an earlier, unpublished bit of verse which is more moving: 'Through the million of million decillions of worlds/As a flash, Thou wilt answer me.'

10. He submitted 'Lucretius' to the Latinist Munro who was his friend. Munro had no fault to find except that 'neat-herds' would be better than 'shepherds'.

11. Lucretius III, 18–24; 'Morte d'Arthur', 260–63. *Odyssey* IV, 566f.

12. I assume it was Jowett, because his reply was a sphinx-like twinkling smile.

13. *Farringford Journal of Emily Tennyson 1853–64*, ed. Hutchings and Hinton. Emily says 'the funny man' was the Ethiopian Singer. Alfred heard some

Ethiopian singers at Tavistock as a bachelor, so it sounds as if 'Nigger Minstrel' was a later Americanism.

14. The Bradleys took a house near Tennyson's and came to delight in him. He was a disciple of Arnold at Rugby.

15. Allingham's *Journal*, Aug. 23, 1867, ed. Grigson 1967. He was born in 1824, met Alfred in 1851, moved to Lymington 1863, and married, at fifty in 1874, the painter Helen Allingham.

16. The hat was less curious then than it now looks. Queer hats were common; D. G. Rossetti had a 'ventilating hat' like a London policeman's helmet. Gladstone when in the country was a still more eccentric sight.

17. Lang and Shannon, Vol. 2, p. 321 and 367.

18. Woolner had married a Miss Waugh, and Holman Hunt married two of her sisters in succession. Woolner had just carved a head of Doctor Symonds, and just been to Tintagel with Palgrave and Tennyson.

19. Because his brother-in-law was a legal official in Jamaica, or because Eyre was a Louth old boy? More likely because of views Alfred had based on the Indian Mutiny. They were not thought to be extreme, and some respectable people held them. It should be understood when reading this account that Tennyson was and had always been wholly against slavery anywhere, but Lincoln shocked him because Alfred felt all reform should be gradual.

Symonds also reports Alfred's theological views at considerable length. They are none of them unexpected.

20. The whole of Symonds' reporting is in Lang and Shannon, Vol. 2, p. 415-21.

21. Lang and Shannon, Vol. 2, p. 334. He had been vaccinated twenty years before, but she felt he needed it again.

22. Ibid., p. 453.

23. For all information about Symonds, see Phyllis Grosskurth's biography of Symonds.

24. Lang and Shannon, Vol. 2, p. 273. His dismissal from the British Institute was discreet. Information is still meagre, but Weld went abroad alone, and the disgrace is undoubted. Emily confided in Edward Lear, but she knew little. Charles Weld had stayed at Farringford and settled near by.

25. In 1871, in response to a letter from Manley Hopkins (senior) he joined a Committee and subscribed to a Christian mission in her kingdom (Lang and Shannon, Vol. 3, p. 21).

26. For example in the charming study *Dear and Honoured Lady*, by Tennyson and Dyson, 1969. The *Letters*, not complete until 1991, reveal a calmer, more ordinary story.

27. Lang and Shannon, Vol. 3, p. 321-5, (with notes) gives a fine display of diplomatic fencing between Victoria and Tennyson (with Hallam as secretary) and Gladstone, in 1885.

28. In 1865 the offer was through the Duchess of Sutherland, Argyll's mother-in-law, so it was not political (Lang and Shannon, Vol. 2, note on p. 309

citing Journals of Walter White, who was a friend and at one time assistant of Charles Weld).

29. Lang and Shannon, Vol. 2, p. 301, 304, 325–7 (a visit described by little Hallam in May 1863) etc. See also Emily's Journal, February 1864.

30. Ibid., p. 551 and note.

31. Simeon was MFH for three years in the 1850s and like the late Duke of Beaufort was familiarly called Master. At least once he invited Alfred to a meet.

32. R. Trevelyan, *A Pre-Raphaelite Circle*, 1978, p. 161.

33. Confirmed late in 1859; the rescue ship *Fox* returned in October and Captain (later Sir F.) MacClintock's diary was published in December. Emily's aunt sent her a copy (Lincoln 3355).

34. Lang and Shannon, Vol. 2, p. 357.

35. Lord Egremont observed a builders' notice saying 'Trespasers will be prosecuted', and rode away in scorn, saying 'Fellow can't even spell.'

36. Lang and Shannon, Vol. 3, p. 84.

37. R. Trevelyan discusses this view in *A Pre-Raphaelite Circle*, 1978, p. 167.

38. See Alexander on the poem in *Old English Literature*, 1983.

39. We must assume Tennyson never heard of Hopkins as a poet, yet Hopkins had an early poem in *Once a Week*, which Tennyson had written in, and Bridges knew Tennyson. When Hopkins sat for Balliol, V. Cracroft Amcott was also a candidate. Hopkins' father reviewed *The Princess* and *In Memoriam* in *The Times*. There is a queer similarity between 'The Wreck' (stanzas 7–12) and 'The Wreck of the Deutschland'.

40. Though Rogers may be a phantom: A. D. Coleridge who recorded the remark may have mistaken the name.

41. Emily's *Journal*, ed. Hoge, 1981. Later Turgenev came to Aldworth, where he and Tennyson became fast friends.

42. See Ann Thwaite, *Edmund Gosse*, 1984, p. 101, for more context; the story itself is fuller in Gosse's *Portraits and Sketches*, 1912.

43. Ann Thwaite's *Gosse*, p. 295–6. The offence of Collins was in Alfred's eyes an infuriating and utterly misleading article about the poet's sources.

44. The poem is printed as Appendix A to the second volume of Lear's *Letters*.

45. *Life and Letters of C. L. Dodgson* (1899), p. 92. He was at Farringford at Easter.

46. 1864, 1868, 1873.

CHAPTER TEN

1. Compton Mackenzie's parents the Comptons, the actor-managers, may be an exception. They were interested both in Tennyson and in Henry James, whose *Guy Domville* they put on successfully at Southport.

2. Sir C. Tennyson, p. 518.

3. Arthur Waugh, *Tennyson*, 1892², describes the public reaction, but of the production Henry Jennings writing in 1884 gives the fullest account.
4. Sir C. Tennyson, p. 535 note.
5. There are a number of witnesses and versions of this story, one in Rosamond Lehmann's memoirs, one by Mr Benson as Archdeacon of Huntingdon in *As We Were*, and one by Compton Mackenzie, who says in the second of his *Octaves* that it happened to his mother.
6. Lang and Shannon, Vol. 3, p. 120–1 etc.
7. I took these details from a bookseller's catalogue (Sanders of Oxford?) about 1970, when the book was for sale for £85.
8. See *Essays in Criticism* 41, 2 (April 1991), a review by Pamela Siska, p. 172.
9. Lang and Shannon, Vol. 3, p. 113, cf. p. 104; *Memoir²*, 526–8.
10. Ibid., 13–14 with note.
11. Dean Stanley was a grandson of Lord Derby, as well as nephew to the first Lord Stanley of Alderley and cousin to the second; he was cousin therefore once removed to the contemporary Lady Carlisle, who made her husband throw a cellar of wonderful wine into his lake; and was Gilbert Murray's mother-in-law and founded a line of famous alcoholics.

    Stanley was Dean 1864–81, and married the Earl of Elgin's daughter. C. Wordsworth, then Archdeacon, protested at his appointment from the pulpit for unorthodoxy. The Dean's reaction was to invite the Archdeacon to lunch. He was Tennyson's friend and the most spectacular success as Dean. Jowett and F. D. Maurice preached for him, and Arnold wrote a fine poem for him. He had a Bach Passion sung in the nave, refused the Abbey to an illiberal Synod, and on occasion gave Communion to Unitarians.
12. Lang and Shannon, Vol. 3, p. 142 n. from Lady St Helier (then Mrs Stanley), *Memories of Fifty Years*.
13. Not quite the Season, but Alfred's London season, mid-March 1877.
14. Horne: Lang and Shannon, Vol. 3, p. 153, and note; Fanny Keats: Marie Adami 1937, p. 193.
15. Tennyson Research Centre, Lincoln. Letters in Lang and Shannon, Vol. 3, p. 178.
16. A London University manuscript of this poem has a number of verbal variants, but Ricks scorns them, and we are probably safe to follow him.
17. See *Memoir*, Vol. 2, 247–8, and Lang and Shannon, Vol. 3, p. 197 note.
18. *Diary*, ed. Grigson, 1967, p. 85–304.
19. R. B. Martin, *With Friends Possessed*, 1985, p. 230 and 257–8.
20. Lang and Shannon, Vol. 3, p. 197 and note.
21. Victoria Glendinning (by birth a Seebohm) tells the story in *A Suppressed Cry* (1969).
22. The poet was fond of them. They were grand in lineage (the Earl of Cork's family) but not hugely rich.
23. *Life of Richard Owen*, Vol. 2, p. 225.
24. Lang and Shannon, Vol. 3, p. 213.

25. Allingham had used the same story in Leigh Hunt's magazine in 1851.
26. Lang and Shannon, Vol. 3, p. 220 f.
27. Ibid., p. 230.
28. Lord Tennyson did vote once or twice, and after his death his son became a Governor of Southern Australia, for which the peerage qualified him.
29. Translated most recently by D. C. Lau, 1963, for Penguin classics.
30. Lang and Shannon, Vol. 3, p. 247.
31. Ibid., p. 321–2 and 314–6.
32. Arnold also backed him, so he got in.
33. Lines 55–65. Hallam says these lines were written at news of Lionel's death.
34. e.g. Lang and Shannon, Vol. 3, pp. 312, 332, 271.
35. *The Romance of Certain Old Clothes*, 1868.
36. A Wellingtonia, planted at his visit in April 1864. A tourist immediately tore off a branch.
37. Luckily one of the few copies of this is in the Bodleian Library.
38. 253–489. The modern Budé edition, by F. Vian, 1969, includes an excellent French translation. Quintus is now called Smyrnaeus; his book is the *Post Homerica*.
39. He deliberately disregards the view which Ovid entertained (*Metamorphoses*, VII, 362) that Paris had killed his and Œnone's son Korythos for loving Helen.
40. Quintus is more romantic, and the mountain is full of ominous bird noises.
41. In Quintus nymphs and herdsmen lament, Œnone weeps like a waterfall, etc.
42. In Quintus herdsmen put the ashes in a golden pot.
43. Its restraint does not echo the flowery flatness of the Greek, in which typically 'the glens replied lamenting'. Indeed such touches as the adder-bitten lamb are original, or based on the source of the first Œnone poem in Ovid's *Heroides*.
44. Birrell used to call Farringford, Wuthering Heights. It was by then an extremely old-fashioned house, lit only by candle lanterns and decorated with very old photographs, with a prehistoric central heating system hardly powerful enough to destroy the wax cylinders that recorded the poet's voice.
45. Lang and Shannon, Vol. 3, p. 396.
46. Lang and Shannon say Admiral Crozier was the Colonel's father; the Colonel lived at Freshwater, his father at Yarmouth.
47. David Peak of Bristol is the authority on these people, and is editing one of their diaries.
48. Sir C. Tennyson, p. 524. Sir Charles remembers these stories: he was a boy of twelve.
49. The nearest he came to that experience was seeing an experimental torpedo sink a ship in 1890. For some minutes afterwards he did not speak. Later he said it was as if all the science of the century had combined to produce a malignant spirit.

50. H. Parry, *Life and Works*, cited in Lang and Shannon, Vol. 3, p. 436–7.

51. Sir C. Tennyson, Life, p. 519.

52. Lang and Shannon, Vol. 3, p. 439.

53. Ibid., p. 444.

54. See Jowett's letter, 18 April 1892, and J. C. Livingston in *Victorian Poetry*, 27, 1989, p. 665. Tennyson needed Arthur Waley's *Real Tripitaka*, which alas lay in the future. I have discussed these pilgrims, who are better known today, in *The Lightgarden of the Angel King* (1975).

55. The spasms (a few) are recorded by R. B. Martin, *Tennyson*, p. 582.

56. 1785, in ten volumes, now at Lincoln. He had many other editions.

57. Roundell Palmer, Jowett's old ally and Tennyson's neighbour.

58. His wife came to lunch in 1889 and 'he praised her husband's feeling for the empire' (*Memoir*, Vol. 2, p. 354).

59. A personal friend who advised on Lord Tennyson's appalling itches on the leg, which were from eczema.

60. The evidence for this is that Val Prinsep painted her once in the Isle of Wight as a beautiful and very young woman in the height of fashion.

ESSENTIAL BIBLIOGRAPHY

TENNYSON'S WORKS

Becket (London, 1884)
The Cup and The Falcon (London, 1884)
Queen Mary: A Drama (London, 1875)
Harold: A Drama (London, 1877)

G.E. Campion, *A Tennyson Dialect Glossary, with the Dialect Poems* (Lincoln, 1969)
C.B. Ricks, ed., *The Poems of Tennyson* (Harlow, 2nd edn., 1987)
S. Shatto, ed., *Tennyson's Maud: a Definitive Edition* (London, 1986)
S. Shatto and M. Shaw, eds., *In Memoriam* (Oxford, 1982)

BIOGRAPHIES OF TENNYSON

W.H. Auden, *Tennyson, an Introduction and a Selection* (London, 1946)
A.C. Benson, *Tennyson* (London, 1912)
H.J. Jennings, *Lord Tennyson, a Biographical Sketch* (London, 1884)
R.B. Martin, *Tennyson, the Unquiet Heart* (Oxford, 1980)
H. Nicolson, *Tennyson: Aspects of his Life, Character and Poetry* (London, 1923)
H.D. Rawnsley, *Memoirs of the Tennysons* (Glasgow, 1900)
J. Richardson, *The Pre-Eminent Victorian: a Study of Tennyson* (London, 1962)
C. Ricks, *Tennyson* (London, 1972)
C. Tennyson, *Alfred Tennyson* (London, 1949)
C. Tennyson and H. Dyson, *The Tennysons: Background to Genius* (London, 1974)
H. Tennyson, *Alfred Lord Tennyson: a Memoir by his Son* (London, 1897)
——, ed., *Tennyson and his Friends* (London, 1911)
H. Walker, *The Age of Tennyson* (London, 1897)
A. Waugh, *Alfred Lord Tennyson, a Study of his Life and Work* (London, 1892)

OTHER BIOGRAPHIES

M. Adami, *Fanny Keats* (London, 1937)
A.O. Allen, *John Allen and his Friends* (London, 1922)
A.C. Benson, *Fasti Etonenses. A Biographical History of Eton Selected From the Lives of Celebrated Etonians* (Eton, 1899)
C.H. and F.M. Brookfield, *Mrs Brookfield and her Circle* (London, 1905)
F.M. Brookfield, *The Cambridge 'Apostles'* (London, 1906)
B. Champneys, ed., *Memoirs and Correspondence of Coventry Patmore* (London, 1901)
K.C. Chorley, *Arthur Hugh Clough: the Uncommitted Mind. A Study of his Life and Poetry* (Oxford, 1962)
P.W. Clayden, *Rogers and his Contemporaries* (London, 1880)
B. Clough, *Prose Remains of A.H. Clough: with a Selection from his Letters and a Memoir* (London, 1888)
S.D. Collingwood, *The Life and Letters of Lewis Carroll* (London, 1899)

S. Dobell, *The Poetical Works of Sydney Dobell, With Introductory Notice by J. Nicol* (London, 1876)

G. Faber, *Jowett, a Portrait with Background* (London, 1957)

J.A. Froude, *Thomas Carlyle: a History of the First Forty Years of his Life, 1795–1835* (London, 1891)

C.M. Gaskell, ed., *An Eton Boy, the Letters of J.M. Gaskell from Eton and Oxford* (London, 1939)

W.H. Griffin, *The Life of Robert Browning: with Notices of his Writings, his Family and his Friends* (London, 1938)

P. Grosskurth, *John Addington Symonds: a Biography* (London, 1964)

A.J.C. Hare, *The Story of my Life* (London 1896–1900)

B. Hill, *Julia Margaret Cameron, A Victorian Family Portrait* (London, 1973)

P. Honan, *Matthew Arnold, a Life* (London, 1981)

M. Howitt, *Mary Howitt: an Autobiography* (London, 1889)

H. James, *William Wetmore Story and his Friends: from Letters, Diaries and Recollections* (Edinburgh and London, 1903)

C. Kent, ed., *Leigh Hunt as Poet and Essayist . . .* (Cavendish Library, 1887)

F.W. Maitland, *The Life and Letters of Leslie Stephen* (London, 1906)

R.B. Martin, *The Dust of Combat: a Life of Charles Kingsley* (London, 1959)

——, *With Friends Possessed, a Life of E. Fitzgerald* (London, 1985)

——, *Gerard Manley Hopkins: a Very Private Life* (London, 1991)

C. Merivale, *An Autobiography of Dean Merrivale, with Selections from his Correspondence* (London, 1899)

H.G. Merriam, *Edward Moxon, Publisher of Poets* (New York, 1939)

M. Mitford, *Recollections of a Literary Life, or Books, Places and People* (London, 1852)

P. Metcalf, *James Knowles, Victorian Editor and Architect* (Oxford, 1980)

G.F. Palgrave, *Francis Turner Palgrave: his Journals and Memories of his Life* (London, 1899)

W.F. Pollock, *Personal Remembrances* (London, 1887)

J. Pope-Hennessy, *Monckton Milnes: the Flight of Youth 1851–1885* (London, 1951)

E.F. Rawnsley, *Canon Rawnsley, An Account of his Life* (Glasgow, 1923)

T.W. Reid, *The Life, Letters and Friendships of Richard Monckton Milnes, First Lord Houghton* (London, 2nd edn., 1890)

R.E. Roberts, *Samuel Rogers and his Circle* (London, 1910)

H.M. Schuester and R.L. Peters, eds., *The Letters of John Addington Symonds* (Detroit, 1967–79)

W. Sharp, *Life and Writings of Robert Browning* (London, 1890)

W. Sinclair, ed., *The Poetical Works of Alexander Smith* (Edinburgh, 1909)

B. Stoker, *Personal Reminiscences of Henry Irving* (London, 1906)

J. Stratford, *Gloucestershire Biographical Notes* (Gloucester, 1887)

H. Taylor, *Autobiography of Henry Taylor, 1800–1875* (London, 1885)

A. Thwaite, *Edmund Gosse: a Literary Landscape, 1849–1928* (London, 1917)

R.C. Trench, *Letters and Memorials, Edited by the Author of Charles Lowder* (London, 1888)

A. Woolner, ed., *Thomas Woolner, R.A. Sculptor and Poet: his Life in Letters* (London, 1917)

LETTERS AND JOURNALS

P. Allen, *The Cambridge Apostles, the Early Years* (Cambridge, 1978)

H. Allingham and D. Radford, eds., *William Allingham, A Diary*, reissued with an introduction by G. Grigson (Fontwell, 1967)

F.H.C. Doyle, *Reminiscences and Opinions . . . 1813–1885* (London, 1886)

M.R.D. Foot, ed., *The Gladstone Diaries* (Oxford 1968 and since)

N.C. Hannay, ed., *A Fitzgerald Friendship, Unpublished Letters . . . to W.B. Donne* (London, 1932)

J.O. Hoge, ed., *The Letters of Emily, Lady Tennyson* (London, 1974)

——, *Lady Tennyson's Journal* (Charlottesville, 1981)

J. Kolb, ed., *The Letters of Arthur Henry Hallam* (Colombus, Ohio, 1981)

C.Y. Lang and E.F. Shannon, eds., *The Letters of Alfred, Lord Tennyson* (Oxford, 1981–1990)

A. McKinley Terhune and A. Terhune, eds., *The Letters of Edward Fitzgerald* (Princeton, 1980)

G.N. Ray, ed., *The Letters and Private Papers of William Makepeace Thackeray* (London, 1945)

H. Ritchie, ed., *Letters of A.T. Ritchie . . .* (London, 1924)

H.J. Schonfield, ed., *Letters to F. Tennyson* (London, 1930)

Lady Strachey, ed., *Letters . . . to Chichester Fortescue, Lord Carlingford and Frances, Countess Waldegrave* (London, 1907)

C. Tennyson and H. Dyson, eds., *Dear and Honoured Lady: the Correspondence between Queen Victoria and Alfred Tennyson* (London, 1969)

A.I. Thackeray, *Records of Tennyson, Ruskin and Browning* (London, 1982)

——, *From the Porch* (London, 1913)

W.A. Wright, ed., *Letters and Literary Remains of Edward Fitzgerald* (London, 1902–3)

AUXILIARY BOOKS

P. Ackroyd, *Dickens* (London, 1990)

A.C. Bradley, *A Commentary on Tennyson's* In Memoriam (London, 3rd edn., 1930)

N. Campbell, ed., *Tennyson in Lincoln: a Catalogue of the Collections in the Research Centre* (Lincoln, 1971)

A. Carlyle, ed., *New Letters and Memorials of Jane Carlyle* (London, 1903)

T. Carlyle, *The Collected Works of Thomas Carlyle* (London, 1857–58)

E.D.C.G. Cecil, *The English Poets* (London, 1941)

C.H. Church, *Europe in 1830, Revolution and Political Change* (London, 1983)

A. Cruse, *The Englishman and his Books* (London, 1930)

J.A. Davies, *John Forster: a Literary Life* (Leicester, 1983)

P.L. Eliot, *The Making of the Memoir* (Greenville, South Carolina, 1978)

T.S. Eliot, *Essays Ancient and Modern* (London, 1936)

——, *Selected Essays* (New York, new edn., 1950)

A.H.R. Elton and M. Elton, *Clevedon Court, Somerset. A Property of the National Trust* (Clevedon, 1963)

E. Fitzgerald, *Euphranor, a Dialogue on Youth* (London, 2nd edn., 1855)

J.A. Froude, ed., *Letters and Memorials of Jane Carlyle* (London, 1883)

E. Gosse, *Books on the Table* (London, 1921)

J.S. Hagen, *Tennyson and his Publishers* (London, 1979)

W. Howitt, *Homes and Haunts of the most eminent British Poets* (London, 3rd edn., 1857)

L. Huxley, ed., *Jane Welsh Carlyle. Letters to her Family, 1839–1863* (London, 1924)

C.B. Johnson, *William Bodham Donne and his Friends* (London, 1905)

M.V. Levey, *The Case of Walter Pater* (London, 1978)

W.L. Lockyer and N. Lockyer, *Tennyson as a Student and Poet of Nature* (London, 1910)

E.J. Morley, ed., *Henry Crabb Robinson on Books and their Writers* (London, 1938)

R.J. Olney, *Rural Society and County Government in Nineteenth-Century Lincolnshire* (Lincoln, 1979)

W.D. Paden, *Tennyson in Egypt. A Study of the Imagery in his Earlier Work* (Lawrence, Kansas, 1942)

N. Page, ed., *Tennyson: Interviews and Recollections* (Basingstoke, 1983)

N. Pevsner, *Cambridgeshire* (Harmondsworth, 1954)

——, *Lincolnshire* (Harmondsworth, 1964)

F.B. Pinion, *A Tennyson Chronology* (Basingstoke, 1990)

R.W. Rader, *Tennyson's Maud: the Biographical Genesis* (Berkeley, 1963)

E.F. Shannon, *Tennyson and the Reviewers* (Cambridge, Mass., 1952)

R.H. Super, ed., *The Complete Prose Works of Matthew Arnold* (Ann Arbor, 1960–77)

C. Tennyson, *Alfred Tennyson and Somersby* (Lincoln, 1974)

——, *Farringford, Home of Alfred, Lord Tennyson* (Lincoln, 1976)

A. Tilney Basset, ed., *A Victorian Vintage: being a Selection of the Best Stories from the Diaries of the Right Hon. Sir M.E.G. Duff* (London, 1930)

R. Trevelyan, *A Pre-Raphaelite Circle* (London, 1978)

T.H. Warren, *The Centenary of Tennyson* (Oxford, 1909)

W. Watkins, *The Birds of Tennyson* (London, 1903)

A.G. Weld, *Glimpses of Tennyson and of some of his Relatives and Friends* (London, 1903)

H. Wolfe, *Tennyson* (London, 1930)

D.C. Woodman, *Unravelling the Franklin Mystery: Inuit Testimony* (London, 1991)

POETRY

W.E. Gladstone and G.W. Lyttelton, *Translations* (London, 1861)

F. Lushington, *Points of War* (Cambridge, 1854)

F. and H. Lushington, *Wagers of Battle, 1854–1899* (London, 1900)

C. Turner, *Collected Sonnets Old and New* (London, 1880)

——, *A Hundred Sonnets*, selected and with an introduction by J. Betjeman and Sir C. Tennyson (London, 1960)

INDEX

NOTE: **bold** references indicate plate numbers. Tennyson's poems are indexed individually.